BIOLOGICAL ANTHROPOLOGY

BIOLOGICAL ANTHROPOLOGY

SECOND EDITION

MICHAEL ALAN PARK
CENTRAL CONNECTICUT STATE UNIVERSITY

MAYFIELD PUBLISHING COMPANY
Mountain View, California
London • Toronto

For Jan

Library of Congress Cataloging-in-Publication Data
Park, Michael Alan.
    Biological anthropology / Michael Alan Park.—2nd ed.
        p.   cm.
    Includes bibliographical references and index.
    ISBN 0-7674-0512-9
    1. Physical anthropology.   I. Title.
GN60.P35   1998
599.9—dc21   98-4068
                                                       CIP

Manufactured in the United States of America
10 9 8 7 6 5 4 3

Mayfield Publishing Company
1280 Villa Street
Mountain View, CA 94041

Sponsoring editor, Janet M. Beatty; production editor, Melissa Kreischer; manuscript editor, Dale Anderson; design manager and cover designer, Susan Breitbard; text designer, Anna George; art manager, Robin Mouat; illustrators, Joan Carol, Alice and Will Thiede—Carto-Graphics, and John and Judy Waller; cover photo, © Frans Lanting/Minden Pictures; manufacturing manager, Randy Hurst. The text was set in 10.5/12 Goudy Old Style by UG/GGS Information Services and printed on 50# Chromatone Matte by Banta Book Group.

To the Instructor

Contemporary biological anthropology is a dauntingly broad field. It studies humans in the same way that zoologists study their subject species—from a perspective that includes *all* aspects of the species' biology and that emphasizes the interrelationships among those aspects. In addition to the traditional topics of the human fossil record and human biological variation, bioanthropology includes primatology, modern technologies in molecular genetics, human demography, development of the individual, life histories, and such applications as forensic anthropology. Bioanthropology also appreciates that our cultural behavior is an integral part of our behavior as a species.

No wonder then, that I (and others I have spoken to) have had difficulty in covering the entire field in a one-semester course. We have ended up leaving out important aspects (or paying them little more than lip service), or we have sacrificed a sense of bioanthropology as an integrated whole to a rushed and encyclopedic inventory of all the field's current topics.

As modern bioanthropology increased in breadth and complexity over the past several decades, so, too, did the size and detail of introductory texts. Several are now more than 600 pages long. To date, attempts to produce shorter introductory texts have consisted of simply cutting out parts of these existing tomes, resulting in rather uneven, sometimes oddly organized presentations of the field.

I wrote this text in order to present a diverse scientific field to beginning students. Here are the major assumptions that guided my writing:

- Because this is a text for introductory courses, I have tried to reduce the field to its most basic information. No part of the discipline has been left out; instead I have achieved brevity by managing the amount of detail and including only the information necessary to clearly and accurately convey the basic themes, theories, methods, and facts of bioanthropology.

- The text assumes that students have limited background knowledge of the material and little understanding of what science is and how it works. The text *explains* rather than simply itemizes facts and ideas, and it does so, as much as possible, in a narrative format. A lesson from the study of folklore is that a story is far more easily understood and retained than is a list of facts.

- I want students to feel that they are reading a text written by a real person who has participated in the field. I have tried to achieve a balance between an informal style and formal style, and I have not shied away from the occasional colloquialism or personal comment.

FEATURES

I've included a number of features that I hope will make this text a more useful learning tool for students.

- *I've used the scientific method as a theme throughout the book to demonstrate the integrity and nature of bioanthropology.* I describe the scientific method and then, because this *is* anthropology, compare science to knowledge garnered from belief systems, discussing the relationship of these two spheres of inquiry and knowledge within cultures. I try to show specifically how scientific reasoning has provided us with the knowledge we have about the topics in bioanthropology. For example, I've presented extended discussions of bipedalism and the issue of modern human origins by posing questions, suggesting answers, and then testing the logic of and evidence for those answers.

- *The text is organized to help students navigate their way through what is still a fairly hefty amount of information.* To help students feel a little less at sea in the midst of new facts and ideas, I regularly refer back to previous topics and ahead to topics that will be covered. The headings I use as signposts are as descriptive as possible (for example, "Natural Selection: The Prime Mover of Evolution").

- *Within chapters, a consistent format helps students better understand material new to them.* Each chapter starts with an **introduction** that sets the stage and context for what's to come, which is followed by a series of **questions** that the chapter will answer. Because science proceeds by asking and answering questions, this format is also used within the body of the text. Important **terms** are in boldface and are defined in the margins at their first appearance. Each chapter concludes with a list of key terms and a **summary** that not only recaps the important points of the chapter but also provides some new ideas and thoughts that help put the chapter into context within the whole discipline. A list of **suggested readings,** made up mostly of nontechnical works, tells students where to find more information about the chapter topics.

- *Two glossaries, a bibliography, and a comprehensive index make informa-tion more accessible.* A Glossary of Human and Nonhuman Primates with a pronunciation guide defines taxonomic names for taxa discussed in the text. In addition to the running glossary within chapters, a comprehensive glossary appears at the back of the book. The bibliography gives complete references for the suggested readings and also lists technical works referred to within the text. The index helps students access information quickly.

- *The text's visual appeal enhances its readability.* Detailed, colorful charts and drawings, as well as full-color photographs, underscore significant points in the text. Captions for the artwork add information rather than simply label the pictures.

NEW TO THIS EDITION

- Given the amount of new information—fossil finds, recalibrated dates, new hypotheses—about the origins of modern humans reported since the first edition, the controversy over this topic has become even harder to explain at the introductory level. This edition addresses that problem in two new chapters:

     Chapter 11, "The Evolution of the Genus *Homo*," covers the hominid fossil record from *Homo erectus* to modern *Homo sapiens*. For clarity of organization, Chapter 11 uses (but does not necessarily endorse) the currently most elaborate interpretation of the fossils—the recognition of six species: *H. erectus, ergaster, antecessor, heidelbergensis, neanderthalensis,* and *sapiens*. This does not ignore other interpretations that lump some of these species in various ways; these interpretations are covered within the chapter and in the next chapter. I just believe that this organization best facilitates the comparison of major models in Chapter 12.

     In Chapter 12, "The Debate Over Modern Human Origins," the two major models are presented and diagrammed, and the supporting predictions for each are listed. Each model is then discussed in light of current data from the fossil record, genetics, and evolutionary theory. An alternative model is presented and evaluated.

- Chapter 13, "The Study of Living Peoples," continues to focus on bioanthropology applied to modern populations and individuals. It now includes a new section on "Disease and Human Populations," which discusses evolutionary trends in the relationship between human groups and diseases and contains what one reviewer called "frighteningly relevant" information on emerging diseases such as AIDS and mad cow disease.

- A "Contemporary Reflections" section at the end of each chapter poses a question that addresses a current topic or concern (for example, Does Science Dehumanize Society? Is It Really Possible to Clone Humans and Dinosaurs? Who Owns Old Bones? Are There Racial Differences in Athletic Ability?). The questions are addressed using specific material from the chapter. As one reviewer said, "The Contemporary Reflections answer many of the most often asked questions by students."

- A section "Race and Modern Human Origins" is included in Chapter 12 to clarify the commonly expressed connection between those two topics.

- Chapter 3 includes an improved description of protein synthesis, Chapter 4 elaborates on the sickle cell anemia example, and Chapter 5 includes an expanded, more accurate discussion of the issue of gradualism v. punctuated equilibrium.

- Chapter 7 on primates now includes a discussion of cladistics and cladistic primate taxonomies.

- Chapter 8 contains updated information on baboon behavior and now includes a separate section on the behavior of the bonobos.

- Chapter 10 includes updated material on the evolution of the early primates, bipedalism, and the first Plio/Pleistocene hominids.

SUPPLEMENTARY MATERIAL

The **Instructor's Manual** includes a test bank of about 500 multiple choice and short answer/essay questions, as well as chapter overviews, suggested activities, and lists of key words.

A **Computerized Test Bank** is available free of charge to qualifying adopters. It is a powerful, easy-to-use test generation system that provides all test items on computer disk for IBM-compatible or Macintosh computers. Instructors can select, add, or edit questions, randomize them, and print tests appropriate to their individual classes.

A set of **Color Transparencies** is also available for use on an overhead projector. Included are charts and diagrams from the text as well as several diagrams created just for classroom use.

ACKNOWLEDGMENTS

I must go back to the very beginning of my career and thank my first teachers in bioanthropology at Indiana University, Robert Meier and Paul Jamison, and the late Georg Neumann.

In the present, special thanks to my friend, colleague, and ofttimes co-author, Ken Feder. Not only has he been a help with this project, but he has, over more than twenty years, been a catalyst, if not a major element in much of my professional activity, particularly my writing.

And thanks, as always, to the folks at Mayfield, particularly sponsoring editor Jan Beatty (whose knowledge of both the publishing business and anthropology provides the holistic vision that makes such projects possible); production editor Melissa Kreischer (whose attention to all of the details made the production go smoothly); art manager Robin Mouat (who transformed my doodles into art); copyeditor Dale Anderson (who polished up some of my sentences and didn't edit out a small joke); and designer Anna George and design manager Susan Breitbard (who made the book so attractive and, therefore, more useful).

I also thank all those who reviewed the manuscript: John A. Alsoszatai-Petheo, Central Washington University; Diane Everett Barbolla, San Diego Mesa College; Ronda A. Burkhart, Pikes Peak Community College; Lynne E. Christensen, San Diego State University; Dana Cope, College of Charleston; Mark L. Fleischman, Syracuse University; Agustin Fuentes, Central Washington University; Richard B. Lane, St. Cloud State University; Jonathan Marks, University of California, Berkeley; Patricia Rice, West Virginia University; Rebecca Storey, University of Houston; and Elizabeth Strasser, California State University, Sacramento. Their suggestions and advice were invaluable. Any errors, of course, remain my responsibility.

To the Reader

The broad field of biological (or physical) anthropology deals with every-thing from evolutionary theory to the human fossil record to the identi-fication of human skeletal remains from crime scenes and accidents. A detailed account of this whole field would result in an unwieldy text that would be a tough assignment for a one-semester introductory course, es-pecially if it were assigned in its entirety.

This text is intended to truly be an *introduction* to biological anthro-pology. It will tell you about the many different kinds of studies bioan-thropologists participate in and how they conduct them; you'll also learn about the scientific theories and data they use. All the important aspects of bioanthropology are covered here but with just the essential amount of detail. When you understand an idea from this book, then you should be able to delve more deeply into the subject if you are interested and you will have the basis for an even more profound understanding.

A major theme of this book is the scientific method. Biological an-thropology is a science, so an understanding of how science works is es-sential. Because the field of anthropology studies the human species in its entirety, however, the text will examine science as a human endeavor, seeing where it fits in the realm of human knowledge.

HOW TO USE THIS BOOK

Each chapter starts with an **introduction** that sets the stage and context for what's to come, followed by a series of **questions** that the chapter will answer. Because science proceeds by asking and answering questions, this format is also used within the body of the text. Important **terms** are in boldface and are defined in the margins at their first appearance. Each chapter ends with a **summary** that not only recaps the important points of the chapter, but also provides some new ideas and thoughts that help put what you have just learned into the context of the whole discipline of bioanthropology. A list of **suggested readings** made up mostly of nontechnical works tells you where to find more information if you are interested in a particular topic.

A Glossary of Human and Nonhuman Primates defines taxonomic (scientific) names for species discussed in the text—names like *Homo sapiens* and *Australopithecus afarensis*—and tells you how to pronounce them. In addition to the running glossary within chapters, a comprehensive main glossary appears at the back of the book. The bibliography gives complete references for the suggested readings and also lists technical works referred to within the text. The index will help you more quickly access information.

Contents

Observe always that everything is the result of change, and get used to thinking that there is nothing Nature loves so well as to change existing forms, and to make new ones like them.

—Marcus Aurelius

CHAPTER

1

BIOLOGICAL ANTHROPOLOGY

Anthropologists study
spiders, right?
—Anonymous caller

If you ask twenty different people to define anthropology, you will probably get twenty different answers. Anthropology is such a broad field that many people, understandably, are not sure just what an anthropologist studies. I have been brought rocks to identify, been asked about the accuracy of the dinosaurs in *Jurassic Park*, and even received a phone call from a man who wanted information about black widow spiders—and he was referred to me by someone within the university where I teach.

In this chapter, we will define anthropology in general and then focus on the subfield of biological anthropology (bioanthropology or physical anthropology). Because fieldwork—where anthropologists make their observations and collect their data—is perhaps the best known aspect of anthropology and is the part that attracts many students to the discipline, I will begin with a brief description of two of my fieldwork experiences.

As you read, consider the following questions:

What is anthropology, and what are its subfields?

What is biological anthropology?

How does the scientific method operate?

In what way is bioanthropology a science?

What are belief systems, and what is their relationship to scientific knowledge?

IN THE FIELD: DOING BIOLOGICAL ANTHROPOLOGY

The wheat fields on either side of the long, straight road in western Saskatchewan, Canada, stretched, as the cliché says, as far as the eye could see. I found myself wishing, on that June day in 1973, that the road went on just as far. I was on my way to an initial visit with my first real anthropological subjects, a colony of people belonging to a 450-year-old religious denomination called the Hutterian Brethren, or Hutterites.

Up to this point I had not felt much anxiety about the visit. Accounts by other anthropologists of contacts with Amazon jungle warriors and New Guinea headhunters made my situation seem rather safe. The Hutterites are, after all, people who share my European-American cultural heritage, number English among their languages, and, far from being hostile, practice a form of Christianity that emphasizes pacifism and tolerance.

At this point, though, those considerations, no matter how reassuring they should have been, didn't help. Nor did the fact that I was accompanied by the wife of a local wheat farmer who was well known and liked by the people of this colony. I simply had that unnamed fear that affects nearly all anthropologists under these first-contact circumstances.

Finally, the road we traveled—which had turned from blacktop to dirt about ten miles back—curved abruptly to the right, crossed a railroad track, and crested a hill, and I saw below us, at the literal end of the road, a neat collection of twenty or so white buildings surrounded by acres of cultivated fields. This was the Hutterite colony, or *Bruderhof*, the "place where the brethren live" (Figure 1.1).

We drove down the hill and into the colony. Not a soul was to be seen. My companion explained that it was a religious holiday, which required all but essential work to cease. Everyone was indoors observing the holiday, but the colony minister and colony boss had agreed to see me.

We entered one of the smaller buildings, which I recognized from pictures and diagrams of "typical" colonies as one of the residential

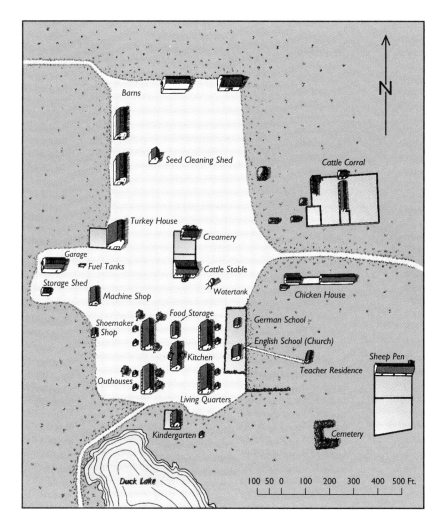

FIGURE 1.1
Diagram of typical Hutterite colony. The variety of buildings and their functions are indicative of the Hutterites' attempt to keep their colonies self-sufficient and separate from the outside world.

buildings. The interior was darkened in conjunction with the holiday, and that fact combined with my nervous excitement have erased all first impressions from my memory. A few minutes later, however, with my bearings straight and the introductions made, I found myself explaining the reason for my visit to two men and a woman.

The men were dressed in the Hutterite fashion—black trousers and coats and white shirts—and they wore beards, a sign of marriage. The older, gray-haired man was the colony minister. The younger man, who happened to be his son, was the colony boss. The woman, the minister's wife, also dressed in the conservative style that has become a trademark of the Hutterites and related groups. She wore a nearly full-length sleeveless dress—a small floral pattern on a black background—with a white blouse underneath. Her head was covered by a polka-dot kerchief or "shawl," as they call it.

My contacts, the wheat farmer and his wife, had already given the Hutterites an idea of what I wanted to do, and this visit had already been arranged. But if they didn't like me or my explanation, they could still decline to cooperate. So I started from the beginning. The three listened in silence as I went through my well-rehearsed explanation. When I had finished, they asked me a few questions, far fewer than I had expected. Was I from the government? (My study involved using fingerprints as hereditary traits, and they apparently knew about them only in the context of law enforcement and personal identification.) Did I know Scripture? (My equivocal answer created no problem.) What would I use this study for? Was I going to write a book? Did I know so-and-so, who had been there two years ago and done medical examinations?

I expected that when they were done they would confer with one another or ask me to come back when they had decided if they would allow me to conduct the study. Instead, the Hutterite minister, who was clearly in charge, simply said, "Today is a holiday for us. Can you start tomorrow?"

And so, for the next month, I took part in my personal version of fieldwork—taking fingerprints, recording family relationships, observing colony life, and getting to know the Hutterites of this and one other Canadian *Bruderhof* (Park 1979) (Figure 1.2).

What exactly had brought me thirteen hundred miles from my university to the northern plains, to this isolated community of people whose way of life has changed little over the last 450 years and whose lifestyle and philosophy differ so much from those of North American culture in general? Essentially, it was the same thing that takes anthropologists to locations from the highlands of New Guinea to caves in the Pyrenees to street corners in New York City: the desire to learn something about the nature of the human species.

FIGURE 1.2
Author (right) and Hutterite informant. I already had the beard, but it was suggested that I keep it so I would look more familiar to the Hutterite children.

In my case, I was pursuing an interest I had developed early in graduate school. An important facet of biological anthropology is the study of the processes of evolution and how they affect humans. I was curious about two of these processes: gene flow and genetic drift (see Chapter 4 for details). Both topics had been described half a century earlier, but their workings and importance, especially with regard to living human populations, were still poorly understood.

To examine the actions of these processes on human populations and to determine their roles in human evolution, I needed to find a human group with a few special characteristics. The group had to be genetically isolated; that is, most members should find their mates within the group. The group had to be fairly small as a whole, but hopefully with large individual families. It was also helpful if the people knew and were interested in genealogical relationships and if their family relationships reflected genetic as well as cultural categories. (All societies have systems of family relationships, but few of these coincide completely with biological relationships.) Finally, individual populations within the group ideally would have been created through the splitting of earlier populations.

The Hutterites fit this description well. (I'll elaborate later.) I discovered them through library research on genetically isolated groups. My opportunity to study them was greatly enhanced by a stroke of luck. A fellow graduate student was the daughter of the wheat farmer and his wife who became my "public relations advisors."

Exactly twenty years later, I found myself standing over an open grave in an old cemetery in the wooded hills of northwest Connecticut. Our team of anthropologists was hoping to find the remains of a native Hawaiian who had been buried here in 1818 and who was now, after 175 years, going home.

A few weeks earlier, Nick Bellantoni, the Connecticut state archaeologist (and a former student of mine) had called me with a fascinating story. In 1808 a young Hawaiian named Opukahaia (O-pu-ka-ha-EE-a) escaped the tribal warfare that had killed his family by swimming out to a Yankee whaling vessel, where he was taken on board as a cabin boy. Two years (and many adventures) later he ended up at Yale University in New Haven, Connecticut. He took the name Henry, converted to Christianity, and became a Congregational minister who helped build a missionary school in Cornwall, Connecticut. His dream was to return to Hawaii and bring his new faith to the people there (see the portrait in Figure 1.5).

Sadly, Henry's dream was never realized. He died in a typhoid epidemic in 1818 at the age of twenty-six, but his vision inspired the missionary movement that was to change the history of the Hawaiian Islands forever. His grave in Cornwall became a shrine both for the people of his adopted land and for visiting Hawaiians, who would leave offerings atop his platform-style headstone (Figure 1.3).

Nearly two centuries later, a living relative of Henry's had a dream in which she envisioned honoring Henry's final wish to once more see his native land. After almost a year of raising funds and making the necessary arrangements, her dream was to come true. And this is where anthropology comes in.

Old New England cemeteries vary widely in the exact placement of headstones relative to the bodies buried beneath them, and the acidic New England soil is unkind to organic remains. Both logically and legally, this was a job for the state archaeologist, and Nick wanted my help in recovering and identifying whatever remains we might be lucky enough to find. He also wanted my help, it turned out, in moving several tons of stone.

Henry's tomb had been carefully and lovingly assembled by the people of Cornwall. They placed the inscribed headstone on a pedestal of fieldstone and mortar. We dismantled this with care, labeling each stone and diagramming its position, since it was to be rebuilt by a stone mason.

FIGURE 1.3
The headstone of Henry Opukahaia.

Under the pedestal, and going down about three feet into the ground, we uncovered three more layers of fieldstone that acted as a foundation for the monument and protection for the coffin and the remains we hoped were still below. When all the stones had been removed and we were into a layer of sandy soil, Nick worked alone, delicately scraping away the dirt inch by inch.

Late on the second day of our excavation, the remnants of the coffin came into view. In fact, the wooden coffin itself had long since decayed. All that was left was the dark shadow of its outline in the soil (Figure 1.4). We began to despair of finding much else, but an hour later Nick's trowel grazed something hard, and in a few minutes the apparent remains of Henry Opukahaia saw the light of day for the first time in 175 years.

We soon learned that the skeleton was virtually complete. But was it *Henry?* As Nick slowly freed each bone from the soil and handed it up to me, we recorded it and compared it with what we knew of Henry from written descriptions and a single portrait. The skeleton was clearly that of a male and, at first glance, conformed to that of a person in his late twenties of about the right size. Henry had been described as being "a little under six feet," and the long bones of the arms and legs appeared to be

FIGURE 1.4

Excavating the grave of Henry Opukahaia. The pattern on the floor of the excavation marks the coffin outline.

just a bit shorter than mine, though much more robust. The skull, however, confirmed our identification. As the dirt was brushed away, the face of Henry Opukahaia emerged, the very image of his portrait. (The family has requested that, for religious reasons, photographs of Henry's remains not be published.)

We spent two more days with the bones, this time in the garage of a Hartford funeral home. We cleaned, photographed, measured, and described each bone. Closer analysis supported our graveside conclusions, and more. On the inside surface of the ribs, we found the telltale ashy texture that can be symptomatic of typhoid. The original diagnosis, done in the days before medicine even understood about microorganisms, had been correct.

Finally, we placed each bone in correct anatomical position in spaces cut into heavy foam rubber with which we had lined the bottom of a *koa* wood coffin, specially made and shipped from Hawaii. The following Sunday we attended a memorial service in Cornwall, and then Henry's remains began their long journey back home (Figure 1.5).

FIGURE 1.5
Reverend David Hirano, from Hawaii, speaks over the remains of Henry Opukahaia at his "homegoing" celebration in Cornwall, Connecticut. The koa wood coffin, ti leaves, and flowered lei all have symbolic meaning in Hawaiian culture.

WHAT IS BIOLOGICAL ANTHROPOLOGY?

My experiences as a biological anthropologist range from examining the esoteric detail of evolutionary theory to using my knowledge of the human skeleton for a very personal endeavor. These are just two examples of the many things that biological anthropologists do.

    Biological anthropology (bioanthropology or **physical anthropology)** needs to be defined within the context of anthropology as a whole, and doing this is both simple and complex. **Anthropology,** in general, is defined as *the study of the human species.* Simply put, anthropologists study the human species as any zoologist would study an animal **species.** We look into every aspect of the biology of our subject—genetics, anatomy, physiology, behavior, environment, adaptations, and evolutionary history—stressing the interrelationships among these aspects.

    This kind of approach—examining a subject by focusing on the interrelationships among its parts—is called **holistic.** The holistic approach

biological anthropology: Subfield of anthropology that studies humans as a biological species.

bioanthropology: Another name for biological anthropology.

physical anthropology: The traditional name for biological anthropology.

anthropology: The study of the human species.

species: A group of organisms that can produce fertile offspring among themselves but not with members of other groups.

holistic: Assuming an interrelationship among the parts of a subject.

is the hallmark of anthropology. We understand that all the facets of our species—our biology, our behavior, our past, and our present—interact to make us what we are. We need to study some topics separately, since they can be so complex. Thus, you may be taking courses in history, economics, psychology, art, anatomy, and so on. What anthropologists do is seek the connections among these subjects, for, in real life, they are not absolutely separate.

But here's where it gets complicated. The most characteristic feature of our species' behavior is **culture,** and cultural behavior is not programmed in our genes, as is, for example, much of the behavior of birds, or virtually all of the behavior of ants.

Human culture is learned. We have a biological potential for cultural behavior in general, but exactly *how* we behave comes to us through all our experiences. Take language, for example. All humans are born with the ability to learn a language. Which language each of us actually speaks is determined by what language is spoken in our family and in the broader culture in which we live.

Moreover, cultural knowledge involves not just specific facts, but, more importantly, ideas, concepts, generalizations, and abstractions. For example, you were able to speak your native language fairly fluently before you were ever formally taught the particulars of its grammar. You did this by making your own generalizations from the raw data you heard and the rules they followed, that is, from the speech of others and from trying to make yourself understood by them. Even now when you speak, you are applying those generalizations to new situations. And each situation— every conversation you have, every essay you write, every book you read—is a new situation.

In addition, because culture exists in the context of human social interactions, it must be shared among members of a social group. The complexity of cultural ideas requires this sharing to involve symbols— agreed-upon representations of concepts and abstractions. Human language, of course, is symbolic, as are many visual aspects of our cultures.

In short, culture is highly variable and flexible. It differs from society to society and from one time period to another. It even differs, in its details, from one individual to another. We continually modify our cultural behaviors to fit the unique circumstances of our lives.

All this variability makes the study of the human species complex and challenging, and so anthropology, the discipline that takes on this challenge, is typically divided into a number of subfields.

Biological anthropology looks at our species from a biological point of view. This includes all the topics covered in this book. **Cultural anthropology** is the study of culture as a characteristic of our species and of the variation in cultural expression among human groups. This includes human language, although sometimes anthropological linguistics is considered a separate subfield. **Archaeology** is the study of the human cultural past and the reconstruction of past cultural systems. It also involves the techniques used to recover, preserve, and interpret the material remains of the past.

All anthropologists, then, are trying to do the same thing: learn about the human species. The scope and complexity of the subject require several starting points or focuses. These are the subfields of anthropology.

Each subfield has many specialties. For biological anthropology, these specialties are best expressed in terms of the questions we seek to answer about human biology:

1. What are the *biological characteristics* that define the human species? How do our *genes* code for these characteristics? Just how much do genes contribute to our traits? How much are traits shaped by the environment? How does *evolution* work and how does it apply to us? (These were the questions I was pursuing in my study of the Hutterites).

2. What is the *physical record* of our evolution? This is the specialty referred to as **paleoanthropology,** the study of human *fossils*.

3. What sort of *biological variation* do we see in our species today? What genetic variations does this variation reflect? How did it evolve? What do the variable traits mean for other aspects of our lives? What do they *not* mean?

4. What can we learn about the biology of our close relatives, the non-human **primates,** and what can it tell us about ourselves? This specialty is called **primatology.**

5. What do we know about **human ecology,** the relationships between humans and their environments?

6. How can we apply all this knowledge to matters of current concern? This is often called **applied anthropology.** (The story of the exhumation of Henry Opukahaia is an example.)

The place of biological anthropology and its specialties within the whole discipline of anthropology may be diagrammed as in Figure 1.6.

Individual biological anthropologists undertake numerous and diverse studies. I took fingerprints of members of a centuries-old Christian group to learn something about the processes of evolution that have affected our species. Paleoanthropologist Donald Johanson was with the team that discovered and identified the famous fossil of "Lucy," a 3.2-million-year-old human ancestor. Paleontologist Elwyn Simons studies fossils of nonhuman primates that go even further back in evolutionary time—to the dawn of the apes more than 30 million years ago. Other anthropologists study living nonhuman primates. Shirley Strum, Barbara Smuts, and Linda

culture: Ideas and behaviors that are learned and transmitted. Nongenetic means of adaptation.

cultural anthropology: Subfield of anthropology that focuses on human cultural behavior and cultural systems and the variation in cultural expression among human groups.

archaeology: Subfield of anthropology that studies the human cultural past and the reconstruction of past cultural systems.

paleoanthropology: Specialty that studies the human fossil record.

primates: Large-brained, tree-dwelling mammals with three-dimensional color vision and grasping hands. Humans are primates.

primatology: Specialty that studies nonhuman primates.

human ecology: Specialty that studies the relationships between humans and their environments.

applied anthropology: Anthropology used to address current practical problems and concerns.

FIGURE 1.6
The subfields of anthropology and the specialties of biological anthropology.

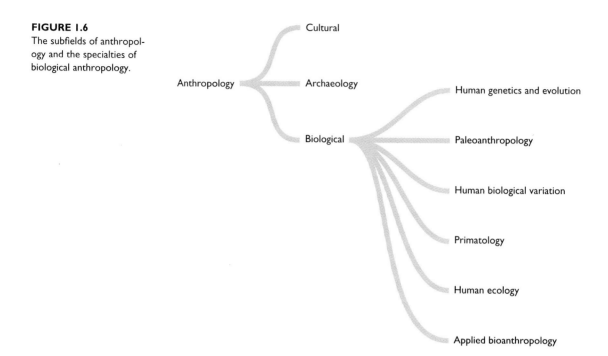

Fedigan, for example, have all observed troops of baboons to understand what their behavior can tell us about our own.

Clyde Snow is a **forensic anthropologist.** He applies his knowledge of the human skeleton to solving crimes and identifying missing persons. He has worked to identify the remains of the victims of death squads in Argentina and has tried (so far without success) to locate the bones of Butch Cassidy and the Sundance Kid in Bolivia.

Melvin Konner has examined the lifestyles of contemporary **hunter-gatherers,** including diet and exercise, to show how those lifestyles differ (mostly for the better) from those of people in industrial societies.

We'll meet these people and their studies, and many more, as we survey the field of bioanthropology. As we do, keep in mind that what connects these varied activities is their focus on *learning about human beings as a biological species.*

The studies of bioanthropologists are also connected in that they are all scientific. In many cases, they may not seem to fit the common conception of science. Most anthropologists don't wear white lab coats and work with test tubes and chemicals. Many anthropologists study things that can't be directly observed in nature or recreated in the lab because they happened in the past. But bioanthropology *is* a science, just as much as chemistry, physics, and biology. We'll see how this is so, and we'll also look at some nonscientific ways in which people try to understand their world.

BIOANTHROPOLOGY AND SCIENCE

A popular image of a scientist is that of a walking encyclopedia. Science is often seen as fact-collecting. While it's fair to say that scientists know a lot of facts, so do a lot of other people. Champions on the TV quiz show *Jeopardy* are not usually professional scientists.

Facts are certainly important to science. They are the raw material of science, the data scientists use. But what scientists really do is *explain* facts, not simply collect them. **Science,** in other words, is *a method of inquiry; a way of answering questions about the world.* But how does science work? Is science the only valid and logical method for explaining the world around us?

The Scientific Method

The world is full of things that need explaining. We might wonder about the behavior of a bird, the origin of the stars in the night sky, the identity of a fossil skeleton, the social interaction of students in a college classroom, or the ritual warfare of a society in highland New Guinea. As people, we strive to understand such phenomena, to know why and how these things occur as they do. As scientists, we must answer these questions according to a special set of rules—the **scientific method.**

We begin by asking the questions we wish to answer or by describing the observations we wish to explain. We then make what are essentially educated guesses about possible explanations. These are called **hypotheses.** In other words, we try to formulate a *general* explanatory principle that will account for *specific* pieces of real, tangible data. This process is called **induction.**

Next comes the essence of science. We must attempt to either support or refute our hypothesis by *testing* it. Tests may take many forms, depending on what we are trying to explain, but basically we reverse the process of induction and go from the general back to the specific by making predictions: *If* our general hypothesis is correct, *then* what other specific things should we observe? This process is called **deduction.** For example, we look for:

1. *Repetition.* Does the same phenomenon occur over and over?
2. *Universality.* If we vary some aspect of the situation, will the phenomenon still occur? How might different situations change the phenomenon?
3. *Explanations for exceptions.* Can we account for cases where the phenomenon doesn't appear to occur?
4. *New data.* Does new information support or contradict our hypothesis?

forensic anthropologist: One who applies anthropology to legal matters.

hunter-gatherers: Societies that rely upon naturally occurring sources of food.

science: The method of inquiry that requires the generation, testing, and acceptance or rejection of hypotheses.

scientific method: The process of conducting scientific inquiry.

hypotheses: Educated guesses to explain natural phenomena.

induction: Developing a general explanation from specific observations.

deduction: Suggesting specific data that would be found if a hypothesis were true.

If we find one piece of evidence that conclusively refutes our hypothesis, we consider it disproved. But if the hypothesis passes every test we come up with, we elevate our idea to the status of a "very good hypothesis." In science, we call this a **theory.**

Notice that I didn't say we "proved" the hypothesis. Scientists should always be skeptical, always look for new evidence, always be open to and even invite change. The best we can honestly say about a theory is that *so far* no evidence has been found that *disproves* it.

Of course, some theories are so well supported that we are safe in considering them to be true and in using them as a basis for further investigation. The theory of gravity, the theory of evolution, and the theory of relativity are all concepts central to many aspects of our thinking because they are ideas supported by every test applied to them and refuted by none.

We don't stop investigating when we have developed a theory, however. No theory is complete. The theory of gravity establishes that some force that we call gravity exists, but we still don't understand exactly what gravity is and how it works. Science is now testing several hypotheses that attempt to explain the nature and operation of gravity.

Science is often popularly conceived of as the study of visible, tangible, and present-day objects—chemicals, living organisms, planets, and stars. But notice that gravity, for example, is decidedly *not* visible or tangible. We can't see gravity, but we know it exists because all our deductive predictions support its existence (Figure 1.7).

FIGURE 1.7

Light bent by gravity. Einstein predicted that a strong gravitational field could bend light. His prediction was verified when light from stars that should have been blocked by the sun could be seen during a solar eclipse. The effect is greatly exaggerated in this drawing.

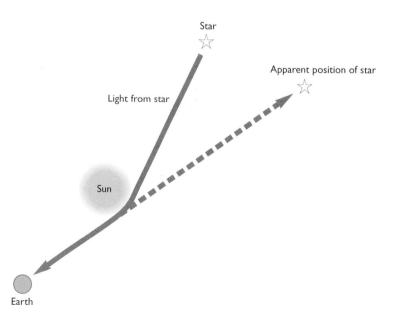

Similarly, past events can't be seen or touched. They can't be experimented upon directly or repeated exactly. The evolution of plants and animals is an example. But again, we now accept that evolution occurred because the idea has passed all our tests. The idea of evolution explains observations of the real world. We have observed everything we predicted we would *if* evolution occurred. We'll look more closely at how science has derived and supported the theory of evolution in Chapters 3 through 6. We will also see how the accepted fact of evolution is itself further explained by the theory of natural selection and other processes of genetic change. (See also the "Contemporary Reflections" for this chapter.)

Finally, we often think of the scientific method as applying only to stereotypical scientific matters like gravity, chemistry, and evolution. In fact, we all use the scientific method every day for issues somewhat more down-to-earth than gravity. Remember, science is *a way of thinking.* Any time you solve some problem—say, how to most efficiently organize all your activities for a certain day or how to repair a broken household item—you use a version of the scientific method.

Science answers questions about our lives and about the world in which we live. For an answer to be defined as scientific, it must be testable. Put another way, it must be possible to find data that would refute or falsify it. As Galileo said—speaking in metaphor—and as Pope John Paul II repeated centuries later, scientific inquiry tells us "how heaven *is.*" That is, science tells us what the world is really like and how it works. In contrast to science are belief systems. They tell us how the world *should* be, or, as Galileo put it, "how to *get* to heaven."

Belief Systems

Some questions about the world, even in a technologically complex society like ours, remain beyond the scope of science.

Scientific inquiry, as powerful and important as it is, doesn't answer everything. Though we have some well-established theories about how the universe evolved once it began, the ultimate origin of the universe remains, for the moment at least, outside the realm of science. For most human societies throughout most of our species' history, many questions could not be addressed scientifically.

Nor does science tell us how to behave. In our society, for example, we treat medical matters scientifically. But science does not, and cannot, inform us how best to apply medical knowledge. Who should practice medicine? How are medical practitioners trained and administered by society? How should they be compensated? What should their relationship be with their patients? Is everyone equally entitled to medical care? Society and the medical profession answer these questions through laws and regula-

theory: A hypothesis that has been well supported by evidence and testing.

Contemporary Reflections

Is Evolution a Fact or a Theory?

It may come as a surprise, but the answer to this commonly asked question is *both*. Evolution can be seen as a fact because so much evidence supports it. But it can also be seen as a theory because the scientific method is not a nice, neat, linear series of steps from first observation to final theory—even though it may seem like that from basic descriptions (including, perhaps, the one in this chapter). Rather, the inductive and deductive reasoning of science must be applied constantly to the different aspects of the same general subject, for data and hypotheses should always be re-examined and each theory itself becomes a new observation to be questioned, tested, and explained.

Observations of the world of organisms—fossils, the geological formations in which they are found, and the biology of living creatures—find explanation in the theory of evolution, the idea that living things change through time and that organisms are related as in a huge branching family tree, existing species giving rise to new species. There is so much evidence in support of evolution that this tried and tested theory may reasonably be considered a fact. Of course, new data could conceivably change that, but with an idea as well supported as evolution, it is highly unlikely.

A good analogy is the accepted fact that the earth revolves around the sun and not, as people thought for so long, the other way around. But how do we *know* the earth revolves around the sun? It certainly appears, upon basic daily observation, to do just the opposite. We accept the heliocentric theory because there is so much evidence in its support. It makes so much sense that we consider it a fact and take it for granted. I would be very surprised to read in tomorrow's newspaper that some new evidence refuted the idea. A fact then can be, as Stephen Jay Gould says (1983:255), a theory "confirmed to such a degree that it would be perverse to withhold provisional assent." Similarly, that evolution occurred and accounts for the nature of life on earth, then, is for all intents and purposes a fact.

But that fact poses new questions. A big one (the one that confronted Darwin) is *how* evolution takes place. The fact of evolution now becomes a new observation that requires explanation through the generation of new hypotheses and the subsequent testing and retesting of those hypotheses. Darwin proposed a mechanism he called natural selection and then, over many years, examined this hypothesis against real-world data. The mechanism of natural selection is now so well supported that we call it, too, a fact. But an overall explanation for how evolution works—a theory to explain the observed fact of evolution—is far from complete. We know that mechanisms in addition to natural selection account for evolution. The relative importance of all these mechanisms is still debated. The broad picture of evolution—the "shape" of the family tree of living things—is a matter of much discussion as well. The specific genetic processes behind all evolutionary change are only beginning to be glimpsed as new technologies are letting us look closer and closer at the very code of life. So, evolution is also a theory, in the sense that we are still examining hypotheses to account for *how* it takes place.

The next five chapters will detail how the scientific method has been and is currently being applied to the fact and theory of biological evolution.

tions. For example, the Hippocratic Oath, taken by all doctors, says, in part, "I will not permit considerations of religion, nationality, race, party politics or social standing to intervene between my duty and my patient; . . ."

Finally, there are questions that can never be answered by science—matters like the meaning of life, the existence of a higher power, the proper social relationships among people within a society, or the purpose of one's own life.

All these sorts of questions are addressed by **belief systems**—religions, philosophies, ethics, morals, and laws. Belief systems differ from science in that they cannot be tested, cannot be disproved. Their truths are taken on faith, and that, of course, is the source of their power. They provide stable bases for our behavior, for explanations of what is beyond our science, and for the broad, existential questions of life. Belief systems change, but they only change when *we* decide to change them, either as a society or as individuals.

The existence of a supreme being is an example of a value inherent in one's belief system. Two of us with opposite views on the subject could debate the issue endlessly, but no scientific test could support or refute either view. If I were to change my mind on the matter, it would be because of a personal decision. The supreme being is not to be found in a test tube or in an observation through a telescope.

Belief systems don't apply only to these big questions. I had a friend in graduate school from a West African society that was polygynous—men could have several wives. Having more than one wife is normal for his society, whereas in mine, one wife (at least one at a time) is the norm. We discussed the pros and cons of these two systems at length one day, but we never, of course, arrived at any "answer." His belief was the norm for his society as was mine for my society. We each took it on faith that this was so.

Although we often perceive science and belief systems as being eternally and inevitably at odds with one another, nothing could be further from the truth. Conflicts do arise, as they do among facets of any society. But it should be apparent that, for a society to function, it needs both scientific knowledge and beliefs because neither, by itself, addresses all the questions.

To repeat Galileo's statements, while science tells us "how heaven *is*," belief systems tell us "how to *get* to heaven." Or, in the words of biologist John Maynard Smith, science tells us what is "possible," and beliefs tell us what is "desirable." No culture can function without both.

⋁   ⋁   ⋁

SUMMARY

Anthropology is the study of the human species. Cultural anthropology studies human culture, cultural systems, and their variation. Our species' most characteristic feature today is our cultural behavior, which is expressed in a great variety of ways among different societies.

belief systems: Ideas that are taken on faith and cannot be scientifically tested.

Most human cultural systems existed in the past and have left us only meager physical remains of their presence and nature. A second major subfield of anthropology recovers and interprets these remains; this subfield is archaeology.

Biological anthropology studies the human species the way biology studies any species, examining our biological characteristics, our evolution, our variation, our relationship with our environment, and our behavior, including our ability to have culture.

Bioanthropology, as a scientific discipline, asks questions about the human species and then attempts to answer them by proposing hypotheses and by *testing* those hypotheses, looking both for evidence in their support and for anything that would refute them.

Scientific knowledge is important for any society, but it must be mediated by the nonscientific values of belief systems—the untestable ideas of philosophy, law, and religion that are taken on faith. Societies need both, interacting in harmony, to fully function.

KEY TERMS

biological anthropology

bioanthropology

physical anthropology

anthropology

species

holistic

culture

cultural anthropology

archaeology

paleoanthropology

primates

primatology

human ecology

applied anthropology

forensic anthropologist

hunter-gatherers

science

scientific method

hypotheses

induction

deduction

theory

belief systems

SUGGESTED READINGS

For more personal experiences of biological anthropologists, see Part 1 of my *Biological Anthropology: An Introductory Reader.*

For more information on the Hutterites, see John Hostetler's *Hutterite Society.*

For a longer discussion of the nature of science and the scientific method, see Kenneth L. Feder's *Frauds, Myths and Mysteries: Science and Pseudoscience in Archaeology*, third edition. The relationship between science and belief systems is nicely covered by John Maynard Smith's article "Science and Myth" in the November 1984 issue of *Natural History*.

The field of anthropology in general is covered by Emily Schultz and Robert Lavenda in *Anthropology: A Perspective on the Human Condition*, second edition, and in a series of contemporary articles by Aaron Podolefsky and Peter Brown in *Applying Anthropology: An Introductory Reader*, third edition.

THE EVOLUTION
OF EVOLUTION

One touch of Darwin
makes the whole
world kin.
—George Bernard
Shaw

Evolution and its application to the human species—how we descended from nonhuman ancestors, how we have changed over time into modern *Homo sapiens*, and how we are still changing—is a central theme of bioanthropology. As noted in Chapter 1, the *fact* of evolution is well supported by scientific examination—the idea has passed every scientific test applied to it. Scientists, however, are still debating the details of evolution and are still refining the *theory* that explains exactly how evolution operates. It took some time, though, for the scientific method to be applied to this idea.

> How did our knowledge of the history of living organisms move from the realm of belief systems to the realm of science?
>
> How did the scientific evidence for evolution develop?

"ON THE SHOULDERS OF GIANTS": EXPLAINING THE CHANGING EARTH

FIGURE 2.1
Portrait of Charles Darwin in 1869.

The Englishman Charles Darwin (1809–1882) is usually, and correctly, associated with our understanding of biological evolution (Figure 2.1). He is also popularly given credit for the very idea of evolution and for explaining and therefore proving it. This, however, is not entirely correct. Like any great scientific accomplishment, Darwin's was based on the work of many who came before him. He stood, as Isaac Newton said of himself, "on the shoulders of giants." Darwin's genius was in being able to take massive amounts of data and assorted existing ideas and, using an imagination possessed by few humans, put them all together into a logical, cohesive theory that made sense of the world and that could be examined by the methods of science.

The idea of evolution is simple enough: Species of living things change over time, and sometimes this change is extensive enough to produce new forms of living organisms. This idea was not new in Darwin's time. Anaximander, a Greek of the sixth century B.C., proposed that humans had arisen from other forms of life. He incorrectly thought we arose directly from fish, but he explained his idea using reason rather than basing it on the supernatural, and his reasoning was based on the question of how animals survive in their environments, a question that would form the cornerstone of Darwin's idea (Harris, 1981).

Many others over the next two thousand years also contemplated the origins of living things, but the modern story of evolution theory really begins in Europe in the seventeenth century, where the influence of the Bible was felt in all aspects of life, including science. Specifically, the ancient Judeo-Christian creation story—Adam and Eve, the Garden of Eden, the flood and Noah's ark—was generally considered to be literally true. Thus, it was thought that the entire universe was created by supernatural powers over a period of six days and that, except for the matter of the great flood, the earth and its inhabitants were pretty much the same now as they were when created. One scholar, Irish archbishop James Ussher (1581–1656), even used the assumption of biblical truth, as well as certain historical records, to help him calculate the date of creation, and thus the age of the earth. In 1650 he reckoned that the creation began at noon on Sunday, October 23, in the year 4004 B.C. The earth was thus just under 6000 years old.

The literal interpretation of the Bible, in turn, was probably influenced by two old but persuasive ideas that go back to Plato and Aristotle, Greek philosophers of the fourth and fifth centuries B.C. One idea is called "essentialism"—the notion of ideal types. It is the concept that there is an ideal or essential form of every natural entity and that the entities we see are mere inexact copies of the ideal. The variations we see, for example, among the members of some species of living organism—for example, breeds of dogs—are just deviations from the essential dog form. Applied to biblical creation, essentialism promoted the idea that one ideal form of each living thing had been created and that the present-day variations—breeds of animals or races of people—are departures from those ideals.

The second idea is called the "great chain of being." It says that the ideal or essential forms of things are not just a list of equals but are arranged in a ladder or chain, from least complex to most complex and from least perfect to most perfect. There are two different creation stories in Genesis, one where humans are created last, after all the animals (Gen. 1), and one where humans are created first (Gen. 2). Whichever order one accepts, however, there is the clear implication that humans are the most perfect form of creation. These two philosophical ideas would also have a strong influence on the later science of evolution, as we will see.

Dependence upon the Bible for knowledge of the natural world was not to last. About the time Ussher was making his calculations, others were beginning to seek knowledge about the earth from the earth itself. What these "natural scientists" or "natural philosophers" saw forced them to begin changing their minds about what seemed to be the obvious lessons from the book of Genesis.

For example, **fossils** of plants and animals—once thought to be mere quirks of nature—were recognized by another seventeenth-century scientist, Robert Hooke (1635–1703), as the remains of creatures that had become extinct or that still existed but in different form. Living things, in other words, had changed.

CHAIN OF BEING—
LEAST PERFECT →
MOST PERFECT

IMMUTABILITY—
NO CHANGE

evolution: Systematic change through time; here, with reference to biological species.

fossils: Remains of life forms of the past.

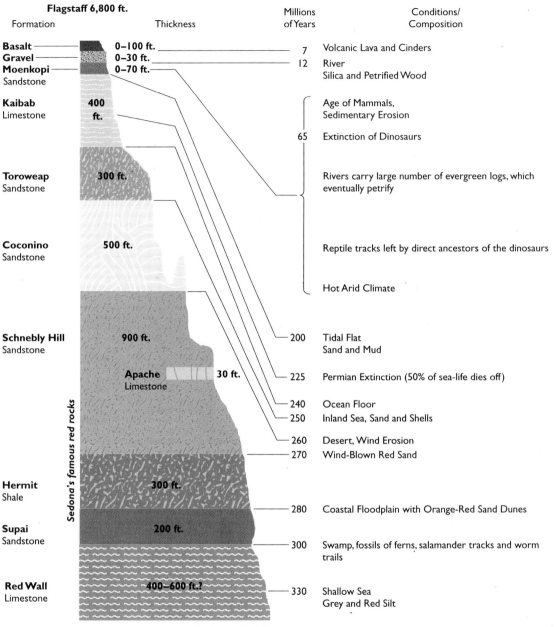

Flagstaff 6,800 ft.

Formation	Thickness	Millions of Years	Conditions/Composition

Basalt — 0–100 ft. — 7 — Volcanic Lava and Cinders

Gravel — 0–30 ft. — 12 — River

Moenkopi Sandstone — 0–70 ft. — Silica and Petrified Wood

Kaibab Limestone — 400 ft. — Age of Mammals, Sedimentary Erosion

65 — Extinction of Dinosaurs

Toroweap Sandstone — 300 ft. — Rivers carry large number of evergreen logs, which eventually petrify

Coconino Sandstone — 500 ft. — Reptile tracks left by direct ancestors of the dinosaurs

Hot Arid Climate

Schnebly Hill Sandstone — 900 ft. — 200 — Tidal Flat, Sand and Mud

Apache Limestone — 30 ft. — 225 — Permian Extinction (50% of sea-life dies off)

240 — Ocean Floor

250 — Inland Sea, Sand and Shells

260 — Desert, Wind Erosion

270 — Wind-Blown Red Sand

Hermit Shale — 300 ft.

280 — Coastal Floodplain with Orange-Red Sand Dunes

Supai Sandstone — 200 ft.

300 — Swamp, fossils of ferns, salamander tracks and worm trails

Red Wall Limestone — 400–600 ft.? — 330 — Shallow Sea, Grey and Red Silt

Sedona's famous red rocks

Sedona 4,500 ft.

FIGURE 2.2
Geological cross section of the area around Sedona and Flagstaff, Arizona, showing the variation in composition and thickness of the strata and some of the events represented in those strata.

Moreover, Hooke attributed these extinctions and changes to the fact that the earth itself had been continually undergoing change since the creation. He even proposed a naturalistic explanation for Noah's flood; it was, he said, probably caused by earthquakes. So, since the earth is in a continual state of change, so are its inhabitants, changing as their environments are altered or becoming extinct if that alteration is too great.

Evidence for this idea of a changing earth came from the examination of the layers of rock and soil below the earth's present surface. These are the earth's **strata** (singular, stratum), and their study is called **stratigraphy** (Figure 2.2). One of the earliest scientists to discuss this was a Dane, Nicholas Steno (1638–1686). He suggested that the strata represented layers of sediments deposited by water in a *sequence*, the lower layers earlier and the higher layers later. The nature of the rock and soil of each stratum, and its fossil contents, showed the natural conditions at the time the stratum was deposited: what creatures existed, whether the area was under sea or on land, and so on. It became clear that neither the earth nor its inhabitants were stable and unchanging. It was also clear that the record of past change could be read by observing the present-day world.

Steno and Hooke, however, still believed in a biblical chronology. To Steno, the water-deposited layers of the stratigraphic sequences represented two events—the original water-covered earth on which God created land and plants and animals (Gen. 1) and the waters of Noah's flood (Gen. 6–8). The geological record, however, shows a vast amount of change, and the Bible only provides six thousand years of the earth's history. To bring about so much change in so short a time, thought Steno and Hooke, required the presence of global catastrophic events—such as earthquakes and volcanos—associated with the creation and the flood. Steno and Hooke and others who ascribed to this explanation are often referred to as **catastrophists.**

One well-known proponent of catastrophism was the French naturalist Georges Cuvier (1769–1832). Cuvier thought that a "prototype" of each creature had been created and that it and its environment had been planned to fit each other. The influence of essentialism is obvious here. Differences in climate, felt Cuvier, could bring about alterations in these prototypes, but such changes were limited, producing minor variations in the created types. He also thought that he could reconstruct the prototypes by using fossil remains of creatures. He compared the fragments of ancient creatures to living ones to try to picture what the whole organism looked like. In doing this, he pioneered the method known as **comparative anatomy,** still used today to infer missing parts of fossil organisms.

Cuvier also knew that life on earth had undergone major changes as well because, he felt, the entire plan of creation had been changed several times by the creator. These changes were manifested in a series of global catastrophes that brought about the extinction of existing forms of life

strata: Layers; here, the layers of rock and soil under the surface of the earth.

stratigraphy: The study of the earth's strata.

catastrophists: Those who believe the history of the earth is explained by a series of global catastrophes.

comparative anatomy: Comparing the anatomical features of various species. Used to reconstruct a fossil species from fragmentary remains.

and prepared the way for newly created forms. Thus, as science historian John Greene put it, Cuvier "recognized change but not development" (1959 : 130). In other words, he accepted that the world had changed but not that it had evolved, with new forms of life being modifications of older forms. Moreover, since humans were only included in the latest creation (although Cuvier did admit to the possibility that they might have been around before), there was the implication that humans were somehow the creator's highest, most perfect form of living thing—an idea clearly influenced by the idea of the chain of being.

Catastrophism enjoyed a degree of popularity because it seemed to reconcile natural evidence with a biblical timeframe. But strict catastrophism did not stand up to further scientific observation and examination. The French scholar the Comte de Buffon (Georges-Louis Leclerc) (1707–1788) concluded that, although catastrophic events do occur, they are rare and so "have no place in the ordinary course of nature." Instead, the earth's history is mainly explained by "operations *uniformly* repeated, motions which succeed one another without interruption [emphasis mine]." The motions Buffon spoke of were mainly the motions of the sea—tides and currents—operating to form the earth while the earth was still completely covered by water and while the strata were still being deposited. Phenomena such as wind and water erosion, occurring on land, he thought were not particularly important. But he did establish a new model: Much of the earth's geological history could be explained by normal, everyday, uniform processes—the things we can see taking place before our eyes. This idea is called **uniformitarianism.** For such processes to account for all the changes recorded in the earth's strata, however, the earth would have to be older than 6000 years. Buffon was among the first to propose a longer history for the planet.

It was a Scotsman, James Hutton (1726–1797), who brought uniformitarianism onto the land. Hutton said that the history of the earth, as seen in its strata, is the result of three general processes: (1) the deposition of strata under the waters of the oceans; (2) the compacting of these strata by pressure and their uplifting above sea level by subterranean heat; and (3) the erosion of land by water, wind, and decay. Hutton saw these processes as part of a self-regulating system: Erosion produced soil in which plants grew. Plants, in turn, fed animals and humans (for whom, he thought, all this had been created in the first place). New land was continually being formed under the sea from sediments produced by erosion, which would ultimately provide new sources of soil, and so on. Again, such a system would require far more than 6000 years, and Hutton suggested that the earth was much older. Indeed, he thought it was virtually timeless, having "no vestige of a beginning—no prospect of an end."

Charles Lyell (1797–1875) was born in Scotland the year Hutton died, and it is his name that is usually associated with uniformitarianism.

This is in part because his version of that idea was so extreme. He advocated, as had Hutton, the uniformity of processes throughout time, that is, that present-day processes are the key to explaining the past. He also believed that the rate of geological change was uniform—slow and steady through countless eons, with no need to invoke global catastrophes.

Furthermore, he believed that the earth itself was fairly uniform through time. The earth has been, and will be, always basically the same. Changes certainly occur, but they occur, said Lyell, just in the details, not in the overall appearance of the earth or in its life forms. Moreover, these changes occur in great cycles. He thought, for example, that dinosaurs, though extinct at the moment, would eventually reappear.

At this point, it would be a good idea to briefly describe where modern scientific knowledge stands on all these issues. We now agree with the major parts of the uniformitarian position, which are as follows:

1. Processes that formed and changed the earth in the past—as seen in its stratigraphic record—are the same processes that take place in the present.

2. By studying the stratigraphic record, we can reconstruct the past history of the earth (an idea that goes back to Steno).

3. For known geological processes to account for the changes recorded in the strata, an immense amount of time is required; we know now that the earth is about 4.5 billion years old (Figure 2.3).

FIGURE 2.3
Utah's Bryce Canyon shows the results of geological processes, especially the laying down of strata and subsequent erosion, over millions of years.

uniformitarianism: The idea that present-day geological processes can also explain the past history of the earth.

We also now understand that Lyell was far too restrictive in his idea about uniform rate. Not all processes are slow and steady. Catastrophic events may seem relatively rare to us, but they do take place and have taken place many times during the history of the earth. Even Lyell acknowledged that most are localized events like volcanos and earthquakes that affect the geology and life of a particular area. However, some events are catastrophic on a global scale. At least five times during the four-billion-year history of life on earth, a major catastrophe has taken place, bringing about the extinction of, in one case, over 90 percent of the earth's species. The most famous of these cataclysms (though not the biggest) occurred 65 million years ago when a comet or asteroid collided with the earth and caused such radical environmental change that 75 percent of the world's marine species became extinct along with many terrestrial species, including the dinosaurs. (See Chapter 6.) These are not the series of biblically associated catastrophes of Steno, Hooke, and Cuvier; rather, they occur irregularly and are of natural origin. They have, nonetheless, radically altered the history of the planet.

Today we understand that Lyell's idea about the earth changing only in its details and in great cycles is also incorrect. The earth's history is a complex chain of events leading to other events, a continual sequence of changes—major and minor—never to be repeated. The dinosaurs are extinct; they will never return.

Despite what turned out to be some incorrect notions, Lyell's influence was great. Not only did he expand upon the work of Hutton and others; he also began the explicit examination of geological data, bringing it fully into the realm of natural science. For example, he attempted to estimate the age of the Mississippi Delta (Figure 2.4). Because the rate of deposition of sediments at the mouth of the river can be measured and because the size of the existing deposit in the delta can be estimated, the time required for the delta to be formed can be reckoned by assuming a uniform rate of deposition. Lyell arrived at an age of about 100,000 years (1873:44–47). (Lyell was incorrect; the delta is not that old. Deposition rates are not constant, nor were existing measurement techniques precise enough.)

Through the work of Hooke, Steno, Hutton, Lyell—and many others—the study of the earth was made natural rather than supernatural. Data about earth's history were sought in the earth itself, not within the presuppositions of belief systems. As a result, by the early nineteenth century, our world was viewed through the interacting perspectives of constant change brought about by observable processes over vast amounts of time.

Lyell put these ideas down in a major scientific work, his three-volume *Principles of Geology*, first published between 1830 and 1833. The book

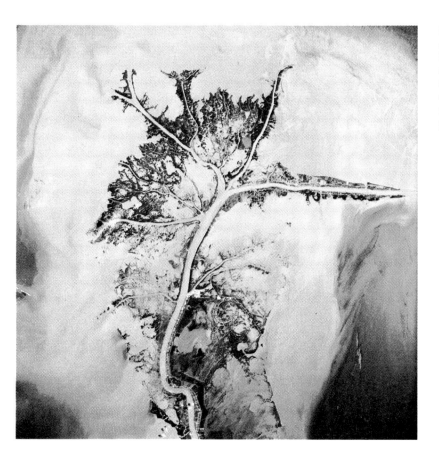

FIGURE 2.4
Aerial view of the Mississippi Delta. By estimating the amount of material deposited in the delta, Charles Lyell concluded (although incorrectly) that it was 100,000 years old.

was highly influential. It was enthusiastically received by supporters of the uniformitarian approach, strongly criticized by those who continued to explain earth's history as a series of global catastrophes, and pored over by those still examining the data. Among the latter was a young British naturalist who took the first volume of Lyell's book with him as he embarked, in 1831, on a round-the-world voyage of scientific exploration. This was Charles Darwin.

"COMMON SENSE AT ITS BEST": EXPLAINING BIOLOGICAL CHANGE

The view of life on earth as static and unchanging is exemplified by Carl von Linné (1707–1778), better known to us as Carolus Linnaeus, whom we will discuss in detail in Chapter 7. Linnaeus, who devised the system of scientific names we still use to classify living things, initially thought that all species of plants and animals had been divinely created in their present forms and numbers. But Linnaeus, a keen observer of nature, came to recognize (as had Robert Hooke before him) that some sort of change had taken place—that fossils, for example, represented species that had become extinct, and that new species could arise. Still, Linnaeus saw any change as divinely preordained and as taking place within the constraints and limits of the original creation—he thought, for example, that new species arose through hybridization between originally created species. This is another example of essentialism.

Gradually, though, through the observations and interpretations of all those discussed so far, it became clear that life on earth had undergone change, just as had the earth itself, and that this change required scientific explanation using a uniformitarian approach. But this idea—then referred to as the "transmutation of species"—was a somewhat more controversial matter than the idea of a changing earth. For if other forms of life had arisen and changed over eons of time by uniform natural processes, then it followed that the same should apply to humans. It was, in part, in reaction to this idea that Cuvier attempted to apply catastrophism with a divine basis to an explanation of biological change. So, even after it became obvious that life had "evolved" (as we now phrase it), just *how* this had taken place mattered a great deal.

There were many who addressed this issue from a uniformitarian position, including Charles Darwin's grandfather, Erasmus Darwin (1731–1802), but one of the most influential was the French naturalist Jean Baptiste de Lamarck (1744–1829). Lamarck emphasized Hooke's conclusion that plants and animals are **adapted** to their environments; that is, that each kind of living organism has physical traits and behaviors that allow it to survive under a given set of natural circumstances. When environments change—as the stratigraphic record shows they do—organisms must change if they are to continue to exist.

Lamarck was quite correct that organisms underwent "possibly very great" change and that this change is connected to the environment. He erred, however, in his explanation for how this change occurred and in his idea as to the overall direction of evolution. Like others, he could not bring himself to see biological change as having no particular direction. Rather, he saw it as **progressive,** going from imperfect to perfect by a process of increasing complexity. This is another example of the influence of the idea of the chain of being. It should be obvious which species Lamarck thought was the most perfect and complex. This was the appeal of the idea of progressive evolution: If life itself changed through time, at least *we* were what it was changing toward.

Moreover, Lamarck's mechanism for this progressive change was fairly foolproof. It is called the **inheritance of acquired characteristics** (Figure 2.5), an old idea that Lamarck formalized in his 1809 *Philosophie zoologique*.

Environmental change leads to need for greater stature

Future generations born with increased stature

FIGURE 2.5
Schematic diagram of Lamarck's model of evolution as exemplified by the long necks of giraffes.

He wrote:

> When the *will* guides an animal to any action, the organs which have to carry out that action are *immediately stimulated* to it by the influx of *subtle fluids*. . . . Hence it follows that numerous repetitions of these organised activities strengthen, stretch, develop and *even create* the organs necessary to them. . . . Now every change that is wrought in an organ through habit of frequently using it, is subsequently *preserved by reproduction*. . . . Such a change is thus handed on to *all succeeding individuals* in the same environment, without their having to acquire it in the same way that it was actually created [emphases mine]. (Harris 1981 : 116–17)

For example, Lamarck explained the long necks of giraffes in the following way: In the past, giraffes were short, but some environmental change altered their food source, placing the foliage they ate high up in the trees. Confronted with this problem, each giraffe was able to stretch itself enough to reach the leaves. This greater height was automatically passed on to the giraffes' offspring, who had to make themselves even taller, and so on.

One reason that Lamarck's idea was popular was that it was one of the first detailed, lengthy, scientific treatments of evolution. Lamarck even spelled out how he used the scientific method by specifying the data that would be required to falsify his model. It was also a comfortable explanation for an uncomfortable topic. It had become clear that life had changed over time. At least, according to Lamarck's hypothesis, life changed in a particular (and very human-oriented) direction, and it changed by a process that was unfailing and dependent upon something inherent to the organism—Lamarck called it "will." It even followed that no organisms ever become extinct. Creatures represented only by fossils are simply creatures that have undergone so much change they now look very different.

adapted: When an organism has physical traits and behaviors that allow it to survive in a particular environment.

progressive: In evolution, the idea that all change is toward increasing complexity.

inheritance of acquired characteristics: The incorrect idea that traits acquired during an organism's lifetime can be passed on to its offspring.

FIGURE 2.6

Biological variation. Variation within a population represents the raw material for natural selection. The tiger swallowtail butterflies (upper right and bottom) are members of the same species. The dark one is a mimic of the pipe-vine butterfly (left), which is protected from predation by its foul taste.

But observation and logic produced some major objections to Lamarck's concept. Traits acquired during an organism's lifetime cannot be inherited by its offspring. A bodybuilder's children will not automatically be born with bulging muscles. Further, it was hard to see how an organism's "will" could change its color or produce a new organ or even make a giraffe taller. And just what is the "subtle fluid" that is supposed to bring all this about?

Thus, Charles Darwin was born (in 1809, the same year Lamarck's book was published) into a world that accepted the *fact* of biological change, but was still in search of a *mechanism* for that change. Although many, like Lamarck, held to a uniformitarian position, others, like Cuvier, still adhered to a catastrophic explanation. It was Darwin who would provide the mechanism that has withstood over a century of scientific examination.

The story of Darwin's life and scientific work is a fascinating one (see, for example, Bowlby 1990). For the purpose of our story, however, we can simply say that Darwin recognized an important fact not fully appreciated by many of his predecessors or many of his contemporaries. In his work in his native England and especially on his famous voyage around the world on H.M.S. *Beagle* (1831–1836), Darwin realized the incredible degree of variation that exists within each living species (Figure 2.6). If Lamarck were correct, one would expect every member of a particular species to look pretty much the same because they all would have responded identically to the same environmental circumstances. Darwin saw this was clearly not the case. Variation always exists, no matter how well adapted a species might be. What tipped Darwin off to this fact of nature were his observations of domestic species like pigeons, carefully bred for certain features but still showing physical variation every generation. Therefore, in each generation, breeders would have to choose for mating only those individuals possessing the features they desired, using the assumption that offspring tend to resemble parents. The goal was to eliminate undesirable traits and accumulate desirable ones.

Darwin reasoned that the same thing happened in nature. Some of the natural variation within a species would make a difference in the success, or **fitness,** of individuals. The better adapted individuals would tend to be more reproductively successful. Their traits would be passed on to more offspring than would those of the less well adapted. Over time, then, some traits would accumulate while others would decrease in frequency or even be eliminated. If the environment to which a species is adapted changes, it stands to reason that the fitness value of certain traits might change, so the process described might proceed in a different adaptive direction—what was once adapted might now be neutral or perhaps even poorly adapted.

So, while Lamarck thought that variation arose *when it was needed*, Darwin understood that variation *already existed*. Because Darwin lived before genetics were known, he did not understand where this variation came from, but his observations showed it was a fact; and he realized that nature, like a plant or animal breeder, "selects" the better adapted individuals for more successful reproduction. Darwin called this process **natural selection** (Figure 2.7).

Several important ideas follow from natural selection:

1. It becomes clear that evolution by natural selection has no particular direction. Organisms do not "progress" to increasingly complex forms

fitness: The relative adaptiveness of an individual organism, measured ultimately by reproductive success.

natural selection: Evolutionary change based on the differential reproductive success of individuals within a species.

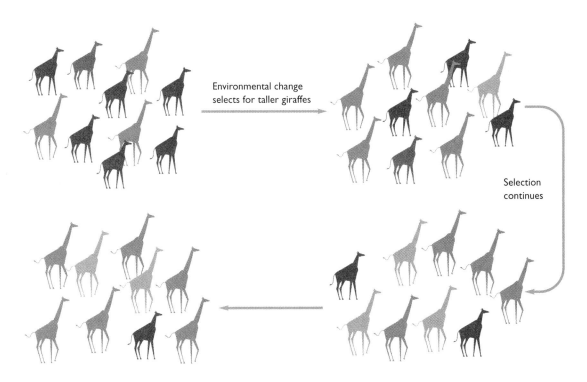

FIGURE 2.7
Schematic diagram of Darwin's model of evolution.

as Lamarck thought but evolve to simply stay adapted to their environments or, if possible, become re-adapted to changed environments. Variation is not "willed." It results from random processes that we now understand as the processes of genetics (see Chapter 3).

2. It is also clear that such a process, using random rather than directed or "willed" variation, is not foolproof. It doesn't always work. Species do become extinct, usually when the environment changes so extensively or rapidly that none of the existing variation within a species is adaptive. Extinction is, in fact, the norm. Nine-tenths of all species that have ever lived are now extinct.

3. It follows that *new* species can arise from this basic process. If populations within a species become environmentally separated, these populations will be under different selective pressures—different traits will be differently adapted to each environment. Moreover, different variations will be produced in each population. Natural selection will have different raw materials to work with. Over time, then, a single species may give rise to one or more new species. This, in fact, was what Darwin was ultimately trying to explain, as indicated by the title

of his most famous work, *On the Origin of Species by Means of Natural Selection*, first published in 1859.

Darwin's idea generated some controversy, which was perhaps what caused him to delay publishing it. We know he understood natural selection sometime in the late 1830s, yet it was not until over twenty years later that he made it public. Even then, he only did so because a younger, less well known naturalist, Alfred Russel Wallace (1823–1913), independently came up with the same idea, and Darwin was urged by friends to rush his conclusion into print.

The controversy centered not around the idea of uniformitarian evolution itself—which was generally well accepted by that time—but around the fact that Darwin's idea, unlike Lamarck's, did not involve a particular progressive direction nor the direct control or will of the organism. Darwin also acknowledged extinction. These ideas were not always comfortable. But, to Darwin's surprise, by the time his book sold out on its first day of publication, the scientific community and much of the informed public were ready to accept the idea, even with its implications. Natural selection—the mechanism of evolution—was hailed as a major scientific breakthrough and remains today a classic example of scientific reasoning, what Darwin's friend Thomas Henry Huxley called "common sense at its best."

At about the time Darwin was writing *Origin of Species*, a monk in what is now the Czech Republic was answering Darwin's question about the source of variation. After years of undocumented research on several species of plants and animals, Gregor Mendel (1822–1884) derived the basic laws of genetics by experimenting with the pea plants in the garden of his monastery. These laws (which we'll cover in the next chapter) not only explained one source of biological variation, but also showed why and how offspring tend to resemble their parents. Basic laws of genetics and biological variation are crucial to natural selection and the origin of new species.

Mendel died in relative obscurity (Darwin never learned of his work), and his writings languished in libraries until 1900, when they were rediscovered independently by three European scientists. They realized that Mendel's work carried implications far beyond some interesting facts about pea plants. (This had been the reaction to his work during Mendel's life—that he had found some interesting facts about peas.) They understood that genetics filled in those pieces that Darwin acknowledged were missing from his process.

During the twentieth century, many scientists have added to Darwin's idea of natural selection and Mendel's work on genetics. There have been new details, changes of emphasis, and major discoveries, such as the breaking of the genetic code in the early 1950s. But all the work of the last

Contemporary Reflections

Has Science Dehumanized Society?

To many, the story recounted in this chapter is one of science *versus* belief systems, specifically religious belief. A popular assessment of Darwin's contribution is that by "proving" evolution he "disproved" the Bible. As we will see in Chapter 5, there is still a substantial contingent today who feel that the very idea of evolution is anti-religious.

And it's not just the science of evolution. From Mary Shelley's *Frankenstein* (published in 1818) to modern blockbuster movies like *Jurassic Park* and *The Lost World*, science in general is seen as a potential evil, something that is far too easily abused and that, when abused, wreaks havoc on people and their societies. People often use the phrase "playing God" when referring to scientific endeavors—genetics studies in particular—that they perceive as being an affront to human spirit and individuality. Science is blamed for many of today's social and environmental ills—and there *are* plenty of them—from global warming to radioactive contamination to the proliferation of high-tech weaponry.

There are three errors in this view of science. First, although science has put forth, and scientists have embraced, ideas that resulted in human suffering, one of the hallmarks of science is its ability for self-correction. The eugenics movement, for example—which held that many human behaviors were hereditary and that therefore selective breeding could improve the species—resulted (even in this country) in the forced sterilization of many individuals who were deemed less fit because of some characteristic that society felt undesirable (below average intelligence, for instance, or having borne illegitimate children). This is abhorrent, but through scientific progress we now know much more about the nature of human heredity, and such mistakes are at least unlikely in the future.

Second, this view of science ignores the fact that *anything* may be a danger if used incorrectly or for nefarious purposes. One has but to examine world history to see that religious ideals are not always put to positive use. Indeed, several present bloody hostilities are based on religious conflicts—in some cases involving religions that specifically prohibit the taking of human life.

Third, in focusing on the negative results of science, we all too easily forget about the positive results. People today who are the most vocal critics of science still promote their ideas over television, write them down on computers, travel in airplanes, and enjoy all the medical and nutritional benefits of a modern scientific society. The late astronomer Carl Sagan (1996) tells of asking a group of people how many of them would not be alive today if it weren't for modern medical technology. Most raised their hands. (I tried this with a class of undergraduates, average age about twenty, and still about half raised their hands.)

But still, didn't Darwin set the stage for this seeming conflict by disproving the Bible with his theory of evolution? Not at all. He *did* show that one literal interpretation of one part of one book of the Bible failed to account for observations of biology in the real world. In no way, however, did his idea of evolution refute a whole religious world view, nor need it conflict with one's personal sense of the spiritual. Indeed, Darwin himself, in the last paragraph of *The Origin of Species*, wrote (emphasis added), "There is grandeur in this view of life, with its several powers, having been originally breathed *by the Creator* into a few forms or into one."

It is not knowledge or ideas, scientific or otherwise, that are dangerous, but how they are used. Ignorance is far more dangerous. It is ignorance that dehumanizes us.

TABLE 2.1
Chart of Important People and Ideas Associated with Evolution

	Approx. Date of Publication	Contribution
James Ussher (1581–1656)	1650	Calculated age of earth using biblical data.
Robert Hooke (1635–1703)	1660s–90s	Fossils as evidence of change. Importance of environmental change.
Nicholas Steno (1638–1686)	1669	Stratigraphy.
Carolus Linnaeus (1707–1778)	1758	System of scientific names. Recognized extinction and possibility of new species.
Comte de Buffon (1707–1788)	1749	Uniformitarianism. Longer timeframe.
James Hutton (1726–1797)	1795	Uniformitarianism. Natural cycles. Longer timeframe.
Jean Baptiste de Lamarck (1744–1829)	1809	Adaptation. Inheritance of acquired characteristics. Progressive evolution.
Georges Cuvier (1769–1832)	late 1700s, early 1800s	Ideal prototypes. Climatic alterations. Extinction. Catastrophism.
Charles Lyell (1797–1875)	1830–33	Uniformitarianism. Scientific investigation.
Charles Darwin (1809–1882)	1859	Natural selection. The origin of species.
Gregor Mendel (1822–1884)	1860s	The laws of inheritance.
Alfred Russel Wallace (1823–1913)	1859	Natural selection.

nearly one hundred years has been built upon the thoughts and discoveries of people like Darwin and Lyell and Hooke, and many others. All the men and women whose investigations have led to our modern theory of evolution (which we will cover in the next three chapters) would freely agree that they have stood on the shoulders of these giants (Table 2.1).

▽   ▽   ▽

SUMMARY

The Judeo-Christian belief system, as set down in the Bible, was long seen as informing its followers not only "how to get to heaven" but also "how heaven is." That is, it was seen as both a belief system and as a source of literal knowledge. As scholars began looking more objectively at nature itself, however, their observations and the rational conclusions they drew from them showed clearly that knowledge of the heavens, the earth, and the earth's inhabitants required the methods of science. As the scientific method was applied to the study of the earth, scientists gradually learned to give up their presuppositions.

Charles Darwin, adhering faithfully to the spirit of scientific methodology, was able to synthesize his observations and thoughts with those of many others and to formulate a theory that made possible the work that has led to our modern knowledge of the nature and evolution of living things.

KEY TERMS

evolution	uniformitarianism	fitness
fossils	adapted	natural selection
strata	progressive	
stratigraphy	inheritance of	
catastrophists	acquired	
comparative anatomy	characteristics	

SUGGESTED READINGS

The history of the study of evolution is covered in C. Leon Harris's *Evolution: Genesis and Revelations*, which contains numerous sections from original works, and in John C. Greene's *The Death of Adam*. The impact of Darwin's work on modern knowledge in general is the theme of Philip Appleman's *Darwin: A Norton Critical Edition*.

A new biography of Darwin that focuses on the man as well as the scientist, and nicely shows how the two aspects of his life were related, is John Bowlby's *Charles Darwin: A New Life*.

Paleontologist and science historian Stephen Jay Gould has written many wonderful essays about the history of evolution and the personalities involved. These can be found throughout his books *Ever Since Darwin*, *The Panda's Thumb*, *Hen's Teeth and Horse's Toes*, *The Flamingo's Smile*, *Bully for Brontosaurus*, *Eight Little Piggies*, and *Dinosaur in a Haystack*. These are all highly recommended.

EVOLUTIONARY GENETICS

The laws governing
inheritance are for the
most part unknown.
—Charles Darwin

wo important features of Darwin's natural selection were the seemingly contradictory facts that offspring tend to resemble their parents but that, at the same time, there is continual production of biological variation among members of a species and from generation to generation. Both facts were obvious enough to careful observers like Darwin. But, as Darwin freely admitted, science was largely ignorant of the source of those facts, in other words, of how inheritance worked.

A popular idea of Darwin's time assumed that inheritance was "blending"—a mixture of some material from both parents. Certainly there are sufficient examples of offspring with combinations of parental traits to make this idea seem logical. For example, new flower colors can be produced by crossbreeding other colors, much like paints are mixed to make new shades. Breeds of dogs can be crossbred to get combinations of the parents' physical and behavioral characteristics in the hybrid offspring. But offspring are often born with characteristics that resemble neither parent's or, as with one's sex, are definitely *not* mixtures.

Observations of nonblending traits may have led Gregor Mendel to begin experiments to determine just how inheritance operates. The laws he derived are still recognized today as the basis of genetics although, of course, they have been added to greatly. The most basic and perhaps most important of Mendel's contributions was his conclusion that inheritance did not involve the blending of substances but, rather, was **particulate.** He showed that traits are passed on by individual particles according to very specific principles. Mendel called these particles "factors"; we call them **genes.** We'll now survey the aspects of modern genetics pertinent to bioanthropology by addressing the following questions:

> **How do genes produce the traits that make a pea plant or a human being?**
>
> **What are the basic laws of inheritance?**
>
> **What processes bring about the variation we see among members of a species and between parents and offspring?**

HOW GENES WORK

We begin to see how genes work with something Mendel could not possibly have understood. Although he concluded that the particulate factors we now call genes produce the features of an organism and provided us with the basic model for how traits are inherited, Mendel possessed neither the background knowledge nor the technology to figure out just how the genetic code operates at the chemical level.

We now understand that the genetic code is a set of instructions for the production (or synthesis) of **proteins** from **amino acids,** which are

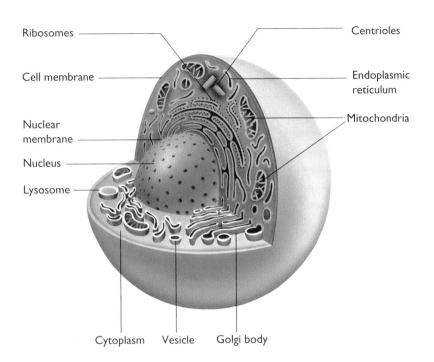

Ribosomes

Cell membrane

Nuclear membrane

Nucleus

Lysosome

Centrioles

Endoplasmic reticulum

Mitochondria

Cytoplasm   Vesicle   Golgi body

FIGURE 3.1
A typical cell and its important parts. This cell represents all types of cells from the more complex single-celled organisms like ameobas to the cells in the human body. The ribosomes are the sites of protein synthesis (see Figure 3.3). The mitochondria are the cells' energy factories, converting energy stored in nutrients into a form the cells can use to perform their various functions (see Chapter 12).

particulate: The idea that biological traits are controlled by individual factors rather than by a single hereditary agent.

genes: Those portions of the DNA molecule that code for specific traits.

proteins: Molecules that make cells and carry out cellular functions.

amino acids: The chief components of proteins.

enzymes: Proteins that control chemical processes.

chromosomes: Strands of DNA in the nucleus of a cell.

deoxyribonucleic acid (DNA): The molecule that carries the genetic code.

nucleotide: The basic building blocks of DNA and RNA, made up of a sugar, a phosphate, and one of four bases.

codons: The sections of DNA that code for specific amino acids.

found in the cytoplasm of the cell. Proteins are the basic building blocks of an organism's cells and, in a form called **enzymes,** are responsible for the cells' chemical reactions. All organisms are composed of cells (Figure 3.1), so it can logically be said that all living things are based on proteins. Even the nonprotein substances found within a living organism—like the calcium in your bones—is regulated by proteins.

The genetic code is found in the nucleus of cells, on long strands called **chromosomes** (see Figure 3.6). A chromosome is made up of proteins and a nucleic acid. It is the nucleic acid—**deoxyribonucleic acid (DNA)**—that carries the code.

DNA is like a ladder with the ends twisted in opposite directions (Figure 3.2). This shape is referred to as a double helix. The sides of the ladder are for structural stability. The rungs of the ladder carry the code. They are made up of pairs of bases (a family of chemicals) joined or bonded in the middle. Each base and the portion of the side of the ladder to which it is connected is called a **nucleotide.** Only four bases are involved: adenine (A), thymine (T), cytosine (C), and guanine (G), and they are only paired in A-T or T-A and C-G or G-C combinations. Thus, if we know the sequence of bases on one side of the DNA helix, we can correctly predict the sequence on the other side.

The strings of these bases are divided into groups of three, called **codons.** Codons are like words made up of three letters. Each word stands

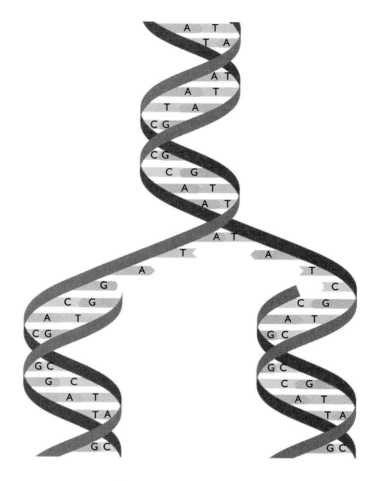

for a particular amino acid. A string of words—a genetic sentence—thus stands for a chain of amino acids. A chain of amino acids is a protein. Therefore, a sequence of codons codes for the linking together of amino acids to make a protein. This process is known as **protein synthesis** (Figure 3.3). We can carry our analogy further. Because sentences need beginnings and ends, some codons serve the function of punctuation, separating one codon sentence from the next.

But the genetic code, it should be noted, is not as neat and precise as we once thought. In some cases, for example, two codon sequences may overlap and one may even be embedded within another. Most amazing of all, between 90 and 97 percent of human DNA is noncoding; that is, it does not carry instructions for making proteins. Some noncoding DNA is even found *within* a coding sequence. Most of this DNA appears to do nothing, or to have functions yet to be discovered, but some noncoding DNA serves as instructions for the "turning on" of nearby genes. The functions of the rest of this DNA, how it originated, and, indeed, the very definition of a gene, all remain a matter of debate. (See Marks and Lyles 1994 for more detail.)

1. Section of DNA molecule with base pairs.

2. DNA molecule temporarily separates at bases. mRNA lines up its bases (with U replacing T) with their complements on the coding side of the DNA.

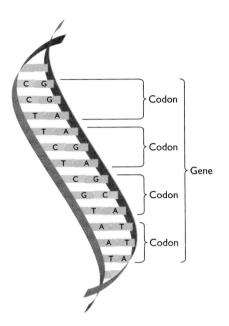

3. mRNA moves out of cell nucleus to ribosomes. As ribosomes move along mRNA, tRNA picks up amino acids and lines up along mRNA according to base complements. Each tRNA transfers its amino acid to the next active tRNA as it leaves, resulting in a chain of amino acids.

4. This chain of amino acids forms a protein.

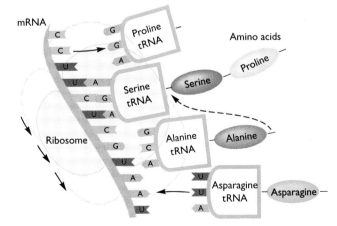

FIGURE 3.3
Protein synthesis as described in the text. In reality, no protein is only four amino acids long, but the process works exactly as shown.

protein synthesis: The process by which the genetic code puts together proteins in the cell.

FIGURE 3.4

Skin color variation in modern humans provides an example of a polygenic trait with a wide range of phenotypic expressions.

For our purposes here, we will define *gene* in a functional way, that is, as that portion of the DNA molecule that carries the codon sequence for a particular protein. It is common, because of the varied ways *gene* is used, to also use the term **locus** (pl. **loci**) for this sequence of codons, referring to the position (locus) of those codons on a chromosome. To summarize then:

FEATURE	ANALOGUE	MEANING
base (A, T, C, G)	letter	
codon	word	amino acid
gene (locus)	sentence	protein

How does protein synthesis work? As you read this description, follow along in Figure 3.3. First, the code must be read. The DNA molecule unwinds, breaking apart at the middle of the "rungs" where the bases are joined. Only half of the DNA molecule, that is, only one base of each pair, carries the code. Another nucleic acid, **messenger ribonucleic acid (mRNA)**, in which uracil (U) replaces thymine (T), transcribes the code by lining up its bases to match their complement bases exposed on the unwound DNA. Remember, A must always pair with T (or U), and C with G. The mRNA, now a mirror image of the DNA code, then moves out of the nucleus into the cytoplasm of the cell.

In the cytoplasm are free amino acids (there are only about twenty different amino acids in all living organisms) and yet another nucleic acid, **transfer ribonucleic acid (tRNA)**, which translates the code into a protein. The tRNA bases are in the original code letters (but with U still replacing T). The tRNA molecules pick up the corresponding amino acids and then line up along the mRNA with bases paired as in the original DNA molecule back in the nucleus. The lined-up amino acids bond to form the specified protein, which can now perform its functions in the cell.

It's still a long way from a protein to a trait—the observable, measurable physical or chemical characteristics of an organism. Some traits are fairly simple. Hemoglobin, the chemical on red blood cells that carries oxygen, *is* protein. It is made up of two chains of 141 and 146 amino acids. In other words, it is coded for on two loci—two gene sentences with 141 and 146 words.

Skin color, by contrast, is not a simple trait. It involves three different pigments (including red hemoglobin) and other factors such as skin thickness. The color of a person's skin is thus a trait produced by the complex interaction of many proteins and so is coded for on many loci (Figure 3.4). Such traits are called **polygenic.** Traits coded for by a single locus are, obviously, called **monogenic.** Most traits of complex organisms are polygenic.

FROM GENE TO TRAIT

If Mendel possessed neither the technology nor the background knowledge to understand the structure of the genetic code and the process of protein synthesis, what then did he discover about the processes of genetics? We refer to his contribution as **Mendelian genetics.** It involves the basic laws of inheritance, which we will take up in the next section, and some general principles about the relationship between the genetic code and the traits that are the end-product of that code.

locus (plural, **loci**): The location on a chromosome of the genetic code for a specific trait.

messenger ribonucleic acid (mRNA): The molecule that carries the genetic code out of the nucleus for translation into proteins.

transfer ribonucleic acid (tRNA): RNA that lines up amino acids along mRNA to make proteins.

polygenic: A trait coded for by more than one locus.

monogenic: A trait coded for by a single locus.

Mendelian genetics: The basic laws of inheritance, discovered by Gregor Mendel in the nineteenth century.

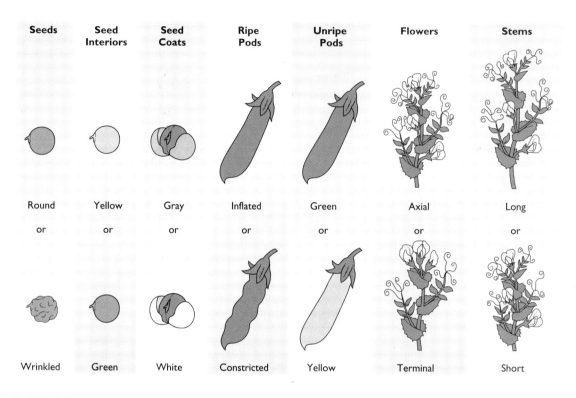

Seeds	Seed Interiors	Seed Coats	Ripe Pods	Unripe Pods	Flowers	Stems
Round	Yellow	Gray	Inflated	Green	Axial	Long
or	or	or	or	or	or	or
Wrinkled	Green	White	Constricted	Yellow	Terminal	Short

FIGURE 3.5
The traits of the pea plant that Mendel observed in his famous experiments.

Mendel conducted at least eight years of extensive breeding experiments, mostly on pea plants, crossing plants that exhibited different expressions of a trait and then crossing hybrids with each other and back with the original plants.

Mendel only used traits that were monogenic (Figure 3.5). He carefully picked these after considering other traits, many of which were polygenic and so were rejected because, like skin color, they did not appear in simple either/or variation. In a sense, Mendel "fudged" his experiment (no modern scientists would simply leave out what didn't fit their expectations), but we forgive him because, in fact, all *genes* work the way he thought even if some *traits* are more complex.

Mendel reached the conclusion that *each organism possesses two genes for each trait—one from each parent. Not only does each organism possess two of each gene (or locus), but loci may come in different versions. We call these alleles.* Although Mendel used pea plants, it might be more interesting for us to use a human example. There is a chemical called PTC (phenylthiocarbamide) that people can either taste or not. (For those who can, it has a dry, bitter flavor. If you find brussels sprouts bitter, you are tasting a thiocarbamide.) This "taster trait" is monogenic, but the locus for the trait has, as you might suspect, two alleles: *T*, which codes for the ability to taste PTC, and *t*, which codes for the inability to taste the chemical.

Because every human possesses two loci for the taster gene—one from their father and one from their mother—we each have one of three possible combinations. These combinations are called **genotypes.** We may have two of the same allele: *TT* or *tt*, a condition known as **homozygous** (from *homo*, the same), or we may have a pair of nonmatching alleles: *Tt*. This is **heterozygous** (from *hetero*, meaning different).

These genotypes are responsible for producing either a taster individual or a nontaster. The observable trait—the result of the genetic code—is the **phenotype.** What phenotype does each genotype produce?

GENOTYPE	PHENOTYPE
TT	taster
tt	nontaster
Tt	taster

Why does the heterozygote *Tt* produce the same phenotype as the homozygote *TT*? Because, as Mendel also reasoned, some alleles are **dominant,** and some are **recessive.** In this case the allele for tasting is dominant (that's why it's written as a capital letter), and so, in the heterozygous genotype, it hides the action of the allele for nontasting. The only way a phenotype can reflect a recessive allele is if the genotype is homozygous for the recessive (*tt*).

It is very important to understand that the words *dominant* and *recessive* have no value attached to them. Dominant alleles are not necessarily better or more common. There are, for example, quite a few human genetic diseases, some lethal, caused by dominant alleles. The terms *dominant* and *recessive* simply mean that if two alleles in this relationship are in a heterozygous genotype, the action of the dominant will be expressed and the action of the recessive will be hidden.

Alleles for most traits do not, in fact, work this neatly. In most cases heterozygote genotypes result in phenotypes that exhibit some action of both alleles. (This is, in part, what led to the mistaken concept of "blending" inheritance.) Such alleles are said to be **codominant,** and they result in a greater number of possible phenotypes. In addition, many loci have more than two possible alleles, resulting in even more potential phenotypes. (Remember, however, that each individual can only possess a *pair* of alleles.)

A single example can demonstrate both these concepts. Your blood type for the ABO system is coded for by a single locus, the *I* locus, which

alleles: Variants of a genetic locus.

genotypes: The alleles possessed by an organism.

homozygous: Having two of the same allele.

heterozygous: Having two different alleles in a gene pair.

phenotype: The chemical or physical results of the genetic code.

dominant: The allele of a pair that is expressed in the phenotype.

recessive: The allele of a pair that is only expressed if homozygous.

codominant: When both alleles of a pair are expressed in the phenotype.

has three possible alleles: I^A, I^B, and I^O. So we have six possible genotypes but only four possible phenotypes. (We can designate the genotypes using only the superscript, but remember that these are alleles of a single locus, not separate genes.)

GENOTYPE	PHENOTYPE
AA	type A
AO	type A
BB	type B
BO	type B
AB	type AB
OO	type O

It's clear that both A and B are dominant over the recessive O. The AB genotype, however, expresses the action of both alleles. The A and B alleles are codominant. (We will discuss the ABO system in greater detail in Chapter 13.)

Most phenotypic traits are coded for by multiple loci, some of which may have more than three possible alleles. In addition, some alleles are in an even more complex relationship, where the action of both is expressed in the phenotype, but one more so than the other.

Some of the pea plant traits that Mendel rejected were probably traits like these. He rejected them because their phenotypic expressions were too complex for him to easily see any regularities. We still have this problem today although, of course, we don't simply ignore data we can't explain. The genetic bases for most phenotypic traits have eluded us because there are multiple loci involved and because the alleles of those loci are not in a simple dominant/recessive relationship to one another.

There is a further complication, and it's an important one. The path between the genetic code and the resultant phenotypic expression can be influenced by outside factors, that is, factors that are not directly part of the reading of the genetic code and the synthesis of proteins. We can call these nongenetic influences **environmental.** Certainly, some traits are unaffected by environmental influences. Your ABO blood type is a direct product of your genetic code—there's nothing that can change what those genes code for except a change in the code itself. Such a change is called a **mutation,** literally a mistake in the genetic code. (We will discuss mutations in the next chapter.)

Other traits, however, are influenced by environmental factors. Your skin color, for example, is certainly coded for in your genes (there are at least four loci involved and probably more). Your specific skin color phenotype at any point in time, however, is influenced by a number of nongenetic factors: the amount of exposure to ultraviolet radiation from the sun, your health status, even your psychological condition (blushing from

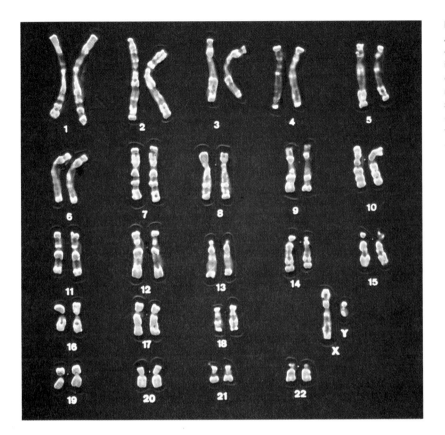

FIGURE 3.6
All twenty-three pairs of chromosomes typically found in a human being. This set of chromosomes came from a man—note the last pair has an X chromosome and a Y chromosome. A woman would have two X chromosomes.

embarrassment, for example). In other words, two of us might have exactly the same genes for skin color but still differ in our phenotypic expression of that trait. In fact, different parts of your own body can have different skin colors at the same time depending upon environmental influences, as many of us learn every summer when we're not careful about exposure to the sun. Mendel noticed such variation even in some of the simple traits he worked with in peas, some of which may have been the result of different environmental effects on individual plants.

HOW INHERITANCE WORKS

Genetic loci come in pairs. So do the chromosomes that carry these loci. Thus, the members of a pair of genes are found on a pair of chromosomes. Species differ in number of chromosomes. In humans, there are forty-six chromosomes, which come in twenty-three pairs (Figure 3.6). In general, the more complex the organism, the more genetic loci it has. This general

environmental: Here, any nongenetic influence on the phenotype.

mutation: Any mistake in an organism's genetic code.

FIGURE 3.7
Mitosis. The process by which the cell copies its genetic material and divides to make two identical daughter cells.

FIGURE 3.8
Meiosis. The process of producing gametes (sex cells), during which the chromosome pairs, and therefore the pairs of genes, are halved.

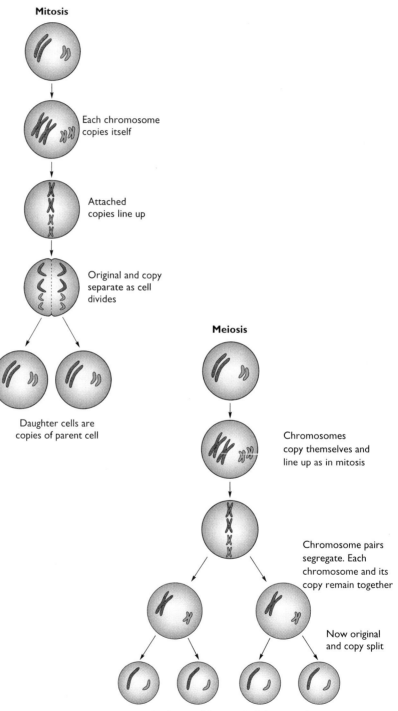

Mitosis

Each chromosome copies itself

Attached copies line up

Original and copy separate as cell divides

Daughter cells are copies of parent cell

Meiosis

Chromosomes copy themselves and line up as in mitosis

Chromosome pairs segregate. Each chromosome and its copy remain together

Now original and copy split

Each sex cell has one-half the normal number of chromosomes

rule does not necessarily hold true for the chromosomes that carry the genes, however. Chimpanzees, for example, have forty-eight chromosomes, wheat plants have forty-two, and dogs have seventy-eight.

When cells divide—as the organism grows or to replace cells that have died or been lost—each chromosome copies itself. It does this by unwinding and splitting at the bond between the bases A, T, G, and C, as in the first step of protein synthesis. Each strand now picks up nucleotides with the proper complementary bases (which are in solution within the cell) and thus replaces its other half. There are now *two* pairs of each chromosome. When the cell divides, each "daughter cell" receives a full set of chromosome pairs. This process is known as **mitosis** (Figure 3.7).

Some single-celled organisms reproduce in this fashion, but other single-celled organisms and nearly all multicellular organisms reproduce sexually, that is, by the joining of specialized cells from two parents. Such specialized sex cells are called **gametes** (sperm and egg in animals, for example). Now, if each gamete had a full set of chromosome pairs and thus a full set of gene pairs, the resultant fertilized cell, the **zygote,** and all the cells of the offspring, would have *twice* the normal number of chromosomes and *twice* the normal number of genetic loci.

This duplication does not occur, however, because when gametes are produced, the chromosome pairs—and thus the gene pairs—separate. Mendel called this **segregation.** Each gamete, then, has only one member of each chromosome pair and so only one member of each pair of genes. The process of producing gametes is **meiosis** (Figure 3.8). When the gamete from the male fertilizes the gamete from the female, the zygote once again has two of each chromosome and two of each genetic locus. But, because the members of each pair come from different parents, the combination of alleles at each locus may well be different from that of either parent.

Adding to the differences between parents and offspring that result from fertilization are differences caused by two other phenomena, **independent assortment** and **crossing over.** Independent assortment, described by Mendel, says that, as long as genes are on different chromosomes, their alleles will segregate independently during the production of gametes. For example, all the traits Mendel observed in pea plants (see Figure 3.5) are on different chromosomes and therefore assort independently. One expression of stem length is not linked to a particular expression of seed texture or to a particular expression of seed color. All combinations are possible. If, on the other hand, two genes are on the same chromosome, they are said to exhibit **linkage** and, therefore, their alleles will not assort independently and variation is reduced.

But sometimes, during meiosis, portions of chromosome pairs break and are "spliced" back together, but to the *other* member of the pair. This is crossing over. Thus, alleles are exchanged between chromosome pairs,

mitosis: The process of cell division that results in two copies of the original cell.

gametes: The cells of reproduction, which contain only half the chromosomes of a normal cell.

zygote: The fertilized egg before cell division begins.

segregation: In genetics, the breaking up of allele pairs in the production of gametes.

meiosis: The process of cell division in which gametes are produced.

independent assortment: When genetic loci on different chromosomes segregate to gametes independently of one another.

crossing over: When sections of chromosomes switch between chromosome pairs.

linkage: When genetic loci occur on the same chromosome and are inherited together.

Contemporary Reflections

Is It Really Possible to Clone Dinosaurs and Humans?

The premise of the novel and movie *Jurassic Park* seemed eminently logical. Since prehistoric insects (including mosquitos) are found intact within amber (fossil resin from plants), perhaps some of those mosquitos still contain blood cells from now-extinct creatures, including dinosaurs. If we can extract and identify dinosaur cells, we should be able to produce dinosaur clones. In *Jurassic Park,* that's exactly what happens—with, of course, disastrous results.

The problem with the story stemmed from a basic fact of developmental genetics. Although each cell in our body (with the exception of red blood cells and gametes) contains *all* of our genes, they are not all operative. Our cells have differentiated since we were a single fertilized zygote. Our bodies are made up of skin cells, nerve cells, muscle cells, bone cells, and so on. The only genes in a skin cell that are working are those genes that make it a skin cell. When the story was written, we knew of no way to reactivate all the genes in an adult cell so the descendants of that cell would themselves differentiate into all the kinds of cells that make up an adult body. In other words, you can't make a whole *Tyrannosaurus rex* from one *T. rex* cell, even if you could get one—which, so far, hasn't been done, despite all those bugs in all that amber.

But then, in 1996, along came Dolly. Dolly, a Scottish sheep, was cloned from a single cell. And it was a cell from an *adult* ewe. The investigators (Wilmut et al. 1997) took the nucleus from a mammary tissue cell of an adult ewe and transferred it to an unfertilized sheep egg cell that had its nucleus removed. The embryo was then placed in a recipient ewe, where it developed into a normal lamb. The egg cell, in other words, reprogrammed the genetic material from the donor cell to "start from scratch" and go through the processes of cell differentiation as if it were the DNA of the egg to begin with.

So the answer to part of the question must be that, yes, it *is* possible to clone humans. The technique that worked for a sheep, another mammal, should work on us. But—in contrast to many popular accounts of human cloning—such a procedure *would not* produce an exact copy of the donor human. There are a great many steps between the genetic code and the final, fully formed organism, most importantly, all the environmental influences on phenotype. For humans, the most important environmental influence is our culture and all its effects on our growth and development—physically, emotionally, and intellectually. A clone of one of my cells would most decidedly not produce another me. He would look like me for the most part, and might even have some of my general behavioral tendencies. But, because there is no way our environments could be exactly the same, we would be different people. A clone of Michael Crichton would not necessarily write bestsellers like *Jurassic Park.*

Now, about those dinosaurs. Sorry, it's impossible. Any dinosaur DNA we could extract would no doubt be incomplete; DNA doesn't preserve too well for 65 million years! So we wouldn't have a complete genetic code. Anyway, it wouldn't be living DNA in a living cell, and the Dolly experiment only worked because the donor cell was living and had a complete complement of DNA (which, in fact, had to be at a certain stage of cell division for the procedure to work). Further, we would need a living dinosaur egg cell—and a mother dinosaur to put it in. As Stephen Jay Gould notes (1995:227): "A complex newborn animal is not an automatic product of its molecular code—for the code needs to work in, and interact with, the proper environment for embryological growth. . . . Moreover . . . maternal genes must produce products and chemical signals needed by the fertilized egg nucleus for its early divisions and differentiations." *Jurassic Park,* then, remains—and probably always will remain—great science fiction.

and this adds to the possible genotypic combinations that linkage reduces. This phenomenon is called **recombination.**

Recombination, independent assortment, and crossing over (together with mutations, the mistakes that change the code itself) account for the variation within a species that Darwin observed but could not explain. Recall that without the continuous generation of variation, natural selection—and therefore evolution—could not take place.

We can demonstrate Mendelian inheritance using the taster trait. Suppose we have two individuals who are both phenotypic tasters and who are both heterozygotes, that is, their genotypes are Tt. Because chromosomes carrying allele pairs segregate during meiosis, each person will produce some gametes that receive the dominant allele and some that receive the recessive. At fertilization, then, depending upon which sperm fertilizes which egg, three possible genotypic combinations are possible in the zygote. A device called a Punnett Square illustrates this (Figure 3.9).

The cells of the Punnett Square represent the possible fertilizations. If a T sperm fertilizes a T egg, the zygote is homozygous dominant. If a T sperm fertilizes a t egg, the zygote is heterozygous, and so on. Notice that two individuals with exactly the same genotype and phenotype can produce offspring with all three possible genotypic combinations and even, in the case of the homozygote tt, a different phenotypic expression. Two tasters, in other words, can give birth to a nontaster. This variation between parents and offspring is the result of the processes of segregation and fertilization. Variation is the raw material of evolution, the topic of the next chapter.

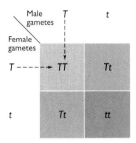

FIGURE 3.9
Punnett Square illustrating the possible genotypic combinations when two heterozygotes for the taster trait reproduce. Note that, because of the hidden recessive, two tasters have a one-quarter chance of producing a nontaster offspring.

SUMMARY

This brief account of the basic facts of genetics demonstrates two important points relative to evolution:

1. It is important to understand that all phenotypic traits are, initially, the products of the genetic code. Thus, evolutionary change is, at its most basic level, genetic change. But the pathway from the genetic code to phenotypic traits is a complex one. A gene simply codes for the synthesis of a protein. Proteins build cells and run their chemical reactions; cells make up tissues, which, in turn, make up the body of a living organism—humans as well as pea plants. Moreover, this complex process is affected by environmental factors so that the genetic code is most definitely *not* solely responsible for the final form and function of a living being. As we try to explain the phenotypic

recombination: The genetic change that results from crossing over.

changes we see in evolution, we must keep these ideas in mind, for if the genetic process itself is complex, so, then, are the processes of evolution that act to change it.

2. The very process by which organisms pass on traits from parent to offspring also accounts for the variation seen between generations and among members of a species. If inheritance produced offspring that were exact copies of their parents, no change would ever take place and there would be no evolution—no adaptation, no change through time, and no new species. But segregation, recombination, independent assortment, and crossing over mix existing genetic combinations (sort of like shuffling a deck of cards), and mutation produces new genetic variation.

We will look more closely at sources of variation and the processes of evolution in the next chapter.

KEY TERMS

particulate
genes
proteins
amino acids
enzymes
chromosomes
deoxyribonucleic acid (DNA)
nucleotide
codons
protein synthesis
locus
loci
messenger ribonucleic acid (mRNA)

transfer ribonucleic acid (tRNA)
polygenic
monogenic
Mendelian genetics
alleles
genotypes
homozygous
heterozygous
phenotype
dominant
recessive
codominant

environmental
mutation
mitosis
gametes
zygote
segregation
meiosis
independent assortment
crossing over
linkage
recombination

SUGGESTED READINGS

For additional detail on the workings of genes and inheritance, try the genetics chapter of John H. Relethford's *The Human Species: An Intro-*

duction to Biological Anthropology, third edition, or the genetics section of any good introductory biology text, for example, *Focus on Human Biology* by Carl E. Rischer and Thomas A. Easton.

A nicely illustrated article on the basics of genetics, with information about genetic engineering, is "Changing Life's Genetic Blueprint" by Robert F. Weaver in *National Geographic* (December 1984).

For a brief discussion of Mendel and an excerpt from his writing, see Harris's *Evolution: Genesis and Revelations*.

CHAPTER

4

THE PROCESSES
OF EVOLUTION

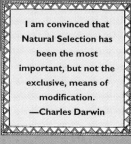

I am convinced that
Natural Selection has
been the most
important, but not the
exclusive, means of
modification.
—Charles Darwin

One of the scientists who "rediscovered" Mendel's work in 1900 was the Dutch botanist Hugo de Vries (1848–1935). De Vries had been trying to explain the variations that sometimes spontaneously appeared in plants (and, of course, in animals)—such as a single flower of the wrong color or an individual that was far smaller or larger than other members of its species. Breeders called these oddities "sports." De Vries called them mutations. When he read about Mendel's experiments, De Vries realized that these mutations were the results of sudden changes in Mendel's "factors." We now say that a mutation is any change in the genetic mechanism.

With De Vries's contribution, all the major pieces were in place to articulate a *basic theory of evolution*, which may be stated as follows:

A particulate genetic code is initially responsible for the form and function of an organism. Mutations in the coding portion of DNA continually add genetic, and therefore phenotypic, variation to a species. Segregation, independent assortment, recombination, and crossing over shuffle existing genotypic combinations at reproduction and thus provide additional genetic and phenotypic variation. Phenotypic variation is affected by the process of natural selection, where the better adapted individuals will be more reproductively successful and will thus disproportionately pass on their phenotypic traits to future generations. The results of natural selection are the maintenance of a species' adaptive relationship to existing environmental conditions, the alteration of a species' phenotypic variation under circumstances of changing environmental conditions, and, ultimately, the development of new species.

As research continued throughout this century, scientists realized that other processes also play roles in the production of the variation on which natural selection acts. Research still goes on into the relationships and relative importance of all these processes in the evolution of species.

What are species?

What are the processes of evolution?

How do these processes interact to bring about evolution as we understand it today?

SPECIES: THE UNITS OF EVOLUTION

We observe evolution as the change in species over time and the development of new species. Evolution does not take place in individuals. You and I don't evolve in this sense. Evolution takes place in *populations* of organisms, and the basic population in nature is the species.

A species is *a population of organisms whose members can, under natural circumstances, freely interbreed with one another and produce fertile offspring.* Humans and chimpanzees, despite our 99 percent genetic similarity, cannot (even under *un*natural circumstances) interbreed and produce offspring because our two species have different numbers of chromosomes. But any two normally healthy humans of the opposite sex, no matter how different they may appear phenotypically, can reproduce, and their offspring will be fertile. Thus, humans and chimps are different species, but all human beings are members of a single species, *Homo sapiens*.

Horses and donkeys can mate and produce offspring, known as mules. But mules are nearly always sterile. Two mules can't reproduce and make more mules. Thus, horses and donkeys are considered separate species.

In captivity, lions and tigers have been known to produce hybrid offspring that are, in many cases, fertile. But lions and tigers don't interbreed in the wild. Though their ranges overlap (in India), the specific environmental **niche** of each animal is different, as are their behaviors, including mating behavior. Thus, lions and tigers are separate species.

Similarly, domestic dogs and wolves can reproduce and the hybrid offspring are fertile. Indeed, in a genetic sense, dogs and wolves are still identical. This leads many authorities to lump them into the same species, *Canis lupus*. But dogs and wolves do not freely interbreed under natural circumstances; wolves are wild and dogs are domestic (and thus, in a sense, unnatural). Dogs have been manipulated by humans for about 12,000 years and have become adapted to *our* environment. We have even produced some breeds that, because of their size, could not possibly mate with a wolf, or with other breeds of dogs, or carry and give birth to the fetuses from such matings. So other authorities indicate this difference by giving dogs a different species name, *Canis familiaris*.

It is not surprising to us that humans and chimps are separate species because, very simply, we don't *look* like the same species, although we do differ in only 1 percent of our genes. Horses and donkeys, on the other hand, do look pretty similar and yet are different species. Lions and tigers look like different species but can still produce fertile offspring, although only under artificial conditions. And some breeds of dogs look so similar to wolves as to obviously belong to the same species, although other breeds only faintly resemble their wild ancestors (Figure 4.1).

If the species is the natural basic unit of evolution, then why is the distinction among various species sometimes so vague? Why aren't all species equally distinct—separate from one another to the same degree and for the same reasons? And why are scientists who specialize in classifying species (called **taxonomists** or **systematists**) sometimes at odds with one another over which populations belong to the same species?

The answer to all these questions is that while the origin of new species from existing species usually happens fairly quickly, it does not

niche: The environment of an organism and its adaptive response to that environment.

taxonomists: Those who classify and name living organisms.

systematists: Synonym for taxonomists.

FIGURE 4.1

Wolflike and very un-wolf-like dogs. The German shepherd (top) closely resembles the wolf, the ancestor of all dog breeds. The West Highland terrier bears little resemblance to that ancestor. Both breeds, however, are genetically the same as wolves and could potentially interbreed with them.

happen instantly. It is a *process* that takes place over time (a subject we'll examine in Chapter 5). Thus, there is usually a period when two or more emerging species still blend with one another and are therefore difficult to define—as is the case with dogs and wolves.

In addition, all species did not emerge at the same time. They appeared at different times, they evolve at different rates, and they continue to evolve. Species thus change in relation to one another as time goes on.

We established in the last chapter that, although evolution results in phenotypic change, it must also involve genetic change. So, if species change over time, we need to characterize populations within a species in genetic terms in order to fully examine their evolution. We do so by using the concept of **gene frequency,** which is also and more accurately called **allele frequency.**

Going back to our example of the taster trait, suppose every human on earth was homozygous for the dominant (T) allele. The allele frequency would be $T = 1.0$ (or 100 percent). The phenotypic result of this would be that every member of the species would be a taster.

Now, suppose that a mutation occurred somewhere that changed a T allele to a t allele and that, over time, the mutated allele was passed on to many generations of offspring so that at some point 25 percent of the alleles at the taster locus in our species were recessives (t). Now the gene (allele) frequencies for this locus would be .75 (75 percent) T and .25 (25 percent) t.

This alteration in frequency would, of course, have a phenotypic effect. Most individuals will still be tasters since T is still the most frequent allele and, as you recall, heterozygotes are also phenotypically tasters. But there will be some homozygous recessives (tt) who will be nontasters. The species will have changed phenotypically over time as a result of a genetic change. Thus, evolution operates by *changes in gene (allele) frequency through time*. Anything that changes allele frequency is therefore a process of evolution.

We will now describe those processes that produce evolutionary change within species and that, ultimately, bring about the origin of new species.

MUTATIONS: NECESSARY ERRORS

A mutation is any change in the genetic code. Some mutations involve a single incorrect base in a codon (one letter of one word). These are known as **point mutations.** Some point mutations may be inconsequential, but some might result in the wrong amino acid in a protein, which could have disastrous results for the organism. (An example is sickle cell anemia, a genetic disease, which we'll cover at the end of this chapter.)

Other mutations may involve a whole chromosome or a large portion of one. These are called **chromosomal mutations.** They are almost always deleterious because many genes are affected. For example, humans who have three of chromosome 21, instead of the usual pair, have Down syndrome, or Trisomy 21, which results in mental retardation and other phenotypic effects (Figure 4.2).

Mutations are random; that is, a specific mutation doesn't occur for a specific reason or at a specific time. Mutations occur continually, but exactly *what* mutation occurs is totally unpredictable, nor do mutations occur *because* they are needed. Some mutations are the results of environmental influences like cosmic radiation, other forms of radioactivity, or chemical

gene frequency: The percentage of times a particular allele appears in a population.

allele frequency: The same as gene frequency, and the preferred term.

point mutations: Mutations of single codons.

chromosomal mutations: Mutations of a whole chromosome or a large portion of a chromosome.

FIGURE 4.2
A child with Down syndrome, showing the characteristic facial features that are some of the multiple phenotypic effects of the presence of the extra chromosome. This girl has just won a medal in swimming at the Special Olympics.

pollutants. Most, however, are simply mechanical errors that occur during the complex process of gene replication at cell division or during the even more complex process by which the genetic code is read, translated, and transcribed into proteins.

As you might imagine, then, mutations are frequent. They are occurring in the cells of your body as you read this. The mutations that occur during the reading of the code just affect the individual. The process of aging, for example, is partly a result of the accumulation of cells with mutations that make them in some way abnormal, though they are still alive and able to divide.

The only mutations that concern us in an evolutionary sense are those that occur in the gametes or in the specialized cells that produce gametes. These mutations are the ones that are passed on to future generations and thus bring about genetic change through time. Therefore, mutation changes gene frequency through time by making new versions of a gene (as in the taster trait example above) or by otherwise altering the details of the genetic code. Mutation is a process of evolution.

Because mutations are mistakes—deviations from the normal genetic code—many are deleterious. They produce a phenotypic result that is abnormal and therefore, to one degree or another, maladaptive. Individuals with such traits may not be as reproductively successful as most members of their species, and so the mutant gene or genes will not be passed on as often, if at all. In other words, natural selection will select *against* those genes. But mutations may also produce alleles that are neutral, making no difference to an individual's fitness, or they may produce alleles that result in even *better* adapted phenotypes and are thus selected *for* by being passed on more often.

Mutation, in other words, changes allele frequency and, as it does so, adds genetic variation to a species' **gene pool.** Mutations are the price living things pay for the process of evolution. Without mutation—if the first life forms had reproduced themselves absolutely without error—nothing would have changed, and the first living things would be the *only* living things. Mutations are thus one of the basic processes of evolution.

NATURAL SELECTION: THE PRIME MOVER OF EVOLUTION

By now, you should have a pretty good idea how natural selection operates. The genetic variation produced by mutation, segregation, independent assortment, and recombination results in phenotypic variation within a species. Much of a species' phenotypic variation may make little difference to the fitness and reproductive success of individuals. We have come to see that nature is more tolerant of variation than Darwin thought. He felt that *every* variation made a difference. We now know this is not the case.

At the same time, however, some phenotypic variation *does* make a difference. How much of a difference, of course, depends upon what traits are important for the adaptation of a particular species to a particular environment at a particular time. What's adaptive for one species—say, large size or a certain color—will not necessarily work for another species. As environments change, a trait that *was* adaptive for a species may no longer be adaptive, or a trait that was once neutral, or even nonadaptive, may now be adaptive.

Perhaps the most famous example of natural selection demonstrates the basic features of the process. There is a moth in England called the peppered moth, because when it was first described, before the Industrial Revolution, most members of the species were light multicolored. This color pattern provided the moths with camouflage when they landed on tree trunks covered with lichens (a combination of an algae and a fungus). Birds, the moth's major predators, had a hard time seeing them.

Every generation, however, some peppered moths would appear that would be uniformly dark in color, the result of a different allele (or alleles) for coloration. These moths were more easily seen by the birds, so relatively fewer of them survived and reproduced. Thus, the multicolored members of the species were more common and the dark ones were rare (Figure 4.3).

When extensive coal burning in the nineteenth century killed off the sensitive lichens and blackened tree trunks with soot, the once-rare dark moths had an adaptive advantage. Less easily seen by predators, they now reproduced relatively more successfully than the multicolored members of their species and so passed on more of the allele(s) for dark coloration. The frequency of the allele(s) involved changed over time, causing the average phenotype of the species to change.

Recently, with less coal burning and better pollution control, the lichens are returning and, as you probably guessed, the multicolored moths are becoming increasingly frequent, from 10 percent of the population in 1959 to over 80 percent in 1995. The same phenomenon has also occurred among a North American population of the same species (Yoon 1996).

The example of the peppered moths makes two very important points:

1. Adaptation within a species is *relative to a specific set of environmental circumstances*. Mixed coloration was adaptive under one set of environmental conditions, while dark color was adaptive when those conditions changed.

2. Notice that the dark coloration did not appear *when* it was needed. It was, perhaps fortunately for the peppered moth, *already present* as a result of genetic variation within the species. If the color variation of

gene pool: All the alleles in a population.

FIGURE 4.3
Peppered moths. Where trees are light and covered with lichens, the light form of the moth has an obvious selective advantage in being better camouflaged. Where trees are blackened by soot, the dark form has the advantage.

the moths had been of a different sort, or if there had been no variation in color, natural selection would have had different materials to work with and a quite different series of evolutionary events would have taken place. Natural selection does not create adaptive variation. It uses the variation already present.

It follows from these points that natural selection is not always successful in maintaining a species' adaptation and survival in the face of environmental change. If a change is too rapid or too extensive, the nat-

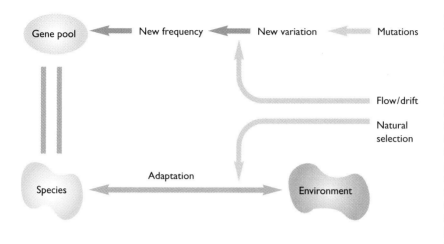

FIGURE 4.4
The processes of evolution. A species is in an adaptive relationship with its environment. This relationship is maintained by natural selection. Environments, however, are constantly changing, so the adaptive characteristics of species change through time. In addition, the gene pool of a species is always changing, altering the phenotypes upon which selection acts. Processes that alter a species' gene pool are also, by definition, processes of evolution because they change allele frequency. Mutation provides new genetic variation by producing new alleles or otherwise altering the genetic code. Flow and drift mix the genetic variation within a species, continually supplying new combinations of genetic variables.

ural variation within a species simply may not be enough to provide any individuals with sufficient reproductive success to keep the species going. When that comet or asteroid hit the earth 65 million years ago and radically altered the earth's climate, perhaps hundreds of thousands of species, the dinosaurs and many others, were unable to adapt and thus became extinct. Natural variation within a species cannot predict what environmental change may take place in the future. Adaptation to change is a matter of luck. Indeed, for over 90 percent of all species that have ever existed, their luck ran out; they are extinct.

Recognition that extinction is commonplace was another reason for Charles Darwin's delay in making his idea of natural selection known to the public. Natural selection does not produce change in a particular direction, nor is it always successful in ensuring the survival of a species. Darwin thought, perhaps correctly at first, that these implications were too uncomfortable for most people to accept. By 1859, however, the Victorian world of rapid social, industrial, economic, and political transformation had come to accept change as the norm, for nature as well as for itself. Moreover, the logic of *Origin of Species* was so lucid and well presented that its conclusions were seen as obvious. Darwin's book was a bestseller, and his idea was, except for a few holdouts, well accepted, at least within science.

Mutation and natural selection are the major processes of evolution. Mutation provides new genetic variation. Natural selection selects phenotypes for reproductive success based on their adaptive relationship with the environment. But because evolution is technically defined as change in allele frequency, two other processes must also be considered as processes of evolution (Figure 4.4).

FIGURE 4.5
Demes. The members of a species of lowland, non-aquatic animal (dots) are un-evenly distributed within that species' range because of mountain and water bound-aries. The separate popula-tion concentrations—the demes—may show genetic and phenotypic differences.

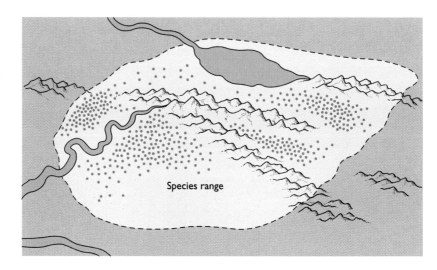

Species range

GENE FLOW: MIXING POPULATIONS

By definition, members of a species can and do interbreed with one an-other. The members of a species, however, are usually unevenly distributed over that species' range. Populations within a species can be to some de-gree separated from other populations by environmental barriers, geo-graphic distance, or, in the case of our species, social and cultural distinc-tions like political, religious, and ethnic boundaries. Such populations are called **breeding populations,** or **demes.** Individuals tend to find mates within their own deme (Figure 4.5).

Although belonging to the same species, demes may exhibit genetic differences. There are two reasons for this. First, demes may exist in somewhat different environmental circumstances from each other, as in Figure 4.5. Natural selection will have been favoring different pheno-types, and thus different allele frequencies, in adaptive response to these environments.

Second, other genetic events (such as mutations and the processes to be covered below) tend to be concentrated within demes because that is where breeding is concentrated. What happens genetically in one deme will differ from what happens in another.

However, because demes *are* still members of one species, interbreed-ing between them does take place. This is called **gene flow.** When mem-bers of different demes interbreed, new genetic combinations may be pro-duced in the offspring. Genes within a species, in other words, "flow"

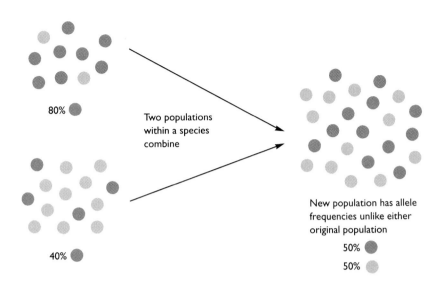

80%

40%

Two populations
within a species
combine

New population has allele
frequencies unlike either
original population

50%

50%

among the populations of that species, altering the allele frequencies
in those populations and adding still more genetic—and thus phenotypic—variation to the species as a whole (Figure 4.6).

This process of evolution is particularly effective in a mobile species
like ours, where our populations are continually moving around and mixing genes. For example, half of all Hutterite marriages take place between
colonies, the bride moving to the colony of her husband. The woman thus
brings her genes into the population and contributes them to subsequent
generations. In one of the colonies I visited, 70 percent of the female
parents came from other colonies, and marriages involving these women
produced nearly 60 percent of the children of the next generation. In the
other colony, 75 percent of female parents "flowed" in, and their marriages
produced 47 percent of the next generation. Changes from one generation
to the next in a Hutterite colony are greatly affected by this continual
mixing or flowing of genes among populations, and it is the same for the
human species as a whole.

GENETIC DRIFT: RANDOM EVOLUTION

The several processes that fall under this heading can be demonstrated by
the following experiment: Take 100 coins and arrange them so you have
50 heads and 50 tails. Mix them up and without looking (that is, at

breeding populations:
Populations within a spe-
cies that are genetically
isolated to some degree
from other populations.

demes: Same as breeding
populations, but some-
times implies physical
distinctions.

gene flow: The exchange
of genes among popula-
tions through inter-
breeding.

FIGURE 4.7
Fission and the founder effect. Notice that this diagram is basically the reverse of that representing gene flow (Figure 4.6).

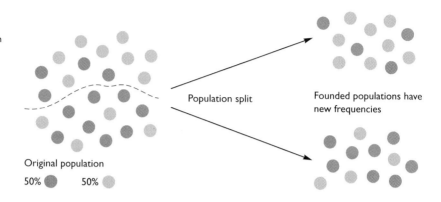

random) select 10 coins. They will probably *not* be 5 heads and 5 tails, 50 percent of each as in the original group. The odds are against it (about 4 to 1). Your sample of 10 is not usually representative of the whole population of coins. It is usually a nonrepresentative sample, and this effect is called **sampling error.**

Similarly, when a population within a species splits, each new population will most likely exhibit a nonrepresentative sample of the genes, and therefore the phenotypes, of the original. The splitting of a population is called **fission** and is the opposite of gene flow (Figure 4.7). When one of the new populations is drawn from a small sample of the parental population, it will be strikingly different genetically (as with the coins above). This phenomenon is called the **founder effect.**

The Hutterites again provide an example. Hutterites have one of the highest recorded birth rates, an average of about ten children per family. After such rapid population growth for about fifteen or twenty years, a colony becomes so large (130 to 150 people) that social and administrative problems arise, and there is increasing duplication of labor specialists. The colony will then fission or, as they call it, "branch out," half the colony families staying in the original location and half founding a new colony. As a result, the 3 original North American Hutterite colonies, founded in 1874 and 1875, have now become over 300, and the original 300 Hutterite immigrants have become 30,000.

In fact, the situation is more pronounced than that. Of the 300 original North American Hutterites, only 90 contributed genes to future generations. So most of the 30,000 present-day Hutterites can trace most of their genes back to fewer than 100 ancestors. (Some people have joined the group from the outside in the last 120 years.) When a founder population is a very small percentage of an original group, it is referred to as a **bottleneck.**

The founder effect can have interesting and sometimes tragic results. In a population of 333 Pennsylvania Dutch, 98, nearly one-third, were found to have the gene for Tay-Sachs disease, a fatal condition that kills recessive homozygotes by their fourth year of life (see also Chapter 15). The high frequency of this lethal recessive allele can be explained by the fact that these 333 people are all descended from one couple who founded the group in the last century. One of them, no doubt, by sad circumstance, carried the gene (Diamond 1991).

Fission, the founder effect, and gene flow, are particularly important in the evolution of our species. For most of human history we have been divided into many populations, defined by such things as religion, politics, and ethnicity; and, of course, we have been separated by our ability to live all over the globe in nearly all natural environments. Our populations, however, have always mixed genes, and they have often split up to found new populations. Cultural boundaries, in addition, are temporary, so the definitions of populations change. Gene flow and fission are processes caused by population movement, and our species is among the most mobile.

The other form of genetic drift is called **gamete sampling.** Just as genes are not sampled representatively when a population fissions, they are not sampled representatively when two individuals produce offspring. An organism passes on only one of each of its pairs of genes at a time, and only chance dictates which one will be involved in the fertilization that produces a new individual.

For example, two humans who are each heterozygotous for the taster trait will possess one of each allele at the taster locus (Tt). But they will not necessarily, in their reproductive lifetimes, pass on an equal number of each allele. It's a matter of chance. It's possible that they could pass on only their dominant allele, or only their recessive, or both but in a proportion other than 50 : 50. In other words, the very act of reproducing—with the genetic processes of segregation and fertilization—can change allele frequency from one generation to the next.

This example refers to a single couple, but the combined effects of this phenomenon on a whole population can bring about a great deal of change between generations. This is especially true in small populations of 100 or under (about the size of the average Hutterite colony). Here, the change produced by one set of parents is not likely to be balanced by change in the opposite direction produced by another set.

Gene frequencies, then, may change at random across generations, "drifting" in whatever direction chance takes them. The change may be great enough that certain alleles may be completely lost, while others may reach a frequency of 100 percent—all with no necessary relationship to natural selection based on the fitness of those alleles.

sampling error: When a sample chosen for study does not accurately represent the population from which the sample was taken.

fission: Here, the splitting up of a population to form new populations.

founder effect: Genetic differences between populations produced by the fact that genetically different individuals established (founded) the populations.

bottleneck: A severe reduction in the size of a population such that only certain genes survive and come to characterize the descendant population.

gamete sampling: The genetic change caused when genes are passed to new generations in frequencies unlike those of the parental generation. An example of sampling error.

FIGURE 4.8
The distribution of frequencies of the sickle cell allele. Compare this with the map of high frequencies of malaria (Figure 4.10).

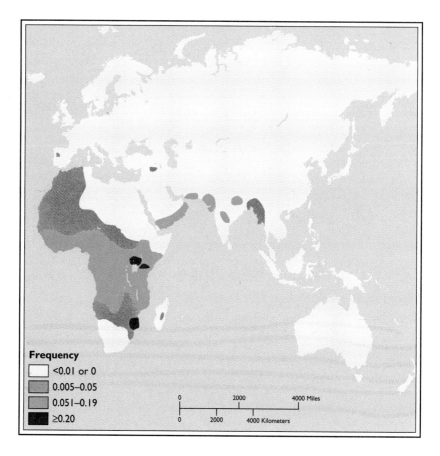

Frequency
<0.01 or 0
0.005–0.05
0.051–0.19
≥0.20

SICKLE CELL ANEMIA: EVOLUTIONARY PROCESSES IN ACTION

We can now take the ideas covered in the last two chapters and see how they work in a real example. Sickle cell anemia is a genetic blood disorder; it is often associated with Africans and African Americans because it is found in high frequency in a band across central Africa. It is also found in north Africa, Southwest Asia, India, and Southeast Asia (Figure 4.8).

Sickle cell anemia is the result of a mutation affecting hemoglobin, the protein on the red blood cells that carries oxygen from the lungs to the body's tissues. Hemoglobin, as you recall, is made up of two pairs of amino acid chains, the alpha chain of 141 amino acids and the beta chain of 146. Mutations no doubt occur all along the codes for these proteins. But if the codon CTC for glutamic acid mutates to CAC for valine in the sixth position of the beta chain—one particular wrong word in a sentence of 146 words—an abnormal form of hemoglobin results.

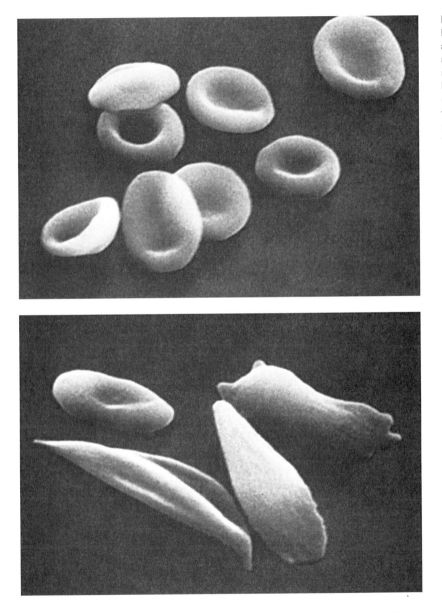

FIGURE 4.9
Normal red blood cells (top) and those showing the abnormal shapes (bottom) that result from the presence of hemoglobin with one incorrect amino acid. Such cells fail to transport oxygen properly to the body's tissues.

When this abnormal form is present and stress, high altitude, or illness lowers an individual's oxygen supply, the red blood cells take on peculiar shapes, some resembling sickles (Figure 4.9). When in these shapes, the cells cannot carry sufficient oxygen to nourish the body's tissues. The results include fatigue, retarded physical development in children, increased susceptibility to infection, miscarriage, fever, and severe pain. Sickle cell kills about 100,000 people a year, 85 percent of whom die before their twenties. Even if they do live longer, they live in constant pain and have

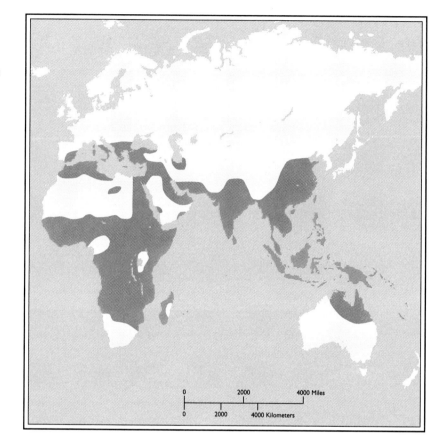

very low reproductive rates. In terms of evolutionary fitness—that is, reproductive success—sickle cell anemia may be considered nearly 100 percent fatal.

The abnormal allele for sickle cell is an example of a codominant
allele. An individual who is homozygous for the allele will have sickle
cell anemia. A heterozygote, who inherits one sickle cell allele and one
allele for normal hemoglobin, will possess only about 40 percent abnormal
hemoglobin. These people are said to have the sickle cell *trait*. In extreme
conditions of low oxygen, they may experience symptoms of the disease,
but usually not as severe as homozygotes and with a great deal of variation
from person to person. The heterozygous condition is not normally fatal.

For a disease that kills its victims, usually without allowing them to
pass on their genes, sickle cell is found in unexpectedly high frequencies
in parts of the world (see Figure 4.8), in some areas as high as 20 percent.
One would expect such an allele to be selected against and to virtually
disappear.

The answer to this puzzle is a perfect example of the complexity of natural selection. Not only do heterozygotes experience less severe episodes of the disease; they also have a resistance to malaria, an often fatal infectious disease caused by a parasitic single-celled organism and transmitted by mosquitos. Malaria, though now treatable, still kills about a million people a year. Red blood cells with abnormal hemoglobin (recall that heterozygotes have about 40 percent of this) take on abnormal shapes when infected by the malaria parasite and die, thus failing to transport the parasite through the body. Sickle cell is found in highest frequencies where malaria is found in highest frequencies (Figure 4.10).

In no environment is there any advantage to being homozygous for sickle cell. In most environments, being heterozygous also confers some disadvantage. But in malarial areas, heterozygotes do have an advantage. They are resistant to malaria and they exhibit a variable and nonfatal form of the anemia. If heterozygotes are the healthiest in such environments and thus are relatively more successful at passing on their genes, then more sickle cell alleles will be inherited than would be expected if sickle cell had no benefit in any environment. Whenever two heterozygotes mate, they stand a one-quarter chance of producing a normal individual, a one-quarter chance of producing an offspring who will die from sickle cell, and a one-half chance of producing an offspring who will die neither from sickle cell nor from malaria but who will possess one sickle cell allele (Figure 4.11). This shows dramatically how adaptive fitness is related to specific environmental conditions. Even a lethal allele may be adaptive under certain circumstances.

The connection between sickle cell and African Americans is an example of the founder effect. African Americans can trace at least some of their ancestry back to the populations from West Africa that provided much of the slave trade to North America. The African-American population was thus, in part, founded by individuals from an area where sickle cell already existed in high frequencies.

But sickle cell is less frequent among African Americans than it is in Africa. Moreover, sickle cell is not limited to persons of African descent in this country. One only has to have the alleles to have the disease. Persons of largely European-American background can also have sickle cell. Both these facts can be explained partly as a result of gene flow. There has been a good deal of genetic mixing between European Americans and African Americans over the last several hundred years. The addition of European genes would lessen the frequency of the sickle cell allele in African Americans because Europe is largely free of the disease. The presence of the disease among a small number of persons of largely European descent might be the result of their having, sometime in the past, an ancestor of African descent who carried the allele. Of course, the mutation that produces the sickle cell allele can occur in people of any geographic or ethnic background, European Americans included.

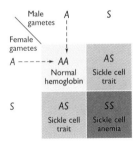

FIGURE 4.11

Punnett Square for sickle cell anemia showing the potential offspring of two heterozygotes. Because heterozygotes have an adaptive advantage in malarial areas but stand a one-quarter chance of producing an offspring with sickle cell anemia, the allele for sickle cell is maintained and passed on in such populations and the disease exhibits high frequencies.

Contemporary Reflections

Are Humans Still Evolving?

As asked by most people, this question has two meanings. Perhaps the most common refers to the direction of future human evolution; in other words, how will we look in so many millions of years? As our minds do more and more of our work—and our bodies do less and less—will we eventually be great big heads atop short, spindly bodies? (This is the image we are often given of aliens from more advanced civilizations. Think of *Close Encounters of the Third Kind, ET,* or *The X-Files.*)

The answer to this meaning of the question is, obviously, who knows? Evolution is so complex, so dependent upon multiple, interacting series of events, that there is really no way of predicting the evolutionary future of any species, especially our species with its ability to control its behavior, the environment, and, indeed, its genes through culture. If we could take a time machine back to the Cambrian Period 530 million years ago and look at its animal life (see Figure 6.5) made up mostly of primitive arthropods (ancestors of modern insects, spiders, and crustaceans), who would predict that a rare little wormy creature only about two inches long, called *Pikaia*, would be the earliest known representative of the chordates, the important group of organisms now represented by fish, amphibians, reptiles, birds, and mammals (Gould 1989; Gore 1993)?

A more sophisticated meaning of the question concerns whether or not we humans have stopped our evolution by so controlling our environment that natural selection is no longer in operation, that genetic variation is no longer an important factor in reproductive success.

There are two parts to the answer. First, as we discussed, there are processes other than natural selection that bring about genetic change from generation to generation in a species. Our control over our environment certainly won't halt the processes of mutation, gene flow, and genetic drift. Indeed, one

Moreover, because malaria is less common in the United States and Canada than in central Africa (although it was a problem in the southern United States until recently), there has been less of an adaptive advantage in possessing the sickle cell trait. Natural selection has thus been producing lower frequencies of the sickle cell allele, even in persons whose ancestors are from one of the areas of highest frequency.

Finally, while we're on the subject, there is evidence (Relethford 1996) that the frequency of malaria increased when people began farming in Africa several thousand years ago. Clearing and planting the land provides the sunlight and the pools of stagnant water that are ideal breeding grounds for the mosquitos that carry the malaria parasite. An increase in malaria would result in an increase in selection for the sickle cell allele, which, in heterozygotes, confers an immunity to the infectious disease.

Thus, the full story of this lethal disease shows the interaction of the forces of evolution and involves not only the genetics behind the cause of the disease, but also a single-celled parasite, an insect, and a human

might argue that we have increased mutation rates through some of our environmental manipulations and that our increasing mobility makes gene flow ever more powerful. So, by its genetic definition, evolution will always be taking place in our species.

But have we buffered ourselves against natural selection? For some genetically based characteristics, yes, we have. Remember that fitness is measured against a particular environment. If, through culture, we change the environment, we then change the adaptive fitness of certain phenotypes and thus of the genes that code for them. If I had lived in, say, *Homo erectus* times (1.8 million to maybe 100,000 years ago), I'd no doubt be dead by now. If my infected appendix hadn't killed me (which it would have), my nearsightedness would have prevented me from being a very effective hunter or gatherer. Our present environment, however, includes all sorts of techniques and devices to improve one's eyesight. I wear glasses and see my optometrist once a year, so my poor vision (which, for the sake of the example, we'll say has a genetic basis) does not put me at any survival or reproductive disadvantage. You can probably think of dozens of other examples.

We have not, however, completely eliminated all relevant genetic variation. There are plenty of genes for diseases that place severe, or absolute, limits on a person's ability to reproduce and thus pass on those genes. Tay-Sachs disease, for example, is lethal well before reproductive age. Sickle cell anemia lowers reproductive rates in the few individuals that live long enough to reproduce.

And let's end on a hypothetical note (keeping in mind my precaution about predicting future evolution). There could well be some genetic variables that will make some difference in reproductive success in the near future. Suppose there is genetically based variation in humans' abilities to withstand less-than-optimal air quality, or severely crowded living conditions, or high levels of noise pollution. As these conditions worsen, it is certainly conceivable that genes for such tolerances would become more frequent as their possessors were less reproductively affected by the modern environment.

cultural practice. The story of sickle cell is a perfect example of the holistic perspective of anthropology.

SUMMARY

A basic theory of evolution involves the production of new genetic variation by mutation and the continual mixing of that variation at reproduction. Gene flow and the forms of genetic drift (fission, the founder effect that results from fission, and gamete sampling) act to randomly change gene frequencies within populations of a species. The resulting phenotypic variation becomes the raw material for natural selection that selects individuals for reproductive success, thus accumulating adaptive traits across generations and decreasing the frequency of poorly adapted traits.

The basic unit of evolution is the species, an interbreeding population that is reproductively isolated from other populations. Because the evolution of new species is a process that occurs over time and at differing rates, species are not always equally distinct from one another and can often be difficult to define. Species are characterized genetically by gene (allele) frequency, the percentage of times each possible allele of a gene occurs. Evolution is thus technically defined as a change in allele frequency over time.

The processes of evolution, based on this definition, are:

1. *Mutation*—mistakes in the genetic mechanism that add new variation to a species' gene pool.

2. *Natural selection*—the differential reproduction of individuals based upon the relative adaptive value of their traits.

3. *Gene flow*—the mixing of genes as populations within a species move about and interbreed.

4. *Genetic drift*—the splitting of populations to found new populations with new sets of gene frequencies (fission and the founder effect) and the nonrepresentative sampling of genes as each new generation is produced (gamete sampling).

Sickle cell anemia not only provides an example of the processes of evolution at work but is also an example of anthropology's holistic approach—the search for connections among the various aspects of its subject.

KEY TERMS

niche	chromosomal	sampling error
taxonomists	mutations	fission
systematists	gene pool	founder effect
gene frequency	breeding populations	bottleneck
allele frequency	demes	gamete sampling
point mutations	gene flow	

SUGGESTED READINGS

An extended discussion of genetics and evolutionary processes within the context of anthropology can be found in John H. Relethford's text, *The Human Species: An Introduction to Biological Anthropology*, third edition.

It includes a chapter that covers sickle cell and many additional examples of evolution in action within human populations.

A highly technical but very readable text on all aspects of evolution is *Evolution* by Mark Ridley. The nature of species and the evolutionary processes that affect them are nicely covered in Edward O. Wilson's *The Diversity of Life*, a book about the importance of maintaining the biological diversity of the planet.

A discussion of the definition and origin of species, that also relates to the next chapter, is Stephen Jay Gould's article in *Discover* (December 1992) called "What Is a Species?"

CHAPTER

5

THE ORIGIN OF SPECIES AND THE SHAPE OF EVOLUTION

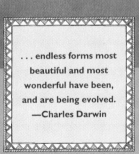

. . . endless forms most
beautiful and most
wonderful have been,
and are being evolved.
—Charles Darwin

The examples of evolution in action that we discussed in the previous chapter—the peppered moth responding to a human-caused environmental change and populations of our own species interacting with malaria—have focused on changes within single species. Darwin's book, however, was called *The Origin of Species*. What Darwin was ultimately trying to explain was how new species arise, the "mystery of mysteries," as he called it in his introduction.

How do existing species give rise to new species?

How do the processes of evolution contribute to the origin of new species?

How do species diversify?

What does the "family tree" of species look like?

Are there any challenges to the idea of evolution? Are they valid?

NEW SPECIES

Species are, by definition, reproductively isolated from other species. Members of two species cannot mate and produce fertile offspring. Members of the same species can. What prevents interbreeding between species?

Any difference that prevents the production of fertile hybrid offspring between two populations under natural conditions is called a **reproductive isolating mechanism.** These isolating mechanisms fall into several general categories (based on Dobzhansky 1970):

1. *Ecological.* Members of the populations are adapted to different environmental niches. Even though their ranges may overlap, their specific environments don't—as is the case with lions and tigers. Ecological isolation probably explains the origin of the **hominids,** the group to which our species belongs (see Chapter 10).

2. *Seasonal.* Mating within each population or the flowering of plants of two related species takes place at different times of the year.

3. *Sexual.* Behaviors that attract one sex to the other (called courtship behaviors) are different in the two populations.

4. *Mechanical.* The organs of reproduction (genitalia or flower parts) are incompatible.

5. *Different pollinators.* In flowering plants, different species, even though closely related, attract different insects, birds, or bats to facilitate pollination.

6. *Gamete isolation*. The cells of reproduction may be incompatible or may not be able to survive within the body of a member of the other species, thus preventing fertilization even if mating takes place.

7. *Hybrid inviability*. Fertilization may occur, but the hybrid zygotes do not survive.

8. *Hybrid sterility*. Hybrids survive but do not produce functional gametes. Mules are normally an example, although on some occasions they are fertile.

The origin of new species, then, is the evolution of *any* of these differences between populations that prevent the production of fertile offspring. As biologist Edward O. Wilson puts it, "In order to spring forth as a species, a group of breeding individuals need only acquire *one* difference in *one* trait in their biology. . . . When that happens, a new species is born [emphases mine]" (1992:68).

How do such differences arise? It is important to understand that reproductive isolating mechanisms do not evolve *in order to* produce a new species. It is an accident that the differences in traits end up as isolating mechanisms. The differences themselves evolve through the processes of mutation, gene flow, genetic drift, and natural selection acting differently on different populations.

To take the simplest model, a species inhabits a wide geographic range, and populations (demes) at opposite ends of the range exhibit slightly different adaptive responses to the particular environmental circumstances found there. Now, some environmental change—say, a river changing its course, the destruction of some important resource, or the advance of a glacier—splits the species, geographically isolating one deme from another. Over time, each population will continue to adapt to its environment but without being able to exchange genes with the other deme. In other words, there is no gene flow. Each population will accumulate different genetic and phenotypic traits. Quite possibly one or more of these will, by chance, be a reproductive isolating mechanism. If, at some later point, the geographical barrier were removed and the two populations *could* mix, they would not be able to interbreed. They would be separate species, and we would say that **speciation** has occurred (Figure 5.1).

Even if a species is adaptively homogeneous, with very little variation, speciation can occur if a small population becomes isolated from the rest of the species. As in the example above, the processes of evolution, responding to the local environment of that population and acting just on that population, may evolve a trait or traits that end up as reproductive isolating mechanisms. Over time, the descendants of the small population will become a separate species from the parental population. Even if reunited, they will not be able to interbreed and produce fertile offspring.

reproductive isolating mechanisms: Any difference that prevents the production of fertile offspring between members of two populations.

hominids: Modern human beings and our ancestors, defined as the primates who walk erect.

speciation: The evolution of new species.

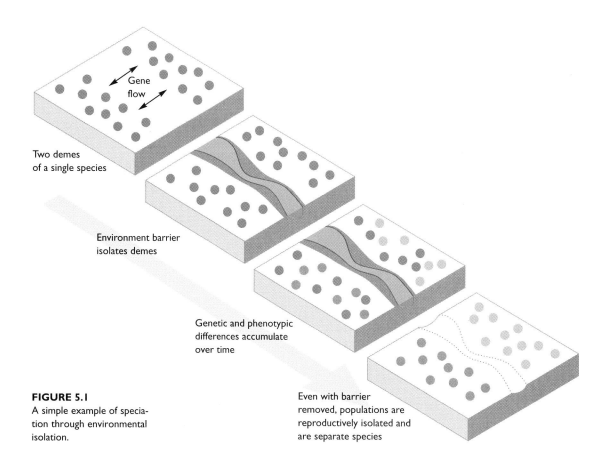

Gene flow

Two demes
of a single species

Environment barrier
isolates demes

Genetic and phenotypic
differences accumulate
over time

FIGURE 5.1
A simple example of speciation through environmental
isolation.

Even with barrier
removed, populations are
reproductively isolated and
are separate species

Speciation may be accelerated when a breeding group within a species shares a mutation with extensive phenotypic effects. Such mutations are called **macromutations.** Most macromutations are, as you would expect, deleterious. But, by chance, some macromutations might be neutral or even beneficial. In such a case, they would be retained by natural selection, and they might serve to very rapidly make a small population within a species adaptively isolated from the rest of the species. Speciation is given a "head start" by the macromutation.

A famous example is that of the salamanders, who begin life as aquatic larvae much like tadpoles. Eventually they develop functioning lungs and legs and spend their adult life on land. The axolotl from Mexico (Figure 5.2) is a salamander that never grows up. Because its pituitary gland fails to supply its thyroid with a certain hormone, the axolotl becomes sexually mature but does not finish developing physically and retains into adult-

FIGURE 5.2
An axolotl (upper left) with larval (lower left) and adult salamander (upper right). Note the similarity between the axolotl
and the immature salamander. The axolotl is, in a sense, a salamander that never completely matured.

hood the external gills and fully aquatic lifestyle of salamander larvae. It
is a separate species. If injected with the missing hormone, the axolotl will
mature and live on land. The difference, in other words, is a simple
one—the presence of a hormone—but the mutation that brought about
the difference served to immediately reproductively isolate its possessors
from the rest of their species. The speciation that produced the axolotl
was nearly instant. (Obviously, more than one salamander would have to
have shared the mutation. Perhaps the mutation occurred during the production of a group of eggs and so all the salamanders that developed from
those eggs were actually axolotls.)

The processes of evolution that bring about genetic and phenotypic
variation (see Figure 4.4) are constantly in action. So are the processes
that alter environmental circumstances. It stands to reason, then, that the
conditions that produce new species are ever-present and that speciation
must be a very common occurrence indeed.

macromutations: Muta-
tions with extensive and
important phenotypic
results.

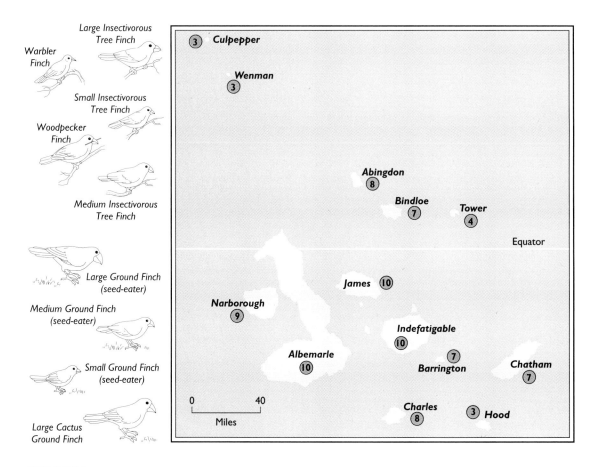

FIGURE 5.3
The various species of Darwin's finches evolved when small groups from an original species underwent adaptation to the varying environmental conditions found throughout the Galápagos Islands. The numbers on the map represent the number of finch species found on each major island. The drawing represents some of the variation observed among the species of Darwin's finches.

ADAPTIVE RADIATION: THE EVOLUTION OF LIFE'S DIVERSITY

No one is sure how many species of living things inhabit the earth, and we have no idea how many have *ever* lived on this planet. There are about 1.5 million *named* species living today; the total is certainly many times that number.

Even in modern times, new species are still being discovered. In 1997, for example, a new species of marmoset (a monkey) was discovered in Brazil—the seventh new monkey species found in that country in the last seven years. New species of small mammals, mostly rodents and bats, are described at an average rate of sixteen per year. New species of bacteria are being found by the thousands, some recent ones discovered to be living in small spaces within rocks nearly two miles below the surface of the earth and at temperatures of over 235°F.

Indeed, some microbes (single-celled organisms) that live at extreme conditions in superheated water near volcanic vents on the ocean floor, for example, or in water so salty it would kill most creatures, have been shown to be far more common than previously thought. Genetic tests of these and other microbes have shown them to belong to a whole new branch of life and have indicated that microbes comprise the bulk of the world's biomass—a measure of the weight of organic matter (Gould 1996). The actual number of species in the world must be, as one scientist put it, "staggering."

Despite the great array of living creatures, however, there is a great degree of similarity among them all. All living things, for example, use the same genetic code; they are built from the proteins that are the products of that code using the same basic twenty amino acids. We assume, then, that life on earth had a single origin. This being the case, all those millions upon millions of species have descended from a common ancestor and have come about by the process of speciation.

For a potential new species to persevere, it must survive the adaptive trials of natural selection. Put another way, it must have a place to go, an environment to which its traits are adapted, an "ecological opportunity." When such opportunities are extensive, speciation may take place numerous times, and a group of related species may spread into a number of niches. This spread of related species is called **adaptive radiation.** Evolution has been a story of the adaptive radiation of species into different environments and the subsequent actions of the processes of evolution on those species.

Ecological opportunities come about, and can foster adaptive radiation, under these three general circumstances:

1. when an environment is empty, that is, when no similar and therefore competing species live there,
2. when extensive extinction empties a set of environments of competing species, and
3. when the new group of related species are adaptively **generalized** (as opposed to **specialized**) and are able to disperse successfully into different niches and displace species already there.

An example of the first situation is the famous case of Darwin's finches, a group of thirteen (some authorities recognize fourteen) related bird species that inhabit the Galápagos, a volcanic archipelago of some nineteen islands in the Pacific about 500 miles west of Ecuador (Figure 5.3). This was one of Darwin's stops on his voyage around the world.

From a small group of original migrants, blown out to the islands from the mainland of South America an estimated half-million years ago, these birds have radiated into niches that were unoccupied by other birds. Today

adaptive radiation: The evolution and spreading out of related species into new niches.

generalized: Here, species that are adapted to a wide range of environmental niches.

specialized: Species adapted to a narrow range of environmental niches.

FIGURE 5.4

The fossil remains of *Archeopteryx* ("ancient bird"), about 150 million years old. It is actually a small, bipedal dinosaur with feathers. These feathers, modifications of dinosaurian scales, are an example of a sudden but sizable alteration in a species' genetic makeup that eventually gave rise to a whole new group of organisms.

there are species of ground-dwelling finches that feed on seeds of different sizes and have bills shaped accordingly. There are several species that feed on cactus, and several that live in trees and eat insects. Their beaks, too, are adapted for the specific foods they eat. One species is a tool-user, holding a cactus spine or twig in its bill and using it to probe for insects in tree trunks. The ground finches on two of the smaller islands peck the skin of larger birds and drink the blood that results. Not surprisingly, they are referred to as "vampire finches."

In fact, birds in general are an example of adaptive radiation into empty niches. Birds first evolved some 150 million years ago from dinosaurs (Figure 5.4). There was little competition for species possessing the new attributes of feathers and, for some, flight. This evolutionary novelty radiated into a wide variety of niches resulting currently in about 9000 species of birds of incredible diversity. All are variations on the same basic theme.

The mammals are an example of a group of species that were able to take advantage of the niches opened up by a major extinction—the one that killed off all the dinosaurs and many other species 65 million years ago. The mammals were among the survivors. At the time they were mostly small, **nocturnal,** shrewlike or rodentlike creatures, but they now had a world of niches open to them that were free of previous competitors. The mammals radiated rapidly, and by about 40 million years ago most major types of mammals we know today had evolved. (Birds, too, survived this extinction.)

We can look to our own group of mammals, the primates, for examples of species that were able to radiate because they were generalized and could fairly easily disperse into diverse niches. When monkeys first evolved, over 35 million years ago, they proved more generalized than their **prosimian** ancestors, the so-called primitive primates. The monkeys were larger-brained, **diurnal,** and well adapted to an active **arboreal** life eating a mixed diet of leaves, fruits, and insects. As the monkeys underwent speciation and radiated into new niches, they displaced the prosimians. In the New World (Central and South America), there are only monkeys; the North American prosimians apparently became extinct. In the Old World (Europe, Africa, and Asia), prosimians were pushed into marginal areas. A few species live on the mainland of Africa, but most inhabit isolated islands of Southeast Asia and the island of Madagascar, which had separated from mainland Africa prior to the monkeys' evolution (see Chapter 10 for more detail).

On the scale of a single species, we will see this pattern repeated when we look more closely at our own evolution. At least once during the evolution of our group of primates, a new and more generalized species of hominid spread geographically and ecologically, displacing an existing hominid species (see Chapters 10, 11, and 12).

THE SHAPE OF THE FAMILY TREE

What is the pace of speciation and what, as a result, is the shape of the evolutionary "family tree" of species?

Charles Darwin felt that natural selection was responsible for speciation and that it was a process of almost unlimited power. He said that natural selection brought about "the accumulation of innumerable slight variations, each good for the individual possessor," and he added:

> What limit can be put to this power, acting during long ages and rigidly scrutinizing the whole constitution, structure, and habits of each creature,—favoring the good and rejecting the bad? I can see no limit to this power, in slowly and beautifully adapting each form to the most complex relations of life. (1898:267)

In other words, Darwin saw natural selection as "fine-tuning" each species to its environment, constantly favoring or rejecting any difference among individuals, no matter how "slight." This constant selection eventually changes one species so much it may be considered a new species.

nocturnal: Active at night.

prosimian: Primate with primitive features, most closely resembling the ancient primates, as well as those most ancient primates themselves.

diurnal: Active during the day.

arboreal: Adapted to life in the trees.

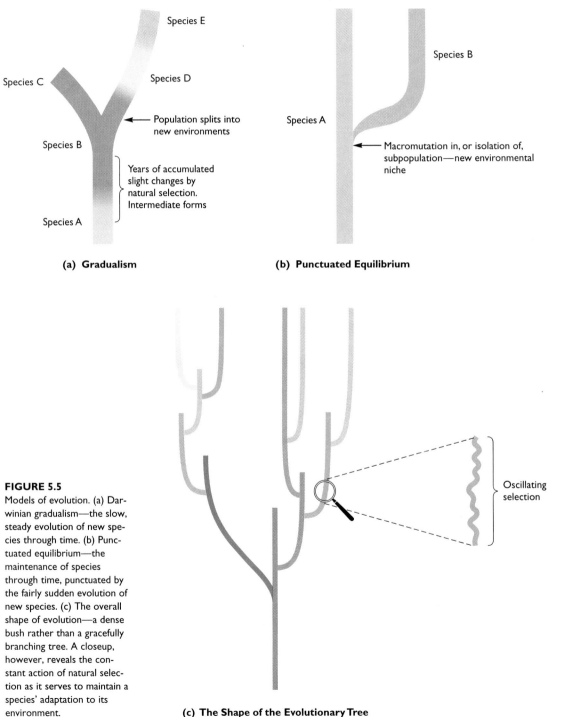

(a) **Gradualism**

Species E

Species C

Species D

Species B

Population splits into
new environments

Years of accumulated
slight changes by
natural selection.
Intermediate forms

Species A

(b) **Punctuated Equilibrium**

Species B

Species A

Macromutation in, or isolation of,
subpopulation—new environmental
niche

FIGURE 5.5
Models of evolution. (a) Darwinian gradualism—the slow, steady evolution of new species through time. (b) Punctuated equilibrium—the maintenance of species through time, punctuated by the fairly sudden evolution of new species. (c) The overall shape of evolution—a dense bush rather than a gracefully branching tree. A closeup, however, reveals the constant action of natural selection as it serves to maintain a species' adaptation to its environment.

Oscillating
selection

(c) **The Shape of the Evolutionary Tree**

In the process, selection can produce "varieties" within each species as populations become differently adapted to slightly different environments. These varieties will eventually become so distinct that they will be separate species. For Darwin, this process was slow and steady. Indeed, we refer to it as **Darwinian gradualism.**

According to this model, the family tree of species has gracefully diverging branches. These represent the slow but steady pace at which individual species change through time and at which populations within species slowly become distinct from one another under the "scrutiny" of natural selection. The tree of evolution represents, in Darwin's words, "an interminable number of intermediate forms . . . linking together all the species . . . by [fine] gradations" (1898:271–72) (Figure 5.5(a)).

Here, however, Darwin was uncharacteristically incomplete. For one thing, the fossil record has failed to show intermediate forms with fine gradations for all evolutionary lines. Instead, fossil species often tend to remain relatively stable for long periods of time and changes—new species—show up rather suddenly. For example, the first bird we know of for sure in the fossil record is not a mix of birdlike and dinosaurlike traits, a 50/50 combination, as one might expect if evolution were slow, gradual, and steady. Rather, *Archeopteryx* (see Figure 5.4) is a perfectly good dinosaur with perfectly good feathers. Clearly, evolution here was not a slow, steady accumulation of many small changes, but was focused on the evolution of feathers and may have occurred fairly quickly. (It is important to remember that "quickly" in evolutionary perspective is, of course, a relative term and may mean *tens* of thousands of years or more.)

Similarly, the origin of our own group, the hominids, did not occur slowly and steadily, gradually producing a humanlike form from an apelike one. The first fully accepted hominid fossils, from over 4 million years ago, are, to exaggerate only slightly, apes that stood upright (see Chapter 10). The change was not gradual, but was focused on bipedalism and was quick enough so that few other evolutionary changes had time to occur.

A second problem is more theoretical. If, as according to Darwin, each "slight variation" that natural selection favors is "good for the individual possessor," then we have to assume an adaptive benefit for *each small step* in the development of some trait. But can one-hundredth of a feather, then one-tenth of a feather, then one-quarter of a feather, and so on, each benefit its possessor enough to make a reproductive difference? It could happen, but we have come to realize that natural selection is not as creative as Darwin imagined. It cannot "scrutinize" a species, as if through a powerful microscope, and favor or reject *each* little difference among individuals. If this were the case, species would not show as much variation as they do and still be well adapted. Rather, natural selection acts only on differences that make a difference in reproductive success.

Darwinian gradualism: The view, held by Darwin, that evolution is slow and steady with cumulative change.

This does not mean, of course, that natural selection is bringing about *no* change during a species' time on earth. Traits that are important to a species' survival may change back and forth as environmental conditions change. For example, a pioneering study was conducted on Darwin's finches by Peter and Rosemary Grant (Weiner 1994). The Grants' data indicate that a slight difference in beak size among members of a finch species—as little as a millimeter or two—can be of adaptive importance during sudden, prolonged, or radical environmental changes such as droughts that significantly affect food sources. Such differences make the difference between life and death in terms of acquiring food and so, after such an environmental change, the average beak size of an affected finch species could be altered. When conditions—and, thus, food sources—returned to normal, the average beak size often returned to its previous measurement. Such back-and-forth selection is known as "oscillating selection."

So, natural selection is a conservative force, rejecting what doesn't work and allowing whatever does to reproduce. The role of natural selection is basically to maintain the adaptation of a species to its environment. Natural selection is not the author of evolution so much as the editor. Thus, species normally change little over the course of their tenure on earth, and new species seem to arise fairly quickly as a result of the isolation of populations within species through geographic separation, mutation, or a combination of both. Natural selection, of course, *then* plays an important role in screening the isolated population in terms of adaptive fitness.

We may describe this model of evolution as follows: The adaptive equilibrium of species with their environments is punctuated (interrupted) by the evolution of a new species from a population of the parental species. The parental species, in the meantime, may remain unchanged, at least for a time. This model is called **punctuated equilibrium** and is represented not by a tree with gracefully diverging branches but by a bush with many twigs. These twigs are evolution's experiments, potential new species. Many twigs are short, since the species they represent became extinct in a short time. Some are longer, however, and give rise to yet more new species (Figure 5.5(b)).

No doubt, both modes of evolution—Darwinian gradualism and punctuated equilibrium—occur. It is currently being debated whether one or the other is the more common mode. Likely, we will find examples of both as the fossil records of various evolutionary lines become better understood (Figure 5.5(c)).

At any rate, the evolution of life on earth cannot be depicted as a ladder or a chain representing the steady march of progress toward complexity, as Lamarck and other early scientists believed. Nor is it a gracefully branching tree, as Darwin pictured it. Instead, it is, in the words of Stephen

Jay Gould (1994:91), a "luxuriant bush," more complex than we will probably ever know—a "blooming and buzzing confusion," says Gould (1985:355) or, to use Darwin's words, like the "tangled bank" of a stream.

EVOLUTION QUESTIONED: THE PSEUDOSCIENCE OF "SCIENTIFIC CREATIONISM"

All the information about the theory of evolution presented in these last two chapters has been developed and tested, using the methods and principles of science, over the past several hundred years by many people and from many different perspectives. Evolution is so well supported we consider it a fact, and it is the central concept of all biology, although we continue to apply the scientific method to our investigation of specific details. Our ideas about the generation of genetic variability, adaptation by natural selection, and the origin of species from existing species—all these explain everything we observe and understand about the living world.

We benefit from this knowledge every day of our lives. We eat foods from species of plants and animals bred according to the principles of genetics and selection. We know the causes of many of the illnesses that beset us because we understand the genetic operations of our cells, and we have insight into how some organisms (like viruses and bacteria) are adapted to other organisms (like us), and vice versa. Many of the antibiotics and other medicines that help us treat those illnesses work only because of the interrelatedness of all life. And this interrelatedness has also allowed us to manipulate the genes of other organisms, like bacteria, to "trick" them into producing human insulin for the treatment of diabetes; human growth hormone; and interferon, a chemical in our body's immune system.

So it is truly astounding that some people, even today, question the fact that evolution actually occurred. Think back to our discussion of science from Chapter 1. Science and belief systems are both important for the operation of any society, and ideally, they operate in harmony with one another. They are still, however, distinct realms of knowledge, distinguished by the *testability* of science and the *faith* of belief. What about ideas that have characteristics of both?

Suppose someone holds a scientific idea (an idea that is testable) but treats it as a belief by taking it on faith and by not testing it or recognizing the results of tests that have been applied to it, even if those tests refute it.

Here's an example: There are people who believe that the lines in the palms of your hands and on your fingers hold information about your

punctuated equilibrium: The view that species tend to remain stable and that evolutionary changes occur fairly suddenly.

FIGURE 5.6
Strata of the Grand Canyon in Arizona. Scientific creationists contend that these strata and all the fossils they contain are the results of the biblical flood. Real scientific data show that the canyon's strata represent geological and biological events that took place over nearly 2 billion years of time. (See also Figure 2.2.)

personal character and even, perhaps, about your future. This belief is called palmistry, and its precepts are quite scientifically testable. I tested them (Park 1982–83), and, not surprisingly, they failed. But will palmists all over the country close up shop because some anthropologist says their ideas are false? Hardly. Palmists take their ideas on faith. In other words, they treat a scientifically testable idea like a belief system. Thus, palmistry is a **pseudoscience** or "false science."

Although pseudoscientific ideas like palmistry, astrology, or the power of crystals may be harmless enough, other examples contain implications that may not be so benign. Some pseudoscientific ideas find support within established belief systems. There are—believe it or not—still people who want to think the earth is flat and who refuse to acknowledge the masses of scientific evidence to the contrary (Schadewald 1981–82). It turns out that a major source for this belief comes from literal interpretations of several biblical passages, for example, Matthew 4:8: "Again, the devil taketh him [Jesus] up into an exceedingly high mountain, and sheweth him all the kingdoms of the world. . . ." How, the flat-earthers ask, could Jesus have seen all the kingdoms of the earth unless the earth were flat?

Although most people recognize the allegorical sense of this and similar passages in both testaments of the Bible, there is a danger that some might find the issue terribly confusing. On the one hand, scientific evidence tells us unequivocally that the earth is a sphere. On the other hand, an interpretation of the chronicles of two major religions seems to say the earth is flat. Must one choose between science and religion? There are those who think so, and, in the process, both science and belief suffer.

The idea of a flat earth is utterly ridiculous, but there is another pseudoscience, relevant to our topic here, that is far more complex and difficult to evaluate. It's called **scientific creationism.** It proposes that the entire universe, including the earth and all its inhabitants, were created spontaneously by untestable forces around 10,000 years ago. Except for minor changes within "kinds" of plants and animals (breeds of dogs, for example, or regional varieties of a wild species), no changes in living organisms have occurred. Certainly no *new* species have arisen. What about the layers of rock and soil and the fossils they contain? Those are the results of "a primeval watery cataclysm" (Morris 1974:22), a great flood, in other words (Figure 5.6).

Sound familiar? It should. It is derived directly from a literal interpretation of the first eight chapters of the Book of Genesis, and it is clearly in direct opposition to all the data and ideas accumulated and tested by science. A hundred years of scientific inquiry tell us that the universe, including the earth and its inhabitants, arose through knowable, natural processes. The universe is at least 12 billion years old, the earth 4.5 billion, and life on earth nearly 4 billion years old. Living organisms do change through time, and species give rise to new species. The geological and fossil records are the records of these billions of years of change.

"Scientific creationism" is thus a pseudoscience—a testable set of ideas that, even in the face of contrary evidence, are accepted on faith. But scientific creationism goes further. Its proponents claim its ideas are, indeed, supported by scientific evidence that also refutes the accepted theory of evolution. That the creation model coincides with one interpretation of Genesis merely shows, they say, the scientific accuracy of the Bible. Because advocates of scientific creationism claim both models are scientific, they feel both should be taught in science classes as viable alternative explanations for the origin and diversity of life.

The argument is persuasive, especially in a society like ours, concerned with religious freedom and with our American senses of fair play and equal time. *But equal time is for equivalent things.* There is not a single shred of scientific evidence in support of the creation model.

To teach scientific creationism alongside evolution would be to violate the religious freedoms of those who do not subscribe to a strict creationist interpretation. It would also badly confuse those trying to learn how science really operates and what conclusions about our world science has arrived at. The distinction between science and belief would be blurred, interfering with the harmonious and important relationship between the two.

pseudoscience: Scientifically testable ideas that are taken on faith, even if tested and shown to be false.

scientific creationism: The belief in a literal biblical interpretation regarding the creation of the universe, with the connected belief that this view is supported by scientific evidence.

Contemporary Reflections

Can We See Evolution in Action?

When we look around us, it seems as if the world is a fairly stable place, biologically speaking, anyway. Certainly we hear of species becoming extinct at a rapid rate (see the "Contemporary Reflections" for Chapter 6), but otherwise we don't see much change. There doesn't seem to be any evolution still going on. But there is, of course.

The problem is one of scale. We tend to see the world from our perspective—as large mammals with large brains that afford us a great deal of control over our environments. We have an amazing ability to live in a wide variety of environmental conditions and to withstand a wide range of environmental extremes. But most creatures are a lot smaller than we are, and most are far more at the mercy of their environments. And we rarely see things from the point of view of our genes.

By definition, evolution is phenotypic change across generations involving, at the most basic level, genetic change. Much genetic change is brought about by the processes of mutation, gene flow, and genetic drift (fission and the founder effect, and gamete sampling). These processes are *always* taking place. Indeed, given the mobility of our species and our proclivity for exchanging genes, gene flow and the forms of genetic drift might be seen as particularly powerful processes of evolution for us. The human species is evolving all the time, by these processes alone.

What about natural selection? As noted in the "Contemporary Reflections" for Chapter 4, natural selection is certainly still taking place in our species, although, again because of scale—especially our long life spans—we might not always perceive it. But look to some other species.

In the woods in back of my house there are numerous small stands of young pine trees. Where the trees are very young, a foot tall or less, they can grow in quite dense concentrations. I counted six small trees growing in a 1-square-foot area of forest floor. A square foot, however, is hardly enough space for

The quality of our lives now and in the future depends on the continued progress of our testable scientific knowledge, mediated by the values of our belief systems. We need to understand what these two areas of knowledge are and how they interact, and we must promote free access to, and sharing of, all knowledge.

SUMMARY

The evolution of new species is an obvious result of the interacting processes of genetic variation, natural selection, and environmental change. New species arise when a population within an existing species becomes isolated. Isolation is usually geographic but may also be the result of a macromutation. In isolation, this new population experiences the pro-

six full-grown pines. There will be fewer plants there next year, fewer still the next year, and fewer the next. Many years from now, with luck, there will be one adult tree in that space. Only one will have the characteristics that will allow it to out-compete the others—greater height to catch more sun, greater ability to withstand insects, cold, and drought—whatever makes successful pine trees successful. Only one will be left to reproduce and pass on those traits that made it successful. Natural selection right in my backyard. Evolution in action.

But evolution in its broadest sense involves the origin of new species. Can we see this? Think about how new species evolve, but *don't* think on our human scale. There must be new species of small organisms evolving all the time. Speciation in microbes must be very common indeed. And even with larger organisms, whose generation times are longer, we can see distinct evidence of evolution. Although we recognize and name thirteen species of Darwin's finches on the Galápagos, the Grants (page 92) noted that some of those species can interbreed when altered environmental circumstances cause their niches to overlap. In other words, they are still in the process of becoming completely separate species. With Darwin's finches, we have caught speciation in the act.

In another striking example, a recent study (Johnson et al. 1996) has indicated that the basin of Lake Victoria in East Africa was completely dry only 12,000 years ago. And yet, there are 300 distinct but closely related species of cichlid fishes in the lake, species found *nowhere else*. (Cichlids are common fishes in home aquariums.) Clearly all these species have arisen in the last 12,000 years from, according to DNA studies, a single ancestral species. Apparently, cichlids are poor swimmers that prefer certain habitats and don't move around much. They may also have a tendency not to select males outside their local group. So small populations could quickly become isolated, and this could account for what seems to be the world's record for speciation rate in a vertebrate (Yoon 1996).

Evolution—even the origin of new species—is happening all around us. We just have to look carefully enough.

cesses of genetic variation and phenotypic adaptation separate from the parent species. Among the differentiating traits that result may be characters that act as reproductive isolating mechanisms, meaning that even if the populations once again have the opportunity to interbreed, they will probably not be able to do so. They are separate species.

The process of speciation, occurring countless times over the billions of years of life's history, has produced the incredible array of living forms we know today and see in the fossil record. The species we know about only hint at the variety that exists today and has existed in the past. When species have the opportunity, they are able to adaptively radiate into new niches, and the diversity of living forms is the result. It must be remembered, however, that all these forms are variations on the single theme of life that originated on this planet. All life, through speciation and adaptive radiation, is descended from a single origin.

We can depict evolution as a luxuriant bush, dense with innumerable twigs, each representing a new species. We use the bush as a metaphor for evolution for two reasons. First, we realize that the conditions for speciation are continuously being produced, so that speciation has probably taken place more often than we can imagine. Second, we understand that Darwin's model of the origin of species driven by the steady, gradual "fine-tuning" of natural selection is not entirely accurate. Natural selection is a conservative force, acting largely to maintain a species' adaptation. What produces new species is geographic or genetic isolation, and these processes act relatively quickly.

The evidence for evolution is overwhelming. We are still examining the specific details of evolutionary theory, but the fact of evolution and our knowledge of the essential processes involved are hypotheses that have passed numerous scientific tests and failed none. They are theories in the scientific sense of the word. The evidence for evolution is as strong as, say, the evidence for the idea that the earth revolves around the sun. Nonetheless, some people, for reasons that have nothing to do with science, claim that evolution did not occur. These claims have been examined scientifically, and they have been shown to be scientifically invalid. Their proponents, however, continue to insist on their accuracy. These claims are thus pseudoscience, and they confuse the important relationship between science and belief systems; for, in fact, there is no necessary conflict between the two.

KEY TERMS

reproductive isolating mechanism	generalized	Darwinian gradualism
hominids	specialized	punctuated equilibrium
speciation	nocturnal	pseudoscience
macromutations	prosimian	scientific creationism
adaptive radiation	diurnal	
	arboreal	

SUGGESTED READINGS

You should certainly have a look at the book that began our modern understanding of evolution, Darwin's *Origin of Species*. The last chapter, "Recapitulation and Conclusion," nicely summarizes his arguments and provides a good idea of his style.

A wonderful book on evolutionary processes, the origin of new species, and the variety of living things is Edward Wilson's *The Diversity of Life*.

For more on Darwin's finches, see Jonathan Weiner's *The Beak of the Finch*.

One of the originators of the model of punctuated equilibrium is biologist Stephen Jay Gould, and many of his articles concern that model. Try "The Episodic Nature of Evolutionary Change" and "Return of the Hopeful Monster," both in *The Panda's Thumb*.

Gould has also addressed the shape of the evolutionary bush. See his informative books *Wonderful Life* and *Full House* and his article in the October 1994 *Scientific American*, "The Evolution of Life on the Earth."

For an idea of the arguments of the scientific creationists, try *Evolution: The Fossils Say No!* by Duane T. Gish. For a refutation of scientific creationism, go once again to Stephen Jay Gould and a series of articles on the subject in *Hen's Teeth and Horse's Toes*.

A BRIEF EVOLUTIONARY TIMETABLE

. . . and there is no new
thing under the sun.
—Ecclesiastes 1 : 9

Anthropology focuses on one group of organisms, the hominids, and deals mostly with a single species of hominid, *Homo sapiens*. Hominids have been around for 5 or 6 million years. According to many interpretations, our species has inhabited the earth for half a million years at most. Although this seems a long period of time to us, it is really just the last tick of the earth's evolutionary clock, one-tenth of 1 percent (0.1 percent) of the history of our planet, and three one-hundredths of 1 percent (0.03 percent) of the estimated history of the universe. If the history of the universe were reduced to a single year, our species would not show up until after 11:30 P.M. on December 31.

So, although we focus on *us*, we need to appreciate the fact that all the processes of evolution apply to all forms of life on earth and that the idea of evolution—change through time—applies to the whole history of the universe.

Before we focus on ourselves, our close relatives, and our immediate ancestors, we need to put human evolution in context, to see it as part of a long and ongoing series of changes that began some 15 billion years ago.

What is the history of the universe, the earth, and life on earth?

What processes and events have affected the overall history of the earth and life on earth?

FROM THE BEGINNING: A QUICK HISTORY

The origin of the universe is shrouded in mystery. We don't, in all honesty, really know exactly how old it is, although 15 billion years is an average of recent estimates. We do know, however, that the universe is expanding in all directions. All the galaxies in the universe (an estimated 50 billion) are constantly traveling farther away from each other. A logical conclusion from this fact is that the universe began at a single location, and evidence indicates that it started as an incredibly tiny, dense, and hot speck (the proper term is a *singularity*) comprised of pure energy that would one day become all the energy and space and matter—including us—of the universe we know.

At the beginning of time—we'll use 15 billion years ago—this speck began to expand, an event commonly called the Big Bang. The details of this are still a matter of intense debate and are among the most complex issues in science. For our purposes here, suffice it to say that as the newborn universe expanded, it cooled, and matter quickly condensed from energy (Figure 6.1). By three minutes after the beginning, protons and neutrons

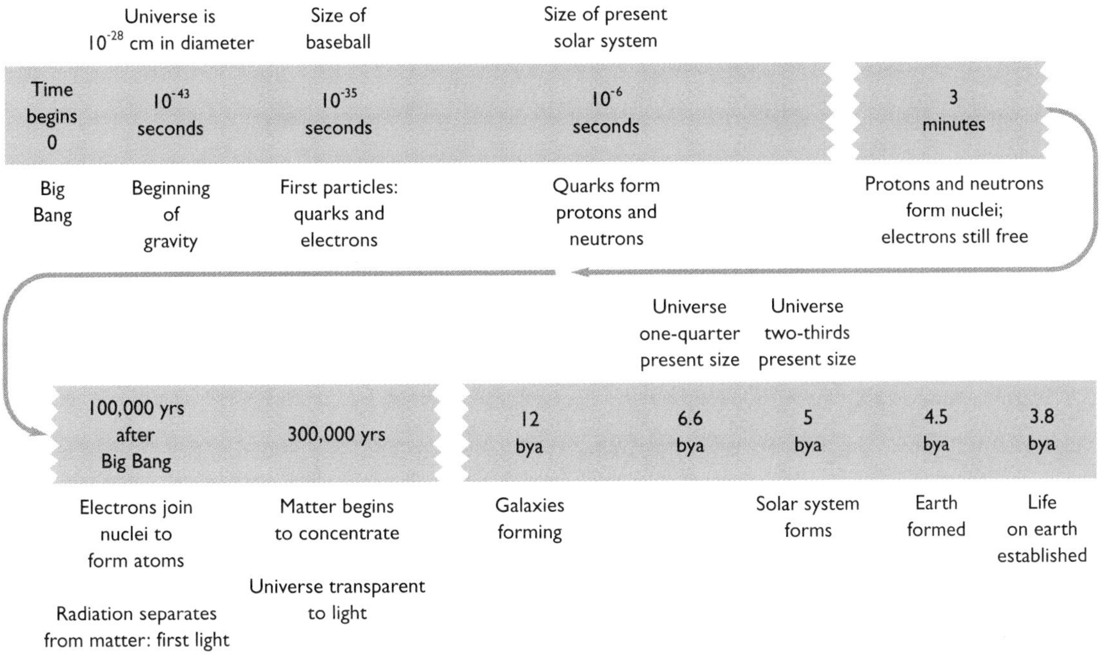

	Universe is 10^{-28} cm in diameter	Size of baseball	Size of present solar system	
Time begins 0	10^{-43} seconds	10^{-35} seconds	10^{-6} seconds	3 minutes
Big Bang	Beginning of gravity	First particles: quarks and electrons	Quarks form protons and neutrons	Protons and neutrons form nuclei; electrons still free

		Universe one-quarter present size	Universe two-thirds present size			
100,000 yrs after Big Bang	300,000 yrs	12 bya	6.6 bya	5 bya	4.5 bya	3.8 bya
Electrons join nuclei to form atoms	Matter begins to concentrate	Galaxies forming		Solar system forms	Earth formed	Life on earth established
	Universe transparent to light					
Radiation separates from matter: first light						

FIGURE 6.1

The history of the universe from the Big Bang to the beginnings of life on earth. The scale of the time line changes because some events are condensed into incredibly small periods while others are stretched over unimaginable spans (bya = billion years ago).

had formed and had joined to make atomic nuclei, but it took another 100,000 years for electrons to join the nuclei to form atoms. At about the same time, radiation separated from matter and there was light, but for the next 200,000 years the universe was still too dense for that light to travel through it.

By 12 billion years ago, galaxies had begun to form as gravity pulled matter together into huge clusters. These were made up of stars that were mainly hydrogen, the simplest element. As a result of the nuclear reactions in these stars, heavier, more complex elements formed. When these early stars died in tremendous supernova explosions, their elements were scattered into space, some eventually to contribute to the formation of new galaxies with all their stars and, in at least one case, planets. (Planets have recently been discovered orbiting another star in our galaxy.)

About 5 billion years ago, when the universe was two-thirds its present size, our solar system formed around a medium-sized star in the Milky Way galaxy. Earth, the third of nine planets orbiting that star, came into being 500 million years later. Amazingly, in less than a billion years—3.8 billion years ago—life on earth was established. We know this indirectly from rocks found in Greenland, southern Africa, and Australia (Figure 6.2). In

FIGURE 6.2

Stromatolites in Australia, formed when mats of blue-green algae, single-celled organisms, are covered with sand, silt, and mud, which the algae cement down and then grow over. Fossil stromatolites, and thus the organisms that made them, have been dated to 3.5 billion years ago.

Australia there are also actual fossils of single-celled organisms preserved in stone, many of which were probably already capable of **photosynthesis.**

Just how life came about on the earth is also a matter of debate. For over forty years, scientists have been able to produce carbon-rich **organic** compounds from **inorganic** compounds with a fairly simple laboratory procedure, showing that the process could have occurred quite easily. In fact, they have been able to produce amino acids, which, as you recall, are the building blocks of proteins. But, as you also recall, proteins cannot be built without a nucleic acid code. Evidence now suggests that RNA formed very early in earth's history. RNA was able to replicate itself and act as a code for the synthesis of proteins. Later, DNA took over this role (Orgel 1994). It is still, of course, a long way from amino acids and RNA to a living organism, and the details of this path remain unclear.

Whatever happened, it happened fast (about 700 million years from the formation of the earth to life *is* fast, in the geological time scale), but once established, life at first evolved slowly. The world's first organisms were simple single cells like bacteria (Figure 6.3). It wasn't until about 2 billion years ago (bya) that complex single-celled organisms containing nuclei and organelles evolved (see Figure 3.1). Multicellular organisms first appeared about 1.7 bya. The earliest evidence for life on land—bacteria or perhaps fungi—dates to 1.2 bya.

All these early single-celled organisms reproduced **asexually** by splitting and making copies of themselves. Evolutionary change relied entirely on mutations. About a billion years ago, some organisms began to reproduce **sexually.** Sexual reproduction may have begun as a mechanism of genetic exchange to replace defective genes. Soon, however, it proved to be an accelerator of evolution. Now, in addition to mutation, fertilization also provided genetic and phenotypic variation, and evolutionary change quickly started to gain speed. Figure 6.4 summarizes what is known about the timing of important events in the evolution of life on earth.

About 543 million years ago (mya), complex multicellular organisms burst on the scene. Some even possessed hard parts like shells. So sudden and rapid was this event that it is referred to as the Cambrian Explosion. In a mere 5 million years, all major body plans of multicellular animals had evolved, including ancestors of the **vertebrates,** animals with backbones (Figure 6.5). In fact, there are Cambrian fossils representing several body plans that no longer exist. So far, there are no explanations for this "explosion" that everyone agrees upon, but it is clearly a major event in the history of life. The evolution of animals since the Cambrian has been, essentially, variations on the themes set during that relatively brief time (Gould 1989, 1995).

By 425 mya, fish had evolved, and plants and animals began to colonize the land. Insects appeared about 400 mya; by 350 mya, some of them had evolved wings. Reptiles showed up around 350 mya as well, and the reptilian form that is thought to have given rise to the mammals was found at about 256 mya. Dinosaurs began evolving around 235 mya, with true mammals appearing about 220 mya. Sometime around 150 mya, a small dinosaur with feathers signaled the beginning of the evolution of birds (see Figure 5.4). Flowering plants appeared only a little more than 100 mya, and the primates, the group to which humans belong, showed up about 55 mya.

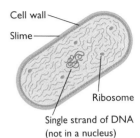

Cell wall
Slime
Ribosome
Single strand of DNA
(not in a nucleus)

FIGURE 6.3
A typical bacterium, representing some of the earliest forms of life on earth and, in terms of time and numbers, still the dominant forms.

photosynthesis: The process by which plants manufacture their own nutrients from carbon dioxide and water, using chlorophyll as a catalyst and sunlight as an energy source.

organic: Molecules that are part of living organisms. They are based on the chemistry of carbon and contain mostly hydrogen, oxygen, carbon, and nitrogen. Even carbon-based molecules that are not found in living things are sometimes referred to as organic.

inorganic: A molecule not containing carbon.

asexually: Reproducing without sex, by fissioning or budding.

sexually: Reproducing by combining genetic material from two individuals.

vertebrates: Organisms with backbones.

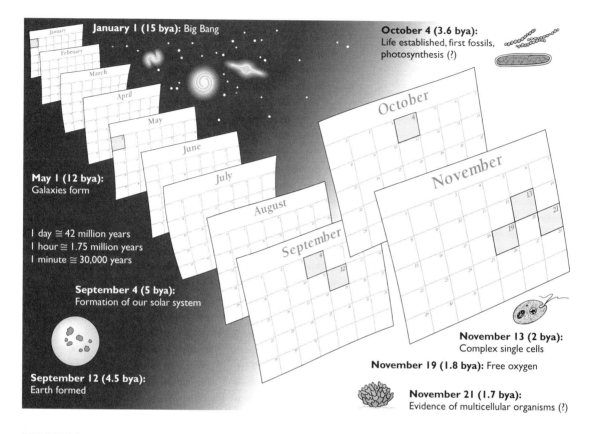

FIGURE 6.4
Astronomer Carl Sagan likened the history of the universe to a single calendar year in his 1975 Pulitzer Prize–winning book *The Dragons of Eden*. This calendar has been recalculated to show the currently accepted dates for important events. Numbers in parentheses are actual dates given in billion years ago (bya) or million years ago (mya). One calendar day equals approximately 42 million years.

DRIFTING CONTINENTS AND MASS EXTINCTIONS: THE PACE OF CHANGE

During all this time, life was not the only thing evolving on earth. The earth itself was also evolving as the continents changed shape and position, a phenomenon known as continental drift that operates through the process of **plate tectonics.** The outer layer of rock on the earth, the crust, is in a constant state of change. It is broken into some sixteen pieces of various sizes called plates that fit together like a huge spherical jigsaw puzzle. The motion of the molten rock (magma) below the crust causes the plates to change shape and location. In some areas, magma seeps up between the plates and solidifies, pushing the plates apart. Something has to give, and at other boundaries, called "subduction zones," one plate is pushed under another and plunges deep within the earth, where it melts and adds to the magma. Clearly, then, the continents—those parts of the

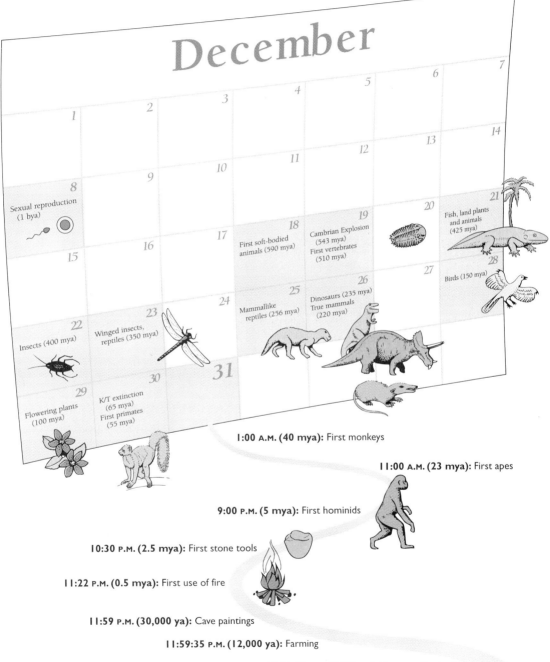

December

1

2

3

4

5

6

7

8 — Sexual reproduction (1 bya)

9

10

11

12

13

14

15

16

17

18 — First soft-bodied animals (590 mya)

19 — Cambrian Explosion (543 mya) First vertebrates (510 mya)

20

21 — Fish, land plants and animals (425 mya)

22 — Insects (400 mya)

23 — Winged insects, reptiles (350 mya)

24

25 — Mammallike reptiles (256 mya)

26 — Dinosaurs (235 mya) True mammals (220 mya)

27

28 — Birds (150 mya)

29 — Flowering plants (100 mya)

30 — K/T extinction (65 mya) First primates (55 mya)

31

1:00 A.M. (40 mya): First monkeys

11:00 A.M. (23 mya): First apes

9:00 P.M. (5 mya): First hominids

10:30 P.M. (2.5 mya): First stone tools

11:22 P.M. (0.5 mya): First use of fire

11:59 P.M. (30,000 ya): Cave paintings

11:59:35 P.M. (12,000 ya): Farming

11:59:55 P.M. (2,000 ya): Common Era begins

11:59:59 P.M. (500 ya): Renaissance

FIGURE 6.5

Cambrian fauna, mostly arthropods, the group consisting of modern day insects, spiders, and crustaceans. The large creature in the center grew to 3 feet long. The flowerlike animals on the right are unclassified.

plates that protrude above sea level—have shifted over time and will continue to do so (Figure 6.6). It should also be noted that plate tectonics accounts for important geological phenomena. Where the plates meet and move against one another, tremendous forces are produced that cause earthquakes, volcanos, and mountain building.

By the time the dinosaurs and early mammals had appeared, all the continents had drifted together to form a huge supercontinent we call **Pangea,** literally "all lands." This is why, for example, we find fossils of the same type of dinosaur in what are now such widely separated places as China, North America, and Antarctica. Around 200 mya, Pangea began to break up, and the resulting landmasses—the ancestors of our present-day continents—drifted over the globe, producing a diversity of environments and geographical boundaries that has profoundly affected the nature of life on earth as we know it today.

From all we've discussed so far, it would seem that the evolution of the earth and of life—influenced by continental drift and the environmental changes it brings about—has been a steady process. And basically, it has been—relative to the immense amount of time involved. But the fossil record shows that at least five times in the planet's history, some

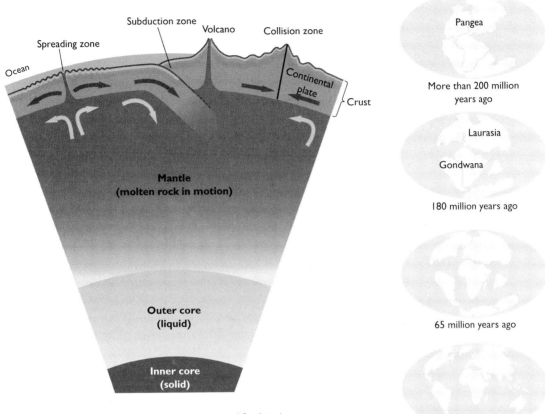

FIGURE 6.6

Cross section through the earth showing the process of plate tectonics and the resultant drift of the continents over the past 200 million years. Continental drift, of course, occurred prior to 200 mya and will continue into the future as well.

change has taken place that was so rapid and extensive that it radically altered the course of biological evolution by causing a mass extinction.

For example, about the time the continents were drifting together to form the supercontinent of Pangea—at the end of the Permian period (250 mya)—over 95 percent of all species of marine and terrestrial organisms suddenly became extinct. Some changes occurred to which none of the variants within all those species were adapted. The cause for this greatest of all mass extinctions is not known for sure, but a new hypothesis suggests it was the result of massive volcanic eruptions in what is now Siberia that altered the planet's climate. At any rate, such a catastrophe certainly had a major effect on the future course of life's evolution.

plate tectonics: The movement of the plates of the earth's crust caused by their interaction with the molten rock of the earth's interior. The cause of continental drift.

Pangea: The supercontinent that included parts of all present-day landmasses.

FIGURE 6.7

This painting, by the late Rudolph Zallinger, reflects some now outdated ideas about the appearance and behavior of the dinosaurs. It does show, however, some of the variety of these creatures as they existed over 170 million years of time (from left to the right in the mural). The dinosaurs once dominated the earth's environments.

Other mass extinctions do not have such a "down-to-earth" explanation, and one of these directly affected the evolution of our small section of the evolutionary bush. About 65 million years ago, the dinosaurs were the dominant form of land animals and were present in the oceans as well. Mammals were also around, and had been for nearly as long as the dinosaurs. In terms of ecological niches, however, mammals didn't have many places to go because those niches were already occupied (Figure 6.7).

Then one day—literally—a comet or an asteroid, thought to measure 6 miles across, crashed through the earth's atmosphere and into the crust where the north coast of the Mexican Yucatán is now. The impact made a crater 200 miles in diameter. The comet or asteroid may have broken apart on impact with the atmosphere, and pieces may have hit in other locations as well.

This collision created a blast like that of a nuclear explosion. Thousands of cubic miles of vaporized rock, water vapor, and small particles and dust were shot into the atmosphere, where they were carried around the world. Heat from the impact caused massive forest fires that created smoke and ash. One hypothesis suggests that the impact produced shock waves that bounced inside the earth and were focused on the opposite side of the planet, causing large-scale volcanic activity that put even more smoke and ash into the air. It has recently been noted that the Yucatán is rich in sulfur, suggesting that the impact might have produced sulfuric acid in the atmosphere, causing acid rain. All this matter would have created a blanket that blocked sunlight, cooling the earth and preventing green plants from carrying out photosynthesis.

These extensive environmental changes proved disastrous (a word that means, appropriately, "bad star"). Dinosaurs became extinct, along with every other species of land animal weighing more than about 55 pounds, many plants, and much of the ocean's plankton, the small organisms that provide a great deal of the world's oxygen and that act as an important source of food at the base of the food chain.

Somehow, many of the mammals survived. Perhaps, by a stroke of luck, they were adapted to withstand adverse, changing conditions already. Now, with the dinosaurs suddenly gone, a whole world of new niches was open to them and to many other creatures that made it through the catastrophe. This group included the birds, thought by many to be the dinosaurs' only living direct descendants (Figure 6.8).

So rapid was the mammals' adaptive radiation that within about 10 million years, all major types of mammals we know today had appeared—everything from bats to whales to a group of tree-dwelling creatures possessed of acute eyesight, dexterous hands, and large, inquisitive brains. These are the primates, and it is this group that we shall focus on in the next chapters.

▽ ▽ ▽

FIGURE 6.8
The wild turkey (below) shows a striking similarity to bipedal dinosaurs, further evidence of the evolutionary relationship between dinosaurs and birds.

SUMMARY

This narrative of the history of the universe has been necessarily brief, but it does point out three themes that are important to remember as we continue.

First, it could be said—by virtue of human numbers (nearly 6 billion) and our impact on the planet—that we are the dominant species on the earth today. But our evolutionary history makes up a small fraction of the whole history of the universe and even of the earth. We are the new kids on the evolutionary block, and we have not as yet even proved ourselves successful by the criterion of longevity. Cockroaches have been around hundreds of times longer than we have; bacteria have been around since the beginning of the fossil record. By these standards, our species is in its infancy.

Second, as the Bible says, "there is no new thing under the sun." Indeed, although we often speak of the "origin of the earth" or the "origin

Contemporary Reflections

Are Mass Extinctions a Thing of the Past?

Extinction is part of evolution. For one reason or another, species become extinct all the time. An estimated 95 percent of all species that have ever existed are now extinct.

But the idea of some intense event that can bring about the extinction of up to 90 percent of the earth's living forms over a short period of time seems inconceivable to us. And yet, at least five such events have occurred in the 3.8-billion-year history of life on this planet. The best known of these wiped out the dinosaurs—a long-lived and very successful group of species—65 million years ago. Surely, we think, these events were part of the earth's "formative" years and could not happen again. Sadly, this view is incorrect—for two reasons.

First, we are fairly certain that the mass extinction that included the dinosaurs was initiated by the impact of a huge asteroid or comet, and impacts are associated with some of the other mass extinctions as well. Although impacts were more common in the past, asteroids, comets, and fragments of them are far from used up. Lots of them still orbit through our solar system. Go outside on any clear night, look up long enough, and you're bound to see one of the smaller ones burn up as it hits the earth's atmosphere. These are so-called shooting stars. Bigger ones, parts of which survive the atmosphere, hit the earth regularly (although most are neither seen nor found).

And, on occasion, we encounter very large ones. A few years ago, an asteroid large enough to do serious damage missed the earth by a mere 250,000 miles—the distance between the earth and the moon, a near miss on the cosmic scale. It was not seen until it had already passed us!

In 1908, a large portion of an asteroid or a fragment of a comet nucleus exploded 6 miles up in the atmosphere over Siberia. The shock waves were heard 600 miles away and flattened trees over 770 square miles. It's altogether possible, then, that our planet will be hit by another large object from space in the future, and, if it's big enough, devastating consequences will follow, including the extinction of many species.

But there is a second reason why mass extinctions are not things of the past—a reason even more disturbing since (unlike the situation with asteroids) we *could* do something about it. There is, in fact, a sixth mass extinction in earth's history, and it is happening right now.

Starting about 10,000 years ago, species began becoming extinct at a rate faster than usual. At present, species are disappearing at a rate at least as fast as, and probably faster than, during any of the previous five mass extinctions (Eldredge 1991, 1995; Leakey and Lewin 1995). Estimates vary, but the earth may be losing species at a rate of 27,000 a year—that's 3 every hour. Now, one might argue that, given what we know of earth's history, extinctions—even mass ones—are "natural." Well, they have been; but this one is different. Unlike the other extinctions, where the conditions causing the problem eventually went away, this situation is unlikely to get better because, as biologist Niles Eldredge says (1995:128), "the irritant . . . remains on the scene." That "irritant," of course, is us.

Since we figured out how to control natural food sources through farming and animal husbandry some 12,000 years ago, our species' population has grown at an ever-increasing rate. Our need for resources, energy, and space has grown along with our numbers. We have pushed other species into marginal areas, destroyed their habitats and resources, and hunted or otherwise exploited them to extinction. We are well into the process of changing the very climate of the earth as our emissions into the atmosphere are causing the world's climate to warm.

Although we may not be seeing the catastrophic death and destruction of an asteroid impact, we are—*right now*—in the midst of what may be the biggest, fastest of all mass extinctions. Decidedly *not* a thing of the past.

of life," the only *real* origin is that of the universe itself. All the events listed above have been *rearrangements* of what already existed: matter condensing from energy as it cools; large atomic particles forming from smaller ones; stars coming together from cosmic dust; heavy elements being created from lighter ones in the nuclear furnaces of those stars; the elements of inorganic molecules being rearranged to form the molecules of life; and the shuffling of the genetic code producing the extraordinary multitude of living things that have inhabited this planet.

Third, and perhaps most humbling, the specific history of the universe, including the earth and its life, could have happened in countless other ways. Each event in our story is contingent upon preceding events. For example, our evolution as we know it is dependent upon the specific sequence of events that came before it. If those events had been different, *we* might be different—or we might not be here at all. Imagine if that comet or asteroid had *not* hit the earth 65 million years ago. In other words, the evolution of humans—or anything else for that matter—was not inevitable. We're lucky we're here.

KEY TERMS

photosynthesis	asexually	plate tectonics
organic	sexually	Pangea
inorganic	vertebrates	

SUGGESTED READINGS

There are many good books on the subject of the history of the universe, the earth, and life. I especially recommend Timothy Ferris's *Coming of Age in the Milky Way* for a discussion of the science behind our understanding of this history. *The Book of Life*, edited by Stephen Jay Gould, is an especially complete and beautifully illustrated book. For a more technical, but still readable work, try *History of Life* by Richard Cowen.

The Cambrian Explosion is covered in Stephen Jay Gould's *Wonderful Life* and in an article by R. Gore in the October 1993 *National Geographic*, "Explosion of Life: The Cambrian Period."

The subject of mass extinctions is discussed in E. O. Wilson's *Diversity of Life* and in an article in the June 1989 *National Geographic*, "The March Toward Extinction."

Evolution as a series of contingent events is a second theme of Stephen Gould's *Wonderful Life* and of his article in the October 1994 *Scientific American*, an issue devoted to the subject of life in the universe.

CHAPTER

7

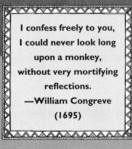

THE PRIMATES

I confess freely to you,
I could never look long
upon a monkey,
without very mortifying
reflections.
—William Congreve
(1695)

"The proper study of mankind is man," said the poet Alexander Pope. The last few chapters should have convinced you that even biological anthropologists, who by definition focus on the study of mankind (or, more properly, humankind), simply cannot limit their interests to just our own species. The processes that have produced modern *Homo sapiens* are the processes that have produced every single species that has ever inhabited this planet. Additionally, all those species are part of an integrated whole, comprised of all environments and all living things in complex interaction with one another across geographical space and through evolutionary time.

Moreover, were we to limit our study just to our species, or even to the hominids in general, we would lose a great deal of perspective. We need to compare ourselves to other forms of life to see in what ways we are similar and in what ways we differ. This comparison is made all the more important because we *are* the species we are studying, and so it can be difficult to be objective about ourselves. Thus, the study of primatology is an important part of anthropology.

In this chapter we will address several important questions:

What is our place in nature; that is, where do we fit—from a scientifically objective point of view—in the world of living things?

What are the characteristics of the primates—the group of animals of which we are a part?

In what ways are humans like the other primates? In what ways are we unique?

NAMING THE ANIMALS

We have already discussed the concept of the species, the unit of classification in nature. Each organism belongs to a specific species (the words come from the same root), a group of potentially interbreeding individuals that are reproductively isolated from other groups.

The most cursory examination, however, shows clearly that there are larger units of classification of living things. Some species are more similar to one another than they are to other species. The book of Genesis, for example, does not name each species that God creates, but lists general categories: "the fish of the sea," "the fowl of the air," "every herb of the field," "every beast of the earth."

The idea that species had similarities so struck Swedish botanist Carl von Linné (1707–1778) that he devised a taxonomic system to name and

TABLE 7.1
Taxonomy of Five Familiar Species

	Human	Chimpanzee	Bonobo	Gorilla	Wolf
Kingdom	Animalia	Animalia	Animalia	Animalia	Animalia
Phylum	Chordata	Chordata	Chordata	Chordata	Chordata
Class	Mammalia	Mammalia	Mammalia	Mammalia	Mammalia
Order	Primates	Primates	Primates	Primates	Carnivora
Family	Hominidae	Pongidae	Pongidae	Pongidae	Canidae
Genus	Homo	Pan	Pan	Gorilla	Canis
Species	sapiens	troglodytes	paniscus	gorilla	lupus

thus categorize all living creatures. A **taxonomy** is a classification based on similarities and differences. I have, for example, accumulated thousands of notes, articles, and other important individual pieces of paper in my years as a bioanthropologist. If I simply stored all these together randomly, I'd never find anything when I need to refer to it. Instead, I file my papers according to general categories and subcategories nested within them. For instance, I have a file cabinet marked "Biological Anthropology." One of its drawers is marked "Evolution," and within that drawer is a file folder marked "Taxonomy," where I keep notes and copies of articles on Linné and the related matters I'm now writing about.

Similarly, Linné (who used Latin names and even latinized his own name to Carolus Linnaeus) devised a system, published in final form in 1758, that used four nested categories—class, order, genus, and species. Modern taxonomy recognizes seven basic categories but may use additional categories when needed. Table 7.1 shows a traditional Linnaean taxonomy for five familiar species. We'll detail the taxonomy of our species to show what Linnaeus's system accomplishes.

It should be noted that a species is never referred to by just the species name, listed in the bottom row of the table. The species name is usually descriptive, and so there may be many species that share the same name. Many African animals have the species name *africanus*, for example. The chimpanzee shares its species name, *troglodytes*, with the winter wren, a small North American bird (the name conveying the erroneous assumption that these species were cave dwellers). It takes *both* the genus and species names to denote a particular species. We are, for instance, *Homo sapiens*.

taxonomy: A classification based on similarities and differences.

FIGURE 7.1
Amphioxus, a chordate, with a notochord but no bony spine. (Shown about four times life size.)

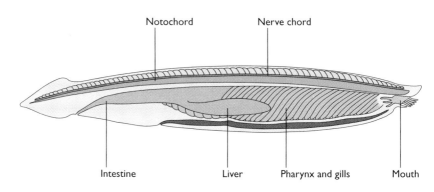

Notochord   Nerve chord

Intestine   Liver   Pharynx and gills   Mouth

Humans are members of the kingdom called Animalia. We share this grouping with the other four species on the chart by virtue of the fact that we all ingest our food, have sense organs and nervous systems, and are capable of intentional movement. We are not members of any of the other three kingdoms of eukaryotes (organisms whose cells have nuclei): complex single-celled organisms (amoebas and the like), fungi (mushrooms, mildews, molds), or plants (roses, ferns, broccoli, pine trees). (There are, in addition, two main groups of prokaryotes, single-celled organisms that lack nuclei: bacteria and archaea. These are the microbes, referred to in Chapter 5, that may make up the bulk of the earth's biomass.)

Within kingdom Animalia are about thirty phyla (singular, phylum), which include groups such as sponges, jellyfish, starfish, three types of worms, mollusks, arthropods (insects, spiders, crustaceans), and chordates. We are members of phylum Chordata because we have a bony spine, the evolutionary descendant of a **notochord,** a long cartilaginous rod running down the back to support the body and protect the spinal chord, the extension of the central nervous system (Figure 7.1). Chordates with a bony spine are grouped into a subphylum, Vertebrata. All five species on Table 7.1 are chordates and, more specifically, vertebrates.

There are seven classes within the vertebrates: the jawless fishes (an ancient group represented by only a few existing species), cartilaginous fishes (sharks and rays), bony fishes (guppies, tunas, and so on), amphibians (frogs, salamanders), reptiles (snakes, lizards, alligators), birds, and mammals. All our sample species are members of class Mammalia because they maintain a constant body temperature (that is, they are called "warm blooded"); have hair; give birth to live young; nourish the young with milk from mammary glands; and have relatively large, complex brains.

We need to stop here for an important point. You may have noticed that some of the traits listed for mammals are also possessed by other classes. Birds, for example, are also warm blooded; so, according to many, were some of the dinosaurs, and so are a number of other creatures, including great white sharks. Some sharks, some bony fishes (like guppies), and some snakes give birth to live young. On the other hand, you might know two mammals that do not possess all the mammalian traits. The spiny anteater and the duckbill platypus, both from Australia, lay eggs. Obviously, though, birds, dinosaurs, and great white sharks are *not* mammals, while the spiny anteater and platypus *are*. What's the resolution to this seeming contradiction?

The answer is that inclusion into a taxonomic category is more than simply a matter of possessing a list of traits. The traits of an organism make possible that organism's *adaptation*, and it is adaptation, measured by reproductive success, that is the criterion of natural selection. Thus, taxonomic categories become statements about adaptation, with each taxonomic level becoming more specifically focused. Mammals, whether they lay eggs or not, are animals that are adapted through active lifestyles and a reliance on learned behavior facilitated by a set of shared traits. Mammalian young, therefore, require a great deal of direct care and nurturing, and mammals require a constant body temperature to sustain their level of activity, and hair (or in the case of whales, a thick layer of fat) to maintain that temperature. That's not a very concise definition of a mammal, but the real world doesn't always make things easy for those of us who try to describe it.

Within class Mammalia are about nineteen existing orders—nineteen rather specific adaptive strategies and resulting sets of characteristics. There are, for example, the flying bats; the fully aquatic whales and dolphins; the partially aquatic seals, sea lions, and walruses; two orders of hoofed plant eaters (the difference being a skeletal feature of the feet); the rabbits and hares; the rodents; the meat eaters; the insect eaters; the pouched marsupials (kangaroos, opposums); and a group of large-brained, tree-dwellers with three-dimensional vision and dexterous hands. These are the members of order Primates.

At the level of order, our five sample species (from Table 7.1) differentiate. The wolf belongs to order Carnivora (the meat eaters), while the other four are primates. Humans split from the other primates in this table at the level of family. The gorilla, while similar to the remaining two, is different enough to be placed in a separate genus (plural, genera). The chimpanzee and bonobo (or "pygmy chimp"), similar enough to once be considered members of the same species, are now recognized as different species within the same genus. The Linnaean taxonomic system thus indicates the relative relationships among named organisms.

Linnaeus's goal was to describe the system that, as he believed, God had in mind when he created all the earth's living things. Linnaeus was a creationist, as were just about all scientists of his time. But, as you can probably see, to modern scientists, his taxonomy indicates not only present-day similarities and differences but evolutionary relationships as well. The *reason* the chimp is more similar to the bonobo than to a human

notochord: The evolutionary precursor of the vertebral column.

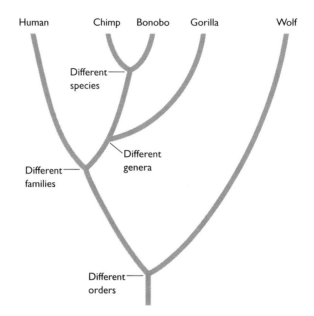

is that the chimp and bonobo diverged from each other more recently than they did from humans. The chimp and bonobo are thought to have had a common ancestor from which they split about 1.5 million years ago. Humans and the chimp/bonobo line branched about 5 million years ago. Humans and chimps have had a longer time to evolve in different ways than have the bonobo and chimp, which is why they are more different *and* why they are placed in different taxonomic families.

So, from a Linnaean taxonomy, we may create a family tree, indicating when the classified species branched from one another in their evolutionary history. Of course, a taxonomy can't tell us the exact dates of divergence. Evolutionary rates differ in different evolutionary lines and at different times. But a taxonomy can tell us the relative times of branching. Figure 7.2 shows a family tree for the five species in Table 7.1.

This tree, however, demonstrates the basis of a current debate within taxonomy. The tree was *inferred* from traditional taxonomic categories, which were based largely on physical comparisons of living species. Many evolutionary trees drawn in this way prove quite accurate with regard to the relative times of branching and, thus, the overall pattern of branching. But as we learn more about the fossil ancestors of living creatures, and as we improve our techniques for comparing the genes of organisms, we also learn more about the details of the evolutionary relationships among those organisms—particularly, about the specific times of their evolutionary divergence.

Current knowledge from the fossil records and from genetic compar-

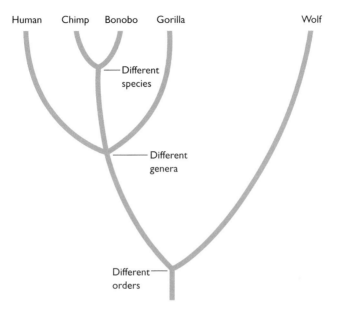

FIGURE 7.3
Evolutionary tree for the five species in Table 7.1 based on cladistic interpretation. Cladists also recognize families, but they don't show in this particular example.

isons indicates that the human, chimp/bonobo, and gorilla lines diverged from one another at about the same time. The genetics of these species show 98 or 99 percent similarity (depending upon the exact measure used) and show the three lines to be about equally distinct. Although we are all separate species, and are clearly distinguishable phenotypically, we all share genetic characteristics as well as phenotypic features that are derived from a relatively recent common ancestor. The actual family tree should not look like Figure 7.2, then, but more like Figure 7.3. There seems to be a contradiction between the taxonomic names and categories for these species and the evolutionary relationships of these species.

An alternative taxonomic system that attempts to resolve this problem is called **cladistics** ("clade" means branch). It places organisms in taxonomic categories based on the order of their evolutionary branching, regardless of how their present-day appearances might assort them into groups. Branching order is determined in two ways: by shared derived characteristics, and by genetic comparisons. If two groups of organisms share phenotypic features not found in other groups, it is assumed that they derived those features from a common ancestor, and they are therefore lumped into the same taxonomic category at the appropriate level.

For example, birds are quite physically distinct from dinosaurs, and dinosaurs appear far more similar to reptiles. Traditionally, then, birds have been placed in one taxonomic class (Aves) and dinosaurs lumped into another (Reptilia). However, dinosaurs all share a trait of the pelvis that no reptile has but that all birds do. In addition, birds all share certain

cladistics: A classification system based on order of evolutionary branching rather than on present similarities and differences.

traits possessed only by some dinosaurs. It seems, then, that dinosaur and reptile evolution is separate and that birds evolved from a group of dinosaurs, from which they derived their main features. As a result, many authorities using cladistics include both dinosaurs and birds under a single taxonomic category (sometimes called Dinosauria).

Branching order is also determined by genetic comparisons. It would seem intuitively clear that humans should fall into one group and that chimps, bonobos, and gorillas are all African "apes." The traditional taxonomy recognizes this obvious grouping by placing us in one family (Hominidae) and the African apes in another (Pongidae). But the fact that humans, chimps/bonobos, and gorillas are pretty much equally distant genetically would seem to warrant placing them all in the *same* taxonomic family. Since, by the rules of taxonomy, the earliest name used would take precedence, all these species would be lumped into family Hominidae, leaving the differences in genus and species names to indicate the separate subsequent evolution of each line.

At present, there is no agreed-upon resolution to this debate, and we tend to pick and choose the taxonomy that fits the way we each see the data for particular groups of organisms. For the situation of apes and humans, this book will continue to use the traditional categories of Pongidae for all the apes and Hominidae for all humans and their ancestors (defined as the primates that walk upright), recognizing, of course, what the evolutionary family tree actually looks like. My justification for this choice is that, *no matter how they got to be that way*, the condition of these five species at present clearly assorts them into two phenotypically and adaptively distinct groups—us and the apes—and a traditional taxonomy reflects this.

Now, let's focus on the mammalian adaptive strategy and the phenotypic traits that characterize the members of order Primates.

WHAT IS A PRIMATE?

There are about 200 living species of primates. We're not sure how many have existed during the order's evolutionary history of around 55 million years. Primates range from the very small, such as the mouse lemur of Madagascar, which weighs less than 3 ounces, to the gigantic—an extinct ape from China, Vietnam, and India that may have stood 12 feet tall and tipped the scales at half a ton (Figure 7.4). Some primates inhabit small, very specific environmental ranges and spend their lives slowly moving through the trees, eating fruits, leaves, or insects; one species of primate lives in every environment and produces its own food.

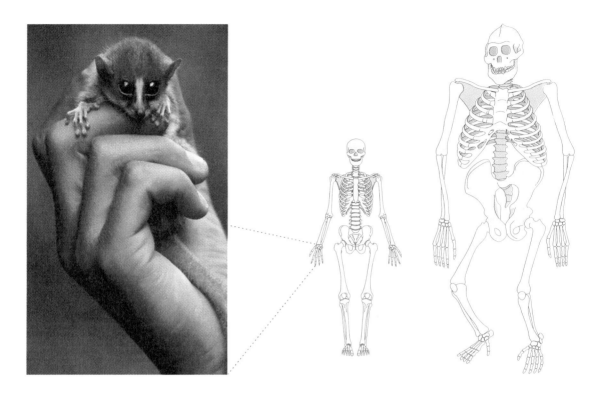

FIGURE 7.4
A mouse lemur, the smallest living primate, compared to a human and to *Giganto-pithecus,* now extinct, the largest primate ever (see Chapter 10).

This wide variety makes it a bit difficult to define the primate order in a simple sentence. The primates are best defined by looking at the characteristics that they have in common and in seeing how these traits facilitate the primate adaptive strategy. We'll look at the primate traits by using the following categories: (1) the senses, (2) movement, (3) reproduction, (4) intelligence, and (5) behavior patterns.

The Senses

Bats and dolphins live in worlds of sound. Dogs live in a world of smells. The primates live in a visual world. Vision is the predominant sense for the primates.

Most primates see in color, and all primates see in three dimensions. They have true depth perception, technically called **stereoscopic vision**—possible because the eyes face forward and see the same scene from slightly different angles (Figure 7.5). The nerves and muscles of primate eyes are protected by being enclosed within a bony socket. If you look around the place you're now in, you're seeing it just as the majority of primates would.

stereoscopic vision:
Three-dimensional vision; depth perception.

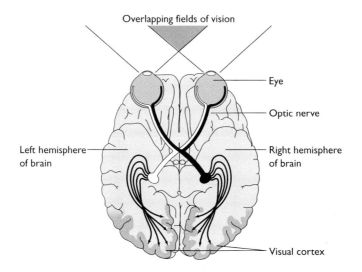

Other senses are not as acute as in many mammals. Primates lack the auditory (hearing) and olfactory (smell) senses of such familiar animals as dogs, cats, and cattle. Furthermore, and obviously related to the less acute sense of smell, primates tend to lack a snout and so are rather flat-faced in profile. There is, as you might expect for a group of 200 species, some variation. Many members of one group of primates (the prosimians that we'll discuss in the next section) are nocturnal and lack color vision, but they have better senses of smell and hearing than do monkeys, apes, and humans.

Movement

Primates, like most mammals, are, with one exception, **quadrupedal;** that is, they walk, climb, and leap using all four limbs. Although many primates can stand or even walk on two legs for short periods, humans are the only habitually **bipedal** primates. Unlike most mammals, the limbs of primates are extremely flexible, and the hands (and, in many cases, the feet) of primates have the ability to grasp objects. That is, they are **prehensile** (Figure 7.6).

In addition, most primates are able to touch their thumbs to the tips of the other fingers, allowing them to pick up and manipulate small objects. This capacity is called **opposability.** Finally, most primates have nails rather than claws on the tips of the fingers and toes. These provide support for the sensitive tactile sense receptors of the fingers. In short, primates have manual dexterity. Some have a great degree of dexterity in the feet as well (see Figure 7.13).

Reproduction

Most primate species give birth to one offspring at a time. Some, such as some of the marmosets from South America and some of the lemurs from Madagascar, normally produce twins or triplets. As is typical of mammals, primate parents take an active role in the protection, nurturing, and so-cialization of their young. Mostly because of their large, complex brains and because of the importance of learning, the primates take a long time to mature. How long, of course, depends upon the size of the primate species. During this time, the young primates are dependent upon adults. The primates, relative to size, have the longest period of **dependency** of any mammal.

Intelligence

Intelligence can be defined as the relative ability of an organism's brain to acquire, store, retrieve, and process information. These abilities are related to brain size and brain complexity. A bigger brain has more room for all the complex nerve connections that make it work, just as a very sophisticated computer must necessarily be larger than a simple one. But brain size must also be looked at in a relative way: How big is the brain compared to the body it runs? A sperm whale, with its 20-pound brain, has a brain size ten times that of the average human's. A sperm whale's body, however, is over *five hundred* times the size of ours. We have bigger

quadrupedal: Walking on all fours.

bipedal: Walking on two legs.

prehensile: Having the ability to grasp.

opposability: The ability to touch the thumb to the tips of the other fingers.

dependency: Here, the period after birth during which offspring require the care of adults to survive.

intelligence: The relative ability of the brain to ac-quire, store, retrieve, and process information.

FIGURE 7.7
The human brain with major parts and their functions. The lobes and the motor cortex are all part of the neocortex.

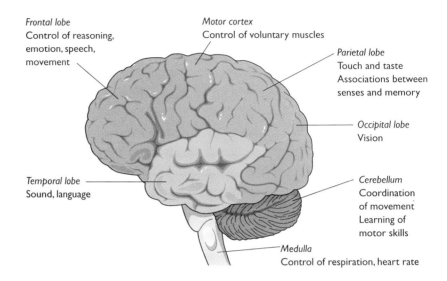

Frontal lobe
Control of reasoning, emotion, speech, movement

Motor cortex
Control of voluntary muscles

Parietal lobe
Touch and taste
Associations between senses and memory

Occipital lobe
Vision

Temporal lobe
Sound, language

Cerebellum
Coordination of movement
Learning of motor skills

Medulla
Control of respiration, heart rate

brains than a whale *relative to* the size of our bodies; we run less body with more brain, which is true of the primates in general. Of all land mammals, the primates have the largest relative brain sizes. The human brain, however, is three times the size one would expect for a primate of our body weight (Passingham 1982:78). (Some sea mammals, like dolphins, have brains relatively larger than apes', but the meaning of this in terms of their intelligence is still debated.)

In addition, the primate brain is complex, especially in the neocortex, that part of the brain where memory, abstract thought, problem solving, and attentiveness take place (Figure 7.7). In short, the primates are smart.

Behavior Patterns

Primates are social animals. Most primate species live in groups. Many other animals do too, but even those few primate species—like orangutans—that usually remain solitary still interact with other members of their species in ways that are far more complex than are the ways that antelopes in a herd interact. The difference is that primates recognize individuals, and the individual primate holds a particular status relative to others in its group and to the group as a whole. A primate group is made up of the collective relationships among all its individual members. We will see these relationships in action when we examine primate behavior more closely in Chapter 8.

As physical evidence of the importance of these relationships, it may be noted that primates are among the most colorful of mammals, and most of the color patterns of anthropoid primates are on their faces (Figure 7.8).

FIGURE 7.8
Some colorful primate faces, including that of one primate that purposely enhances the color. Colorful faces are evidence of the importance of individual recognition within primate societies. Clockwise from upper left: Chinese white-handed gibbon, mandrill, human, bald uakari.

FIGURE 7.9
Male baboon protecting
mother and young. The fe-
male holding her baby at left
was being threatened by the
boisterous play of a group
of adolescent males, out
of the picture to the right.
The adult male in the center
stepped in and barked at the
group, which quickly took its
play elsewhere.

The attention of one primate to another is drawn to the face, to the primate's identity as an individual.

In some primates—baboons and chimpanzees, for example—each individual may have rather specific status within the group. Some have more social power and influence than others. They are said to be dominant, and the structure of the relative power and influence of all a group's individuals is called a **dominance hierarchy.** In addition, most primate species recognize a special status for females with infants, and these mother-child units are well protected by other members of the group, even those who are not directly related to them (Figure 7.9). Among chimpanzees and baboons we even see lasting relationships that can only be described as friendship.

Primate social groups are maintained through communication. Primates have large repertoires of vocalizations, facial expressions, and body gestures. Touch is also an important form of communication among primates and often takes the form of **grooming,** an activity that serves the practical purpose of removing dirt and parasites but also acts as a source of reassurance to maintain group harmony and unity (Figure 7.10).

FIGURE 7.10
Chimpanzee communication. (Top) A chimp exhibiting a "pant-hoot," a call used when a food source is found, when two groups join together, or to communicate over distances. (Bottom) Chimps grooming, an activity that rids them of dirt and parasites and, more importantly, helps maintain group unity and harmony.

dominance hierarchy: Individual differences in power, influence, and access to resources and mating.

grooming: Cleaning the fur of another animal, which promotes social cohesion.

How, then, may we characterize the primate adaptive strategy? First, it is important to acknowledge the environment that the primates are adapted *to*. The basic primate environment is arboreal—primates live in trees. To be sure, several species—gorillas, for instance—spend more time on the ground than in the branches, and we humans are thoroughly terrestrial. But most primates spend most of their time in the trees, and the primate traits in the preceding discussion all evolved in response to an arboreal environment. Even the partially and completely terrestrial primates possess features that are variations on the arboreal adaptive theme. So, we can define primates in the following way:

> The primates are mammals adapted to an arboreal environment through well-developed vision, manual dexterity, and large, complex brains that rely on learned behavior; the latter is aided by the birth of few offspring and the direct and extensive care of those offspring during a long period of dependency while they are socialized into groups based upon differential relationships among individuals.

Such a complex group of organisms requires a lengthy description.

A SURVEY OF THE LIVING PRIMATES

Figure 7.11 is a simplified traditional taxonomy of the approximately 200 species of living primates. For the sake of space, some groups are indicated only by the number of those groups within a category; for instance, there are six families of prosimians. One of the first things you should notice is that there are new categories here compared to those shown in Table 7.1. Suborder, infraorder, and superfamily have been added between the traditional Linnaean categories of order and family. Sometimes a **taxon** of organisms has many species adapted to a wide variety of geographical locations and environmental niches; consequently, additional taxonomic categories need to be added to accurately capture what seem to be natural divisions. (A complete taxonomy of insects, for example, a class with over three-quarters of a million *known* species, is, as you can well imagine, incredibly complex.)

The order Primates is traditionally divided into two major suborders, Prosimii and Anthropoidea. Prosimians ("pre-apes") represent the most primitive primates, that is, those that most closely resemble the earliest primates. At first widespread, prosimians were pushed into marginal areas as newer, more adaptively flexible primates evolved. Some modern prosimians live on the mainland of Africa and India and on the isolated islands of Southeast Asia, but the majority inhabit the island of Madagascar (Figure 7.12).

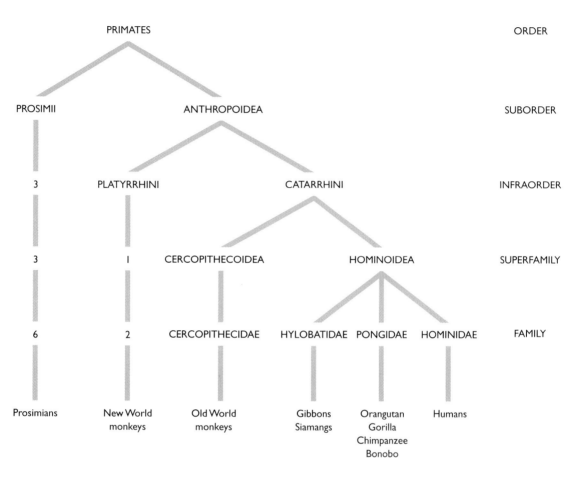

FIGURE 7.11
Primate taxonomy using traditional categories. Numbers refer to living primate groups in that category when the specific group names are not given.

The forty or so living species of prosimians exhibit a number of differences from the general primate pattern (Figure 7.13). About half of the prosimian species are nocturnal and so lack color vision. They have large eyes that can gather more light and better than average senses of smell and hearing. To aid their olfactory sense, they have a protruding snout with a large smell receptor area (the mucous membranes within the nose) and a moist, naked outer nose (like a dog or cat) to help pick up the molecules that make up the olfactory signal. Prosimians do have the stereoscopic vision characteristics of primates because they need to judge distances in bushes and trees, and many use their three-dimensional vision to help catch insects, a favorite food of many prosimian species.

Prosimians have prehensile hands and feet, but the opposability of their thumbs is limited. Many can only touch the thumb with the other four digits together; their digits don't move independently. Some prosimians have claws instead of the typical primate nails on a couple of fingers

taxon: Any category within a taxonomic classification.

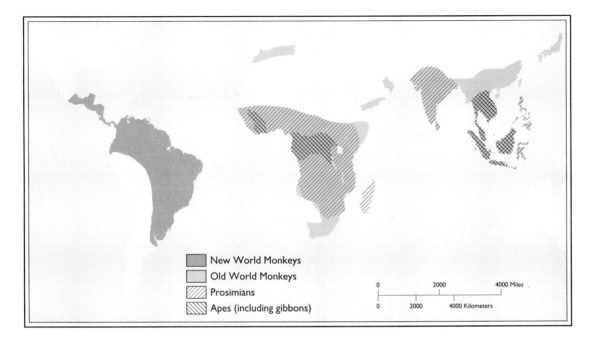

FIGURE 7.12
Distribution of the living nonhuman primates.

FIGURE 7.13
Two prosimians. The slender loris of India and Sri Lanka (above) has the large eyes and moist, naked nose characteristic of this suborder. Note also the prehensile hands and feet and the grooming claw on one toe of the foot at the top of the picture. The crowned lemur of Madagascar (right) displays a posture that is part of the locomotor pattern called "vertical clinging and leaping." All the Madagascar primates are endangered.

FIGURE 7.14
The Philippine tarsier. Note the huge eyes (each eye is as big as the entire brain) for nocturnal vision, the enlarged finger- and toetips, and the powerfully built legs.

or toes. These are known as "grooming claws" and are used both for that purpose and to help acquire food.

A few species of lemurs from Madagascar give birth to twins or even triplets on a regular basis. Transporting them through the trees, however, is no problem because an adult male or an older brother or sister often helps the mother carry and care for her infants. At other times, the infants are kept in a nest.

A particularly interesting prosimian is the tarsier of Southeast Asia (Figure 7.14). Weighing just 4 or 5 ounces, this little insect eater has powerful hindlimbs for jumping, enlarged fingertips and toetips for added friction, and the ability to turn its head 180 degrees in either direction like an owl. Its name comes from its elongated ankle, or tarsal, bones, which make its legs look like they bend too many times.

The tarsier is at the center of another specific debate within primate taxonomy. Because of its flat face, upright posture when clinging to trunks and branches, lack of the moist, naked nose of other prosimians, and some recent genetic comparisons, some authorities suggest placing the tarsier in the second primate suborder, Anthropoidea. Cladists go further. Focusing on the fact that all prosimians have the moist nose, but no anthropoids do, they suggest dividing the order Primates into suborders based on that trait. The former prosimians would be in suborder Strepsirhini ("nose with curved nostrils"), and the anthropoids would become suborder Haplorhini ("simple nose"). The latter group would include the tarsier because of its nose, color vision, and other traits. Both versions are found in the literature; here we will use the traditional classification.

The anthropoid ("humanlike") primates include monkeys, apes, and humans. Suborder Anthropoidea is further divided into two infraorders, Platyrrhini and Catarrhini. This division is based on a geographical separation of early primates into a Western Hemisphere, or New World, group and an Eastern Hemisphere, or Old World, group. All the New World platyrrhine primates are monkeys. The Old World catarrhine primates are made up of monkeys, apes, and humans. Despite the fact that humans now inhabit the entire globe, the hominids first evolved in the Old World, in Africa.

Several features distinguish New World from Old World primates. The most obvious is the nose. Platyrrhine means "flat nose," and the noses of the Central and South American monkeys have widely spaced nostrils separated by a broad septum (Figure 7.15). Compare this with a typical Old World catarrhine nose ("with nostrils close together and facing downward") by looking in the mirror. Platyrrhine monkeys have more teeth than catarrhines, with twelve premolars (bicuspids) as compared to eight. Because New World monkeys are almost entirely arboreal, they have evolved long limbs, and some have clawlike nails. Several species also have evolved prehensile tails and so effectively have five grasping limbs. No Old World monkey evolved this adaptation. Finally, two groups of platyrrhines, the marmosets and tamarins, normally give birth to twins.

The Old World primates are divided into two superfamilies. The monkeys of Europe (now limited to Gibraltar), Africa, and Asia make up superfamily Cercopithecoidea. Apes and humans are in superfamily Hominoidea, divided into three families.

There are about seventy-five species of cercopithecoids (Figure 7.16). They have the nasal shape and tooth number of all Old World primates, and most have tails. Males tend to be larger than females, a trait not common in New World species. Also unlike the platyrrhines, the Old World monkeys have fully opposable thumbs. The monkeys of the Eastern

FIGURE 7.15
A New World monkey—the wooly spider monkey, or muriqui, of Brazil. Notice the widely separated nostrils and the prehensile tail.

FIGURE 7.16
Old World monkeys, the olive colobus from West Africa. Note the more closely spaced nostrils compared to the New World monkey's. This species is not colorful; its drab coat acts as camouflage against predators—which include a fellow primate, the chimpanzee (see Chapter 8).

FIGURE 7.17
White-handed gibbon from Southeast Asia suspended by one arm. Notice the long, hooklike fingers and that it is also grasping with its feet.

Hemisphere seem more adaptively flexible than those of the West. At home in the trees, many cercopithecoids are equally comfortable on the ground. They live everywhere from the deserts of Africa and the Middle East to the mountains of northern Japan.

Superfamily Hominoidea contains the larger, tailless primates. The hominoids—the apes and hominids—are generally larger than the monkeys and have larger brains, both relatively and absolutely. Their brains also have larger neocortexes, meaning that the hominoids are more intelligent as we have defined that term. Finally, a series of traits make the hominoids good "suspensory climbers and hangers"; they are adapted to an arboreal environment through the ability to climb and hang from branches with their arms. The traits behind this ability are a flexible shoulder joint, a shoulder blade that is farther back than in monkeys, and a stronger collar bone (clavicle) for added support. Although modern humans do not display this ability as often or as well as the apes, we still possess it, as is evident by watching athletes on the high bar or rings.

Family Hylobatidae includes the gibbons and siamangs of Southeast Asia and Malaysia. Sometimes referred to as "lesser apes," they are noted for their mode of locomotion, an arm-over-arm swinging through the branches called **brachiation** (Figure 7.17). They also have an unusual social organization for primates. Male and female hylobatids form a monogamous pair, though not a permanent one.

There are four species within family Pongidae, the "great apes": the orangutan of Southeast Asia and the gorilla, chimpanzee, and bonobo of Africa (Figure 7.18).

The pongids are large (a male gorilla in the wild may weigh 450 pounds), with heavy, powerful jaws used for eating a wide range of fruits, nuts, and vegetables. Chimps and bonobos also eat meat on occasion. The apes are quadrupeds, although chimps, gorillas, and, especially, bonobos are fairly good at upright walking for short distances. Orangutans are solitary, but the other apes live in social groups marked by some degree of dominance but otherwise with fairly loose organization and changeable group membership.

The apes have relatively large brains; a large chimp, for example, may have a brain half the size of the smallest modern human brain. Apes are intelligent. They have, for example, an intimate knowledge of a large number of food sources, many of which ripen seasonally or grow in limited areas.

Some chimpanzees can make simple tools, the best known of which is their termite "fishing stick," a modified twig or blade of grass they insert into a hole in a termite mound and wiggle around to stimulate an attack by the insects. The termites cling to the "invader," and the chimps draw out a tasty meal (Figure 7.19). Other chimps have been seen to use rocks to break open hard-shelled nuts. Chimps are also known to cooperatively hunt small animals, including other primates, and meat is the one food source that chimps will share with one another.

Finally, apes have a large repertoire of calls, facial expressions, and body gestures with which they communicate information, mostly about emotional states. Though this form of communication is nothing like human language, some individuals from all the great ape species have been taught to use nonvocal versions of human languages, most notably American Sign Language (AMESLAN), developed for the hearing impaired. It is said by some researchers that with this skill they can communicate at the level of a 4- or 5-year-old human.

The third hominoid family is Hominidae, the hominids. This includes all living human beings and several extinct species. We need, of course, to detail the traits of this group.

brachiation: Locomotion using arm-over-arm swinging.

FIGURE 7.18
The great apes (clockwise from top left): orangutan of Southeast Asia; gorilla, bonobo, and chimpanzee of Africa.

FIGURE 7.19
Chimps using tools they have made to extract termites from their mound.

THE HUMAN PRIMATE

Each of the 200 living primate species has its own unique expression of the primate adaptive strategy. Humans are no exception. Let's describe the hominids by using the same categories with which we characterized the primates in general.

The Senses

Our senses are essentially the same as those of the anthropoid monkeys and the apes. There may be some minor differences, but, basically, all these species hear, smell, and, especially, see the same world.

Movement

Bipedalism is the characteristic that, in broad evolutionary perspective, defines the hominids. We are the only primate that is habitually bipedal,

and we have been for over 4 million years. (Our big brains came along much later.) The bones and muscles of our back, pelvis, legs, and feet are all structured to balance us and hold us upright. Because our legs are the limbs of locomotion, they are longer and more muscular than our arms—just the opposite of the arms and legs of the apes. Completely freed from locomotor functions, our hands have become organs of manipulation. We have the most precise opposability of any of the primates and the relatively longest and strongest primate thumb.

Reproduction

Like most primates, we usually have one offspring at a time. Though we are not the largest primate (the gorilla is), we have the longest period of dependency and we take the longest time to mature. Chimps, for example, reach sexual maturity at about 9 years and physical maturity at about 12. For humans, the averages are 13 and 21. In addition, we are born even more helpless than other primates.

Our sexual behavior, too, is different. The other primates, like most mammals, engage in sexual activity, for the most part, only when it can lead to reproduction. Thus, mating occurs when a female has ovulated, has produced an egg that is ready to be fertilized. She undergoes hormonal changes that make her sexually receptive and lead her to solicit male attention, and she gives off signals that sexually stimulate males. During this time, the female is said to be in **estrus** (popularly, "in heat"). In many mammals the estrus signals are in the form of olfactory stimuli; in many primates, they are also visual (Figure 7.20).

Humans, of course, have lost the signals of estrus, a condition sometimes referred to as "concealed ovulation." Human males don't automatically know when a human female is fertile. This may seem a rather inefficient way to perpetuate the species, but, as we are all aware, humans have replaced unconsicous, innate sexual signals with sexual consciousness. Sexuality has become part of our conscious thought, tied up with all the other reactions and attitudes and emotions we have toward other members of our species and toward ourselves. You might say we are potentially continually in estrus. Although humans exhibit the most extreme example of this form of reproductive behavior, we will see it foreshadowed, in the next chapter, in some of our close relatives.

Intelligence

We are clearly the most intelligent primate, as we have defined that term. We can store, retrieve, and process more information in more complex ways. Our cultural behavior—our languages, societies, belief systems, norms of behavior, and scientific knowledge—all attest to these abilities. Our intellect is made possible by our large, complex brains, especially our neocortex, the outer layer where abstract thought takes place.

Behavior Patterns

Like most Old World primates, humans live in societies that are based on the collective conscious responses of a group of individuals. The difference is that our groups are structured and maintained by cultural values—ideas, rules, and behavioral norms that we have created and shared through complex **symbolic** communication systems.

∀   ∀   ∀

SUMMARY

The study of the nonhuman primates has been a traditional aspect of biological anthropology. We *are* primates, after all, and the characteristics of our relatively new species have evolved out of the basic primate traits and the adaptive strategy that they facilitate. We can only fully comprehend ourselves as a biological species by understanding where we fit into the natural world.

Taxonomy provides us with a way of naming and categorizing species so as to indicate their biological relationships. It also gives us an idea as to the evolutionary relationships among species. At present, there are two major schools of thought about taxonomy. One (traditional) names and classifies according to both comparisons of phenotypic features and data on evolutionary relationships. The other (cladistics) uses only evolutionary relationships.

estrus: In nonhuman primates, the period of female fertility or the signals indicating this condition.

symbolic: Here, a communication system that uses arbitrary but agreed-upon sounds and signs for meaning.

Contemporary Reflections

Should Nonhuman Primates Have Rights?

This question is part of a larger question that has become one of today's most contentious issues: Do animals share with us any of our basic rights and do they, consequently, deserve considerations equal to those accorded humans? Opinions on this issue vary enormously. One animal rights advocate (Francione 1996) argues that we should not consider animals as property and so should treat them as independent, autonomous individuals and not in any way exploit them. At the other extreme is a letter I recall in a local newspaper in which the author claimed that God put animals on earth to sustain people, assist them in work, entertain them at circuses, and provide fur coats for women.

Ideas on the subject vary even more when put into actual practice. Many supporters of some form of animal rights adamantly refuse to eat mammals or birds but continue to eat seafood—drawing some sort of ethical line (I guess) between warm-blooded and cold-blooded creatures. Many who are sickened at the sight of a fur coat still wear leather shoes. Hunters easily justify killing wild creatures for sport while at the same time treating their hunting dogs as members of the family. Veterinary researchers, interested in promoting the health of animals, will subject other animals to experimentation and practice surgery. Clearly, this is a complicated issue involving, for any thinking person, many aspects of their moral, emotional, and material lives.

The question is perhaps most profound and intense with regard to our closest relatives, the nonhuman primates, especially the great apes. These species have always struck us as being very much like our own, and we know now that these apes share with us up to 99 percent of our genes. The African apes and we share a recent common ancestor. Five or 6 million years ago, we and they were the same creature.

Some have claimed that this genetic closeness makes obvious the need to extend basic human rights to apes (see, for example, some of the essays in Cavalieri and Singer 1993). But, in a review of that book (1994), Jonathan Marks notes that the precise degree of genetic similarity depends upon what genes are being examined and how, and that genetic data like these pose the related problem of where to draw the line. *Is* there a line? The African apes and we are 99 percent genetically similar. The Asian orangutan shares about 96 percent of our genes. Is that enough dissimilarity to warrant doing things to orangs we would not do to a human? What about monkeys, who are even less similar, or prosimians, or nonprimates?

The detailed genetic data are not really relevant to this issue. There are, however, *relevant* similarities and differences that could be considered. For example, vegetarians are often sarcastically asked how they can kill and eat plants. There is a serious answer: since plants lack nervous systems and sense organs, they don't feel pain or emotion. This is a natural, documented, and *relevant* difference. The intellectual differences between us and the apes are certainly relevant in some regards; no one would suggest giving bonobos the right to vote. But there are also relevant *similarities*. The reason apes are used as human surrogates for medical experiments—that they are genetically so similar—is the very reason we might consider *not* so using them. Experimenting on apes is the same as experimenting on humans in terms of the physical and emotional stress and pain some experiments cause their subjects. What we know factually about the anatomy, physiology, and behavior of apes lends support to such a view.

Many people (me included) constantly struggle with the emotional, philosophical, and practical questions involved in this issue. Even those who agree that some human rights should be extended to apes must still cope with such moral matters as balancing our needs against theirs in such areas as medical experiments. But—especially after considering the question from the point of view of our closest biological relatives—the one thing one cannot do with this issue is ignore it.

The primates are one of nineteen orders of mammals. They may be characterized as adapted to arboreal environments through manual dexterity, visual acuity, and intelligence. There are about 200 living species of primates, each a unique manifestation of the general primate theme. The human primate's major uniqueness is in its form of locomotion; we are the only primate that is a habitual biped, a trait that evolved over 4.2 million years ago. Since then, our other distinguishing feature has evolved—our big brain, capable of such complex functions that we can create our own adaptive behaviors, expressed as our various cultural systems. It is to the possible precursors of our behaviors that we will turn next.

KEY TERMS

taxonomy	prehensile	grooming
notochord	opposability	taxon
cladistics	dependency	brachiation
stereoscopic vision	intelligence	estrus
quadrupedal	dominance hierarchy	symbolic
bipedal		

SUGGESTED READINGS

An excellent technical book on the primate order is by Napier and Napier, *The Natural History of the Primates*. Noel Rowe's *The Pictorial Guide to the Living Primates* is a beautifully illustrated, up-to-date, and informative reference to all living primate species. For a look at the endangered lemurs of Madagascar, see the article in the August 1988 *National Geographic* by primatologist Alison Jolly called "Madagascar's Lemurs: On the Edge of Survival." The National Geographic Society has also produced a beautifully illustrated book on the great apes, *The Great Apes: Between Two Worlds*, by Nichols, Goodall, Schaller, and Smith, that not only discusses the four species of apes but also talks about the scientific studies conducted on them in the wild as well as the dangers they now face from their close relative.

A comprehensive and readable book comparing humans with other primates is Richard Passingham's *The Human Primate*. For an interesting, though somewhat speculative, discussion of the evolution of the human brain, try Carl Sagan's Pulitzer Prize–winning *The Dragons of Eden*.

I'll recommend some more books on the behavior of humans and our fellow primates in the next chapter.

PRIMATE BEHAVIOR AND HUMAN EVOLUTION

Often I have gazed into
a chimpanzee's eyes
and wondered what
was going on behind
them.
—Jane Goodall (1990)

Just as we look to the anatomy of our close relatives to get some idea about the basic set of phenotypic traits from which we evolved, we may also look at the behavior of the other primates to gain some insight into why we behave the way we do. Because we share common ancestors, some of our behavior patterns—just like some of our physical features—may be variations on the same evolutionary theme.

In this chapter we will look at two types of nonhuman primates in particular, the several species collectively called baboons (genus *Papio*) and the two species of genus *Pan*, the common chimpanzee and the "pygmy chimp," or bonobo. The reasons for choosing these primates will be explained as well.

> How do we organize a study of something as complex as behavior?
>
> What are some of the scientific cautions that must be exercised in doing so?
>
> What are some of the relevant behaviors of our close relatives?
>
> What light do they shed on the evolution of the behavior of the hominids?

STUDYING BEHAVIOR

The idea of studying nonhuman primate behavior is based on the same premise as is our use of physical comparisons with other primates: We share a common heritage with the other primates and so have inherited our shared features from the same source, a common ancestor. It is not a coincidence, for example, that all the primates have prehensile hands. Our common prehensile ability comes from the same ancient ancestor and, in this case, serves the same basic function. Such traits, shared by multiple species through inheritance from a common ancestor, are called **homologies.** Thus, we gain some perspective on our prehensile hands by fully examining the prehensile appendages of species with whom we share an ancestor from whom we all derived the trait.

It should be noted that homologous traits need not share a common function. Your arms and the wings of a bat, though they are used for different things, are homologies. The traits are similar by virtue of having evolved from the same source, an early mammal.

The wings of a bat and the wings of an insect, however, though they share a similar function, have evolved independently and are not at all similar in structure. These functional but evolutionarily unrelated similarities are known as **analogies.** We can certainly learn something about

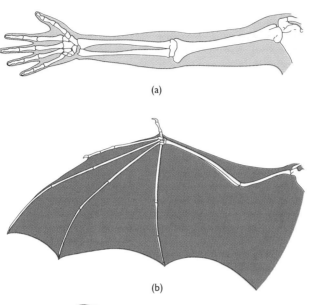

(a)

(b)

(c)

FIGURE 8.1
Homology and analogy. The arm of a human (a) and the wing of a bat (b) are homologous—they have different functions but share the same evolutionary source. The wing of a bat (b) and the wing of an insect (c) are analogous—they share a function but are evolutionarily different.

the physics of flight by comparing these wings, but there is a limited amount of information we can get about the wings of *bats* by studying the wings of *insects* because they evolved quite separately from one another (Figure 8.1).

Just as organisms pass on anatomical and physiological features in their genes, they also pass on behavioral characteristics. In some groups—ants, for example—whole behavioral repertoires are passed on. Ants rely completely on built-in instinct; they don't really think or, in fact, have much of anything to think *with*. So, even though ants live in highly complex societies and act in elaborate ways, all their behaviors are coded in their genes, to be triggered by outside stimuli but with little or no flexibility or variation in the response.

homologies: Traits shared by two or more species through inheritance from a common ancestor.

analogies: Traits shared by two or more species that are similar in function but unrelated evolutionarily.

Other organisms, with larger and more complex brains, can vary their behavior as needed to cope with specific situations. Their behavior is flexible. They have behavioral *potentials* or *themes* carried in their genetic codes, and they respond to their environments by building onto these potentials—taking in information from the outside, remembering it, retreiving stored information, and utilizing it in appropriate circumstances. In other words, they *think*.

The nature of the inborn behavioral potentials in complex organisms is still a matter of debate, especially when humans are the topic. There have been those who argue that we are born as "blank slates," or, in a more modern image, as computers with internal hardware but nothing programmed. The extreme opposite view says that our brains come equipped with *specific* behaviors that are only modified to a small degree by our individual experiences—like a computer with many applications already in the system.

The reality is no doubt somewhere in the middle. Certainly we come into this world with some basic behavioral responses built in. Facial expressions like smiling, nursing behavior among infants, the bond between a mother and her offspring, the drives to walk upright and learn language—these are all recognized as universal in our species and as preprogrammed in our biology. But just as certainly, we are not programmed for *particular* ways of expressing these and other behaviors. Language ability, for example, may be instinctive, but the specific language you speak is learned within a specific cultural and individual context.

There is a scientific study that looks for evolutionary explanations for behaviors, especially social behaviors. It is called **sociobiology,** and two of its ideas are particularly relevant here. The first, **inclusive fitness,** refers to the fact that your close relatives share many of your genes. As a result, the fitness of *your* genes is not just measured by your own adaptive success (the usual definition of fitness); it also "includes" the adaptive success of your relatives. Thus, any behavior that has evolved through time that causes you to aid your close relations also serves to help your genes get passed on.

A good example is the case of **altruistic** behavior. If, for instance, I perform some action that saves my sister's life but costs me mine in the process, I might not pass on any more genes, but I have helped increase the possibility that some of my *genes* will get passed on, because my sister and I share, on average, 50 percent of our genetic endowment.

Of course, humans have moral reasons for altruistic actions, but altruistic behaviors are seen in many other species, where there could be no cultural motivation. It may not seem logical that a behavior that might endanger the individual could have evolved by natural selection. But, if we look at the genes rather than just the "packages" they come in, we can see how this could be the case. The altruistic behavior was selected for because it helped individuals possessing genes for that behavior to be reproductively successful, even if a few individuals were sacrificed in the process.

The second idea concerns **reproductive strategies.** Put simply, individuals have evolved behaviors that maximize their reproductive success. Male and female mammals, however, differ in their contributions to reproduction, so their evolved behaviors may differ as well. Females, of course, carry, nurture, and raise offspring—largely by themselves in most mammalian species, including most primates. Males, on the other hand, contribute sperm. Thus, behaviors have evolved that help females raise healthy offspring and that allow males to try to impregnate as many females as possible.

If it is the case that at least behavioral themes can be inherited, then we can shed light on our behaviors by looking into those of other creatures. In doing so, however, we need to take into account the concepts of homology and analogy. In comparing the behaviors of humans and chimpanzees or bonobos, it is highly likely that a behavior is shared because it is the *same* behavior, derived by all three species from our common ancestor of 5 or 6 million years ago. Understanding the nature and function of that behavior in chimpanzees or bonobos is likely to provide insight into the origin of the behavior in humans because the behavior in question is homologous.

A specific behavior similar in humans and baboons is less likely to be homologous. Our two species have evolved independently for over 20 million years, so there is a greater chance that the behaviors evolved separately, under separate environmental circumstances and for different adaptive reasons. Still, they may be variations on some *general behavioral pattern* common to the primates and inherited from an early common ancestor.

The chance of two behaviors being analogous increases as we compare species that are less and less closely related. Some investigators have compared the behavior of humans with that of social carnivores like lions, wolves, and African wild dogs. There are strikingly "human" behaviors in these species. All three hunt cooperatively. Wolves and wild dogs have complex social relationships, they use vocal and gestural signs to maintain them, and both actively feed their young. Wolves, especially, are territorial. These collections of similarities, however, are probably not derived from a common ancestor, but have, at most, evolved quite independently from some general mammalian traits of social interaction, care of young, and relatively large, complex brains allowing for flexibility of behavior. What we do learn from the behavior of such species is that one possible route to adaptive success for mammals is through complex social behavior

sociobiology: The scientific study that examines evolutionary explanations for social behaviors within species.

inclusive fitness: The idea that fitness is measured by the success of one's genes, whether possessed by the individual or by that individual's relatives.

altruistic: Behavior that benefits others without regard to one's own needs or safety.

reproductive strategies: Behaviors that evolve to maximize an individual's reproductive success.

and that this behavior is common in species that include meat in their diet, especially meat from large animals. But it is only one route; other carnivores—the fox and the leopard, for example—are solitary hunters. Lions, though they hunt cooperatively, never share food with their young.

Comparing analogous behaviors, then, can be informative and can point out possible clusters of adaptive traits. But analogies must be used with the understanding that the more evolutionarily distant the species, the less useful is the comparison. Ants live in highly complex societies to which investigators often apply human names (slave, caste, queen, nurse, soldier), but studying the social behavior of ants probably tells us nothing directly about our own societies.

We can now look at the behavior of some other species that have, to varying degrees, been used as models for the origin and evolution of our own behavior. For years, nearly all our information about other species came from studies of their behavior in the artificial environments of zoos and laboratories. Only when the science of **ethology**—studying creatures in the wild, under natural conditions—became popular and possible could we see how they were *really* adapted. And only then did we begin to learn some of the truly remarkable adaptations that our fellow primates possess.

BABOONS

There are five distinguishable types of baboon that live in the African woodland and **savanna,** all grouped within genus *Papio*. (Some authorities consider them to be subspecies of a single species because, where their ranges overlap, they can and do interbreed and produce fertile offspring. Other taxonomists think that the physical and behavioral differences are sufficient to warrant giving them five different species names.) These primates have long been of interest to anthropologists because of the complexity of their social organization and because of their savanna habitat—an important habitat for our early hominid ancestors (Figure 8.2).

Baboon groups range in size from 20 to 200 individuals. One of the most striking aspects of baboon behavior is the aggressive competition for dominance among the males, who may be nearly twice the size of females and who are endowed with huge, sharp canine teeth (Figure 8.3). The male who is the largest, strongest, most aggressive, smartest (whatever traits are important to baboons) becomes, for a time, the dominant animal, a position recognized and acknowledged by the whole group. The dominant male is the group's leader and decision maker. He has first rights to food and often to females. He produces the most offspring, perpetuating those traits that allowed him to achieve and maintain dominance. It is

also the role of the dominant male and his immediate subordinates to
protect the more vulnerable members of the group—the females and infants—from danger (see Figure 7.9).

Males are also, in general, dominant over females. In the hamadryas
baboon of Ethiopia, males gather a group of females with whom they have
exclusive mating rights. Such a group is referred to as a "harem," and
proximity of and sexual access to the females in a harem is maintained by
male aggression and violence. Many harem females show the literal scars
of such treatment.

Observations of these behaviors led early investigators to depict baboon social organization as almost militaristic—centered around and
totally dominated by a hierarchically arranged group of males, and maintained through violent (though not always bloody) confrontations. Indeed, baboon groups have traditionally been called "troops." A female's
role was seen as the bearing and raising of offspring, her individual identity

ethology: The study of the
natural behavior of animals
under natural conditions.

savanna: The open grasslands of the tropics.

FIGURE 8.3
Baboon threat. A male ba-
boon shows his long canine
teeth and flashes his white
eyelids in a "threat gesture,"
probably directed at a less
dominant male.

defined by that role, and her position in baboon society as subordinate to
that of all males and specifically determined by the position of the male
with whom she mated.

More recent studies have shown, however, that baboon societies are
far more complex and variable (Fedigan and Fedigan 1988; Smuts 1985,
1995; Strum 1987). While male baboons do vie for dominance, achieve
differential social power and influence, and protect the group from other
baboons and from predators (see Figure 8.3)—and while hamadryas males
do maintain harems through violent coercion—a formal, permanent,
tightly structured dominance hierarchy among males does not seem to be
at the center of social organization in all cases. Among other types of
baboons, for example, the olive baboons of equatorial Africa, social structure is based on "a network of social alliances" (Fedigan and Fedigan
1988:14), including friendships between females and between females and
males. These friendships may be so strong that a male will aid his female
friend's infants even though he may not be their father (see Figure 7.9).
Such friendships, rather than the social position of the males, may be what
determines who mates with whom.

Differential social positions exist, but they are based not on those
"masculine" traits mentioned previously but on an individual's "experience, skill, and . . . ability to manipulate others [and] mobilize allies" (Fedigan and Fedigan 1988:15). If there is any subgroup that is central to a
troop and that ties generations together, it is that made up of related
females, the males being more mobile and less a stable part of the troop
than was previously supposed. In fact, the competition that may be most

important to the troop is not that among males, but that among females, competing with one another "over access to the resources necessary to sustain them and their offspring" (Fedigan and Fedigan 1988:5). Finally, it appears that mate choice is more a female prerogative. Males make overtures toward estrus females, but it is the females who decide with whom they will mate. These behaviors are examples of inclusive fitness and male reproductive strategy. The male baboons have evolved protective behaviors toward females and offspring in their troop because those offspring *may* be theirs, and perhaps because those females may one day bear their offspring. Moreover, they try to keep away males from other troops to enhance their own reproductive success. At the same time, males are more mobile than females and will also try to contribute sperm to females in other troops.

The females, on the other hand, by forming alliances with related females and by selecting the males with whom they will mate, are helping ensure their own reproductive and child-rearing success, as well as the success of their genes via the reproductive success of their close relatives. Keep in mind, however, that the baboons don't have these results consciously in mind. The behaviors have evolved over time because they increase the inclusive fitness of the genes of the individuals who perform them. We don't really know what is going on in the minds of the baboons—what motivates them to act in these ways.

The earlier version of baboon social organization indicated that to survive on the savannas a primate needed a tightly organized, male-oriented and -dominated, almost militaristic society. The obvious conclusion was that the early hominid savanna dwellers probably had a similar set of behaviors and that our modern social systems are, to one extent or another, variations on this theme.

Again, however, we must remember that we can share with baboons only the most general primate homologous traits. Similarities between humans and baboons exist because we have evolved variations of the same primate behavioral themes. Our specific expressions of those themes, though, are the results of separate and independent evolutionary histories.

Nevertheless, those separate histories have produced results that are similar in baboons and humans and, as we shall see, in chimpanzees and bonobos—the adaptive focus of a social structure built around a family unit, friendships, mutual aid within the group, defense of the group, and recognition of individuals. This social structure at least tells us that such a focus is one possible adaptive path among primates, and so it is reasonable to assume that something like it was the key to the survival of the early hominids. Given that our closest relatives, the chimpanzees and bonobos, exhibit this cluster of traits, it seems an even more reasonable assumption.

CHIMPANZEES

Some of the most remarkable results of ethological observations have come from three landmark studies of the great apes: Jane Goodall's study of the chimpanzee, Dian Fossey's of the gorilla, and Biruté Galdikas's of the orangutan. Each of these studies is interesting in its own right and tells us something of the variations possible on the basic primate pattern of social organization.

The orangutan (*Pongo pygmaeus*) is an Asian ape and is separated from us by 12 million years or more. The gorilla (*Gorilla gorilla*), though as close to us genetically as the chimp and while exhibiting many of the same basic social behaviors, is a rather specialized ape. Unlike the chimpanzee, it spends much of its time on the ground, and its almost exclusively vegetarian diet is largely of ground plants. This species is not known to make or use tools. (Orangutans, however, have recently been observed using simple tools.) The species most relevant to our present subject are the chimpanzee and bonobo.

Much of what we know of the ethology of the chimp (*Pan troglodytes*) comes from the more than thirty years of research at Gombe Stream National Park in Tanzania led by Jane Goodall (1971, 1986, 1990). Goodall's studies have shown that, in addition to physical and physiological traits, we share with chimps a number of behavioral characteristics. These are centered on aspects of social interaction, and this is instructive for our understanding of our own behavior.

The bond between mother and infant is strong in chimps, as it is in most mammals. These apes, though, have large, complex brains and have a lot to learn about their world before they can become functioning adults. Thus, the mother-infant bond is particularly long-lived and important, and the nature of that interaction can have a lasting effect on the rest of a chimp's life. Poor treatment by its mother, for example, often makes a chimp a poor mother herself when she bears young. Chimps have been seen to help their mothers with younger siblings, and siblings often remain close into adulthood. Chimps, in other words, *raise* their young, and the family bonds that result may last a lifetime.

The chimps in a group are arranged in a dominance hierarchy. Males are generally dominant over all females, but within females a loose hierarchy exists. Males compete with one another in an attempt to achieve the highest position possible. The rewards are access to feeding places and to females, the latter being another example of male reproductive strategy. Social position, though attained in males through violent-looking but seldom injurious actions (Figure 8.4), is maintained via a series of expressions, gestures, and vocalizations. One of the most important is grooming (see Figure 7.10), which maintains social cohesion, and on occasion is a sign

FIGURE 8.4

A male chimpanzee showing a "full open grin." This is a sign of excitement, often used by a high-ranking chimp displaying close to a subordinate. Compare with the baboon in Figure 8.3.

of dominance when a subordinate male grooms his superior. Other expressions of social interaction include kissing, hugging, bowing, extending the hand, sexual gestures, grinning, and various vocalizations—and we can freely use these terms because the meanings of these actions in chimp society seem to be precisely what they are in human society.

A chimp society, however, is in no way some sort of dictatorship. Instead, it is marked by cooperation and mutual concern, which is seen mostly within the family unit of mother and offspring (because chimps are sexually promiscuous—a female may mate with a dozen males during estrus—the biological father is unknown). Throughout their lives, this family unit will protect and care for each other, especially during illness and injury. Males have even been known to help brothers in their competition for dominance. Care also extends outside the family unit. Offspring are important to the group as a whole, and adults will come to the aid or protection of a youngster threatened with some harm, possibly risking their own welfare, even if the youngster is not necessarily theirs. Once, an adolescent male adopted an unrelated youngster who had been orphaned (Goodall 1990:202). This protectiveness may be another example of inclusive fitness, where genes contributing to a behavior have been selected for because they confer adaptive fitness to individuals as well as to those that individual aids, who may also share those genes.

Group membership is somewhat fluid. Chimps, for various reasons, will leave a group, and outsiders will occasionally enter it. Despite this fluidity, there is a sense of group identity and territory. Small bands of males will sometimes patrol the boundaries of their group's range, and when members of other groups are encountered, they are reacted to as outsiders. This is another case of males performing a behavior that serves to protect their reproductive investment.

With chimps, however, we may reasonably wonder about more conscious motivation for some of these behaviors. In one chilling series of events, for example, males from Goodall's main study group attacked and killed a female and all the males of a group that had broken away to establish its own territory. Goodall thinks the motivation may have been to reclaim the area. A word of caution must be interjected here, however. It has been suggested (Powers 1991, for example) that because the researchers at Gombe interfered with the chimpanzees' normal activities by providing food, they may have influenced the apes' behavior, including this event.

Among the chimpanzee's wide range of food sources is meat. Chimps from some groups, including those studied by Goodall and associates at the Gombe, are hunters (Stanford 1995). Males, and occasionally females, will hunt and kill small pigs, antelopes, and monkeys, including young baboons (Figure 8.5). At Gombe, chimps, often hunting in cooperative groups, kill over 100 red colobus monkeys a year, nearly a fifth of the members of that species within the chimps' range. Meat is the one food that chimps will share, and male chimps are more likely to share with friends than with rivals—they will even withhold meat from rivals. There is evidence, too, that a male will hunt in order to get meat to give as an offering to a female in estrus.

Much of our information about this species comes from Goodall's research, but work on other chimp groups amply bears out her general observations and conclusions and lends support to the idea that chimp behavior is flexible, adaptable, and the result of intelligence and reasoning. It is thus variable from group to group. For example, a chimp group in the forests on the west coast of Africa uses hammerstones to crack open nuts,

something the Gombe chimps don't do, though the Gombe chimps are famous for their termite sticks (see Chapter 7). The West African chimps also have different hunting techniques, relying more on cooperation between hunting males than do the Gombe chimps (Boesch and Boesch-Achermann 1991).

FIGURE 8.5

A chimp in Tanzania, eating the carcass of a baboon he has recently hunted and killed. He may share some of his prize with close friends in his group.

BONOBOS

Recently, even more intriguing information has come to light about the third species of African ape, the bonobo (*Pan paniscus*) (de Waal 1995; Ingmanson and Kano 1993; Kano 1990; White 1996). The bonobo lives in the lowland forests of the Democratic Republic of the Congo (formerly Zaire) and has been estimated by genetic studies (see Chapter 9) to have been separate from the chimp for 1.5 million years.

Not really pygmies at all, the bonobos are as large as chimps, though more slender, with smaller heads and shoulders. They walk upright more often than chimps (Figure 8.6). Like chimps, they do some hunting, but they rarely do so, there is no evidence of cooperative hunting, females are sometimes the hunters, and the game is small (flying squirrels or a tiny antelope) (Ingmanson and Ihobe 1992). Also like chimps, bonobos use tools, but never in acquiring food. Rather, the bonobos use leaves as rain hats and drag branches to serve the social purposes of initiating group movement and indicating direction of movement (Ingmanson 1996).

The bonobos are more peaceful and gregarious than chimps. They have a hierarchy, but it is looser than the chimps' and much less male-oriented. They more readily share food with one another, and the food shared is not limited to luxury items like meat (Figure 8.7). They have never been observed to kill another of their kind, and their sexual behaviors play important roles in group cohesion. In contrast, sexual coercion, as seen in the hamadryas baboons, has been observed among the chimps of Gombe.

Bonobos, especially when feeding, constantly posture toward one another, rubbing rumps or "presenting" themselves as if initiating sexual activity. When sex does follow it is usually face-to-face, unlike the position of other primates and like that of humans. Sexual activity is not limited to opposite-sex partners. Females commonly rub genitalia with other females, and males will mount each other.

Moreover, the signs of fertility, the estrus signals, seem nearly always present in bonobo females. In both chimps and bonobos, the fertile and therefore sexual period is marked by a swelling and coloration of the skin of the genital area, which stimulates sexual interest on the part of the males. In chimps, the swelling only occurs when the female has ovulated and is fertile. In bonobos, however, there is some swelling almost all the time, and they seem almost constantly sexually receptive. Sexual activity in this species has become separate from purely reproductive activity and is responded to on a conscious level. The motivation for sex may be as much psychological and social as it is reproductive.

The function of this friendly posturing and sexual receptiveness seems to be the same as with grooming and as with some of the expressions and gestures among chimps: to prevent violence; to ease tension, especially while feeding; as a greeting; as a sign of reconciliation; or to reassure another group member. Sex or some form of sexual activity, between opposite- or same-sex partners, has even been seen to precede food sharing.

Now, if all the behaviors of the chimp and bonobo sound more than vaguely human, the reason may be simple. We share certain behavioral patterns because we inherited them from a common ancestor. To be sure,

FIGURE 8.6

A bonobo standing bipedally. He is collecting and carrying stalks of sugar cane in his hands, now freed from locomotor activities.

FIGURE 8.7
Bonobo society is characterized by peaceful relationships, with sexual activity and—as seen here on the left—food sharing as mechanisms to maintain harmony, ease tensions, reassure other members, and show reconciliation.

our line and that of the chimps and bonobos have been going their separate and independent ways for 5 or 6 million years, and even shared features have had the chance to become modified by all the processes of evolution—to be changed, eliminated, enhanced, and differently adapted to our species' different niches. Chimps and bonobos are not "living fossils" stuck in some 5-million-year-old rut while our ancestors continued to evolve. But because our common ancestor is relatively recent and there is striking similarity between their bodies and behaviors and ours, we can argue that our shared behaviors are homologous.

This does *not* mean that humans have specific genes for friendship, food sharing, territoriality, or continual sexuality. These are complex behaviors, and humans and apes are complex species. It does hint that, as with the chimps and bonobos, the focus of the human adaptation—the thing that adapted our earliest hominid ancestors and that has been the adaptive theme of our line—is social interaction based on individual recognition, a strong bond centered around family relationships (generally mothers and their offspring), long-term friendships, sexual consciousness, mutual care within the group, and recognition of and defense of the group. It seems reasonable to assume that our hominid ancestors behaved in similar ways. As Jane Goodall says,

> . . . the concept of early humans poking for insects with twigs and wiping themselves with leaves seems entirely sensible. The thought of those ancestors greeting and reassuring one another with kisses or embraces, cooperating in protecting their territory or in hunting, and sharing food with each other, is appealing. The idea of close affectionate ties within the Stone Age family, of brothers helping one another, of teenage sons hastening to the protection of their old mothers, and of teenage daughters minding the babies, for me brings the fossilized relics of their physical selves dramatically to life. (1990:207)

$$\triangledown \qquad \triangledown \qquad \triangledown$$

SUMMARY

As we noted in the last chapter, one way to guide us as we look at our own species is to understand the context from which our species evolved. This approach works for behavior as well as for physical adaptations. The importance of a well-defined social organization is seen among another savanna primate, the baboon, and is a good hint that an analogous behavior was a key to the survival of early savanna hominids.

More useful is the behavior of close evolutionary relatives, especially the chimpanzee and bonobo. Chimp and bonobo behavior differs in specifics from ours and has been evolving separately from ours for 5 or 6 million years. All three species have adapted to different particular niches. The basic patterns for the behavior of all three species, however, are homologous. They are the same because we inherited them from a common ancestor. It is highly likely, then, that our remote hominid ancestors also manifested these patterns in some way.

Such studies indicate to us that the early hominids of Africa may very well have been highly social creatures and that their social organization was built around differing interpersonal relationships, a family unit, conscious sexuality, recognition of group membership and territory, and mutual care at both the individual and the group level.

Contemporary Reflections

Are Some Human Behaviors Genetic?

Since Darwin's time, people have speculated about the possible biological bases of some human behaviors. In the last thirty years especially, a huge number of books have been written suggesting biological bases for human aggression, social practices such as marriage patterns, altruistic acts, morality, territoriality, and many more. The more extreme versions of such ideas claim that we have a genetic program for such behaviors, and that these programs evolved in the past and are maintained today because they confer a reproductive advantage on those who express them. In other words, they have been, and many continue to be, naturally selected for. According to opponents of this idea, a logical, and dangerous, implication of this claim is that variation in the specific expression of a behavior might reflect genetic variation among populations of our species.

Addressing this issue is complicated (and there are just as many books that take some opposing viewpoint), but there are a few guiding concepts we may use to think about it. First, we must remember that genes are instructions for making proteins. It's a long way from the gene to the phenotypic trait, and the more complex the phenotypic trait, the longer the path and the more genes involved. Behaviors are *very* complex phenotypes. In short, just as there is no single "stature gene" that determines my height, there is no "aggression gene," or "marriage gene," or "altruism gene." Even in creatures with less complex nervous systems—ants, for example—whose behaviors *must* be biologically programmed, those behaviors are still complex responses of the whole organism to a whole host of environmental stimuli. There must be very many genes involved.

A behavior's biological program, then, is just a program for a potential or a general theme. Its expression requires some environmental stimulus (that is, something outside the genes themselves) and will vary as the exact nature of the stimulus varies. A biological basis for a human behavior can only be

KEY TERMS

homologies	inclusive fitness	ethology
analogies	altruistic	savanna
sociobiology	reproductive strategies	

SUGGESTED READINGS

The latest thinking on baboon behavior can be found in Shirley Strum's *Almost Human* and in Barbara Smuts's *Sex and Friendship in Baboons*. Jane Goodall's latest work on the chimps and her experiences studying them is *Through a Window: My Thirty Years with the Chimpanzees of Gombe*.

for the most general potential. Our cultural environment, which pervades every aspect of our individual and social lives, is immensely complex, and so the expressions of a behavioral potential must be varied indeed. Thus, the variation in a human behavior from society to society (or even from individual to individual) is largely a result of different cultural environments—different systems of belief and knowledge that mark the variety of humans' ways of life.

Language is a perfect—and fairly uncontroversial—example. All normal humans come equipped with the ability to take in raw data—the speech of the people around them and the responses to their attempts to communicate—and turn it into a working knowledge of their native language. Think about it: you spoke your native language fluently before you ever were formally taught all the grammatical rules in school. And you did it by yourself, using some built-in "software" in your nervous system into which data were fed by your senses. The ability to learn language is biological and thus, at its base, genetic. The complex of genes that give rise to this ability were selected for during our evolution (see Chapters 11 and 12). Linguistic ability conferred a reproductive advantage on our ancestors.

However, *what* language you speak, how well you speak it, what words you know, what accent you have—these are cultural. They vary from society to society and even within societies—not because of genetic differences among populations, but because of variation in the cultural contexts of which they are a part.

Similarly, the social system, with its sexual consciousness, that we see in bonobos may represent a common behavioral theme that we humans have translated into various sets of learned cultural norms like sexual ethics and marriage patterns.

Nature has given us behavioral potentials, ultimately coded in our genes, that we inherited from our evolutionary ancestors and that evolved over the course of our species' history. Culture has given rise to our specific expressions of those behaviors. In this way, yes, some of our behaviors may be said to have a genetic basis—but only in this limited way.

For more technical information on primate behavior, see *The Evolution of Primate Behavior* by Alison Jolly, *Patterns of Primate Behavior* by Claud A. Bramblett, and Agustin Fuentes and Phyllis Dolhinow's *The Nonhuman Primates*.

Dian Fossey recounts her study of gorillas in *Gorillas in the Mist*; her own story, in turn, including her murder, is told by Farley Mowat in *Woman in the Mists* and in the 1988 movie *Gorillas in the Mist*. Biruté Galdikas tells about orangutans in *Reflections of Eden: My Years with the Orangutans of Borneo*.

Bonobos are described in Frans de Waal's *Bonobo: The Forgotten Ape*, which has outstanding photographs by Frans Lanting.

CHAPTER

9

STUDYING
THE HUMAN
PAST

The present contains
nothing more than the
past, and what is found
in the effect was
already in the cause.
—Henri Bergson

The study of the human past—our evolutionary history—is a central part of biological anthropology. To understand the human species today, we need to know where, when, how, and from what we evolved. But the past *is* the past. We can't see past events as they were happening. We can't make them happen again. All we have are the present-day results of series of past events, like the living species of primates we discussed in the last two chapters. In some cases, we have the physical remains of past events, such as the fossils of extinct species, but these have themselves undergone change since they were part of a living creature.

The present, however, can be a powerful tool. Recall, from Chapter 2, how Hooke and Steno used fossils and stratigraphy to plot the events of the past and how Hutton and Lyell used the idea of uniformitarianism—that the past can be explained by present-day processes—to understand how past events took place.

In this chapter, we will address the methods used by bioanthropologists to answer questions about our past.

What are the features of the primate skeleton and how can knowledge of them help us identify fossil remains?

How do we locate, recover, and date fossil remains?

How are fossils formed, and what affects the condition of the fossils we find?

What can we learn about our past from new technologies in the study of genetics?

BONES: THE PRIMATE SKELETON

Most of the physical remains we find of the evolutionary past are in the form of preserved bone. Only in rare cases are we lucky enough to discover soft tissue remains of an ancient organism (see Figure 15.1). Therefore, knowledge of the skeletal structure, or **osteology,** of primates is vital. The first thing we need to do, of course, is determine what species the skeletal remains are from. The human skeleton is a variation on the basic mammalian skeletal theme and, more specifically, on the primate skeletal theme. Figure 9.1 compares the skeletons (with the major bones labeled) of a domestic cat, a gorilla, and a modern human.

The bones are not separate from the muscles, nerves, blood vessels, and other soft tissues of the body. Rather, they all develop together and are adapted to function together. For example, the skull serves to protect the brain; therefore, the skull is a good indicator of the shape and size of the brain it once protected. Muscles are attached to bones, and so the location, size, and shape of the point where the muscle attaches to a bone

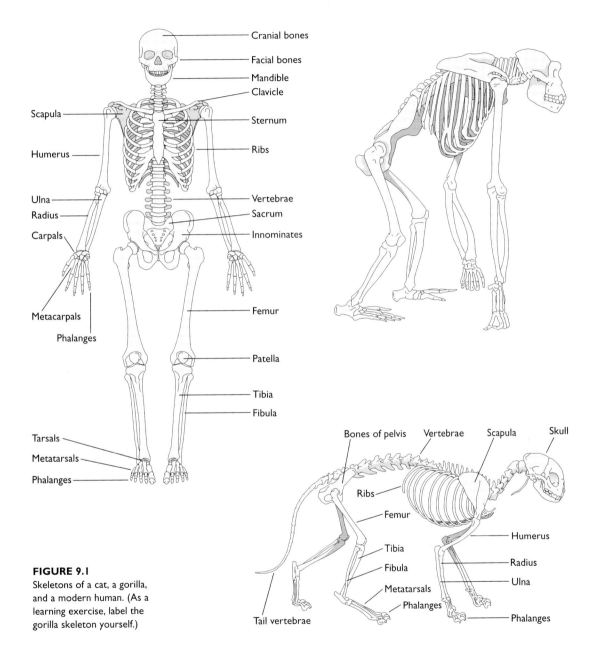

Cranial bones
Facial bones
Mandible
Clavicle
Scapula
Sternum
Humerus
Ribs
Ulna
Radius
Vertebrae
Sacrum
Carpals
Innominates
Metacarpals
Phalanges
Femur
Patella
Tibia
Fibula
Tarsals
Metatarsals
Phalanges

Bones of pelvis   Vertebrae   Scapula   Skull
Ribs
Femur
Humerus
Tibia
Fibula   Radius
Metatarsals   Ulna
Phalanges
Tail vertebrae   Phalanges

FIGURE 9.1
Skeletons of a cat, a gorilla, and a modern human. (As a learning exercise, label the gorilla skeleton yourself.)

osteology: The study of the skeleton.

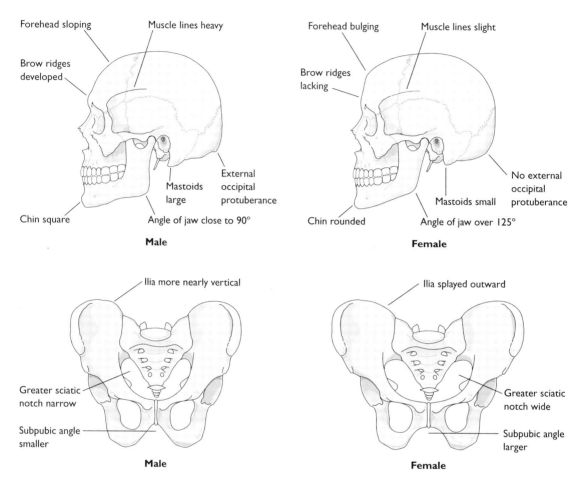

FIGURE 9.2
Sex differences in the skull and pelvis of humans.

will provide some indication of the size and shape of the muscle even though the muscle itself may have decayed long ago. We can tell a lot about a creature from the bones it leaves behind.

One of the more obvious and important things we can tell about a human skeleton is its sex. Humans are a species that exhibits **sexual dimorphism,** notable physical differences between the sexes that are not related to reproductive traits. In general, human males tend to be larger and more heavily muscled than females, a fact that also applies to the apes and to extinct hominid species. The skull and especially, for obvious reasons, the pelvis are the best parts of the skeleton for determining sex (Figure 9.2).

Age at death may also be determined from skeletal remains. The body, including the bones, goes through many physical changes as it develops, matures, and ages, and many of these changes take place at fairly regular times. By determining, on a skeleton, which changes have already taken place and which have yet to take place, we may approximate the age at which these changes ceased, that is, the age at which the individual died (Figure 9.3).

The skeleton acts as a framework for the body, and thus the size and shape of the bones can reveal something of the appearance of the entire living person. We know, for example, from the sheer size and ruggedness of their bones, that a group of humans from Ice Age Europe (the "Neandertals," whom we will discuss in Chapter 11) were big, brawny, and extremely strong. Several investigators have attempted to reconstruct the faces of our ancestors from the shapes of skulls and facial bones. Using their knowledge of human anatomy, they artistically add missing bones, eyes, fatty tissue, cartilage, muscle, and skin to casts of ancient skulls, "fleshing out" our picture of early humans (see Figure 15.2). (This technique is also used in law enforcement to try to identify skeletal remains. We will discuss the application of human osteology to legal matters in Chapter 15.)

The skeleton can also tell us something about the behavior of the organism that possessed it. We have mentioned the importance of bipedal locomotion in our evolution and that this behavior was the first hominid trait to evolve. We know it was first because the nature of the bones of the pelvis and femur, along with the position of the skull atop the spine, suggest posture and movement. Thus, our analysis of the bones of our most ancient ancestors provides indications of how they walked (Figure 9.4).

Moreover, we can discern information about diet from dental and skeletal remains. Look at the dentition of a **carnivore** in your dog or cat, and compare it to the teeth of an **omnivore** in your own mouth. The teeth of the dog or cat, although they show some differentiation, are all pointed and sharp, adapted for grasping, piercing, cutting, and crushing. Our teeth are adapted for a greater variety of operations and, thus, a greater variety of food types. In addition, certain wear patterns on the teeth, when examined microscopically, can reveal whether the diet was made up of soft foods like fruits, or more abrasive, gritty foods like grains and roots (see Figure 10.20). We can even examine the chemical content of ancient bones for the proportion of strontium, calcium, and other elements in them to determine whether plants or meat made up the bulk of the diet of certain populations (Schoeninger 1995).

Finally, we may acquire information about the health status of our ancestors. Many diseases leave characteristic marks on the skeleton. These include such important disorders as arthritis, tumors and other cancers, tuberculosis, leprosy, anemias, syphilis, osteoporosis, typhoid (as in Henry Opukahaia), and various infections. Injuries, too, leave their marks, as do other behaviors, including scalping and **trephination,** a prehistoric surgical procedure that involved cutting a hole in the skull (Figure 9.5).

sexual dimorphism: Physical differences between the sexes of a species not related to reproductive features.

carnivore: An organism adapted to a diet of mostly meat.

omnivore: An organism with a mixed diet of animal and vegetable foods.

trephination: The cutting of a hole in the skull, presumably to treat some illness.

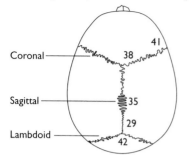

Average dates for cranial suture closure (years)

Coronal — 38, 41

Sagittal — 35

29

Lambdoid — 42

Cranial Suture Closure. The bones of the cranial vault are separate at birth and gradually fuse during a person's lifetime. The numbers indicate the average age (in years) of complete closure at different points along the lines of attachment, the sutures. There are other dates as well, on locations not shown in this view. Because of the great degree of individual variation, this is not a particularly reliable technique.

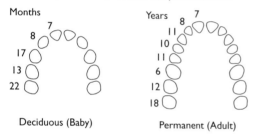

Eruption dates of deciduous and permanent teeth

Months
7
8
17
13
22

Years
7
8
11
10
11
6
12
18

Deciduous (Baby)   Permanent (Adult)

Dental Eruption. Humans have two sets of teeth: deciduous, or "baby," teeth and permanent, or adult, teeth. Each tooth "erupts" through the gum line at a certain average age. We determine age by seeing which tooth was the last to erupt and which unerupted tooth would have erupted next. We recognize this method in our use of the term "six-year molar" for the first adult tooth to erupt. The degree of development of each tooth below the gum line (seen in broken bone or in x-rays) can also be used.

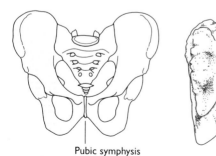

Pubic symphysis

Ages of epiphyseal union (years)

Elbow	14
Hands and feet	15
Ankle	16
Thigh (top)	17
Knee	18
Wrist	19
Shoulder	20
Hip	21
Clavicle	28

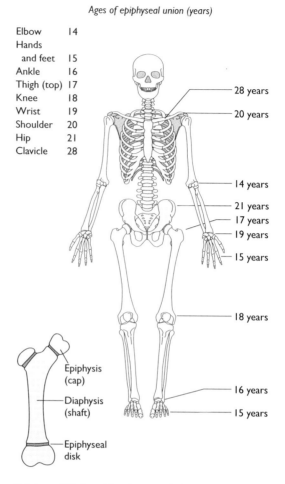

28 years
20 years
14 years
21 years
17 years
19 years
15 years
18 years
16 years
15 years

Epiphysis (cap)

Diaphysis (shaft)

Epiphyseal disk

Epiphyseal Union. Many bones, including those of the arms, legs, hands, and feet, grow in sections: a shaft, or diaphysis, and caps, or epiphyses. When growth is complete, the cartilaginous disks between caps and shaft turn to bone and a single bone results. Ages for epiphyseal union are known and are uniform enough to provide a reliable aging method. The ages shown indicate that all the sites at any one location fuse at about the same time. For example, at the elbow the far (distal) end of the humerus and the near (proximal) ends of the radius and ulna all fuse at 14 years.

Pubic Symphysis. The inner surface of the bones where the pelvis meets in front is called the pubic symphysis. Between the ages of 18 and 50+, the appearance of this surface undergoes characteristic changes. By assessing the phase to which a specimen belongs, we can approximate the age of a specimen at death. The symphyseal face shown is Phase VIII, giving an age of 40 to 44 years. (Redrawn from Todd 1920.)

FIGURE 9.3
Techniques used to determine the age of hominid bones.

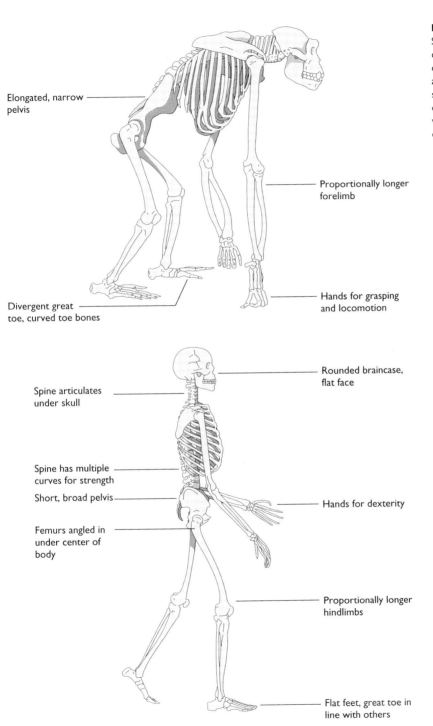

Elongated, narrow pelvis

Proportionally longer forelimb

Divergent great toe, curved toe bones

Hands for grasping and locomotion

Spine articulates under skull

Rounded braincase, flat face

Spine has multiple curves for strength

Short, broad pelvis

Hands for dexterity

Femurs angled in under center of body

Proportionally longer hindlimbs

Flat feet, great toe in line with others

FIGURE 9.4
Some of the important physical differences between a quadrupedal ape (the gorilla) and a modern human. The size and shape of the muscles of posture and locomotion would also reflect this difference.

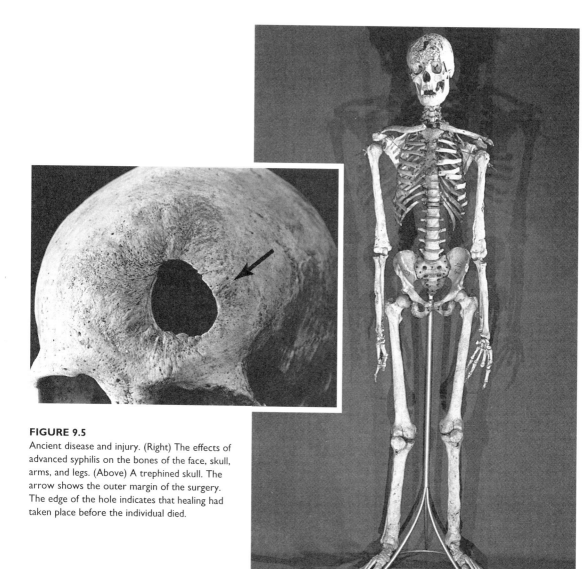

FIGURE 9.5
Ancient disease and injury. (Right) The effects of advanced syphilis on the bones of the face, skull, arms, and legs. (Above) A trephined skull. The arrow shows the outer margin of the surgery. The edge of the hole indicates that healing had taken place before the individual died.

OLD BONES: LOCATING, RECOVERING, AND DATING FOSSILS

Most creatures that have ever lived, including humans, have left no remains. Fossilization (which we'll discuss in the next section) is a rare occurrence. A fossil, therefore, is really a priceless treasure, and finding

one is an uncommon event—even in those **sites** that, because of their geological history and nature, yield many remains. Olduvai Gorge in Tanzania (Figure 9.6) has provided us with some of the most important hominid fossils, yet Louis and Mary Leakey lived and worked there for over twenty years before finding one. How then, do we even decide where to begin looking?

A lot, of course, depends upon just *what* we're looking for. If it's dinosaurs we're interested in, we look in rock strata that date from the time of the dinosaurs. For hominid fossils, we need strata that were deposited in the last 5 or 6 million years.

It helps, too, if those strata are exposed by geological processes. Layers that are far under the surface might contain important fossils, but purely practical considerations would make it difficult, time-consuming, and expensive to dig them up. A place like Olduvai Gorge is ideal. There, an

FIGURE 9.6
Olduvai Gorge, Tanzania, one of the world's most productive sites for paleoanthropologists. The strata represent more than 2 million years of evolution.

sites: Places that contain evidence of human presence.

FIGURE 9.7
Paleoanthropologist Bill Kimbel of the Institute of Human Origins uses dental tools, a small drill, and a binocular microscope to chip stone from bone on nearly sixty fragments of a fossil hominid from Ethiopia. The results of his efforts are shown in Figure 10.13.

ancient river cut a canyon 300 feet into the earth, exposing layers of soil and rock that go back about 2 million years. At Omo, in Ethiopia, another important early hominid site, the strata have been tilted by geological forces, so that layers from 1 million to 4 million years old are all on the surface. Walking back and forth at such sites as these is like walking through time. In addition, in such places, natural water and wind erosion helps expose new soil and whatever fossils it may contain.

Of course, just because a location *looks* like it might easily yield fossils doesn't mean that the conditions there were always conducive to fossilization. Paleoanthropologists might inquire as to whether fossils of *any* sort have been found in a potential area of investigation in strata from the time period they are interested in. Both Olduvai and Omo already had reputations as rich fossil areas before the search for hominid fossils began at those sites.

Recovering fossils once they are located can be a tricky business. Fossils are old and often very fragile. Many old bones are **petrified**—turned to stone—and so are hard to distinguish from the stone in which they were found (Figure 9.7). Raymond Dart, the discoverer of one of the most famous hominid fossils (both of whom we shall meet in the next chapter), took seventy-three days to separate the tiny fossil from the limestone in which it was encased. The excavation tools of the paleoanthropologist, then, are not so much the backhoe or even the shovel, but rather the mason's trowel, the dentist's pick, and the artist's brush.

A fossil sitting on a shelf in a lab, or on display in a museum, may be beautiful, intriguing, and provocative, but it is scientifically useless unless we know precisely where it was found, its **provenience.** To keep track of the proveniences of fossils, recovery is carried out with the utmost care directed at detailed and accurate record keeping. After all, once fossils are removed, a site is destroyed, and we must have records of the relative locations of all the important items contained in that site.

Many early hominid fossils are simply found on the surface of the ground, exposed by wind and water erosion. Many, however, are dug out of the ground or are found associated with particular strata.

The depth at which a fossil is found relative to other fossils and to the natural strata of the soil or rock is, of course, an indication of relative age. This is the principle of stratigraphy, the idea that the deeper a layer is the older it is. It is an important dating method and is referred to as a **relative dating technique;** that is, it indicates the age of one fossil in comparison to that of another (Figure 9.8). In the absence of any natural stratigraphy, the excavator of fossils must establish one. For example, the investigator may dig down by regular increments, perhaps only centimeters at a time, recording the precise depth of any item of interest.

Similarly, the horizontal location of each fossil is important. Often a paleoanthropologist—like the archaeologist looking for human cultural remains—uses a grid system. A site is divided into squares, or grids, and each grid is excavated separately (Figure 9.9). Again, the precise location of a fossil, relative to that of others at the same level, is recorded through photographs and maps.

Besides relative dating, there are also **absolute dating techniques** (also called chronometric techniques). These tell us the actual age of a fossil. Among the best known are **radiometric** techniques, such as **carbon dating,** which can be used to date fossils back to about 60,000 years ago and so is relevant to the later period of human evolution. It works as follows: Carbon, in the form of carbon dioxide, is found in all living things, which continually exchange it with the environment through respiration and metabolism. Most carbon is ^{12}C, indicating that there are twelve particles

petrified: A fossil that has turned to stone.

provenience: The precise location of something.

relative dating technique: Dating method that indicates the age of one item in comparison to another.

absolute dating techniques: Dating methods that give a specific age, year, or range of years.

radiometric: Referring to the decay rate of a radioactive substance.

carbon dating: A radiometric dating technique using the decay rate of a radioactive form of carbon found in organic remains.

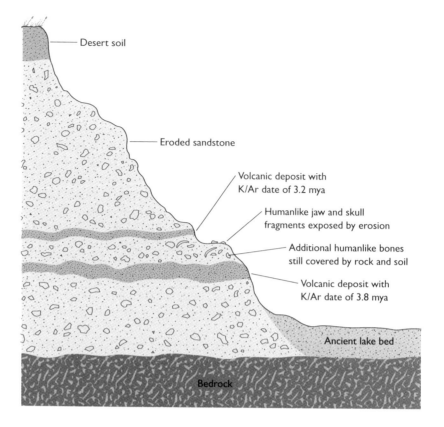

FIGURE 9.8
Hypothetical stratigraphic sequence. The humanlike remains are between two layers of volcanic rock that can be dated using the K/Ar method. They must be younger than the volcanic deposit below and older than the one above.

Desert soil

Eroded sandstone

Volcanic deposit with K/Ar date of 3.2 mya

Humanlike jaw and skull fragments exposed by erosion

Additional humanlike bones still covered by rock and soil

Volcanic deposit with K/Ar date of 3.8 mya

Ancient lake bed

Bedrock

FIGURE 9.9
Grid system diagram of a portion of an excavation from Ambrona, Spain, dated at around 350,000 years ago (see Chapter 11). The grid helps record the precise location of each bone and artifact. Notice how much less information is conveyed by the solid part of the drawing, which does not show the grid.

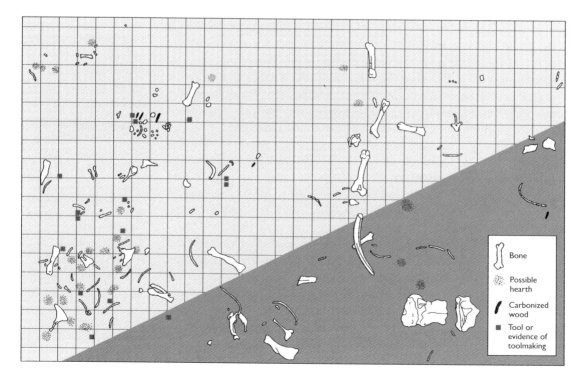

Bone

Possible hearth

Carbonized wood

Tool or evidence of toolmaking

in the nucleus (six protons and six neutrons). Some carbon, however, is "carbon 14," or ^{14}C, because it has two extra neutrons. It is formed when cosmic radiation hits nitrogen atoms in the atmosphere. We know the proportion of each form (called an isotope) of carbon in a living organism. Once an organism dies, however, it is no longer taking in new carbon, and so its ^{14}C—an unstable or radioactive isotope—begins to decay back into nitrogen, and it does so at a constant rate called a **half-life.** The half-life of ^{14}C is 5730 years. In that time, one-half of the ^{14}C will have decayed. In another 5730 years, half of the remaining half will decay, leaving a quarter of the original, and so on.

Now, if we find some organic remains—bone, for example, or even burnt wood from a fire—we can test it to see how much ^{14}C is left compared to how much the organism contained when alive. We know how much ^{14}C a living organism should contain, and we test the amount left as we would test any radioactive substance, with a device like a Geiger counter that measures the amount of radiation emitted. Suppose that our specimen has one-quarter of the living amount. Two half-lives have passed, or 5730 times 2, or 11,460 years. Beyond 60,000 years ago there is not enough ^{14}C left to accurately measure. So how do we date the really old fossils, like those of the early hominids?

We could use another important method called **potassium/argon, or K/Ar, dating.** Radioactive potassium (^{40}K), found in volcanic rock, decays into stable argon gas; its half-life is 1.31 billion years. Organic matter contains ^{40}K as well but loses the argon gas that it decays into. Volcanic rocks, formed during eruptions, have a crystalline structure that traps the argon. Using the same reasoning as for carbon dating, we test volcanic rock for the amount of argon, work backward, and date the rock. Now, organic remains may be dated relatively. Any fossils found in a layer of volcanic rock are as old as that rock. Fossils found just above are younger; those found just below are older, and so on (see again Figure 9.8). Recently, a new technique called **argon/argon dating,** which uses the decay of radioactive ^{39}Ar into argon gas (^{40}Ar), has provided more accuracy in dating volcanic rock. Using lasers, it can be performed on a sample as small as a single crystal.

Two other techniques have recently become more widely used and have provided new dates for some fossil sites (see Chapters 11 and 12). One is called **electron spin resonance (ESR) dating**. Natural radioactivity can excite electrons in crystalline material to higher energy levels, where they are "trapped." The number of trapped electrons in such material is related to the nature of the material, the amount of natural background radiation, and, most importantly, the amount of time since the material formed. By measuring the number of trapped electrons, age can be calculated for materials such as tooth enamel, mollusk shells, cave deposits, corals, and volcanic rock. This technique has been particularly useful for

half-life: The time needed for one-half of a given amount of a radioactive substance to decay.

potassium/argon (K/Ar) dating: A radiometric dating technique using the rate that radioactive potassium, found in volcanic rock, decays into stable argon gas.

argon/argon dating: A radiometric dating technique that uses the decay of radioactive argon into stable argon gas. Can be used to date volcanic rock with greater accuracy and smaller samples than does K/Ar dating.

electron spin resonance (ESR) dating: An absolute dating technique that measures the number of electrons excited to higher energy levels by natural radiation and trapped there. Can be used to date tooth enamel, shells, corals, mineral cave deposits, and volcanic rock, but does not work well on bone.

TABLE 9.1
Dating Methods

Dating Method	Age Range	Material Dated	Basis
Amino (aspartic) acid racemization	1,000,000–2000 B.P.	Bone	Shift in polarity of amino acids
Electron spin resonance	100–10 million B.P.	Teeth, cave deposits	Electrons produced by natural radiation become trapped in crystalline materials at a regular rate
Fission track dating	1,000,000–100,000 B.P.	Volcanic rock	Radioactive decay leaves microscopic damage "tracks" in rock at regular rate
Obsidian hydration	800,000 B.P.–present	Obsidian (volcanic glass)	Regular buildup of "hydration layer" caused by chemical reaction of obsidian with water over time
Paleomagnetism	2000 B.P.–present	Material with magnetic minerals	Movement of earth's magnetic pole and known dates of the position of the pole
Potassium/argon and argon/argon	100,000–billions B.P.	Volcanic rock	Decay of radioactive potassium (or argon isotope) to stable argon gas
Radiocarbon	100s–60,000 B.P.	Organic remains	Decay of radioactive carbon isotope to stable nitrogen
Thermoluminescence	To 800,000 B.P.	Fired clay, pottery, bricks, burned rock	Measure of amount of energy captured in material from decay of radioactive elements in surrounding soil; amount of energy captured is proportional to age
Uranium series	350,000–1000 B.P.	Calcium carbonate	Decay of radioactive uranium to a series of other elements

sites too old (more than 60,000 years) to be dated with radiocarbon. It does not, however, work well on bone.

Luminescence dating, like ESR dating, measures electrons that have been trapped at higher energy levels by background radiation but dates mostly artifacts like fired clay, pottery, bricks, and burned rock such as would be found lining a hearth. The more energy trapped, the older the material. Here, the trapped energy is released in the lab using heat (a process called thermoluminescence, or TL) or light (optically stimulated luminescence, or OSL) and is seen in the form of a light glow (luminescence). It is useful to about 800,000 years ago. This technique has also been applied to soil sediments, but there is, at present, still some debate over the accuracy of this application.

Other dating techniques also exist (see Table 9.1). Several date volcanic rock; others can be used directly on organic remains. In many cases, more than one of these methods may be applied, and, when they agree, we have a well-established date for a geological stratum or a fossil. Most of the dates that will be presented in the following chapters are reasonably well confirmed through the use of one or more of these techniques.

HOW FOSSILS GET TO BE FOSSILS

Most animals and plants that have inhabited the earth have left no fossil remains. There are probably whole taxonomic groups that we have no idea of because we've found no clues to their existence. Why is this so?

The conditions under which an organism, or some of its parts, can be preserved are quite specific. In New England, where I live, the soil is very acidic, due largely to the annual fall of leaves and pine needles. Organic remains tend to disappear very quickly. This is why we were surprised to find the entire, intact skeleton of Henry Opukahaia (see Chapter 1). His bones were preserved because he was buried on a hill in sandy soil, so water, with all its related chemical and biological decaying activity, could not accumulate around him, and probably because the cemetery was regularly cleared of leaves.

Organic remains tend to be preserved under several conditions. In cases of extreme dryness, even soft tissues, usually eaten by everything from bacteria to insects to scavengers, may mummify. Natural mummies were created in normal burials in the desert sands of ancient Egypt, even before the Egyptians began artificial mummification. In 1972, eight human bodies were found in graves in a rock overhang in western Greenland (Hansen et al. 1985). These Inuits (Eskimos) had been naturally mummified by a combination of low temperatures, drying winds, and protection from the elements by the rock, and they had been preserved for over 500 years (Figure 9.10). (See Chapter 15 for another famous example—the Ice Man from the Alps.)

Lack of oxygen also contributes to preservation. Such conditions are found in the thick mud at the bottom of some lakes and ponds. With no oxygen, there is little bacterial action, and organic remains decay very slowly. Many important fossils have been found in places that were once lake bottoms.

Of course, the longer ago the organism lived, the less likely we are to find remains, simply because there is more chance that they will have been crushed, dissolved, eaten, washed away, and so on. But in some cases, minerals may crystallize out of water around the bones or shells of a creature, or in rare cases around slowly decaying soft tissue, and may fill in the spaces left by the decay of organic matter. In this case, the fossil becomes petrified; it literally turns to stone and so is harder, more resistant to pro-

luminescence dating: An absolute dating technique that measures trapped electrons by releasing their energy in the form of light. Can be used to date fired clay, pottery, brick, and burned stones. It may have some application to soil dating.

FIGURE 9.10
Mummy of Inuit baby found in Greenland, about six months old when he died.

cesses of decay and no longer edible, although, naturally, some anatomical detail is lost. The dinosaur fossils with which we are so familiar as well as the remains of the earliest hominids are all stone. Luckily for us, the creatures that left these remains perished in just the right situations. Most creatures aren't so considerate.

A fossil is more than just an indication of the type of organism of which it was once a part. A fossil also contains clues as to how the animal died and what happened to it after its death. The study of these factors is called **taphonomy** (from *taphos*, dead), and it has been important in our understanding of our own evolution.

For example, some early hominid bones have been found in limestone caves in South Africa along with the bones of other mammals. These findings led investigators to believe that our early ancestors inhabited those caves and were hunters who brought their kills back home. More recent taphonomic analysis, however, reveals that the hominids were the hunted, not the hunters. The bones were the leftovers of leopard kills. Leopards often drag their prey up into a tree where no other predator or scavenger can get at it, and they eat it over several days. As the prey is eaten and, later, as the remains decay, the bones fall to the ground. Now, although much of South Africa is dry, the limestone caves hold moisture, and so trees tend to grow well around the mouths of the caves. As leopard kills hanging in these trees fell apart, the bones fell into the caves. Those bones were of antelopes, baboons, and other animals leopards eat, and apparently, our ancestors were on the menu as well (Figure 9.11). One early hominid skull shows twin puncture wounds that appear to have been

FIGURE 9.11
Artist's reconstruction of a leopard with the remains of an early hominid in a tree above the entrance to a South African cave. This behavior probably accounts for the accumulation of bones, including bones of our ancestors, in the area's caves.

taphonomy: The study of how organisms become part of the paleontological record.

the cause of death. The lower canine teeth of a leopard fit exactly into these punctures, providing evidence for the preceding analysis. Taphonomy, although the study of the dead, has thus told us important things about how our distant ancestors *lived*. We will describe another important conclusion from taphonomy in the next chapter when we see how microscopic scratches on bones and teeth reveal something about the diet of the early hominids.

GENES: NEW WINDOWS TO THE PAST

Just as we can reconstruct evolutionary relationships by comparing the anatomical traits of living creatures, we may do the same by making comparisons at the genetic level. In some ways, genetic comparisons are more accurate. Phenotypic traits are normally controlled by a complex interaction of multiple genetic loci, evolutionary processes, and environmental factors. As a result, a trait may look the same in two species, but the expressions of that trait in each species may be based on very different genetics, developmental processes, and environmental interactions, and the two traits may have different adaptive significances.

Stephen Jay Gould (1980) notes the example of the panda's "thumb," which looks like the thumb of primates and is used for grasping. It is actually, however, not a finger at all but an elongated wrist bone that is used solely to strip the leaves off bamboo stalks, just about the panda's only food. One might conclude from this striking similarity in a rather unique feature that pandas are closely related to primates, but the similarity is purely a coincidence. The thumbs of primates and the "thumb" of the panda are analogous, not homologous (see Chapter 8). The panda is a bear, in the order Carnivora, not at all closely related to primates, as an examination of the genes themselves would clearly show.

On the other hand, two species may look very different, but their differences may be the result of extensive phenotypic effects of a very small number of genes, and the species may actually be quite closely related. Humans and chimps are an example.

Comparing genetic differences among individuals, species, and higher taxa (genera, families, and so on) reveals actual biological relationships, no matter what the species look like or how seemingly similar or different some of their traits. In the 1960s, Vincent Sarich and the late Allan Wilson of the University of California at Berkeley pioneered research that used genetic comparisons to determine evolutionary relationships. Because the technology for comparing actual genes was still unknown when they carried out their work, they compared the chemistry of blood proteins. These are large proteins, easily obtained and easy to work with, and, most

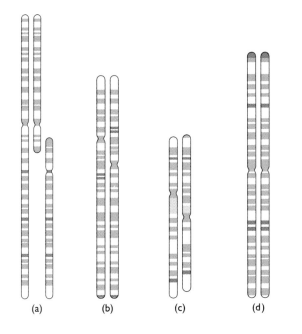

(a)   (b)   (c)   (d)

FIGURE 9.12
Human chromosomes, on
the left in each pair, compared to chromosomes of
chimpanzees. The similarities
in banding pattern are clear.
In the far-lefthand pair, the
pattern of human chromo-
some 2 is similar to that of
two chimp chromosomes.
The far-righthand pair are
virtually identical. This is one
piece of evidence for the 99
percent genetic similarity between our two species.

importantly, the direct products of the genetic code. This research provided some startling conclusions.

It had been assumed at the time that humans and our closest relatives,
the great apes, were separated by 12 to 15 million years of evolution. This
estimate was based on the degree of phenotypic difference between us and
them and on some fossils of that age that *appeared* to show the beginnings
of hominid traits. Wilson and Sarich's research showed that the blood
proteins of humans and chimps were almost identical. In other words, our
genes, at least for those traits, are almost the same. Comparing this difference with that between species whose evolutionary divergence time was
known, Wilson and Sarich calculated that our two species had branched
apart a mere 5 million years ago. These 12-million-year-old fossils, they
said, were not hominids, no matter what they appeared to be. They were
right, as we will see in Chapter 10.

Other methods for making comparisons closer to the genetic level
verified this hypothesis. A protein, you recall, is a genetically coded sequence of amino acids. Proteins may thus be compared for the sequence
of amino acids that constitute them. Again, it turned out that humans
and chimpanzees showed less than 1 percent difference in the amino acid
structure of certain blood proteins—they were nearly identical. Comparison of a bonding reaction of the DNA of chimps and humans and of the
pattern of bands on chromosomes of chimps and humans (an indication
of the nature of their sequence of genes) revealed the same lack of difference (Figure 9.12).

Contemporary Reflections

Who Owns Old Bones?

Recently, the nearly complete skeleton of a *Tyrannosaurus rex* found in South Dakota was at the center of a controversy over ownership. After some complex legal haggling, the owner of the land on which the bones were found was granted permission to sell them. The skeleton went up for public auction in October 1997 and was purchased (with corporate help) by the Field Museum of Natural History in Chicago—for $8.36 million! It will now be available for research and, eventually, for public display. In this case, everybody won, but scientists worry that this could set a precedent that would remove important evidence of the past from free scientific inquiry.

The issue of ownership and availability to science becomes even more complex when the remains of the past are human. In these cases, ownership may be a matter not only of landholding, but also of direct biological or cultural descent. The extreme cases are easy enough to sort out. I don't think anyone would object to the excavation and study of early African hominids, even though they are the ancestors of us all. They are simply too far removed in time and their potential scientific value too great. On the other hand, I would object if some anthropologist wanted to dig up my grandparents, examine their bones, and put them in a museum case—and the law would clearly be on my side. Not all situations, however, are as clear-cut.

For years, otherwise well-meaning scientists have enjoyed the freedom to recover, study, and store the skeletal remains of the remote and not-so-remote ancestors of living peoples. In North America, thousands of Native American skeletons have been recovered—many exhumed from the graves into which they were placed by members of their societies. Although these remains have provided much information about the original inhabitants of this continent, Native American groups began to object, for obvious reasons. In 1990 the Native American Graves Protection and Repatriation Act (NAGPRA)

Recently, we have developed the technology to compare the very structure of the genes themselves—the sequence of bases (A, T, G, and C) of the DNA. A multinational project known as the Human Genome Initiative (the genome is the total genetic endowment of a species) is attempting to map the locations of the 100,000 human genes and to determine the sequence of all the 3 billion base pairs that make up our species' genetic code. The year 2003 is still being projected as the completion date (Rowen et al. 1997).

The technology involved has allowed us to make great strides in such matters as personal identification in criminal and missing persons cases. For example, blood samples from crime scenes can be genetically compared with blood from suspects. DNA sequencing also helps in locating genes involved in various diseases. At least one gene on each of the twenty-three human chromosomes has been found to be linked to a human ailment. Examples are ALS or Lou Gehrig's disease (a fatal degenerative nerve disease), some cases of breast cancer, a form of kidney disease, Tay-

was passed. It said that lineal descendants had a right to the remains of their buried ancestors housed in institutions or discovered on federal or tribal territory. This has led to the removal of large collections of human remains and associated artifacts from museums and labs and has made new excavations of Native American remains difficult, if not impossible. Indeed, before "naturally shed" remains were excluded from NAGPRA regulations, two local tribes demanded the return of some 10,000-year-old human hair found at a site in Montana, hair that could provide information on the DNA of early Americans (see Feder 1997 and references therein for a more complete discussion of this and related issues).

Is there a compromise between honoring the cultural laws and heritage of peoples and providing science with important data—data that may even shed light on the history of the people in question? Each case, in the end, must be examined and judged on its own merits. Much evidence of early America is in the form of abandoned and naturally covered-over objects and bones, not intentional burials. Much cannot be reasonably affiliated with any specific living group. Such things should be freely open to scientific investigation. On the other hand, scientists should not go into clearly identified burial areas armed with shovels and trowels. As is most often the case, where ancient bones are uncovered by natural processes or accident (say, during a construction project), the group to which those bones are affiliated might allow scientific information to be gathered before the bones are reburied. This is the situation with the well-known African Burial Ground in New York City. A model example for me is the case of Henry Opukahaia (Chapter 1), where the family kindly allowed us to fully examine Henry's bones before preparing and returning them for burial.

Whatever the individual cases, however, there is one overriding consideration that should guide our actions in these matters—no matter how old or from what species, bones were once integral parts of living, breathing, feeling beings. Even when we use them as scientific specimens, they deserve respectful treatment.

Sachs disease (a fatal metabolic disorder), one form of Alzheimer's, PKU (a metabolic disease that results in mental retardation), sickle cell anemia, malignant melanoma (skin cancer), cystic fibrosis (a lung disease), Huntington's disease (a degenerative nerve disease), muscular dystrophy, kidney cancer, psoriasis (a skin disease), osteoporosis (thinning of the bones in women), and many more. For many of these diseases, we can test for the presence of the defective gene even if symptoms have not yet appeared.

These new technologies have also been applied to the study of human evolution because we can now very specifically compare the genes of various living human groups (see Chapters 12 and 14) and other primate populations and compare the genes of humans with those of related species. Such detailed studies have shown us, for example, that the bonobos are genetically distinct enough from the common chimps to be considered a separate species. These techniques also further bear out what older studies indicated—that humans and chimpanzees differ by about 1 percent of their genetic makeup and that this difference, when compared with differences among and between other species, points to a divergence time of about 5 million years. Finally, comparing DNA among living populations is shedding light on the possible relationships between modern humans and various groups of our ancestors (see Chapter 12), and we are beginning to be able to apply DNA analysis to fossils themselves by extracting genetic material from ancient bone (see Chapter 11).

In the next three chapters, we will outline the story of hominid evolution. All the above scientific techniques have been applied to studying this story and have allowed us to achieve what knowledge we have of our evolutionary history.

SUMMARY

Often, when we read a necessarily brief article in the popular media about some new fossil find, we get the impression that the scientists conducted some sort of magic to arrive at their stated conclusions. In the October 3, 1994, issue of *Time*, for example, we read that a small fossil tooth and a few other fragmentary bones from Ethiopia had been discovered and heralded as "a new chapter in the history of human evolution" (Lemonick 1994). On the basis of these bones, a new species of hominid was established, and it is described as having been about 4 feet tall and probably bipedal, having been "ravaged by carnivores," and having lived 4.4 million years ago in the forests. That's pretty specific information from a handful of bones turned to stone.

You should now understand that arriving at such conclusions is not magic at all. Though data like these bones are from a creature millions of years old, we may still use scientific methodology to interpret them. We know what modern mammalian skeletons look like and what previous fossil finds look like, so we can compare our new fossils to them in order to give them a taxonomic assignment. As the fossils were being recovered, exhaustive data were recorded about their provenience, allowing us to generate hypotheses about their environment and, using technologies from physics, their date. We understand how fossils are formed and what their specific condition can tell us about how the creature died and became part of the fossil record. We know, for example, what bones that have been "ravaged by carnivores" look like.

Finally, combining the preceding techniques with new methods from genetics, we have been able to piece together a tentative family tree of the hominids. When a new set of fossils are found, we have a context into which they may be placed and a taxonomic system that can supply them with a name. We will meet this new fossil species and many others in the next chapter, as we see exactly how these fact-finding techniques are applied.

KEY TERMS

osteology

sexual dimorphism

carnivore

omnivore

trephination

sites

petrified

provenience

relative dating technique

absolute dating techniques

radiometric

carbon dating

half-life

potassium/argon (K/Ar) dating

argon/argon dating

electron spin resonance (ESR) dating

luminescence dating

taphonomy

SUGGESTED READINGS

A detailed and beautifully photographed book on the human skeleton, with life-sized pictures, is *Human Osteology* by Tim White and Pieter Folkens. Analysis of the human skeleton in anthropological context is also covered nicely in William Bass's *Human Osteology: A Laboratory and Field Manual of the Human Skeleton*; in *Skeleton Keys* by Jeffrey H. Schwartz; and, for comparative osteology among the primates, in *An Introduction to Human Evolutionary Anatomy* by Leslie Aiello and Christopher Dean.

Techniques of excavation, interpretation, and dating are covered in more detail in Ken Feder and Michael Park's *Human Antiquity*, third edition, and in even more detail in *Archaeology: Discovering Our Past* by Robert Sharer and Wendy Ashmore and *In the Beginning* by Brian Fagan.

Taphonomy is covered by Pat Shipman in *Life History of a Fossil: An Introduction to Taphonomy and Paleoecology* and by Lewis Binford in *Bones: Ancient Men and Modern Myths*.

The new techniques in genetics applied to human evolution is one of the topics in *Blueprints: Solving the Mystery of Evolution* by Maitland Edey and Donald Johanson.

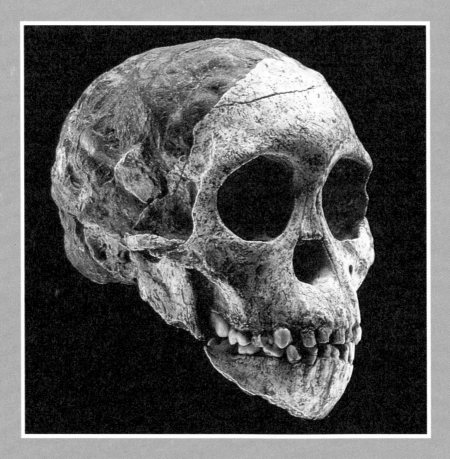

CHAPTER

10

EVOLUTION OF THE HOMINIDS

. . . there are no final
words. Human origins
will always be
enigmatic.
—Donald Johanson

P aleoanthropologists observe present-day species and the fossilized remnants of other species to try to reconstruct the biological past. Similarly, physicists observe and measure the universe as we see it today in an attempt to understand its origin and evolution. Their methods of observation and measurement are highly technical and are considered essentially accurate. Therefore, we know the distances to the stars, the speed with which those stars are moving away from us, and even their chemical makeup.

When these individual pieces of data are put together, however, the story is often confusing and puzzling. Recently, for example, some new estimates of the age of the universe indicate that the universe is *younger* than some of the stars it contains. This obviously can't be. Either some of the observational or measurement techniques are wrong, or they are less accurate than we thought, or different groups of scientists have interpreted the data differently, or—just maybe—the universe is more complicated than we have imagined.

The study of human evolution is also a complicated venture. We have many thousands of individual pieces of data, each observed, measured, dated, and analyzed according to the very latest technologies. But when we try to put them all together, we come up with disagreements, contradictions, and often several equally plausible interpretations. This chapter and the two that follow will give you the most current ideas about our evolution, including all the missing pieces and possible interpretations—at least the ones based on scientific inquiry. We will address the following questions:

What is the evolutionary history of the primates?

When, and under what circumstances, did the hominids evolve, and why was bipedalism so important?

What do we know about the first members of the genus *Homo?*

THE ORIGIN AND EVOLUTION OF THE PRIMATES

There are a large number of fossil specimens of primates, but the fossil record is still spotty. Our identifications of over half of all extinct primate species are based on fragmentary remains, mostly pieces of jaw or sometimes just teeth. Although a particular extinct species may be represented by many specimens, fossils of its contemporaries are lacking, giving us no basis for comparison. There are large gaps in the primate fossil record. Some periods are represented by many fossils, but they all come from one or two sites. Still, we can put together a general, if tentative, picture of the course of primate evolution (Figure 10.1).

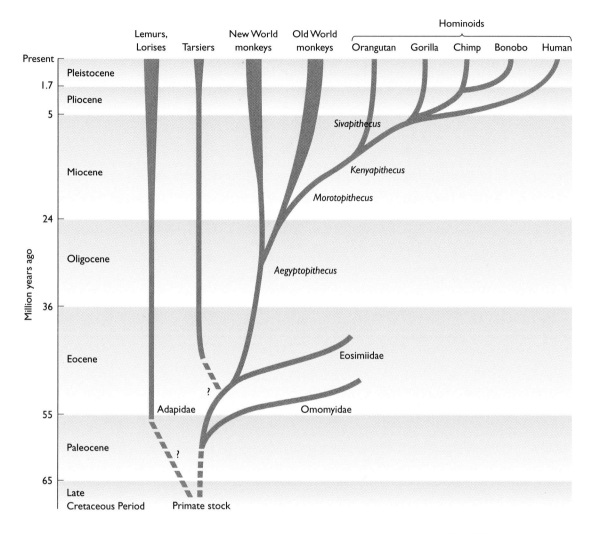

FIGURE 10.1
Simplified evolutionary tree for the primates, with major geological epochs and dates. Question marks and dashed lines indicate insufficient data to establish evolutionary relationships. This represents one of several possible interpretations.

We have few fossils that tell us about the earliest stages of primate evolution. Evidence includes only a few primatelike teeth from Montana dated at 65 million years ago (mya) and some 60-million-year-old bones from Wyoming that have primate features related to climbing behavior. Remember that, at the time, North America and Eurasia were still very close together and possibly still connected in some locations (see Figure 6.6), so the primates probably originated on the large northern landmass called Laurasia, not on what is *now* North America.

Undisputed primates appear about 55 mya. The traits that we associate in modern primates with an arboreal environment (see Chapter 7) may not have first evolved specifically to facilitate that adaptation. After all,

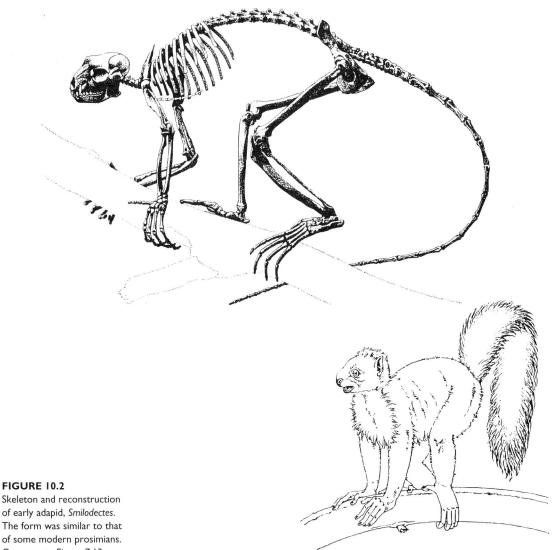

FIGURE 10.2
Skeleton and reconstruction of early adapid, *Smilodectes*. The form was similar to that of some modern prosimians. Compare to Figure 7.13.

other mammals that do not possess these traits are also arboreal. Anthropologist Matt Cartmill (1992) suggests that prehensile extremities and stereoscopic vision may have evolved to aid leaping as a means of locomotion in the forest canopy or the shrub-layer undergrowth and to promote fruit-eating and "visually directed predation" on insects. Modern mouse lemurs, lorises, and tarsiers, for example, all track insects by sight and seize them by hand. As the primates evolved, these basic traits proved a useful adaptive theme for life in the trees.

The early primates come in two groups, both found in North America, Europe, Asia, and Africa. One group, the Adapidae, are lemurlike and so are thought to be ancestral to modern lemurs and lorises (Figure 10.2). The other group, the Omomyidae, are tarsierlike. They may date back as

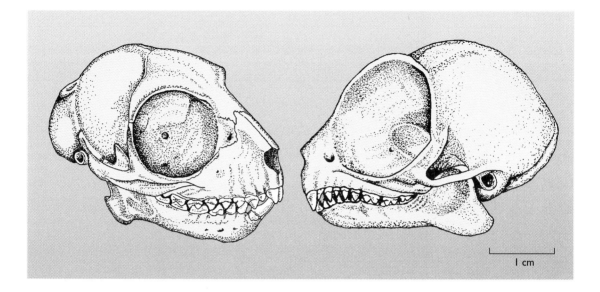

1 cm

FIGURE 10.3
Fossil omomyid, *Necrolemur* (left), compared with modern tarsier (see Figure 7.14).

far as 60 mya and may be ancestral to both tarsiers and anthropoids (Figure 10.3, and see Figure 7.14). A recently discovered group, the Eosimiidae from Asia, may represent the more direct ancestors of monkeys, apes, and hominids (Kay et al. 1997). Important evolutionary shifts that mark the origin of the anthropoids were a change from a nocturnal lifestyle to a diurnal one, less leaping and more climbing through the trees with all fours, and a more herbivorous diet with less emphasis on insects.

By the time the omomyids were evolving, the Eastern and Western Hemispheres were completely separate. We know that all modern New World primates are monkeys, but there are very few monkey fossils from the New World, mostly because the jungle environment leads to quick and complete scavenging or decay of dead animals. Thus, we don't know for sure how the evolution of the primates proceeded in the Western Hemisphere. There are two views on the subject. The first is that the early New World prosimians moved into Central and South America when those areas joined together with North America, and that the prosimians subsequently evolved into modern platyrrhines, the New World monkeys.

The second view is that early monkeys from the Old World "rafted" over to the Americas, floating on logs and branches or "island hopping" over a chain of volcanic islands when the two hemispheres were closer together. These early monkeys replaced any prosimians that still inhabited the New World, and they eventually evolved into the modern New World monkey species. Although there are some distinct differences (see Chapter 7), the basic similarity between the Old World and New World monkeys argues for a single origin and thus for the second scenario. In addition,

FIGURE 10.4

Skull of *Aegyptopithecus* from the Fayum in Egypt, considered an early monkeylike form that may be ancestral to later Old World anthropoids.

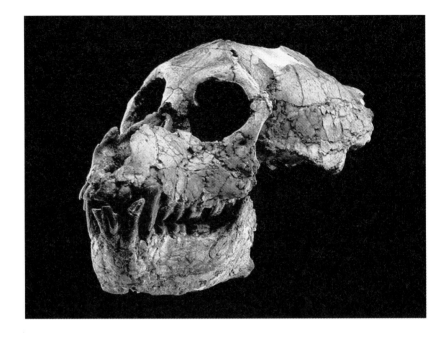

although most of the fossils from the New World are incomplete and therefore hard to evaluate, a recent find from Chile of a 20-million-year-old monkey skull is complete enough to show definite similarities to older monkey fossils from Africa.

We are most interested in primate evolution in the Old World. Much of the history of the Old World anthropoids comes from a single site, the depression formed by an ancient lake in the desert southwest of Cairo, Egypt, called the Fayum. Paleontologist Elwyn Simons began extensive investigations there in the early 1960s that continue today. From this valuable site come a number of monkeylike forms dated from 40 to 25 mya. The most important, perhaps, is *Aegyptopithecus,* from about 34 mya (Figure 10.4). This 10-pound primate shows anthropoid traits as well as several features of the teeth, braincase, and skull that resemble later hominoids (apes and hominids). It may be ancestral, then, to all the modern Old World anthropoids.

As the early anthropoids expanded, they outcompeted the prosimians and pushed these more primitive primates into marginal areas. Most prosimians now live—as endangered species—on the island of Madagascar, which they probably reached by rafting, possibly aided by a land bridge. No other primates invaded Madagascar until humans got there.

Apes appear in the fossil record about 23 mya. We refer to these earliest apes as "dental apes" because it is their teeth, rather than their overall anatomy, that resemble those of modern apes. Especially important is a feature of the molar teeth found only in hominoids and no other primates. It is called the Y-5 cusp pattern (Figure 10.5).

Between 23 and 5 million years ago, there were an estimated thirty or more different types of apes—larger-bodied, tailless, larger-brained primates. Only one lineage, however, gave rise to the modern apes and hominids. Evidence has been scanty, but new fossil finds point to two African genera as candidates for the earliest hominoid (Figure 10.6). *Kenyapithecus*, from 14 mya, has some modern ape features of the jaw, face, and teeth. New fossils of this species indicate other similarities in the arm and ankle bones that are related to the modern chimpanzee's abilities to hang in trees and to rotate the foot, which permits walking flat-footed on the ground and grasping (McCrossin 1997).

A more ancient and more arboreal form, *Morotopithecus* from Uganda, data at 20 mya, also shows similarities. It has a mobile shoulder joint that would have aided in hanging from trees by the arms, as chimps and orangutans do, and vertebrae that suggest a short, stiff spine, a feature of modern apes that allows them occasional upright posture (Gebo 1997).

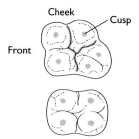

FIGURE 10.5
Y-5 cusp pattern found only in hominoids, and the four-cusp pattern found in all anthropoids. The chewing surface is shown. A look in the mirror will probably give you a first-hand glimpse of a Y-5 tooth.

FIGURE 10.6
Artist's conceptions of *Kenyapithecus* (left) from 14 million years ago and *Morotopithecus* from 20 mya. Both these early African apes have been proposed as the earliest known representative of the ape line that led to modern hominoids.

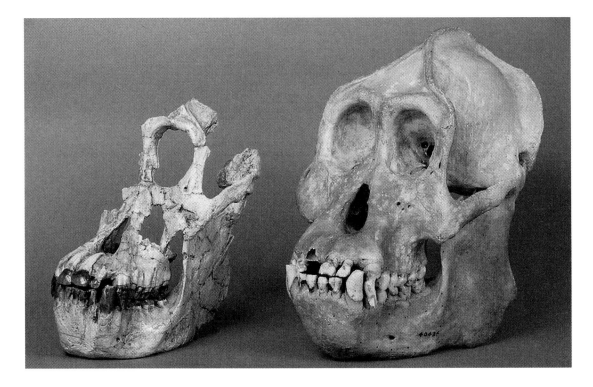

FIGURE 10.7
Skull of *Sivapithecus* (left) compared to that of a modern orangutan. They are essentially identical.

Starting about 12 mya, we find fossils of more ground-dwelling, open-country apes, whose larger back teeth with thicker enamel point to a more mixed vegetable diet that included harder foods such as nuts. Fossils of these apes have been found in Africa, India, Pakistan, China, Turkey, Hungary, and Greece. First evidence consisted of teeth and partial jaws, and an early interpretation claimed they possessed hominid traits. We know now they are too old to be hominids, and as more complete fossils have been recovered, it has become clear they are indeed apes. One group from India and Pakistan, *Sivapithecus*, shares features with the modern orangutan and so is most likely an ancestor of that species (Figure 10.7). A new form from Turkey, *Ankarapithecus*, dated at 9.8 mya, also shows similarities to this group.

Another form, however, *Ouranopithecus*, so far only found in Greece and dated at 10 to 9 mya, shares some features with hominids. Though clearly an ape, about the size of a female gorilla, it is thought by some to be a good candidate for a member of the ape line that eventually led to the hominids (De Bonis and Koufos 1994).

We can't leave this discussion without noting perhaps the most famous, and the biggest, sivapithecid—indeed, the biggest primate ever. It is a giant ape whose fossils have been found in China, northern India, and

Vietnam called, appropriately, *Gigantopithecus* (see Figure 7.4). So far, only jaws and teeth have been found, but estimates from these indicate this primate may have been 10 to 12 feet tall when standing upright and may have weighed from 700 to 1200 pounds. Evidence from the teeth indicate that it was, like the gorilla, a vegetarian. Gigantopithecus lived from about 7 mya to perhaps as recently as 300,000 years ago, recently enough to have possibly encountered modern humans. (One can't help but wonder if these creatures, or at least their bones, may have given rise to legends of the famous "abominable snowman," or yeti, from the Himalayas. In any case, however, there is absolutely no indication that they are still around.)

Current evidence indicates that apes evolved in Africa and Europe about 20 mya and diverged subsequently into a number of evolutionary lines all over the Old World. Gradually, these lines decreased, leaving relatively few forms to evolve into the modern hominoids. One line that we are fairly sure of is that from *Sivapithecus* to modern orangutans. Some African form or an African population of that form gave rise to the line leading to modern African apes and hominids.

THE FIRST HOMINIDS: THE BIPEDAL PRIMATE

The first evidence from the dawn of hominid evolution came in 1925. South African anatomist Raymond Dart was given a fossil found in a limestone quarry at a site called Taung ("place of the lion"). It took Dart seventy-three days to separate the fossil from the limestone around it. When freed, it revealed the face and braincase of a young apelike primate (Figure 10.8), but with two important differences. First, the canine teeth, long and large in apes with gaps to accomodate them when the jaws are shut, were no bigger than those of a human child. Second was the position of the **foramen magnum.** This is the hole in the base of the skull through which the spinal cord extends from the brain, and around the outside of which the top vertebra articulates. In the Taung specimen, this hole was well underneath the skull rather than toward the back, as in apes, indicating an upright, bipedal posture rather than a quadrupedal one. Dart hypothesized that the "Taung Baby," as it came to be known, was an intermediate between apes and hominids. Nevertheless, he named it *Australopithecus africanus*, the "southern ape of Africa"; because of its many apelike traits, he wasn't ready to classify it in the human family.

Further finds in Africa substantiated Dart's assessment of the anatomy of his fossil and his opinion that it represented a new type of primate. They also made it clear that *Australopithecus*, rather than being an intermediary, was, in fact, a hominid, a bipedal primate. (The rules of scientific nomenclature, or taxonomic names, however, require that first-used names

foramen magnum: The hole in the base of the skull through which the spinal cord emerges and around the outside of which the top vertebra articulates.

FIGURE 10.8
The "Taung Baby," the first specimen of *Australopithecus*. Note the naturally formed cast of the brain.

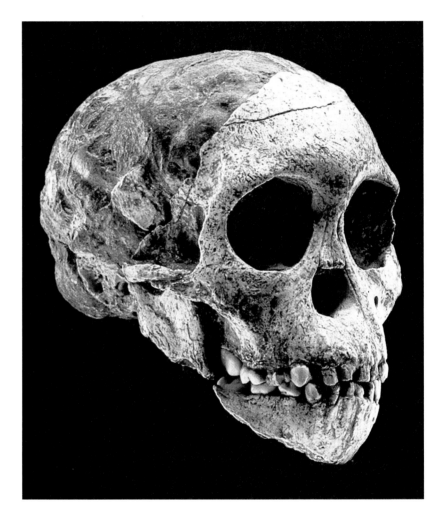

stick even if they later prove to be descriptively inaccurate. Thus, these hominids are still named "southern apes.")

The story of the discoveries and various interpretations of the fossil hominids from the first years of hominid evolution is fascinating in itself. Several of the books listed at the end of the chapter tell that story. Here, we'll look at the story as it stands today. There is still no general agreement on exactly how this part of our evolutionary tree looks, but anthropologists have found fossils with well-established dates (Table 10.1) and locations (Figure 10.9).

First, a general orientation. All the fossils discussed here belong to family Hominidae. Within that family anthropologists now recognize four defined genera, *Ardipithecus*, *Australopithecus*, *Paranthropus*, and *Homo*.

TABLE 10.1
List of Early Fossil Hominid Species*

	A. anamensis	A. afarensis	A. africanus	P. robustus	P. boisei	Early Homo
Dates	4.2–3.9 mya	4–3 mya	3–2.3 mya	2.2–1.5 mya (?)	2.2–1 mya (excludes Black Skull)	2.3–1.6 mya
Sites	Lake Turkana	Hadar Omo Laetoli	Taung Sterkfontein Makapansgat Lake Turkana (?) Omo (?)	Kromdraai Swartkrans	Olduvai Lake Turkana Ethiopia	Olduvai Lake Turkana Omo Sterkfontein (?) Swartkrans (?)
Cranial capacity (in ml)	(no data)	380–500 $\bar{x} = 440$	435–530 $\bar{x} = 450$	520 (based on one specimen)	500–530 $\bar{x} = 515$	500–800 $\bar{x} = 680$
Size (average, in lb.)	114	110	100	105	101	89
Skull	Canines large, but hominidlike canine roots More apelike chin than in afarensis Tooth rows parallel as in apes	Very prognathous Receding chin Large teeth Pointed canine with gap Shape of tooth row between those of ape and human Hint of crest	Less prognathous than in afarensis Jaw more rounded Large back teeth Canines smaller than in robustus, larger than in afarensis No crest	Heavy jaws Small canines and front teeth Large back teeth Definite crest	Very large jaws Very large back teeth Large crest	Flatter face Less sloping forehead Teeth similar to africanus's No crest
Postcranial skeleton	Bipedal knee and ankle joints Fibula intermediate between ape and hominid	Long arms Short thumb Curved fingers and toes Bipedal	Similar to A. afarensis	Hands and feet more like those of modern humans Retention of long arms	Similar to P. robustus	Limited evidence Retention of long arms Maybe retention of primitive features of hand and foot

*Excludes *Ardipithecus ramidus* and *Australopithecus bahrelghazalia*, which are still under study.

Source: K. L. Feder and M. A. Park, *Human Antiquity: An Introduction to Physical Anthropology and Archaeology*, 3rd ed. (Mountain View, Calif.: Mayfield, 1997).

FIGURE 10.9
Map of early fossil hominid
sites.

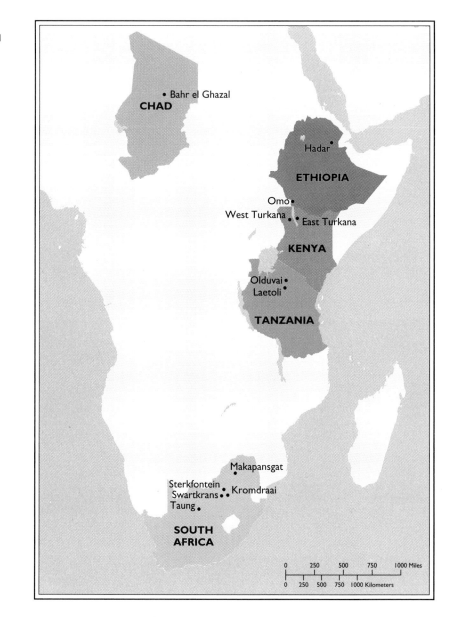

Only the last genus still exists; the other three are extinct. These groups
may be distinguished by the following definitions, on which I'll elaborate:

Family Hominidae: the bipedal primates

Genus *Ardipithecus:* most apelike hominids

Genus *Australopithecus:* small-brained, gracile hominids with a
mixed vegetable diet

FIGURE 10.10
Fossil tooth and a portion of jaw from *Ardipithecus ramidus*.

Genus *Paranthropus*: small-brained, robust hominids with a grassland vegetable diet

Genus *Homo*: large-brained, omnivorous hominids

It should be noted that authorities are about evenly divided on the issue of whether *Paranthropus* is a separate genus or is part of *Australopithecus*. I will use the first option here, in part because I think the evidence warrants it and in part because using a different name makes understanding the evolutionary trends of this complex period of time a little easier.

The earliest hominid fossils discovered so far are among those most recently found. First discovered in Ethiopia in 1992 and 1993, the finds consisted of seventeen fossil fragments including some arm bones, two skull bases, a child's mandible, and some teeth (Figure 10.10). These fossils were different enough from any found previously to warrant creating a fourth hominid genus, and they were called *Ardipithecus ramidus* (the genus name means "ground ape" and the species name means "root" in the local language). The fossils are dated at 4.4 mya. These are the fossils, mentioned in Chapter 9, that had been "ravaged by carnivores." (The only other hominid remains found from between 5 and 4 mya were few,

FIGURE 10.11

A mandible (*left*) and maxilla of *Australopithecus anamensis.* The chinless jaw is apelike, but the vertical root of the canine is clearly a hominid trait (the canine roots of apes are angled).

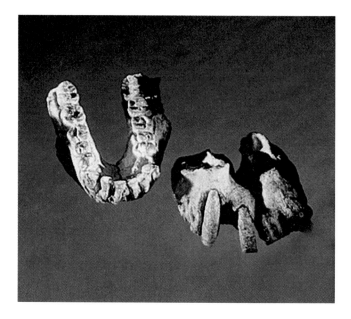

fragmentary, in some cases poorly dated, and their taxonomy not generally agreed upon.)

In 1994, more fossil bones were recovered in Ethiopia, close to the first site. These consisted of ninety fragments representing about 45 percent of a skeleton, including the telltale pelvis, leg, ankle, and foot. These new finds, however, still await published analysis.

Ardipithecus ramidus is considered a hominid because the foramen magnum is more forward than in apes, and because of some detailed features of the elbow joint and the teeth. At the same time, it is "the most apelike hominid ancestor known" (White et al. 1994). Among other things, the canine teeth are larger, compared to the other teeth, than in later hominids. It seems, then, that *ramidus* is very close to the time when the hominids and the apes split and so may be, as the name implies, the "root" hominid species.

However, these fossils remain somewhat enigmatic for the moment. Although the evidence from the foramen magnum indicates that they were bipedal, conclusive evidence from the legs, pelvis, and feet must wait until the newest finds can be fully examined and the results published. Furthermore, along with the fossils of *ramidus* were those of many forest mammals as well as fossilized seeds and wood. It appears *Ardipithecus ramidus* lived in the forests and not on the open plains or savannas, as did the later hominids. As you'll see, all our traditional interpretations of early hominid evolution have been linked to a savanna environment. I'll address this potential problem later.

In August 1995, the newest hominid species was announced (Leakey et al. 1995). Called *Australopithecus anamensis*, it consists, so far, of twenty-one specimens from the Lake Turkana region of Kenya (*anam* means "lake"), including jaws, teeth, a skull fragment, a tibia, and a humerus (Figure 10.11). The specimens are dated at 4.2 to 3.9 mya. Although they exhibit apelike features such as large canine teeth, the root of the canine is vertical as in later hominids rather than angled as in apes, and the tooth enamel is thicker than in apes or in *Ardipithecus ramidus*, and more like in later hominids. Most notably, the leg bones are clearly those of a biped. There appears to be some consensus that this may represent the ancestor of all later hominids, with *Ardipithecus ramidus* representing a side branch of the hominid family.

The next species, by contrast, is well established, and its nature is more generally agreed upon. The species is *Australopithecus afarensis*, and its first and most famous specimen is the 3.2-million-year-old skeleton, also from Ethiopia, known as "Lucy" (Figure 10.12), found in 1974 by Donald Johanson and his team. Lucy is remarkable because, as old as she is, nearly 40 percent of her skeleton was preserved, and all parts of her body were well represented except the cranium, the remains of which are fragmentary. We know—based on the kind of osteological analysis described in Chapter 9—that she was a female and that she stood about 3 feet, 8 inches and weighed about 65 pounds. Although there is some disagreement about details, there is no doubt that Lucy and her kind were bipeds and that they can be grouped together as a distinct species.

Other fragmentary specimens, including a portion of a skull dated at 3.9 mya, were unearthed in Ethiopia and Tanzania and assigned to this species. Based on this evidence, a reconstruction of the head of A. *afarensis* was attempted, but a single complete fossil skull was not found until 1992. In February of that year, Donald Johanson and his team discovered 200 skull fragments, again from Ethiopia. Once reconstructed, the skull closely resembled the previously discovered fragments, except that it was large and rugged, probably the skull of a male. It was dated at about 3 mya (Figure 10.13).

The evidence, so far—over 300 specimens—indicates that there was a single hominid species, A. *afarensis*, that lived from 4 million to 3 million years ago. The great variation in size of the specimens has led some to suggest that there were several species, but the size differences fit the pattern of sexual dimorphism of apes and other early hominids. We are probably looking at the remains of both males (for example, the skull found in 1992) and females (for example, Lucy) of one species.

However, in 1995 a French team found the remains of a partial hominid jaw in Chad, in north-central Africa, dated at 3.5 to 3 mya. The team recently announced that this find represents a second species of hominid living during that time (Simons 1996). The species has been named

FIGURE 10.12
The skeleton of "Lucy," the first specimen of A. *afarensis*.

FIGURE 10.13
Reconstructed by paleoan-
thropologists Bill Kimbel and
Yoel Rak, this skull shows us
the face of *Australopithecus
afarensis*. This individual was
a large male whose worn
teeth indicate he was probably fairly old. He was notably
larger than Lucy, showing
that this early hominid species exhibited sexual
dimorphism.

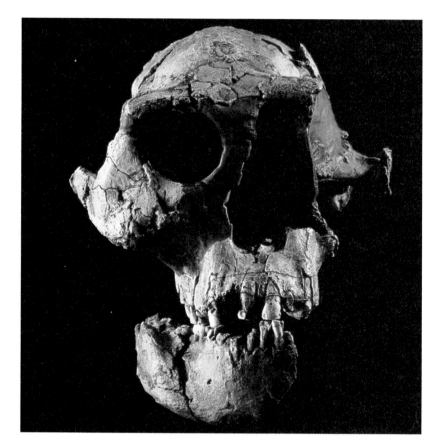

Australopithecus bahrelghazalia (based on an Arab name for a nearby river-
bed), and it suggests that early hominids were more widely spread on the
continent than previously thought. Full acceptance of this classification
and the implications of the fossil await further study.

What did Lucy and her kin look like? They might be described as
"bipedal apes." Their average brain size was about 440 ml (milliliters—a
milliliter is about one-third of a fluid ounce), close to the average for
chimpanzees and with the same maximum size of about 500 ml. They have
the **prognathism** (projection of the lower face and jaws), the pointy canine
teeth, and the gaps in the tooth rows characteristic of apes, though the
canine teeth and gaps are not as pronounced as in apes. There is a hint
of a sagittal crest, a ridge of bone along the top of the skull for the attachment of major chewing muscles. Gorillas have these crests (Figure
10.14). In modern humans, these muscles are attached on the side of the
head. (Put your hand on your head, about 2 inches above your ears, and
then clench and unclench your teeth. You'll feel the muscle.)

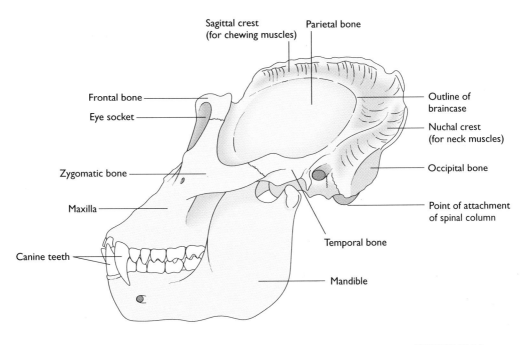

Sagittal crest
(for chewing muscles)

Parietal bone

Frontal bone

Eye socket

Zygomatic bone

Maxilla

Canine teeth

Outline of
braincase

Nuchal crest
(for neck muscles)

Occipital bone

Point of attachment
of spinal column

Temporal bone

Mandible

FIGURE 10.14
Skull of a male gorilla. Compare the sagittal crest with those in Figures 10.19, 10.21, and 10.22.

The arms of A. *afarensis* are about in the same proportion to the torso as are the arms of modern humans, but the legs are relatively shorter, making the arms functionally longer. The hands and feet are relatively longer and show some curvature of the bones. The bones of the shoulders and arms show evidence of heavy musculature. These individuals, though adapted for bipedal walking on the ground, were still good tree climbers.

At first, there was some disagreement as to just how bipedal *afarensis* was, especially considering the apelike nature of much of the rest of its anatomy. All the interpretations, after all, were based on fossilized bones; no one, obviously, had ever actually seen one walk. But in 1976, Mary Leakey recovered the next best thing at a site in Tanzania called Laetoli—a set of footprints made in a fresh layer of volcanic ash that quickly hardened and preserved for us a striking picture of an event that took place 3.7 mya. Two hominids, one large, one small, had walked side-by-side through the ash shortly after an eruption. The hominids' footprints show an anatomy and stride no different from ours today (Figure 10.15).

Clearly, then, bipedalism was the first hominid trait to evolve. We know this because it is, essentially, the only hominid trait in an organism that is otherwise an ape. If bipedalism had evolved slowly, one would expect some other traits to have changed as well. Therefore, bipedalism may be seen as the adaptation that began our family of primates.

prognathism: The jutting forward of the lower face and jaw area.

FIGURE 10.15
The Laetoli footprints from Tanzania, and the reconstruction of the probable scene of their origin at the American Museum of Natural History in New York City.

BIPEDALISM

What's the benefit of standing upright? Under what circumstances was it selected for in our earliest ancestors? Not many creatures use this form of locomotion. Kangaroos do (and many dinosaurs did), but they also use their tails for balance and support. Birds are bipedal, but their feet are able to grasp; they can even sleep standing up. We, on the other hand, attempt to balance our bodies vertically on two small points of contact with the ground. When we walk, we throw ourselves off balance, swing one leg forward, and catch ourselves before we fall flat on our faces. We can't run particularly fast, and we aren't very stable on rough or slippery surfaces. Let's work through an explanation of this early adaptation using the scientific approach of posing questions, suggesting answers, and then testing the logic of those answers.

Remembering that natural selection does not create new traits, but selects from variation already present, we can again look to our close relatives for clues about the beginnings of our family's characteristic posture and locomotion. Most primates, in fact, can walk bipedally on occasion. It has even recently been shown that *Oreopithecus,* an apelike primate from 9 to 7 million years ago, could walk bipedally, at least for short distances. Its lower back, knee, and parts of its pelvis resembled those of early hominids, but its foot was entirely different, with a big toe that stuck out 90° from the others, making a sort of "tripod" (Bower 1997).

The best occasional bipeds are, not surprisingly, the chimpanzees and bonobos, and one of the most common motivations for these quadrupeds to walk upright is the need to use the arms and hands for something other than locomotion—usually to carry something (see Figure 8.6). Assuming that this behavior was true of our common ancestor, we may then offer a general explanation of our bipedalism by saying that this ability was selected for among some group of apes because it conferred an adaptive and reproductive advantage in that group's environment.

Most specimens of hominids from Africa between 4 and 1 million years ago have been found in areas that are, or were at the time, savannas—the great open grasslands that characterize much of eastern and southern Africa today (Figure 10.16). The savannas were even more extensive during the period in question, as the great deserts of North Africa are fairly recent. Could bipedalism be related to this environment?

To a primate, the savannas present a very different set of problems than do the forests. Primates are basically vegetable eaters. Although there are plenty of plants on the savannas, there are not as many that can be utilized by the digestive systems of most primates. Most primates cannot digest cellulose as can the ungulates, grazing animals such as the African savanna antelopes. Edible plants or plants with edible parts are not as

FIGURE 10.16
The climatic zones of Africa
today, except for the large
deserts of the north and
south, were similar when
hominid evolution began
5 mya.

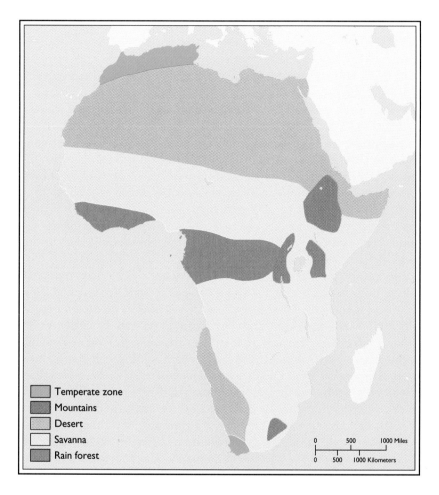

Temperate zone
Mountains
Desert
Savanna
Rain forest

concentrated on the open plains, so primates have to travel over a wider
area to find food. The savannas are more affected by seasonal change than
are the forests, so there may be greater variation in the food supply between
the wet and dry seasons. Finally, there is more danger involved in acquiring
these widely dispersed foods on the savannas. Lions, leopards, cheetahs,
wild dogs, hyenas, and other predators are more than happy to make a
meal out of a small primate, as we saw in Chapter 9.

There are, of course, sources of meat on the savannas. Chimpanzees
are known to hunt, kill, and eat other mammals. They are even known
to scavenge the kills of leopards found hanging in trees. It is unlikely,
though, that our earliest savanna ancestors hunted, and there is no physical evidence that they did. They may well, however, have scavenged kills,
and there is evidence for this, which we will cover later. But, even so, the

prey animals must be located, caught, killed, and then taken away and kept away from other predators or scavenged after the predators have finished. All these are dangerous enterprises on the plains.

Bipedalism, however, could have allowed our early ancestors to accomplish some of the above activities in greater safety and with greater efficiency. Freeing the arms and hands from locomotor activities means that food could be transported from open areas to safer locations like a grove of trees or a rock shelter. This would have been especially important if the food was part of an animal carcass, because other meat-eaters would also find it attractive. Children could be carried while mothers walked in search of food. Perhaps sticks and rocks were carried and thrown to scare predators and scavengers away from a kill.

It has also been proposed that bipedalism, by elevating the head, provides better views of potential sources of food and danger. The vertical orientation, according to another view, also helps cool the body by presenting a smaller target to the intense equatorial rays of the sun and by placing more of the body above the ground to catch what cooling air currents there may be. The savannas can be hot, and the heat built up by hours of steady walking in search of food needs to be dissipated. (This also may be the adaptive significance of another trait, at least of modern hominids—our relatively hairless bodies. Having no hair allows sweat to evaporate more quickly and cool the body more efficiently.)

Finally, data indicate that although bipedalism is an energy inefficient way of *running* compared to quadrupedalism, it is more efficient for walking. Long periods of steady walking in search of food would seem to require less energy if done upright. The importance of this has, however, been called into question (Steudel 1996). Remember that the first hominids did not walk bipedally quite like later members of our family and may not have been any more efficient at walking upright than are chimpanzees. Moreover, it is not certain that what makes our walking more efficient is simply our upright stance. Body mass is related as well. It may be that bipedalism had, initially, all the other advantages listed above and that, once it was established, further changes made it more energy efficient.

At least some of the above hypotheses can be offered as reasonable explanations of why individuals who were better bipeds were better adapted to life on the savannas. Bipeds could search for, find, and transport food to safety, with less heat buildup, less danger, and, perhaps, greater energy efficiency. But does this explain why bipedalism would have made some individuals more reproductively successful? Remember that reproductive success is the measure of natural selection. Simple survival and longevity are only part of it.

Once again, we may get a clue from our close relatives, the chimpanzees and bonobos. Although chimps normally have no need to share resources, they do share meat from a hunt, possibly because it is—in some chimp way—considered a luxury item. The bonobos, on the other hand, even share foods that are plentiful, which serves to avoid conflict and to establish and maintain peaceful coexistence within the group. Food sharing is, in a sense, a symbol of group peace and unity. Moreover, as you recall from Chapter 8, the bonobos use sex to strengthen and maintain group unity and to defuse tension. Sex for them is separate from purely reproductive activity. It has social and psychological meaning as well.

We might speculate that our early ancestors survived by the enhancement of adaptations that focus on peaceful cooperation and group unity. They shared resources, the acquisition of which was made easier and safer by selection for the ability to walk habitually upright. In addition, our sexual consciousness—the fact that, for us, sex is part of our psychological and social beings—may also, as in the bonobos, have both motivated and maintained group cohesion. Of course, sexual consciousness also contributed to the reproductive success of the individuals and thus, in the end, to the evolutionary success of the group.

Such a set of adaptations would certainly have been one way of surviving on the savannas. But two more questions come up. First, what about baboons, another successful savanna primate that survives in that environment *without* bipedalism and food sharing, and whose sexual activity is limited to the estrus periods of the females? Second, what about *Ardipithecus ramidus?* We don't know for certain at this point that they were bipedal. Supposing that they were, however, we need to ask *why* they were. Unlike many subsequent early hominids, they appear to have lived in the forests.

The first question can be answered by remembering that adaptations are relative to a particular species at a specific point in time in response to a specific environment. Just as the primate adaptations are not the *only* successful way of living a life in the trees, neither are the hominid adaptations the only way to survive on the savannas. The different responses of the baboons and the hominids simply show that there is more than one way to adapt to the same environment—even within the same general group of organisms. Even so, despite the important differences, both types of primates focused on social organization in adapting to the savannas.

The answer to the second question is that perhaps bipedalism was actually first selected for survival in the forests, not on the savannas. Bipedal walking is common among the bonobos, as is food sharing and sexual activity with social as well as reproductive meaning, yet the bonobos live in denser forests than do the chimpanzees. In fact, it has been suggested that the bonobos have undergone less evolutionary change than humans or chimpanzees and thus may most closely resemble the common ancestor of all three of these species (de Waal 1995). Their adaptations, then—

focusing on social unity—may simply have been the particular manner in which our ancestral group of apes responded to a forest environment. Later, in response to some change that required life on the savannas, those adaptations turned out to work well in that environment too.

Indeed, there is continuing debate as to just what sort of environmental change would explain the evolution of the hominids. One view (Vrba 1993) suggests that a decrease in global temperature between 6 and 5 mya made Africa drier, shrinking the forests and producing savannas. These changes resulted in the isolation of some populations of our ancestors in that environment and selection for the traits that would become the hallmarks of our family. A further consequence of this drying trend would have been an increased reliance on scavenged meat, a resource that would have been available year-round, in contrast to many plants that would have responded more to seasonal changes.

A second scenario (Coppens 1994) claims that the ancestors of the hominids and modern apes were isolated from one another not by a drastic climatic change but by a geological one—the formation of the Rift Valley in East Africa starting about 8 mya (Figure 10.17). Tectonic movements caused a sinking that formed the valley and a rising of mountains on its western rim. This caused a localized climatic change resulting in the area west of the valley remaining moist and forested, and that east of the valley turning drier and becoming savanna. Today, chimpanzees are found only to the west of the valley. Early hominid fossils, with the exception of the Chad find, are found only to the east.

Yet another view says that at least one site in Kenya reveals no evidence of an abrupt change, but rather indicates that East Africa was a "heterogeneous mosaic" of environments from forests to open plains at the time in question (Kingston et al. 1994:958). The early hominids may not have been so much forced out of the forests but instead may, in some more complex reaction, have taken advantage of new opportunities and less competition (at least from other hominoids) on the savannas. There, their bonobo-like forest adaptations proved equally useful and, over time, were enhanced by natural selection.

Some recent studies have supported the idea that bipedalism was originally a forest, not a savanna, adaptation. Reassessment of the environments of some important early hominid sites have shown them to be more forested than previously thought (see Shreeve 1996 for a summary). The Lake Turkana site where *Australopithecus anamensis* was found, for example, may have been in an arid area, but the lake itself was surrounded by forest. Lucy, the first specimen of A. *afarensis*, probably lived in a mixed forest and bushland area, as did some of the other members of this genus from South Africa. A. *bahrelghazalia*, the new find from Chad, is thought to have inhabited forests with grassy patches.

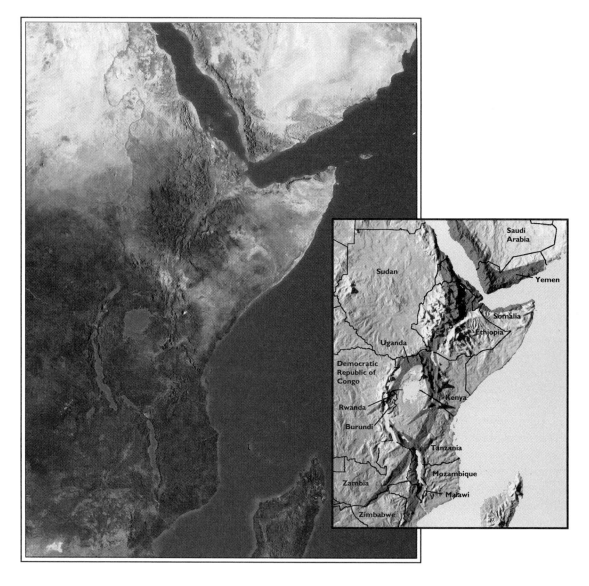

FIGURE 10.17
The Rift Valley. The formation of this valley some 8 million years ago produced major climatic changes that may have influenced hominid evolution.

How to reconcile all this evidence and these differing interpretations? Perhaps anthropologist Richard Potts (1996) has the answer. He says that, rather than climatic change occurring in one direction, there was an increase in the range of global climatic variation beginning 5 million years ago. This brought about great fluctuations in moisture and vegetation. He posits that the evolution of bipedality in the African hominids may have been a response to the presence of *both* terrestrial *and* arboreal settings at the same time and over time—that bipedalism and its associated behaviors

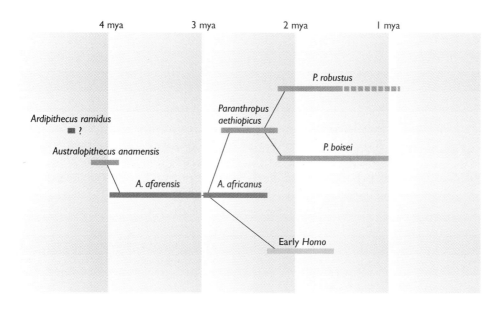

4 mya   3 mya   2 mya   1 mya

P. robustus

Ardipithecus ramidus
■ ?

Paranthropus
aethiopicus

Australopithecus anamensis

P. boisei

A. afarensis   A. africanus

Early Homo

FIGURE 10.18

Known species of early hominids with approximate time ranges. There are at least half a dozen hypotheses regarding the exact evolutionary relationships among these species, each with data and interpretations in its support. The lines here represent one reasonable scheme. (For a detailed comparison of alternative trees see Conroy 1997:245–53.)

afforded our ancestors greater adaptive flexibility "over a span of recurrent [environmental] extremes." He calls this "variability selection" and suggests it may also help account for events in hominid evolution to come.

The details concerning where we stand with our knowledge of the early evolution of our hominid family and its characteristic traits are still being debated. We do know, however, that by 4 mya, the hominid line had been established. We also know that the major adaptation of the hominids—the trait that distinguishes it from the other primates—is bipedalism. We can hypothesize that accompanying upright locomotion was an emphasis on group unity and survival facilitated by food sharing and perhaps by sexual activity separated from purely reproductive functions and linked to emotional, social, and personal relationships.

Whatever happened, it was successful. At least one hominid species was well ensconced on the plains of East Africa by 3 mya and from there our family began its adaptive radiation.

THE HOMINIDS EVOLVE

Somewhere around 3 mya, genus *Australopithecus* branched into at least two lineages, one leading to an extinct form of hominid and the other to the line that would eventually lead to modern humans (Figure 10.18 and refer to Figure 10.9 and Table 10.1).

The basic set of early hominid features represented by Lucy and her kin continued for another three-quarters of a million years. Though little changed from A. *afarensis*, the fossils representing the next period are still called by their original name, A. *africanus* (Dart's "southern ape of Africa"). The remains of this species have been found mostly in South Africa, but there are some fossils from Kenya and Ethiopia as well. They have the same body size and shape and the same brain size as A. *afarensis*. There are a few differences, however. Their faces are a bit less prognathous and they lack a sagittal crest. Their canine teeth are smaller, there are no gaps in the tooth row, and the tooth row is more rounded, as in a human rather than an ape.

The relative sizes and shapes of the teeth of *Australopithecus*, although on the whole larger than those of modern humans, indicate a mostly mixed vegetable diet of fruits and leaves. This is confirmed by taphonomic analysis of microscopic scratches and wear patterns on the teeth (see Figure 10.20). Though there is no direct evidence of meat eating, it is probable that they ate some small creatures and scavenged larger ones.

The essential similarity of A. *afarensis* and A. *africanus* suggests a plausible, and simple, interpretation. We may consider A. *africanus* as a continuation of A. *afarensis*, more widely distributed in South and possibly East Africa, and showing some evolutionary changes. It should be noted that this interpretation is not agreed upon by all investigators and remains hypothetical.

Two distinctly different types of hominid, however, were found to appear between 3 and 2 million years ago. One type retains the chimpanzee-sized brains and small bodies of *Australopithecus* but has evolved a notable robusticity in the areas of the skull involved with chewing. This is genus *Paranthropus*. As noted before, some authorities place these fossils in genus *Australopithecus*, but I will use *Paranthropus* both for clarity and because I lean toward that interpretation of current evidence.

The fossils representing the beginning of this genus are a single skull from Lake Turkana, Kenya, dubbed the "Black Skull" because of its dark color resulting from minerals in the ground (Figure 10.19), and some fragmentary fossils from Ethiopia. These fossils are grouped into a separate species, P. *aethiopicus*, and are dated at between 2.8 and 2.2 mya.

The Black Skull is striking for several reasons. First, at only 410 ml, it has the smallest adult hominid brain ever found. On the other hand, it has the largest sagittal crest of any hominid, the most prognathous face, and an extremely large area in the back of the mouth for the molar teeth. Although no teeth were found, its molars appear to have been four or five times the size of a modern human's.

The Black Skull represents the beginning of a second major type of hominid, sometimes referred to as "robust" hominids. Although they were pretty much the same as *Australopithecus* in brain and body size, the mem-

bers of genus *Paranthropus* were considerably more robust in all those fea-tures involved with chewing. The sagittal crests, broad, dished-out faces, large cheekbones, huge mandibles, and back teeth that are much larger relative to the front teeth—all point to a diet of large amounts of vegetable matter with an emphasis on hard, tough, gritty items like seeds, nuts, hard fruits, and tubers. This is confirmed by microscopic wear pattern analysis (Figure 10.20).

A little over 2 mya, two types of robust hominids appear. We may tentatively consider them two species that branched from the first robust form represented by *P. aethiopicus*. One species, *Paranthropus robustus*, is found in South Africa and dates between 2.2 and 1.5 mya or even later (Figure 10.21). It retains the body size of *Australopithecus*, but there is a slight increase in average brain capacity to about 520 ml. The jaws are heavy, the back teeth are large, and there is a sagittal crest—all indications of a mixed, tough vegetable diet. The crania, though, are obviously not as robust as in *P. aethiopicus*.

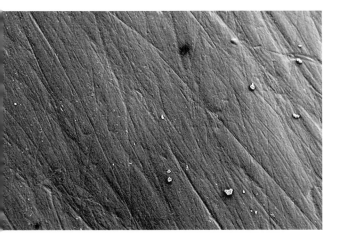 

FIGURE 10.20

Scanning electron microscope pictures of the surfaces of the teeth of early hominids. The enamel of the teeth of *Australopithecus africanus* (above) is polished and scratched, while that of *Paranthropus* is pitted and very rough. This is evidence of the hard, tough, gritty foods eaten by the latter.

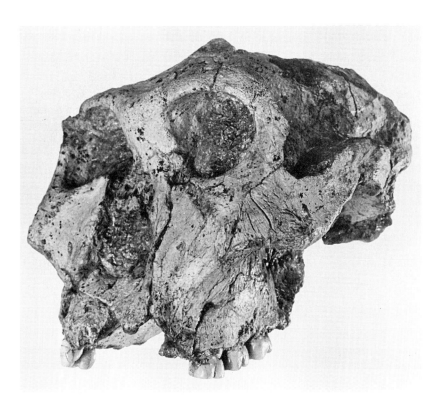

FIGURE 10.21

Paranthropus robustus from Swartkrans, South Africa. Note the remnant of a sagittal crest.

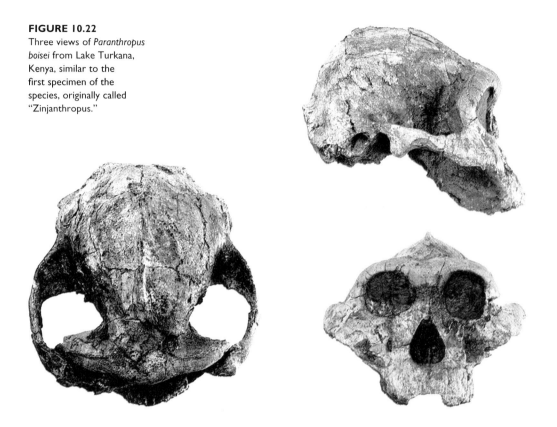

FIGURE 10.22

Three views of *Paranthropus boisei* from Lake Turkana, Kenya, similar to the first specimen of the species, originally called "Zinjanthropus."

The second robust species continues the extreme ruggedness of *P. aethiopicus*, though it is not quite as pronounced. Found in Tanzania, Kenya, and Ethiopia and existing from 2.2 to 1 mya, *Paranthropus boisei* shows features that, along with those of *aethiopicus*, are sometimes referred to as "hyperrobust" (Figure 10.22). The specimen that defined the species is the famous "Zinjanthropus," found by Mary and Louis Leakey in 1959. Dubbed "Nutcracker Man," this specimen showed extremely large jaws and back teeth and a large sagittal crest. Otherwise *P. boisei* has the body and brain size of the South African robust hominids.

A recent *P. boisei* fossil from Ethiopia (Suwa et al. 1997) consists of the first cranium of this species with an associated mandible. The largest known skull of the species, it comes from a new site that extends the species' known range in Africa and is clearly associated with a dry grassland environment. It also shows some physical differences from existing *boisei* fossils that indicate a considerable range of phenotypic variation within the species.

The second new hominid genus that appeared about 2.5 mya is the one to which modern humans belong, *Homo*. We will discuss the first species of our genus in the next section. For now, however, we need to account for the overall shape of the early hominid family "bush" (see again Figure 10.18). What might have caused the branching that founded the new genera of *Paranthropus* and *Homo?* What caused the extinction, around the same time, of genus *Australopithecus?* Finally, what might have caused the extinction of the *Paranthropus* species about a million years ago?

We can't answer these questions with certainty, but there is some evidence (Vrba 1993) that there were further cooling and drying fluctuations, accompanied by a decline of forests and expansion of savannas, at about 2.8 mya and again at about 900,000 years ago (see Kerr 1996 for differing viewpoints). The first change may have selected for both the robust hominids, increasingly adapted to a diet of the tough vegetables found on the open plains, and the genus *Homo*, with its increased brain size and ability to make stone tools. Both these sets of adaptations proved useful on the savannas. The remaining populations of *Australopithecus*, though originally adapted to the savannas, may not have been able to cope with these further changes and may, at the same time, have been out-competed by the new hominid lines.

Although it is intriguing to picture some sort of direct and violent confrontation that caused the extinction of the first hominid genus, and, subsequently, of *Paranthropus*, such a scenario is not necessary. When the niches of several similar species overlap by too great an extent, those species find themselves in ecological competition with one another. As a result, often all but one are pushed out, maybe to the point of extinction. This phenomenon is called **competitive exclusion,** and, with the help of the third climatic and vegetational fluctuation 900,000 years ago, may also account for the fact that genus *Homo*, from that point on, was the only surviving type of hominid.

THE FIRST MEMBERS OF GENUS *HOMO*

When the Leakeys found Zinjanthropus in 1959, they found some simple stone tools at the same level of Olduvai Gorge (Figure 10.23). At first, they thought Zinjanthropus had made the tools, but they began to feel that "Zinj" was too primitive to have made something so sophisticated.

These tools, called "Oldowan" after Olduvai Gorge, seem very simple to us. Also called pebble tools, they are nothing more than water-smoothed cobbles, up to 3 or 4 inches across, modified by knocking off a few chips from one or two faces to make a sharp edge. But, unlike the termite sticks of the chimpanzees, there is nothing in the raw material—the unmodified stone—that immediately suggests the tools that can

FIGURE 10.23
A sample of Oldowan tools. The two at lower right are flake tools. The others are core tools.

be made from it or the method of manufacture. A stone tool requires the maker to be able to imagine within the stone the tool he wants to make and to picture the process needed to make it. Making even a simple Oldowan tool is also a far more complex technological feat than stripping the leaves off a branch to make a stick narrow enough to fit down the hole of a termite mound. (I can attest to the difficulty.) This leap of the imagination and increase in technological skill are what make the first evidence of stone toolmaking so important.

In addition, there is evidence that the earliest stone toolmakers also realized that the flakes chipped off the stone could be used as tools for finer work like scraping small pieces of meat off of a bone. In anthropological terms, they made not only **core tools** but **flake tools** as well.

There is still no accepted evidence that either *Australopithecus* or *Paranthropus* made any tools, although it is likely that, like chimps, they made simple tools from branches or may have used unmodified stone. A recent study (Susman 1994) concluded that the thumbs of *Australopithecus* and *Paranthropus* had features that provide the dexterity required to make stone tools—although this conclusion has been challenged (Gibbons 1997a). Furthermore, some simple stone tools have recently been found in Ethiopia that date to 2.6 mya, 300,000 years earlier than the earliest fossil of *Homo* (Semaw 1997). Still, no hard evidence links any hominid other than *Homo* with the manufacture of stone implements.

It appeared then, and still does, that Zinjanthropus was not a good candidate for having been the maker of the pebble tools. Then, in 1961, the Leakeys found a second hominid from the same time period. Actually, they had found fragmentary fossils of this form in the same year that they found Zinjanthropus, but they had not been fully recognized as something different. They named the new form *Homo habilis*, "handy man" (Figure 10.24).

The reasons for including these fossils in genus *Homo* are twofold. First, there is a notable increase in brain size, from the average of about

competitive exclusion: When one species outcompetes others for the resources of a particular area.

core tools: Tools made by taking flakes off a stone nucleus.

flake tools: Tools made from the flakes removed from a core.

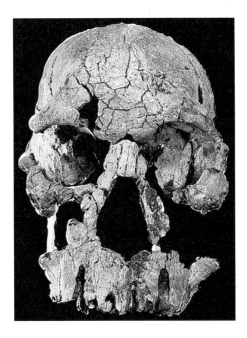
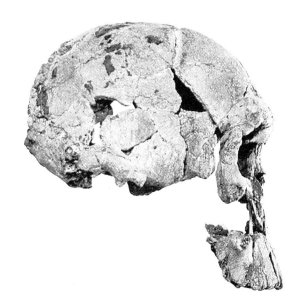

FIGURE 10.24

The well-known skull 1470 from Lake Turkana, Kenya, front and side views. Note the flatter face, smoother contours, lack of a sagittal crest, and more rounded braincase as compared to *Australopithecus* and *Paranthropus*. This fossil was at first classified as *Homo habilis,* and still is by some authorities. Others consider it a separate species, *Homo rudolfensis.*

480 ml for *Australopithecus* and *Paranthropus* to an average of 680 ml with a possible maximum of 800 ml in *H. habilis*. Second, the presence of the stone tools indicated that those larger brains were capable of a complexity of thought not seen in the record of the other two hominid genera. Thus, *H. habilis* seems to mark the beginning of a new trend in hominid evolution—toward bigger brains and greater intelligence. Fossils of *habilis* have now been found in Tanzania, Kenya, and Ethiopia, and perhaps from southern Africa, and have been dated at 2.3 to 1.5 mya.

Although some authorities consider all these fossils as belonging to a single species, *H. habilis*, others feel that some of the specimens from East Turkana, Kenya, are different enough to warrant placing them in a second species, *Homo rudolfensis*. The cranium pictured in Figure 10.24 is an example. Differences include a larger body and brain size than in *H. habilis,* and the lack of a torus (brow ridge) over the eyes (see Tattersall 1992 for a review of this debate).

Other than the larger braincase, early *Homo* still resembles the other two hominids in many respects. The face is a bit less prognathous, but the back teeth are still relatively large, the arms are proportionately long, and the bodies are small. In fact, a partial skeleton of *H. habilis* from Olduvai may be the smallest adult hominid fossil known. These primitive features, in fact, have led some to question whether or not these fossils even belong to genus *Homo*. Most researchers feel that they do, although their exact relationship to later members of our genus remains an open question.

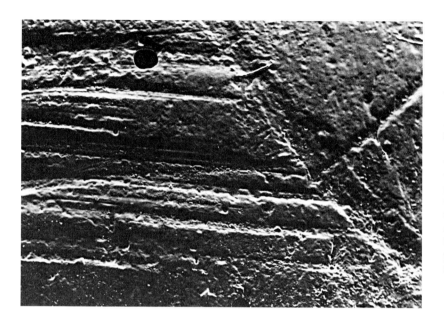

FIGURE 10.25
This micrograph of a fossil bone from Olduvai Gorge shows tool marks (the horizontal lines and the diagonal line beginning at the top of the photo) and a carnivore tooth mark (beginning on the right side and angled toward the center). In this case, the tooth mark overlies the tool mark, indicating that the hominids sliced meat off this part of the bone before a scavenger began eating.

What is it about the stone tools that may have given early *Homo* an edge? Paleoanthropologist Richard Leakey, the son of Louis and Mary, suggests that sharp stone tools allowed these hominids to more quickly cut meat and bones off a carcass, making the addition of meat to the diet through scavenging safer and more efficient. There is evidence for this suggestion.

Ten Olduvai sites from the *Homo habilis* period contain Oldowan tools, flakes, and animal bones. Once thought to be some sort of "home base," these areas are now considered "stone cache" sites (Potts 1984), where hominids left supplies of stones and to which they took scavenged animal remains for quick, safe processing and eating. Analysis indicates that these sites were used for short periods but repeatedly, as one would expect of such places.

Archaeologist Lewis Binford (1985) has analyzed the animal bones from these sites and has found that they are mostly the lower leg bones of antelopes. These bones carry little meat and, along with the skull, are about the only parts left after a large carnivore has finished eating. However, such bones are rich in marrow, so a major activity at the sites in question may have been to cut off what little meat remained on these bones and then to break them open for the nutritious marrow inside.

Finally, Pat Shipman has studied the taphonomy of these and other bones with a scanning electron microscope (1984, 1986). She found that marks left by cutting with stone tools were usually on the shafts of the bones as if pieces of meat were cut off, not near the joints as if an entire carcass had been butchered. Also, the hominid tool marks sometimes overlie carnivore tooth marks, showing that the carnivores had gotten there first (Figure 10.25).

Contemporary Reflections

Where Is the "Missing Link"?

A headline in the December 19, 1912, issue of *The New York Times* proclaimed: "Paleolithic Skull Is a Missing Link." The skull referred to was the now-infamous Piltdown Man, discovered in England, named *Eoanthropus* (the "dawn man")—and forty years later shown to be a fraud (see Feder 1998 for details). At the time, however, it was touted as the "missing link" because it possessed traits that were a perfect mix between those of human and ape. Its cranium was the shape and size of a modern human's and its mandible decidedly apelike. (In fact, it *was* the cranium of a modern human and the jaw of a modern orangutan—modified by the still-unidentified perpetrator to appear ancient.)

For much of the history of evolutionary thought, evolution was conceived of as a ladder or chain—progressing from primitive to modern, with living forms representing points on that chain. Even when it was generally acknowledged that humans had descended from apes, this evolution was thought of as unilinear—a single line of progress from ape to man. Thus, as we go back into the fossil record, we should eventually find something that is intermediate—half ape and half human. Since modern apes were thought of as the remnants of primitive forms that had never evolved further, the missing link (notice the chain metaphor) was conceived of as a mix of the traits of *modern* humans and *modern* apes. In our hubris, we were sure it was our big brains that separated us from the apes and that had evolved first, so the combination fabricated to concoct the Piltdown skull fit the bill perfectly. It had that big brain hallmark of humanity, perched on top of an otherwise apelike jaw.

Indeed, even when evolution was recognized as being a branching tree rather than a ladder or chain, the idea of fossil forms that were intermediates between modern species still held. Famed anatomist Sir Arthur Keith wrote in 1927 (p. 8) that "to unravel man's pedigree, we have to thread our way, not along the links of a chain, but through the meshes of a complicated network." Then, on the next page, he accepted the Piltdown find as authentic.

We recognize today that living species are not leftover primitive links on an evolutionary chain, but are, themselves, the products of evolution. A missing link in the traditional sense—between modern humans and modern apes—simply does not exist. What *does* exist is a common ancestor of humans and our closest relatives, the chimpanzees and bonobos—and it did not look exactly like any of those modern species. Granted, we have reason to think that the common ancestor resembled a bonobo or chimp more than a modern human, but this is just because evolution happens to have taken place at a more rapid pace in hominids than in the apes. The apes are still modern species.

So what we *can* look for is that common ancestor. It is a "link" not in the sense of a chain, but in the sense of being that point where our two evolutionary lines converge. At the moment, that form is still missing. But as we find older and older fossils, we are closing in on our common ancestor.

What will it look like? It should have characteristics shared by both hominids and pongids, but it will look, on the whole, like neither. Genetic evidence, as well as the fact that we have the very apelike form *Ardipithecus ramidus* from 4.4 million years ago, suggests that our common ancestor is around 5 million years old. In fact, anthropologists Robert Boyd and Joan B. Silk (1997:360–61) offer the possibility that *A. ramidus* might *be* the common ancestor.

So if you want to get a glimpse of the "missing link" in the modern sense, turn to Figure 10.10. It's probably *not* the common ancestor of modern apes and humans, but—so far—it's the closest we've come.

We may envision early *Homo* in small cooperative groups, maybe family groups, foraging on the savannas for plant foods and always on the lookout for a carnivore kill, watching for a group of scavengers gathered on the ground or a flock of vultures circling overhead. Their big brains allowed them to better understand their environment and to manipulate it, making imaginative and technologically advanced tools from stone. With these tools they may have cut apart the carcasses they found and took the pieces back to a safe place, maybe where they had stored more tools. There they cut the remaining meat off the bones and, using large hammer stones, smashed open the bones for marrow. It was no doubt a harsh life, but it was successful. The adaptive themes of bipedalism, large brains, social organization, and tool technology set the stage for the rest of hominid evolution.

Fossils indicate that *H. habilis* and *rudolfensis* were around for only about half a million years. Before they disappeared from the fossil record, a new hominid species came on the scene—one that continued and enhanced the trends of big brains and tool technology, adaptations that soon carried it all over the Old World.

SUMMARY

The primates are one of the earliest of the existing mammal groups to evolve after the mass extinction of 65 mya. They appear to have evolved first in what are now North America and Europe, but the success of their adaptations allowed them to radiate over the Old World and into the New World.

About 23 mya, the hominoids appear in the form of primitive apes. This successful group has left fossils all over Africa, Europe, and Asia. It is from one of the African apes that our family, Hominidae, branched off some 5 or 6 mya.

The evolution of habitual bipedalism marks the beginnings of our family and was the major distinguishing characteristic of this family for the first half of its time on earth. Bipedalism may have begun as part of one group's adaptation to the forests. We still see this trait—along with food sharing and sexual consciousness—in today's bonobos. However, these adaptations would also prove useful in Africa's increasingly variable environment, and the hominids soon were well established and radiated into three distinct groups, now classified as separate genera: *Australopithecus*, *Paranthropus*, and *Homo*.

The first two genera, *Australopithecus* and *Paranthropus*, with their chimp-sized brains, remained largely vegetarians and persisted until nearly a million years ago. However, they eventually lost out to a combination of environmental change and competition from the third hominid genus, *Homo,* with its bigger brain and ability to manipulate its environment both mentally and technologically, including the making of stone tools. These adaptations allowed the earliest members of our genus to more safely and efficiently exploit an abundant and reliable new food source, meat scavenged from natural deaths among the great herds of savanna animals. This adaptive base led, as we will see in the next chapter, to the further radiation of this type of hominid, eventually to become one of the earth's dominant species.

KEY TERMS

foramen magnum	competitive exclusion	flake tools
prognathism	core tools	

SUGGESTED READINGS

The primates and their evolution are covered in John G. Fleagle's *Primate Adaptations and Evolution.* The intriguing story of *Gigantopithecus* is told in *Other Origins: The Search for the Giant Ape in Human History* by Russell Ciochon, John Olsen, and Jamie James. For a more technical account of early primate evolution, see R. D. Martin's article in the May 20, 1993, issue of *Nature* called "Primate Origins: Plugging the Gaps."

The story of the study of the human fossil record and of some of the major recent discoveries is told in *Lucy: The Beginnings of Humankind* by Donald Johanson and Maitland Edey, and in a sequel, *Lucy's Child: The Discovery of a Human Ancestor* by Johanson and James Shreeve. A slightly different perspective on much of the same material is found in Leakey and Lewin's *Origins Reconsidered: In Search of What Makes Us Human.* The most recent coverage of this topic is Ian Tattersall's *The Fossil Trail: How We Know What We Think We Know About Human Evolution.* All these are authoritative, readable, and quite enjoyable.

A beautifully illustrated treatment of the subject, based on an exhibit at the American Museum of Natural History in New York is Ian Tattersall's *The Human Odyssey: Four Million Years of Evolution.*

A *National Geographic* series, "The Dawn of Humans," covering the 6 million years of our evolution, appears in the following issues: September 1995; January and March 1996; and February, May, July, and September 1997. The photographs and graphics are, as usual, superb.

It would be a good idea to see what a primary report on an important fossil looks like. A good example is the first report on the discovery of *Ardipithecus ramidus* (at the time, lumped into genus *Australopithecus*). It's by White et al. and appears in the September 22, 1994, issue of the British journal *Nature*.

For a nice summary of the different views on the possible climate change influences on human evolution, see the May 17, 1994, *New York Times* article titled "Fog Thickens on Climate and Origin of Humans" by John Noble Wilford. A nicely illustrated description of the Rift Valley explanation is by Yves Coppens in the May 1994 *Scientific American* titled "East Side Story: The Origin of Humankind."

THE EVOLUTION OF THE GENUS *HOMO*

The great tragedy of
Science—the slaying of
a beautiful hypothesis
by an ugly fact.
—Thomas Henry
Huxley

William of Ockham (c. 1285–c. 1349), an English philosopher, is credited with the principle popularly known as "Ockham's razor." The idea actually goes well back into human antiquity. Ockham said in effect that in logic no more things should be presumed to exist than are absolutely necessary. In other words, "keep it simple."

Ockham's idea, also known as the law of **parsimony,** says that if several possible explanations exist to account for something in science or philosophy, *the simplest is the best*, at least as a starting point. It further means that explanations should be based on facts that are already known rather than on facts that *may* exist. Of course, as new facts come to light, explanations will change, and we may find that the simplest explanation is not the best one.

Applied to the interpretation of the human fossil record, Ockham's razor means that we should begin by creating a tree of relationships among fossil species that has the fewest evolutionary lines allowed by the data. It also means that we should not create new taxonomic categories unless the data support them. Moreover, we should not suggest evolutionary relationships that include a species or other taxonomic unit that may *someday* be discovered when no evidence exists for it at present.

Thus, I believe that the family tree presented in Figure 10.18 is the most parsimonious given the existing data. Most anthropologists would have little or no objection to this model as a *possible* interpretation of that data.

Being simple, however, is not always so easy. There is no universal agreement on the dates of all the hominid fossils, nor on the interpretation of their phenotypic features or their taxonomic categories. There are, as noted, at least a half-dozen different trees for the early hominids, each—according to whoever proposed it—the most parsimonious. If you understand the tree presented in the last chapter, you should then be able to understand all the others if you choose to get deeper into the subject. The "correct" answer, if we can ever find it, awaits more data from the fossil record.

If it is hard for us to agree on the fossils that represent the first 2.5 million years of the human record, it gets worse when we address the latest 2 million. The reason is simple: This is the time during which our genus evolved. The data from these fossils matter to us because they will tell us just who we are and where we came from.

There are widely different interpretations of the nature, dates, and taxonomic affiliations of the human fossils from this period, and there are several divergent schools of thought regarding just what the family tree of our genus looks like. At stake in these discussions is the very identity of the species to which we all now belong. In this chapter, we will address the following questions:

How can we best go about describing and organizing the fossil evidence for the evolution of genus *Homo?*

What do we know about the dates, the distribution, and the physical appearance of the various groups of fossils assigned to this genus?

What can we say about their lives, particularly about their cultural behaviors?

LUMPERS AND SPLITTERS: AN ORGANIZING PLAN

Recall from Chapter 10 that there is disagreement over whether the early small-brained hominids all belong in one genus, *Australopithecus,* or in two genera, *Australopithecus* and *Paranthropus.* In this debate, those who support a single genus are "lumpers," and those who suggest two genera are "splitters." Similarly, placing all early *Homo* into species *habilis* would be lumping, and separating those fossils into *habilis* and a second species, *rudolfensis,* would be splitting.

Splitters tend to focus on differences among fossils and to express those differences by assigning the fossils in question to different taxonomic categories—different species if the distinctions are small, different genera if they are more pronounced. Lumpers, emphasizing the extent of the diversity present in some living species and genera, consider differences among some fossil groups to reflect similar diversity. They believe that the most parsimonious course is to lump fossils into the same taxon unless there is clear evidence that they should be split.

Both these approaches are, of course, provisional starting points. All good scientists understand that hypotheses are open to testing and that new data may require new models—sometimes radically new ones. Time and again, someone's "beautiful hypothesis" is slayed by some new "ugly fact." Moreover, no researcher is always a splitter or a lumper. One scientist's approach can vary from group to group. I favor the two-genus classification of the early hominids (*Australopithecus* and *Paranthropus*), but, as you will see, I favor (at the moment at least) a moderate lumping model with regard to genus *Homo.*

Subsequent to the early *habilis/rudolfensis* stage, the lumping and splitting factions are very much at odds regarding the evolution of genus *Homo.* At one extreme is the viewpoint that all members of *Homo* since *habilis/rudolfensis* belong to a single species, *Homo sapiens.* The other extreme claims six species within genus *Homo* during that 2-million-year period.

parsimony: Use of the simplest explanation in formulating a scientific hypothesis.

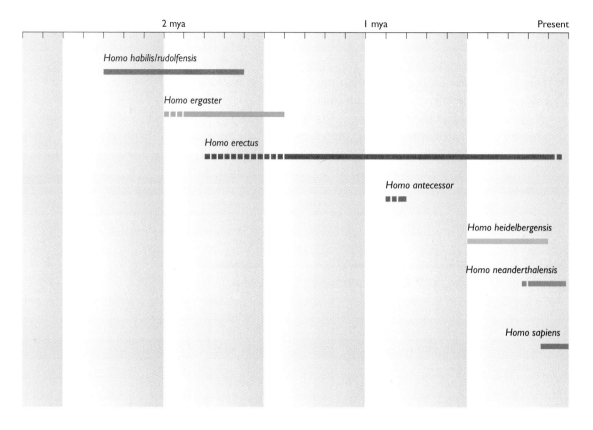

2 mya   I mya   Present

Homo habilis/rudolfensis

Homo ergaster

Homo erectus

Homo antecessor

Homo heidelbergensis

Homo neanderthalensis

Homo sapiens

FIGURE 11.1

Time line of species within genus *Homo* according to the most extreme splitting model. Dashes indicate that some evidence exists for extending the time range of that species as shown. Each species, of course, may be extended in time either way as more fossil evidence is recovered. This model does not necessarily reflect the author's views but is used to clearly sort the fossils into named groups recognized by some authorities as separate species. (Data from Tattersall 1995, 1997; Bermúdez de Castro et al. 1997; Gore 1997 a, b.)

Between these extremes are several intermediate points of view that recognize between one and six *Homo* species. Each model has evidence in its support, and each has opponents with reasonable counterarguments. The issue is by no means even close to being settled. These models are the topic of Chapter 12.

How, then, to begin discussing the fossil evidence for the evolution of our genus if authorities cannot even agree on the names? The simplest scheme would, of course, be the one that lumps all the fossils into *Homo sapiens*—that would certainly cut down on the taxonomic categories. But this view is fairly controversial, and some of those other species names have been in common use for many years. And such an approach would make it difficult to describe and discuss differences among groups of fossils that some authorities feel are enough to merit species distinction.

Instead, let's begin with the extreme splitter model—the currently most complex organization, which divides all later *Homo* into six species (Figure 11.1). We will describe and discuss these species in terms of their phenotypic features, dates, geographic distributions, and behaviors. Then, in the next chapter, we will discuss the various hypotheses for just how many species these groups represent and, most importantly, for how they are related evolutionarily. *Understand that I am not necessarily advocating this model.* I just feel that organizing our discussion in this order will allow

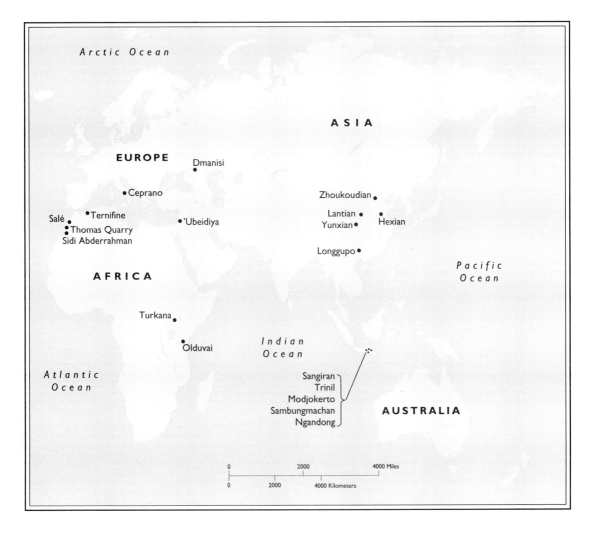

FIGURE 11.2
Map of *Homo erectus/
ergaster* sites.

us to more easily describe the other points of view by lumping species we have already named and defined. I like to think William of Ockham would have approved.

TO NEW LANDS

Most of the fossils in this stage of our story are included in species *Homo erectus*. Some authorities split the fossils of this group from Kenya into a second species, *Homo ergaster* (Figure 11.2 and Table 11.1).

The first finds ever of *H. erectus* were made in Java by the Dutch physician Eugene Dubois in 1891. Dubois chose Java to look for hominid fossils largely because he was already stationed there with the military. But the choice was also a logical one for the time, since most people thought that humans had first evolved in Asia, despite Darwin's clear suggestion that Africa was the hominid homeland. The idea that our evolutionary

TABLE 11.1
Major Fossils of *Homo ergaster* and *Homo erectus*
(the ? indicates that the species identification of that fossil is in question)

Country	Locality	Fossils	Crania	Age (million years)	Est. Brain Size (ml)
Homo ergaster					
Kenya	East Turkana	Cranial and postcranial fragments including mandibles and pelvis and long bone fragments	KNM-ER 3733 KNM-ER 3883	1.78 1.57	850 800
	West Turkana	Nearly complete juvenile individual	KNM-WT 15000	1.6	880
Homo erectus					
Algeria	Ternifine	Three mandibles and a skull	—	0.5–0.7	—
China	Hexian (Lontandong)	Partial skull	"Hexian Man"	0.25–0.5	1000
	Lantian (Gongwangling)	Cranial fragments, mandible	"Lantian Man"	>1	800
	Longgupo(?)	Mandible fragments	—	1.8	—
	Yunxian	Two crania	—	>0.35	—
	Zhoukoudian	Cranial and postcranial remains of 40 individuals	II III VI X XI XII Locality 13	<0.46 <0.46 <0.46 <0.46 <0.46 <0.46 0.7	1030 915 850 1225 1015 1030 —
Georgia	Dmanisi(?)	Mandible fragment, 16 teeth	—	1.8	—
Israel	'Ubeidiya	Fragments	—	1.4	—

line was originally African apparently did not sit well with many Europeans.

When Dubois found a skull cap and a diseased femur at the site of Trinil (Figure 11.3), he thought they represented the "missing link" between apes and humans, and he dubbed the specimens "Pithecanthropus erectus," the upright ape-man, popularly known as "Java Man." Since Dubois's work, numerous other fossils have been located in Java (see Table 11.1) and are now recognized as fully hominid and assigned to our genus, *Homo*. The fossils found in Java are similar in phenotype to the African and other Asian specimens, although their average brain size is larger than in some of the earlier fossils, and many are over 1000 ml. Some new dates

Country	Locality	Fossils	Crania	Age (million years)	Est. Brain Size (ml)
Homo erectus (continued)					
Italy	Ceprano(?)	Cranium	—	0.8–0.9	—
Java	Modjokerto	Child's cranium	—	1.8(?)	—
	Ngandong	Cranial and postcranial fragments from >12 individuals	N-1	<0.1	1170
			N-6	<0.1	1250
			N-11	<0.1	1230
			N-12	<0.1	1090
	Sambungmachan	Large cranial fragment	Sambungmachan	<0.1	1000
	Sangiran	Cranial and postcranial fragments from ~40 individuals	S-2	0.7–1.6	800
			S-4	0.7–1.6	900
			S-10	0.7–1.6	850
			S-12	0.7–1.6	1050
			S-17	0.7–1.6	1000
			1993 cranium	1.1–1.4	856
	Trinil	Skullcap, femur	"Java Man"	<1	940
Morocco	Salé	Cranium	Salé	0.4(?)	880
	Sidi Abderrahman	Two mandible fragments	—	—	—
	Thomas Quarry	Mandible and skull fragments	—	0.5	—
Tanzania	Olduvai(?)	Cranial and postcranial fragments including mandibles and pelvis and long bone fragments	OH9	1.4	1060
			OH12	0.6–0.8	700–800
				Mean	984.79

have recently been suggested for some of these fossils from Java, and we will return to them later.

Perhaps the most famous *Homo erectus* fossils are those from China, particularly from a cave outside of Beijing called Zhoukoudian. Starting in the 1920s, six nearly complete skulls, a couple dozen cranial and mandible fragments, over 100 teeth, and a few postcranial pieces were recovered from the cave. Stone tools and animal bones, including those of horses, were also recovered. The hominid remains are clearly similar to those of other specimens of *H. erectus*. Dating indicates that the cave was first occupied about 460,000 years ago and was used until about 230,000 years ago.

FIGURE 11.3
The skullcap and femur of the "Java Man" *Homo erectus*. The growth toward the top of the femur is the result of a pathological condition.

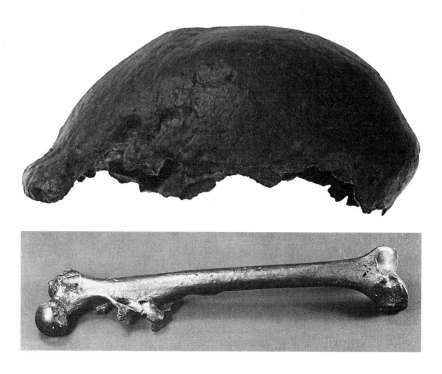

The fame of the Zhoukoudian fossils, called "Peking Man" (from the old spelling of Beijing), lies mostly in the fact that they are missing. When Japan invaded China in 1937, U.S. Marines, attempting to get the fossils out of the country, were captured by Japanese troops. The fossils were never seen again. Their whereabouts remain one of the great mysteries in anthropology. Fortunately, extensive measurements had already been taken on the bones, and accurate casts had been made (Figure 11.4).

Since then, numerous fossils classified as *Homo erectus* have been recovered, and we are filling in—although not without controversy—our knowledge of this important period in hominid evolution. Among the oldest fossils of this group are those that some authorities (see, for example, Tattersall 1997) place in a separate species, *H. ergaster* ("work man," a reference to stone tools found in association with the fossils). The oldest well-established find, from East Turkana in Kenya, is dated at 1.78 mya (Figure 11.5). In some ways it is typical of *H. erectus* crania. It has heavy **brow ridges,** a prognathous face, a sloping forehead, an elongated profile, a **sagittal keel,** a sharply angled occipital bone with a pronounced **torus,** and a cranial capacity of 850 ml (Figure 11.6). The average cranial capacity for this hominid group is about 980 ml, just slightly under the modern human minimum of 1000 ml, but a considerable jump from the 680 ml average for *Homo habilis*. Some *H. erectus* fossils have cranial capacities within the modern human range (see Table 11.1).

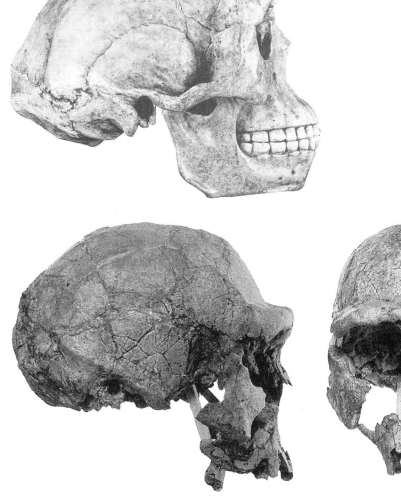

FIGURE 11.4
A cast of one of the "Peking Man" skulls, all of which were lost during World War II.

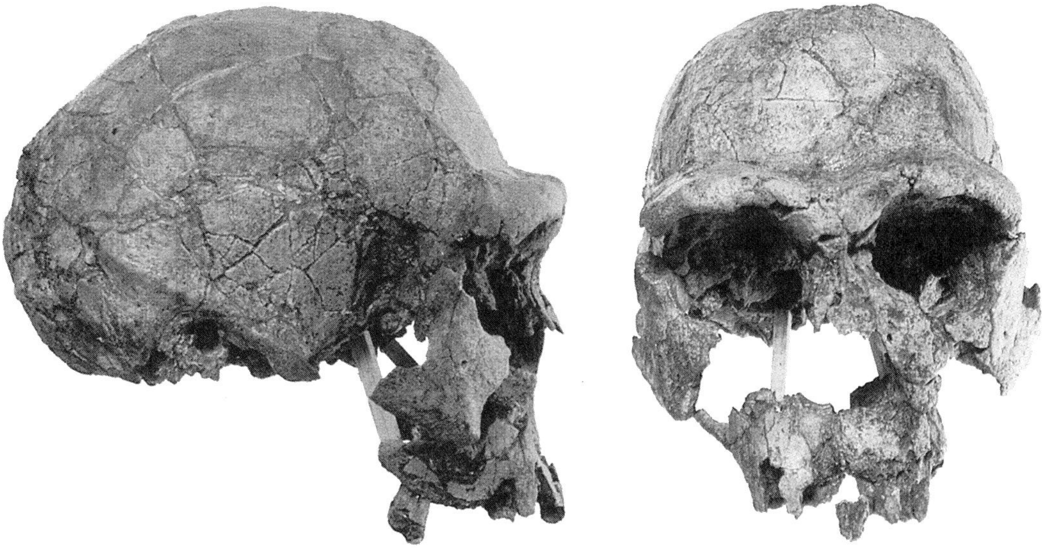

FIGURE 11.5
The *Homo erectus* (or *Homo ergaster*) skull of ER 3733 from Lake Turkana, Kenya, is fairly typical of this group.

brow ridges: Heavy, bony ridges over the eyes.

sagittal keel: A sloping of the sides of the skull toward the top, as viewed from the front.

torus: A bony ridge at the back of the skull, where the neck muscles attach.

FIGURE 11.6
Cranial features of *Homo erectus/ergaster* compared with those of modern *Homo sapiens*.

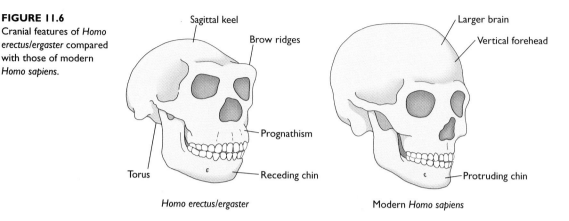

Homo erectus/ergaster

Modern *Homo sapiens*

In other ways, however, the Turkana skull differs from others labeled as *H. erectus*. It is thinner and higher in profile, with smaller facial bones. These modern-looking features are what have led to its placement in the new species *H. ergaster*. The cranium is thought to have belonged to a female. A similar skull from East Turkana dated at 1.57 mya is more ruggedly constructed. It is thought to be a male.

From the neck up, then, *H. erectus/ergaster* is quite distinct from the preceding species, *H. habilis,* in overall size, ruggedness, and especially brain size. The skull, however, still retains primitive features that distinguish it from modern *Homo sapiens*. From the neck down, on the other hand, *H. erectus/ergaster* is essentially modern, and apparently was so from its beginnings.

We know this because one of the oldest fossils of the group—also included in *H. ergaster*—is also the most complete. It is a nearly whole skeleton found at West Turkana in Kenya and dated at 1.6 mya (Figure 11.7). The shape of the pelvis indicates that it was a male. Based on dental eruption and lack of any epiphyseal union, it is estimated that he was 12 years old when he died. The boy was about 5½ feet tall, and he might have been 150 pounds and 6 feet tall had he lived to adulthood.

All other fossils from this group—including those from Africa outside Kenya—are assigned to *Homo erectus* (although a few are awaiting confirmation of their species affiliation). For the moment, we will treat them all as potentially *H. erectus*. The implications of the lumping versus splitting points of view for this group will be discussed in the next chapter.

The *H. erectus* fossils from Africa—except for OH9 from Olduvai Gorge, dated at 1.25 mya—are younger, from 700,000 to 400,000 years old. This means that *Homo erectus* spread throughout the African continent and that populations of the species remained there for over a million years.

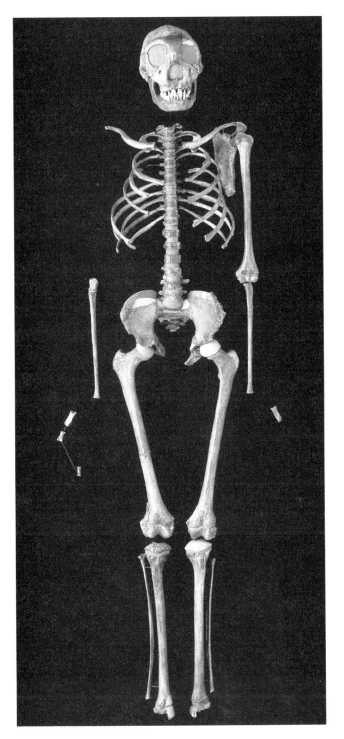

FIGURE 11.7
The "Turkana Boy," *Homo ergaster* fossil KNM-15000, one of the most complete early hominid fossils ever found. The pelvis is clearly that of a male and the epiphyses at the top of his left femur are obviously not fused (see Figure 9.3).

FIGURE 11.8

A veritable river of ice, the Moreno Glacier is located in Patagonia, a region of Argentina.

However, *H. erectus* did not only remain in Africa. According to recent data, members of the species had reached China and Southeast Asia by at least 1 million years ago. What prompted the people of this species to leave the savannas to which they were apparently so well adapted?

We can't know the answer for sure, but a good guess is that the spread of *H. erectus* was simply an outcome of their reproductive success. Their big brains enabled them to exploit the savannas to a greater extent than had the other hominids to date. They had better and more varied tools (which will be discussed later), the ability to learn more about their environment and to reason out the problems that their habitat presented, and, no doubt, a more complex social organization. With these adaptations, H. erectus would have rapidly increased in population size.

Population increase, however, puts pressure on resources and, perhaps, on social harmony as well. So groups of H. erectus probably fissioned and moved outside of familiar areas, in search of less competition over food, space, and two other resources that may have been even more important factors—water and shelter. Water can be scarce on the savannas. There are lakes, rivers, and waterholes, but many of these are seasonal and are dry for months on end. And H. erectus may have needed shelter as well. With bodies virtually the same as ours, they were no longer good tree climbers and so had to seek shelter on the ground, in groves of trees or, if they could locate one, in a cave or rock shelter. But, of course, a leopard or other animal may have already been in residence in the cave and had to be dealt with.

In search of food, water, shelter, and perhaps, space and social harmony, *Homo erectus* wandered the Old World. Those wanderings eventually carried them as far from their African homeland as what is now Beijing, China, and the Indonesian island of Java, and perhaps to Europe as well. Not only did these journeys take them to new climates, but the travels also brought them into contact with the changeable environments of the Ice Ages, known technically as the **Pleistocene.**

Beginning about 1.6 mya and ending 10,000 years ago, the Pleistocene was actually a complex series of extremely cold periods separated by warm phases, some warmer than today. There may have been as many as eighteen cold episodes during the Pleistocene, some lasting tens of thousands of years. We still don't know what caused these cold periods. Suggestions range from increased volcanic activity, with dust and ash blocking the sun's rays, to changes in the earth's orbit.

When the average world temperature drops, ice and snow accumulate over the years at the poles and in higher elevations. The pressure of this accumulation forces the movement of great sheets and rivers of ice—**glaciers** (Figure 11.8). During periods of glacial advances, much of North America, Europe, and Asia were covered by ice, sometimes nearly a mile thick (Figure 11.9). Parts of the world not covered by the glaciers were nonetheless affected, having cooler summers and wetter winters. The advance of the glaciers also had the effect of condensing the world's climatic zones into smaller spaces. Several times during the Pleistocene, the temperate oak and pine forests of Connecticut, where I now live, was like the arctic **tundra** of Alaska and northern Canada. Moreover, with so much of the earth's water tied up in the great ice sheets, sea levels dropped as much

Pleistocene: The geological time period, from 1.6 million to 10,000 years ago, characterized by a series of glacial advances and retreats.

glaciers: Massive sheets of ice that expand and move.

tundra: A treeless area with low-growing vegetation and permanently frozen ground.

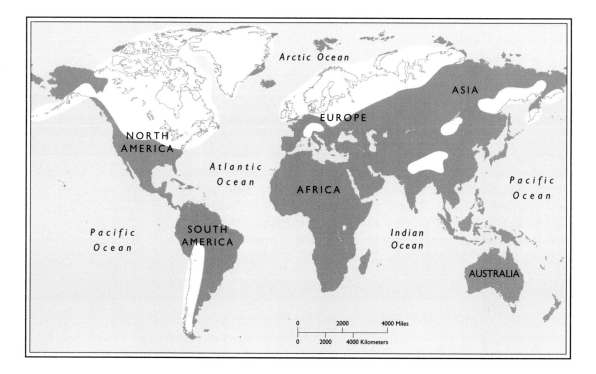

FIGURE 11.9

Maximum extent of the ice sheets during the Pleistocene.

as 400 feet, exposing large areas of land formerly under water. This allowed humans to migrate to areas previously inaccessible, as, for instance, modern *Homo sapiens* migrated to North America.

The world of the Pleistocene was the world through which *Homo erectus* was able to migrate and establish themselves, and we find their remains in some of the far corners of the Old World. They undoubtedly also inhabited the areas in between, but we have yet to uncover fossils in these areas.

Recently, some new dates from Java have posed interesting questions regarding the spread of *Homo erectus* around the Old World. Using new versions of the potassium/argon dating technique, researchers have redated the Sangiran *erectus* fossils to 1.6 mya and the Modjokerto remains to 1.8 mya—twice as old as previously thought, and at least as old as the oldest African *erectus/ergaster* fossil. This could mean that *H. erectus* evolved somewhere other than Africa. But all previous hominid fossils come only from Africa, so it's unlikely that *erectus* evolved anywhere but there.

That leaves two plausible explanations. Perhaps *H. erectus* (or *ergaster*) actually first appeared in Africa earlier than any of the fossils we have— remember how rare fossilization is—and then spread to Asia by these dates. The other possibility is simply that their expansion began very shortly after they first evolved. Science writer James Shreeve (1994:86) notes that Java is 10,000 to 15,000 miles from Africa, depending upon the route, and that Indonesia was connected to Asia at the time by the lower sea levels of the Pleistocene. If *erectus* walked just a mile a year, it would only have taken about 15,000 years to reach Java. That's still pretty fast, considering that they did not necessarily move 1 mile every year *in the right direction*. I think that, if the dates are correct, they probably mean that *H. erectus/ergaster* is older than we now assume based on existing fossils *and* that they began expansion early on.

Another important new date concerns the Java site of Ngandong. There is evidence that some *erectus* fossils there may be younger than 100,000 years—perhaps as young as 27,000 to 53,000 years old. If so, there were populations of *erectus* still around well after modern *Homo sapiens* had evolved, in which case *Homo erectus* would have been a very long-lived species, indeed.

It should be noted that some of the European evidence of *Homo erectus* comes in the form of cultural artifacts dated at times that have been associated with that species from other locations. At the site of Soleihac in France are tools and animal remains dated at 800,000 years. Another French site, Terra Amata on the Riviera, has been proposed as a site where *H. erectus* built shelters and established a village around 400,000 years ago. This interpretation has recently been called into question, however. Someone lived there, but probably not in a village of huts. In Spain, at two adjacent sites called Torralba and Ambrona, dated at 400,000 years ago, are the remains of some large mammals, including elephants, along with some stone tools that suggest a hunting or, more probably, a scavenging site. Until, however, we locate definite fossils of *H. erectus* from Europe—other than the cranium from Ceprano, Italy—we can only conclude that the species was there but was not widespread or, perhaps, that these sites are associated with another hominid species.

What do we know about the lives of *Homo erectus/ergaster*? Like *Homo habilis*, early *H. ergaster* made stone tools by taking a few flakes off a core, just enough to make the "business end." (They also, of course, used the flakes as tools.) But beginning about 1.4 mya, *H. erectus/ergaster* elaborated on this stone toolmaking technique by flaking the entire stone, controlling the shape of the whole core tool. This tool tradition is called **Acheulian,** after the site in France where it was first identified. The core tool produced by the Acheulian technique is the **hand axe.** It is symmetrical, edged and pointed, and **bifacial** (flaked on both sides) (Figure 11.10). It was the all-purpose tool of its time, used for any number of tasks from butchering to cutting wood. My colleague, archaeologist Ken Feder, calls it the "Swiss Army rock."

In addition to hand axes, *H. erectus/ergaster* also made tools with straight, sharp edges called cleavers. Moreover, making a hand axe or cleaver produces a great many flakes—as many as fifty usable ones by one

Acheulian: A toolmaking tradition associated with *Homo erectus/ergaster* in Africa and Europe.

hand axe: A bifacial, all-purpose stone tool, shaped somewhat like an axe head.

bifacial: A stone tool that has been worked on both sides.

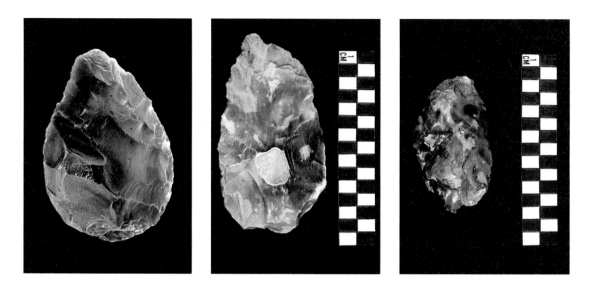

FIGURE 11.10

Bifacially flaked hand axes became one of history's most popular tools and were found in a variety of sizes showing varying degrees of quality.

estimate—so *H. erectus/ergaster* also made flake tools, used either unmodified or further worked to produce a desired shape.

Hand axes appeared in Africa about 1.4 mya and lasted for over a million years. They spread throughout Africa and into Europe. They are, however, rarely found in Asia. Instead, Asian *erectus* populations, like those at Zhoukoudian, made what are called choppers, with flakes removed from one side, and chopping tools with flakes removed from both sides (Figure 11.11). But these tool types, unlike the Acheulian hand axe, were asymmetrical and not flaked over the whole surface.

Perhaps the most striking behavioral advance associated with *Homo erectus* is the purposeful use of fire. There is some evidence, though it is disputed, for the use of fire in Africa at 1.5 mya and France at 750,000 years ago. A rock shelter in Thailand has yielded evidence of fire dated at 700,000 years ago. The earliest well-accepted date (although even it is not without its skeptics) is from the cave at Zhoukoudian sometime after 500,000 years ago (Binford and Chuan 1985; Binford and Stone 1986).

Fire, of course, provides heat, and so it is not surprising that some of the earliest evidence of fire comes from cold northern areas. Fire also provides protection from animals and can be used for cooking, making meat more easily chewed and digestible. But in the long run, perhaps its most important use is as a source of light. Science writer John Pfeiffer (1969) suggests that fire could extend the hours of activity into the night and provide a social focus for group interaction. Sitting around the campfire at night was when people experimented, created, talked, and socialized. Fires have these functions in human cultures today. Moreover, the

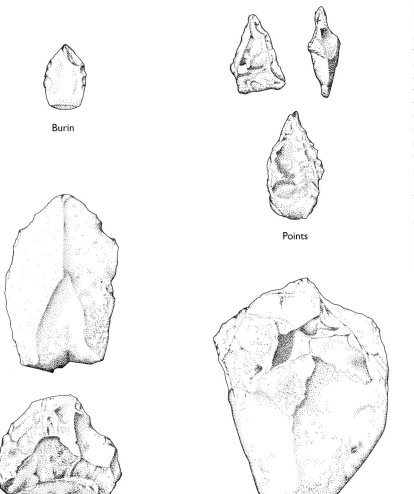

Burin

Points

Scrapers

Chopper

FIGURE 11.11
Flake and chopper tools associated with *Homo erectus* from the cave at Zhoukoudian. Although the functions of these tools is not known for certain, some are named for inferred use. Burins are thought to have been used to etch out thin slivers of antler or bone, which were then further modified into awls or needles. Points may have served as cutting tools for fine work. Scrapers may have helped remove flesh from animal hides, and choppers chopped wood and perhaps broke open bones to extract marrow.

use of fire may well have given people a psychological advantage, a sense of mastery and control over a force of nature and a source of energy. As Pfeiffer says in the title of his article, "When *Homo erectus* Tamed Fire, He Tamed Himself."

Was *Homo erectus* a hunter of big game, as often portrayed, or did this species continue to scavenge for most of the meat in its diet? At the 400,000-year-old Spanish sites of Torralba and Ambrona, two hills on either side of a mountain pass, are the remains of fifty elephants and over sixty other game animals (see Figure 9.9). The traditional interpretation is a rather elaborate reconstruction of a cooperative hunt, indeed, of several seasons of cooperative hunting (see, for example, Time-Life Books 1973). In this scenario, the animals were stampeded, possibly with the use of fire, into a bog where they were killed and butchered. The pieces of the carcasses were then taken to a campsite where they were further cut up, cooked, and eaten. There are some tools at the sites.

Is there evidence for this interpretation? A taphonomic analysis of 3000 bones from these sites found that 95 percent of them were so damaged that the search for specific evidence of human activity was impossible (Shipman and Rose 1983). Scratches on many of the bones, once thought to be stone tool cut marks, turn out, on examination under a scanning electron microscope (SEM), to be merely the results of soil abrasion and root growth. Of the fifty-five bones that could be analyzed, the SEM showed only sixteen cut marks on fourteen bones. The marks are not in a pattern that indicates systematic butchering. There is even little evidence of carnivore tooth marks. Furthermore, the tools found at the site are not associated with the elephants, but with the leg bones and mandibles of horses, deer, and wild cattle—the very parts of the animals that would be gathered by scavenging. At best, it appears that H. *erectus* was present at these sites and cut some meat off animal carcasses found there. There is no compelling evidence for cooperative big game hunting.

Two other alleged kill sites, at Olduvai Gorge and Olorgesailie in Africa, similarly give rise to elaborate interpretations of cooperative big game hunting, but they too are based on questionable evidence. The bones found at these sites are more indicative of scavenging than large-scale hunting. (For a good, detailed discussion, see Johanson and Shreeve 1989, Chapter 8.)

Finally, what about the intellectual and linguistic skills of H. *erectus/ ergaster*? As noted, their average cranial capacity was just a little short of the modern human minimum, and individual *erectus* remains fall within the modern human range. It's difficult to be certain what this fact means. After all, the modern range of 1000 to 2000 ml means that some people have brains twice the size of others, but there is no evidence that within this range brain size has anything to do with intelligence. Was H. *erectus*, then, just a little bit less intelligent than we are?

Anthropologist Ralph Holloway (1980, 1981) has looked at the structure of H. *erectus* brains using the fact that the inside of the skull reflects, rather specifically, some of the features of the brain it once held. By making **endocasts** of the inside surfaces of fossil crania, Holloway can produce images of the very brains of our ancestors (Figure 11.12). One intriguing find is that the brains of H. *erectus* were asymmetrical—the right and left halves of the brain weren't the same shape. This is found to some extent in apes, but to a greater extent in modern humans, because the halves of

FIGURE 11.12
Natural endocasts from South African australopithecines showing the degree of detail possible. Notice the blood vessels, especially in the upper right cast. Such casts may also be made artificially and allow us to compare the brains of our ancestors with those of modern humans.

our brains perform different functions. Language and the ability to use symbols, for example, are in our left hemispheres, while spatial reasoning (like the hand-eye coordination needed to make complex tools) is in the right hemisphere. This hints that *H. erectus* also had hemisphere specialization, perhaps even including the ability to communicate through a symbolic language.

Further evidence of language use by *H. erectus* comes from the use of the anatomy of the cranial base to reconstruct the vocal apparatus. Even though the vocal apparatus is made up of soft parts, those parts are connected to bone, and so the shape of the bone is correlated with the shape of the larynx, pharynx, and other features (Figure 11.13).

Reconstruction work on australopithecines indicates that their vocal tract was basically like that of apes, with the larynx and pharynx high up in the throat. While this allows them to drink and breathe at the same time (as human infants can do up to 18 months), it does not allow for the precise manipulation of air that is required for modern human languages. The early hominids could make sounds, but they would have been more like those of chimpanzees.

endocasts: Natural or human-made casts of the inside of a skull.

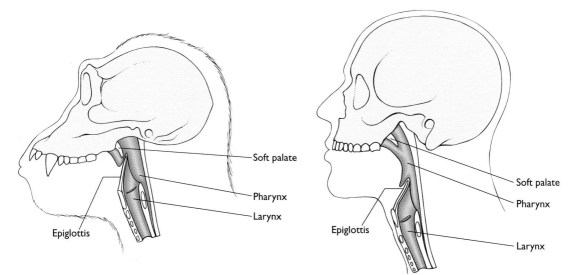

FIGURE 11.13
The vocal tracts of a chimp compared to a modern human's. The high placement of the chimp's makes it impossible for it to produce all of the sounds that are part of modern human languages.

Homo erectus, on the other hand, had vocal tracts more like those of modern humans, positioned lower in the throat and allowing for a greater range and speed of sound production. Thus, *erectus* could have produced vocal communication that involved many sounds with precise differences among those sounds. Whether or not they did so is another question. But, given their ability to manufacture fairly complex tools, to control fire, and to survive in different and changing environmental circumstances, *H. erectus* certainly had complex things to talk *about*. It is not out of the question that *erectus* had a communication system that was itself complex.

By any standards, *H. erectus*, although now extinct, was a smashing success. The species began nearly 2 million years ago in Africa, possibly as an earlier species, *H. ergaster*, and by perhaps 1.8 mya had spread as far as Java. By a half-million years ago, they had reached northern China and Europe. They lasted, in Africa and China, until a quarter-million years ago and may have persisted in Java until less than 100,000 years ago. Their adaptations—now focused on learning, technology, and the cultural transmission of information—allowed them to exploit a number of different environments.

There is some debate over just how much *H. erectus* changed during its tenure on earth. There is a small increase in average cranial capacity over this time (about 180 ml), as well as some refinement in hand axe–making technique and in flake tool variety. These changes, however, are small and slow, so the overall impression is one of stability—not a bad thing in evolutionary terms.

Somewhere around 500,000—and perhaps as early as 800,000—years ago, there was another sudden surge in brain size, to an average matching our own. This marks the beginning of perhaps the most complex part of our story.

BIG BRAINS, ARCHAIC SKULLS

The next three hominid species—still using the six-species model—are marked by brain sizes within the modern human range and, indeed, matching or close to the modern human average, but with other features, especially of the cranium, that retain primitive characteristics. These groups are sometimes collectively referred to as "archaic." The most recent of these, *Homo neanderthalensis*, will be considered separately in the next section. Here, we will discuss the earlier *Homo heidelbergensis* and the even earlier *Homo antecessor* (Table 11.2 and Figure 11.14).

The newest suggested hominid species, only named in mid-1997, is *Homo antecessor* ("advance guard" or "explorer"). Many authorities do not recognize the fossils involved as a separate species, but the discoverers see sufficient distinctions to warrant the new name (Bermúdez de Castro et al. 1997). The fossils were discovered between 1994 and 1996 at the site of Gran Dolina cave in the Atapuerca hills in northern Spain. They consist of more than eighty fragments including skulls, jaws, teeth, and other portions of the skeleton. There are also associated tools. The site has been dated using paleomagnetism (see Table 9.1) at more than 780,000 years old. If that date is correct, these would be the oldest well-accepted fossil humans found in Europe.

The most striking fossil is the partial face of an 11-year-old boy (Figure 11.15). The features present, described by the researchers as "fully modern," include a projecting nose region with a sharp lower margin, hollowed cheek bones (technically, a canine fossa), and several details of the dentition. Analysis of another specimen indicates a cranial capacity of greater than 1000 ml.

On the other hand, other fossils from this site show primitive features such as prominent brow ridges and premolars with multiple roots (modern human premolars have a single root). This unique mix of traits, especially the very modern appearance of the face, is what led the investigators to assign the new species name—and to further suggest that this species is the direct ancestor both of modern humans and of *Homo heidelbergensis* and *H. neanderthalensis* (see Chapter 12).

A logical objection to the analysis of the Gran Dolina boy is that the modern-looking traits seen so clearly in the boy's face might be juvenile features, not present in adults of his group and, therefore, not of diagnostic value for species assignment. The investigators, however, report that some of the other fragmentary facial bones from the site also show these modern

TABLE 11.2
Major Fossils Classified as *Homo antecessor* and *Homo heidelbergensis*
(the ? indicates that the species identification of that fossil is in question)

Country	Locality	Fossils	Age	Est. Brain Size (ml)
Homo antecessor				
Spain	Gran Dolina	More than 80 fragments	>780,000	>1000
Homo heidelbergensis				
China	Dali	Cranium	200,000	1120
	Jinniushan(?)	Nearly complete skeleton	200,000	1350
	Maba(?)	Cranium	130,000–170,000	—
	Xujiayao(?)	Fragments of 11 individuals	100,000–125,000	—
England	Swanscombe	Occipital and parietals	276,000–426,000	1325
	Boxgrove	Tibia, teeth	362,000–423,000	—
Ethiopia	Bodo	Cranium	200,000–400,000	—
France	Arago	Cranium and fragmentary remains of 7 individuals	250,000	1200
Germany	Bilzingsleben(?)	Cranial fragments and tooth	320,000–412,000	—
	Mauer	Mandible	500,000	—
	Steinheim(?)	Cranium	200,000–240,000	1200
Greece	Petralona	Cranium	160,000–240,000	1200
Hungary	Vértesszölös	Occipital fragment	250,000–475,000	1250
India	Narmada	Cranium	150,000(?)	1300
Spain	Sima de los Huesos	Fragments from at least 32 individuals	300,000	—
Tanzania	Ndutu (Olduvai)(?)	Cranium	200,000	1100
Zambia	Kabwe (Broken Hill)	Cranium, additional cranial and postcranial remains of several individuals	>125,000	1280
			Mean	1252.50

traits, and that *later* fossils from a nearby site, Sima de los Huesos, do not (Gibbons 1997b).

The fossil bones from Gran Dolina are striking for their antiquity, but some of the 200 tools found at the site are even older, dating back to a million years ago. These early tools resemble pre–hand axe tools from Africa—cores and simple cutting flakes. Later tools found in the same strata as the human remains are more sophisticated. One long flake has a sharp edge on one side and a dulled, flat edge on the other. It was

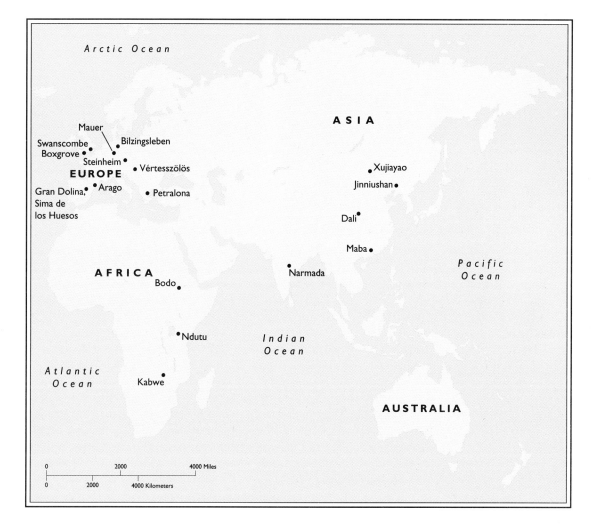

Arctic Ocean

ASIA

Mauer
Swanscombe
Boxgrove • Bilzingsleben
Steinheim •
EUROPE • Vértesszölös
Gran Dolina, • Arago
Sima de • Petralona
los Huesos

• Xujiayao
Jinniushan •

Dali •

Maba •

Pacific
Ocean

AFRICA
Bodo •

• Narmada

Indian
Ocean

• Ndutu

Atlantic
Ocean
Kabwe •

AUSTRALIA

0   2000   4000 Miles
0   2000   4000 Kilometers

FIGURE 11.14
Map of *Homo antecessor* and
Homo heidelbergensis sites.

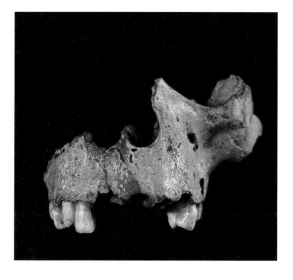

FIGURE 11.15
Fossil ATD6-69 from Gran
Dolina cave, Atapuerca,
Spain. This partial face of
an 11-year-old boy who died
perhaps more than 780,000
years ago is fully modern in
many features, including the
hollowed cheek bone easily
seen here.

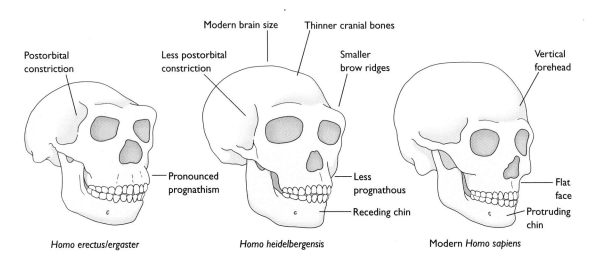

FIGURE 11.16
Cranial features of *Homo erectus/ergaster, Homo heidelbergensis,* and modern *Homo sapiens.*

presumably formed to be used as a knife. None of the tools at the site, however, is as complex as some of the Acheulian tools being made by *Homo erectus* and *H. ergaster* at the same time period or earlier.

Finally, there is some intriguing evidence of the diet of the Gran Dolina people. Bison and deer bones, as well as some from other species, have been found that show stone tool cut marks, implying that the people hunted. According to the investigators, there are also cut marks on some of the human bones that were mixed in with animal bones, suggesting cannibalism (Kunzig 1997).

It should also be noted that there is a site in southeastern Spain, called Orce (or-say), that some contend is even older than Gran Dolina— 900,000 years old or even older. It contains simple stone tools and alleged hominid bones. Other authorities, however, have identified the fragmentary bones as those of wild horses, and the dating is still contested (Bower 1997a). More study is clearly needed at this location.

Table 11.2 and Figure 11.14 show that the fossils assigned to *Homo heidelbergensis* are widespread geographically and range over about 400,000 years in time (longer if one includes *H. antecessor*). The species was first named for a mandible found at Mauer near Heidelberg, Germany, in 1907. Note that the inclusion of several of the fossils is questioned by those who recognize this species.

Members of this group show an average brain size of nearly 1300 ml, a more than 30 percent increase over the average for *Homo erectus*. The brains are also differently proportioned from those of *H. erectus*, with greater emphasis on the forebrain, reflected by steeper foreheads. This may be important because the frontal lobes of the human brain are the areas thought to be most involved in control of voluntary movements, speech, attention, social behavior, planning, and reasoning (see Figure 7.7).

The bones of the cranium, compared to those of *H. erectus*, are thinner; the overall size of the face is reduced; the profile is less prognathous; the brow ridges, though still present, are less pronounced; and the **postorbital constriction,** characteristic of *erectus*, is lessened (Figure 11.16). The postcranial skeletons, essentially modern in overall shape, are more rugged and muscular than in modern humans. The half-million-year-old tibia from Boxgrove in southeast England, for example, is strikingly thicker in cross section than the tibia of a modern person. Figures 11.17 and 11.18 show two of the more complete examples of *H. heidelbergensis* crania.

Given the fragmentary remains of many of these fossils, the fact that some were found early in the history of anthropology or by nonscientists, and the widespread range of the species, fairly little can be specifically said about the lifestyle of these early humans. We do know, however, some things about their tools. For example, by 500,000 years ago, we have evidence from Boxgrove that the hand axe was in use. And about 200,000 years ago, people included in *H. heidelbergensis* invented a new and imaginative way to make stone tools. It appears first in Africa and later in Europe. Called the prepared core, or **Levallois,** technique (after the suburb of Paris where it was first recognized), it involves the careful preparation of the rough stone core so that a number of flakes of a desired shape (up to four or five) can be taken off. The flakes could then be used for cutting, scraping, or piercing. Figure 11.19 shows the steps involved and a photograph of a replica of such a tool.

Finally, an intriguing, but still dim glimpse into the lives of the people of this era comes from another site in Atapuerca, near Gran Dolina (Kunzig 1997). Known as Sima de los Huesos (the "pit of bones"), it is a shaft inside a cave, dated by ESR (see Chapter 9) at about 300,000 years old. It contains the bones of animals and the remains of at least thirty-two humans—many so well preserved that even fingertips and small inner ear bones are included. Most of the bones are from teenagers and young adults, both male and female. Although the bones show signs of chewing by a carnivore, it is unlikely that some predator would select just that age group, and the nonhuman remains in the pit are not from prey animals, but those of foxes and bears, which may have fallen in and chewed on the human bones before dying. Investigators think the bodies were thrown into the pit after death (one seems to have died from a massive infection), probably not as part of a formal funeral ritual (no artifacts were found) but more likely for simple disposal purposes. Perhaps they all died together in some catastrophe, or at least over a short period of time. Many of the bones show signs of childhood malnourishment.

No doubt the peoples labeled *Homo antecessor* and *Homo heidelbergensis* had other mental, cultural, and perhaps physical adaptations to help them deal with the various and changeable environments they encountered as the Pleistocene continued. We certainly know this was true for

postorbital constriction: A narrowing of the skull behind the eyes, as viewed from above.

Levallois: Tool technology involving striking uniform flakes from a prepared core.

FIGURE 11.17
The skull of *Homo heidelbergensis* from Steinheim, Germany. Note the more rounded shape and higher forehead as compared to *H. erectus.* At the same time, note the retention of heavy brow ridges.

FIGURE 11.18
The Kabwe (formerly called Broken Hill) specimen is one of the best-known examples of *Homo heidelbergensis* from Africa. Note the extremely large brow ridges on this skull, which has a cranial capacity of 1280 ml, quite close to the modern mean.

Side Views

Top Views

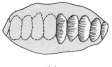

(a)

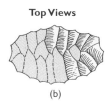

(b)

(c)

(d)

Flake

(e)

Core

FIGURE 11.19

(Above) The Levallois technique: (a) produce a margin along the edge of the core, (b) shape the surface of the core, (c, d) prepare the surface (the "striking platform") to be struck, (e) remove the flake, and return to step b for additional flake removal. (Below) Photograph of a Levallois core and tool (replica).

FIGURE 11.20
The original Neandertal skullcap from Germany. The cranial vault held a very large brain, but the brow ridges indicate an obvious difference from modern humans.

TABLE 11.3
Major Fossils of *Homo neanderthalensis*

Country	Locality	Fossils	Age	Est. Brain Size (ml)
Belgium	Spy	2 skeletons	—	—
Croatia	Krapina	Cranial and postcranial fragments of >45 individuals	120,000	1200–1450
France	Biache St. Vaast	2 crania	150,000–175,000	—
	Fontechévade	Cranial fragments of several individuals	100,000	1500
	La Chaise	Cranium	126,000	—
	La Chapelle-aux-Saints	Skeleton	—	1620
	La Ferrassie	8 skeletons	>38,000	1680
	St. Césaire	Skeleton	36,000	—
Germany	Neandertal	Skullcap	—	>1250
	Ehringsdorf	Cranial fragment	225,000	—
Gibraltar	Forbe's Quarry	Cranium	50,000	—
Italy	Monte Circeo	Cranium	—	—
	Saccopastore	Cranium	—	—
Iraq	Shanidar	9 partial skeletons	70,000	1600
Israel	Amud	Skeleton	70,000	1740
	Kebara Cave	Postcranial skeleton	60,000	—
	Tabun	Skeleton, mandible, postcranial fragments	100,000	1270
			Mean	1478.89

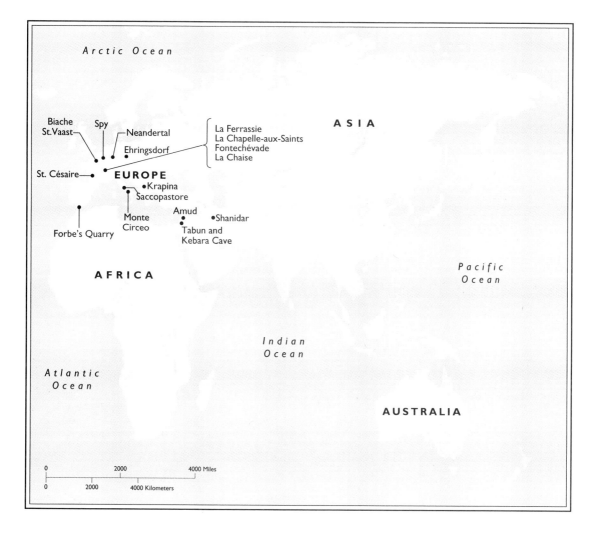

FIGURE 11.21
Map of major Neandertal sites.

one famous group of humans from Europe and the Near East. Some crania from Sima de los Huesos are said to show traits that might be ancestral to this group, the Neandertals.

THE NEANDERTALS

The Neandertals—*Homo neanderthalensis* in the six-species model—were named after one of the first human fossils found and recognized as a human fossil, a skullcap from the Neander Valley in Germany recovered in 1856 (Figure 11.20). This was before Darwin wrote *Origin of Species*. (In German, *thal* means valley and is always pronounced "tal." Recent spelling drops the silent "h," but some still use it, and it remains in the formal species name because that was the spelling when the name was first applied.) Table 11.3 and Figure 11.21 show the basic data for fossils of this species as well as the locations of these finds.

The Neandertals have had an interesting history in anthropology. At one time they were considered brutish, hunched-over, dim-witted members of a dead-end side branch of human evolution. At other times they have been thought of as just an ancient, slightly different-looking form of modern *Homo sapiens* (Figure 11.22). These are both exaggerations. We now recognize the sophistication of the Neandertals' intellectual and cultural achievements. They were certainly similar to modern humans physically, but still different in significant ways. So debate at present centers on whether the similarities place them within our species, or whether the differences make them a separate species (see Chapter 12). Figures 11.23 and 11.24 compare the skulls and skeletons of Neandertal and modern *Homo sapiens*.

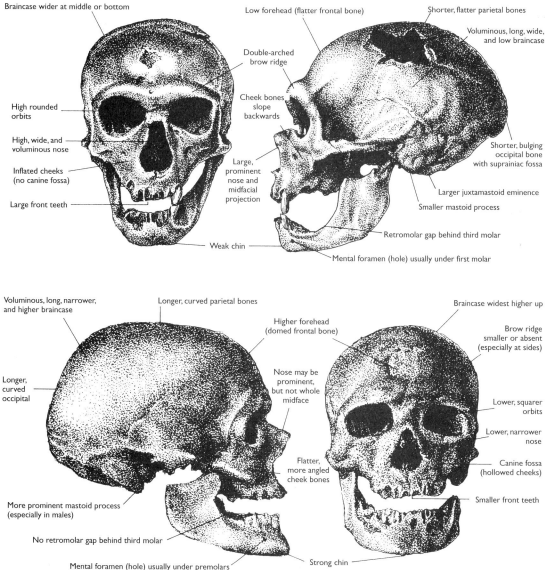

Braincase wider at middle or bottom

Low forehead (flatter frontal bone)

Shorter, flatter parietal bones

Voluminous, long, wide, and low braincase

Double-arched brow ridge

High rounded orbits

Cheek bones slope backwards

High, wide, and voluminous nose

Inflated cheeks (no canine fossa)

Shorter, bulging occipital bone with suprainiac fossa

Large, prominent nose and midfacial projection

Large front teeth

Larger juxtamastoid eminence

Smaller mastoid process

Weak chin

Retromolar gap behind third molar

Mental foramen (hole) usually under first molar

Voluminous, long, narrower, and higher braincase

Longer, curved parietal bones

Braincase widest higher up

Higher forehead (domed frontal bone)

Brow ridge smaller or absent (especially at sides)

Longer, curved occipital

Nose may be prominent, but not whole midface

Lower, squarer orbits

Lower, narrower nose

Canine fossa (hollowed cheeks)

Flatter, more angled cheek bones

Smaller front teeth

More prominent mastoid process (especially in males)

No retromolar gap behind third molar

Mental foramen (hole) usually under premolars

Strong chin

FIGURE 11.23
Cranial features of the La Chapelle specimen of Neandertal (above) compared to modern *Homo sapiens*.

The crania of the Neandertals are strikingly different from those of any modern human. They have, essentially, more pronounced versions of the cranial features of *H. heidelbergensis*. Their cranial capacities ranged from about 1300 ml to 1740 ml, well within the modern range, but their foreheads were still sloped, the backs of their skulls broad, and the sides bulging. The brow ridges were still large, but smaller at the sides than in *Homo erectus*, and they were filled with air spaces (called the frontal si-

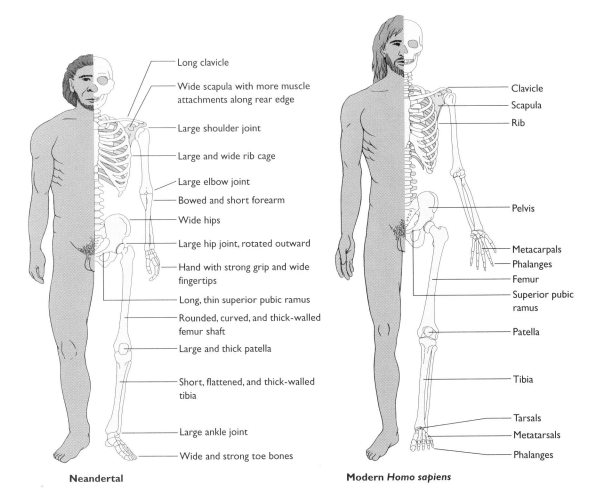

Long clavicle

Wide scapula with more muscle attachments along rear edge

Large shoulder joint

Large and wide rib cage

Large elbow joint

Bowed and short forearm

Wide hips

Large hip joint, rotated outward

Hand with strong grip and wide fingertips

Long, thin superior pubic ramus

Rounded, curved, and thick-walled femur shaft

Large and thick patella

Short, flattened, and thick-walled tibia

Large ankle joint

Wide and strong toe bones

Neandertal

Clavicle

Scapula

Rib

Pelvis

Metacarpals

Phalanges

Femur

Superior pubic ramus

Patella

Tibia

Tarsals

Metatarsals

Phalanges

Modern *Homo sapiens*

FIGURE 11.24
Skeletal features of Neandertal compared to modern *Homo sapiens*.

nuses), unlike the solid ridges of *erectus*. The brow ridges of the Neandertals were also rounded over each eye, rather than forming a straight line, as in earlier archaics. The face was large and prognathous, with a broad nasal opening and widely set eyes. The chin was receding.

From the neck down, there are also striking differences. The bones of the Neandertals, even the finger bones, were more robust and had heavier muscle markings than their modern counterparts. The Neandertals were stocky, muscular, powerful people. This is seen even in the bones of Neandertal children, so it is assumed to be a result of inheritance, not simply of a hard-working lifestyle.

Although very strong and stocky, the Neandertals were relatively short. Estimates put the average for males at 5 feet 6 inches and for females at 5 feet 3 inches. Some of this short stature is a result of relatively short lower legs. The lower arms were short as well. All these physical features hint at adaptations to a strenuous lifestyle and to cold climates. Shorter, heavier bodies with short limbs conserve heat better than narrow, long-limbed bodies (Holliday 1997, and see Chapter 13). As evidence, the limbs of the Neandertals of the warmer Southwest Asia are relatively longer than the limbs of those living in Ice-Age Europe, who faced some of the extreme climates of the glacial advances.

Another possible adaptation to cold has been suggested by several investigators (see Menon 1997). In eight Neandertal skulls, they found triangular bony projections in the nasal cavity unlike anything seen in modern humans or in any other human ancestors. These projections are thought to have provided increased surface area for the nasal mucous membranes, which would have helped warm and moisten the cold, dry air of Europe during the Pleistocene glaciations. It has also been suggested that the large sinus cavities served a similar function. Moreover, it is thought that the larynx of the Neandertals was higher in the throat than in modern humans (see Figure 11.13), which would have prevented them from gulping in cold, dry air through the mouth.

Neandertal fossils date from 225,000 to as recently as 36,000 years ago (see Table 11.3). During this time, it has been proposed, they were responsible for a number of important cultural achievements. What do we know about their behavior?

Among the well-established accomplishments of the Neandertals is an elaboration on the Levallois stone toolmaking technique. Called the **Mousterian** tradition, after the site of Le Moustier in France, it involved the careful retouching of flakes taken off cores. These flakes were sharpened and shaped by precise additional flaking, on one side or both, to make specialized tools (Figure 11.25). One authority has identified no less than sixty-three tool types (Bordes 1972).

Several specific uses of Mousterian tools have been inferred from microscopic wear-pattern analysis on specimens from the Kebara Cave site in Israel. Archaeologist John Shea (1989) notes wear patterns that indicate animal butchering, woodworking, bone and antler carving, and working of animal hides. There are also wear patterns like those produced by the friction of a wooden shaft against a stone spear point. The Neandertals may have been the first to **haft** a stone point.

Though there is still debate on whether or not the Neandertals were big game hunters or mostly scavengers, there is no doubt that they were dependent on the animals that abounded during the Pleistocene—animals like reindeer, deer, ibex (a wild goat), aurochs (wild ox), horse, woolly rhinoceros, bison, bear, and elk. Bones of these creatures have been found in association with Neandertal remains.

From Neandertal times, we find some of the earliest evidence for abstract belief. This evidence comes in the form of burials of the dead.

Mousterian: The culture associated with the European Neandertals.

haft: To attach a handle or shaft.

FIGURE 11.25
Unifacially retouched Mousterian flakes from the original site, La Moustier in France.

Though many of these "burials" have now been attributed to natural causes, at least thirty-six Neandertal sites show evidence of intentional interment of the dead, and in some graves were remains of offerings—stone tools, animal bones, and, possibly, flowers (Figure 11.26).

There is some debate, however, over whether or not these Neandertal burials had ritual significance. Did they represent belief in an afterlife or reverence for the physical remains of the deceased, or were the people simply disposing of a corpse, as seems to have been the case much earlier at Sima de los Huesos? The inclusion of animal bones in the graves may have been the result of the bones of both Neandertals and other animals being dragged by predators and scavengers into caves at the same time and subsequently buried by natural processes. The pollen found in a Neandertal grave at Shanidar, Iraq, may not have been from flowers placed in the grave, but may have been brought in by the burrowing action of rodents, carried in by water, or blown in by wind at the time of burial. The

FIGURE 11.26
The Neandertal burial from La Ferrassie, France. The body was interred in the flexed position with knees drawn up to the chest, perhaps to mimic sleep.

jury is still out on this issue. But, as far as we know, the Neandertals were the first to bury their dead, for whatever reason they did so.

Along the same lines, evidence has traditionally been cited for a Neandertal cave bear "cult" in Europe. The cave bear, now extinct, was a huge, impressive species, about 12 feet tall when standing upright. Caves in Switzerland and France are supposed to contain a number of cave bear skulls placed in special stone chests or in niches in the cave walls. But

FIGURE 11.27
The famous "Old Man" of La Chapelle-aux-Saints in France. Note the typical Neandertal features of the rounded brow ridge over each eye, the broad nasal opening, and the widely set eyes. The mandible and a side view of this cranium are in Figure 11.23.

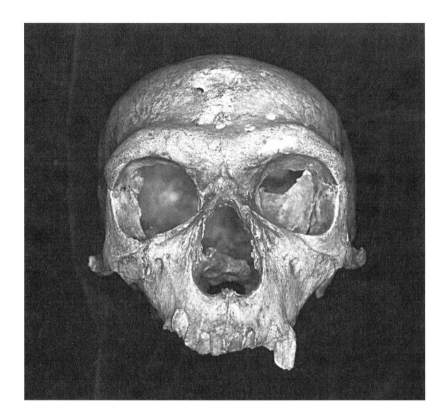

these interpretations were apparently wishful thinking on the part of early investigators. Re-analysis of the site descriptions indicates that the placement of the skulls was the result of natural processes such as clusters of rocks or cave-ins. Moreover, none of the bear bones show any signs of cut marks. This intriguing story has fallen to scientific investigation.

It has also been suggested that Neandertals were among the first to care for their elderly, ill, and injured. The famous "Old Man" of La Chapelle-aux-Saints in France (Figure 11.27) has been interpreted as aged, lacking most of his teeth, and having a debilitating case of arthritis. That he survived for a time with these infirmities, according to an early interpretation, indicates that he was cared for by his group.

Recent reexamination, though, shows that much of his tooth loss was after death and that his arthritis may not have been quite as debilitating as previously thought. Nor was he really old. He died when he was less than 40, probably rather quickly, as did the vast majority of Neandertals. Care of the elderly was probably not something they had to contend with very often.

On the other hand, there is a skeleton of a man from Shanidar, Iraq, that shows signs of injuries that may have resulted in blindness and loss of one arm. He lived with this condition for some time and, therefore, was obviously cared for by his comrades.

Finally, we have the question of the linguistic abilities of the Neandertals. Some investigators have reconstructed the vocal tract of Neandertals based on the structure of the underside of the cranium and have concluded that, because of the higher larynx noted before, they were not capable of making all the vowel sounds of modern humans. On the other hand, a recently found hyoid bone—a horseshoe-shaped bone in the throat—from the Neandertal site of Kebara in Israel appears fully modern. This would mean that the vocal tract of the Neandertals *was* like ours and that they *could* make all the sounds of which we are capable. The point, of course, is—as we said for *Homo erectus*—that the Neandertals had sufficiently complex things to talk *about* and just how they did so is less important than the fact that they did talk.

Archaic members of genus *Homo* were successful in adapting to different environments and, in the case of the Neandertals, harsh and demanding climates. They were clearly intelligent. We will no doubt find more fossils of archaics in new areas in the future, but they weren't exactly like any humans alive today. To begin the story of anatomically modern *Homo sapiens*, we once again return to Africa.

MODERN HUMANS

Beginning perhaps as early as 300,000 years ago, fossils with near-modern or modern features appear, earliest in Africa and later in Southwest Asia, Europe, and East Asia. Later still, modern humans migrated to Australia, the islands of the Pacific, and North and South America. Under the six-species model, fossil forms with modern features are the only ones placed in *Homo sapiens*. There is no general agreement, among proponents of this model, about the exact species affiliation of some transitional forms—fossils with a mix of archaic and modern traits. Table 11.4 and Figure 11.28 give the basic information and locations of some of the more important fossils of early *Homo sapiens* as well as transitional forms.

We call these fossils "anatomically modern" because they lack some features characteristic of earlier hominids and possess features common to humans today. Gone is the prognathous profile. The modern human face is essentially flat. There are no heavy brow ridges. The skull is globular rather than elongated, and the forehead is more nearly vertical. The face is smaller and narrower, and there is a protruding chin. The postcranial

TABLE 11.4
Chronological Listing of Some Important Fossils of Early *Homo sapiens*
(***Trans.*** indicates those considered transitional between archaic and modern *Homo*)

Country	Location	Age
Kenya	Ileret	270,000–300,000 (trans.)
South Africa	Florisbad	100,000–200,000 (trans.)
Ethiopia	Omo	130,000 (trans.)
Tanzania	Ngaloba	120,000 (trans.)
South Africa	Klasies River Mouth Langebaan Lagoon (footprints) Border Cave	84,000–120,000 117,000 62,000–115,000
Israel	Qafzeh Skhul	92,000–120,000 81,000–101,000
Morocco	Jebel Irhoud	100,000 (trans.)
Germany	Stetten	36,000
France	Cro-Magnon Abri Pataud	<30,000 >27,000
China	Zhoukoudian	10,000–18,000
Australia	Lake Mungo	30,000
United States	Midland, Texas	11,600

skeleton is less robust. Refer back to Figures 11.23 and 11.24 and look in the mirror.

Note in Table 11.4 that the earliest fossils are all from eastern and southern Africa and that they are considered, at least by some authorities, as transitional between archaic and modern *Homo*. There is also a transitional form from Morocco (Figure 11.29). The implication is that modern humans—whether a new species or just the modern form of an existing species—arose in Africa. Until recently, the earliest dates for the appearance of transitional forms was about 200,000 years ago from South Africa, but recent finds from Kenya (Bräuer et al. 1997), dated by several methods that appear to correspond well, have pushed this date back to perhaps 300,000 years ago.

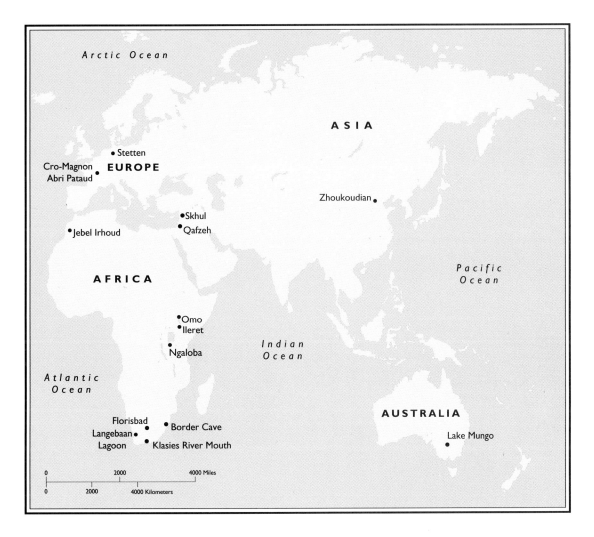

FIGURE 11.28
Map of important early *Homo sapiens* sites in Africa, Asia, Australia, and Europe.

By around 120,000 years ago, we find fossils that represent humans of fully modern appearance. The earliest of these at present are from South Africa and Israel (Figure 11.30). At the South African site of Langebaan Lagoon, a small human, possibly a female, left her footprints in rock claimed to be dated to 117,000 years ago—a moment frozen in time reminiscent of the Laetoli footprints from Tanzania (Chapter 10). As we move farther away from Africa and Southwest Asia, the dates for the early appearance of modern *Homo sapiens* get more recent, a further indication that Africa is the birthplace of modern humans.

With modern anatomy came further advances in technology and expressions of modern behavior patterns. Although much of the tool

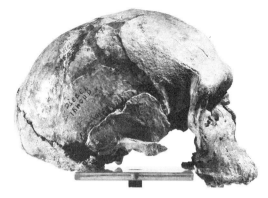

FIGURE 11.29
The cranium from Jebel Ir-houd, Morocco, dated at about 100,000 years old. It is considered by some to be transitional between archaic and modern *Homo.* The braincase is low, the face is relatively large, and it has distinct brow ridges. Other-wise, its features are modern.

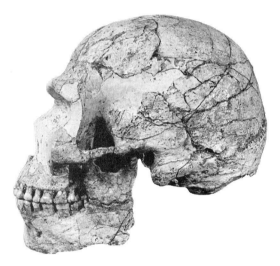

FIGURE 11.30
Examples of early modern *Homo sapiens* (clockwise from top): Skhul, Israel; Border Cave, South Africa; Jebel Qafzeh, Israel. Note the higher foreheads, protruding chins, and flatter faces compared to archaic *Homo.* Despite the rather prominent brow ridges in Skhul, it is still considered fully modern due to its other features.

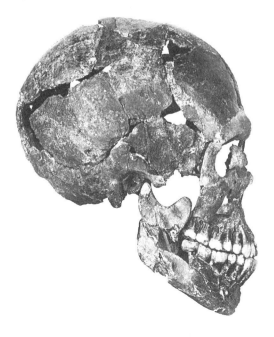

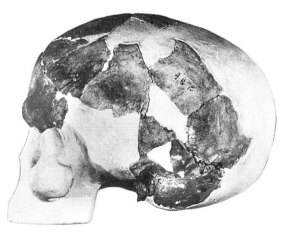

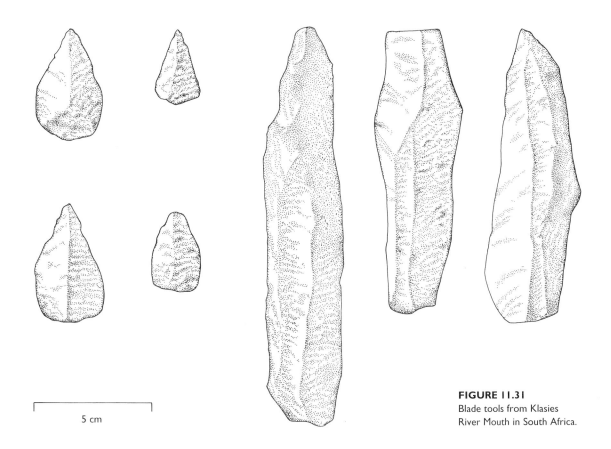

5 cm

FIGURE 11.31
Blade tools from Klasies
River Mouth in South Africa.

technology of early moderns resembles that of archaics, artifacts from one of the oldest anatomically modern sites do show an important advance. From Klasies River Mouth in South Africa, dated to perhaps 120,000 years ago, come long, bifacially worked spear points made from stone blades. These were flaked from cores by the "punch" technique (Figure 11.31). Here, a pointed punch, usually made of antler, is placed on the core and then struck with a stone hammer. This method directs the force of the blow more precisely so that longer, narrower, thinner flakes of predictable shape may be taken off. The same technique shows up much later in Europe.

The Klasies River site also provides evidence that the people there may have hunted adults of such large animals as cape buffalo and eland, a large antelope. The site contains a spearpoint lodged in a buffalo vertebra. Both these animals can weigh up to a ton. Certainly, these people also scavenged and may have hunted only weak or old individuals of these dangerous species. But it appears that there is good evidence of at least limited big game hunting. That behavior, it seems, can be associated with the appearance of anatomically modern humans.

FIGURE 11.32
Bifacially flaked Upper Paleolithic spear points, some of
the finest stonework ever
seen.

FIGURE 11.33
Upper Paleolithic artifacts,
including a shaft straightener
with carved animals (top), a
harpoon carved from antler
(left), and an example of the
famous Venus figurines
(lower right) that may have
served as fertility symbols.

By the time the Neandertals disappeared, about 30,000 years ago, modern *Homo sapiens* had spread all over the Old World, even as far as Australia, and we enter a cultural period called the Upper Paleolithic, known first through finds in Europe. This period is marked by several important cultural innovations. Blades struck off cores become so precisely and beautifully made as to be virtual works of art. In fact, some blades are so thin and delicate we think they may have been just that (Figure 11.32).

Tools in the Upper Paleolithic were also made from bone, antler, and ivory. Some are practical, such as harpoons, spear points, and shaft straighteners. Some have symbolic significance. Even some of the utilitarian items are decorated (Figure 11.33). Indeed, art is seen in the Upper Paleolithic in some of its most striking and beautiful forms. Over a hundred cave sites, mostly in France and Spain, have yielded paintings of animals that rival anything produced today (Figure 11.34). There are also carvings in stone, bone, antler, and ivory, among the most famous of which are the so-called Venus figurines, often thought to be fertility symbols (Figure 11.33, lower right). There is even an engraved antler from about 32,000 years ago that may have been a calendar based on phases of the moon.

There is some evidence of even older art from northern Australia. A hematite "crayon"—used to get red ocher, a pigment—has been dated at almost 60,000 years old at the site of Malakunanja II, and painted ocher figures and carved holes at a rock shelter site called Jinmium may date to between 176,000 and 116,000 years ago. Both sites, however, were dated

FIGURE 11.34
One of many beautiful paintings from the cave of Lascaux in southern France, this depicts an aurochs (an ancient ox) and several horses. There is an antlered animal, probably a deer, in the lower right. Notice that the left front leg of the red horse is separated from the body, adding a three-dimensional appearance. This photograph is really from Lascaux II, a replica near the actual cave, created because of damage to the original from bacteria and carbon dioxide given off by too many visitors. The walls of the replica cave are reproduced to a tolerance of 5 mm, and many of the pigments in the paintings are the same as used by the original artists perhaps 17,000 years ago.

Contemporary Reflections

What Do We Mean by "Human"?

Back in Linnaeus's time, when species were thought to have been separately created, the question of what was "human" was an easy one. People were human, and everything else wasn't. Then, fossils representing the history of other organisms began to appear and to be recognized as the intermediate evolutionary steps from previous states to present ones. And then Charles Darwin explained how this all happened. As anthropologist Ian Tattersall puts it (1994), when, by the end of the nineteenth century, it had become clear that we too had a fossil record and had evolved like other creatures, the issue of humanness became far more complex.

We use the word "human" all the time in different contexts and with different meanings—and we usually communicate and understand those meanings with little ambiguity. Even in a biological context, it is perfectly clear which present-day species the term refers to. We use "human" as precisely as we use "ape" or "monkey." But how about a more scientific definition that takes into account what we know about our evolutionary history and, thus, about our place in nature in a broader context? Put another way, although it's clear that "human" refers to us, who *else* might it refer to?

"Human" could be used as a synonym for "hominid." In the traditional (and still most common) taxonomic sense of this category, human, then, would refer to any habitually bipedal primate and so would include *Australopithecus* and *Paranthropus*, who share few specific traits—other than upright walking—with modern peoples. One cladistic taxonomy (see Chapter 7) includes our sister species—chimpanzees, bonobos, and gorillas—in family Hominidae. In this case, the use of "human" is so broad a category as to be fairly meaningless.

A seemingly more realistic approach is to limit the use of "human" to just *Homo sapiens* (for splitters) or just anatomically modern *Homo sapiens* (for lumpers). No one would deny that modern *H. sapiens* falls into that classification, which could include the criteria of "high intelligence, language, aesthetic sensibilities, and the mastery of complex technologies" (Tattersall 1994:114)—all those things we know define, delineate, and differentiate our species today. Under this use, the other species of *Homo* (*H. neanderthalensis*, for instance) "possessed [almost nothing] even remotely resembling the restless spirit of innovation and inventiveness that informed the lives of Upper Paleolithic peoples. . . . [I]t is only with the Upper Paleolithic that we find evidence for behaviors that would allow us to characterize their possessors as fully human" (115).

But anthropologist Milford Wolpoff (1994—in a rebuttal to the Tattersall piece cited above) argues that this definition is too limited. While older forms of *Homo* may have had less complex cultural behaviors than ours, they nonetheless *had* culture. The makers of the Oldowan tools some 2 million years ago were the first stone toolmakers and the first hominoids to show a trend toward larger brains. Even with our far more complex cultural expressions, we share with these other members of our genus—and *only* with them—these large brains and the abilities they facilitate. It would seem, then, that to limit the use of "human" to just modern *Homo sapiens* would necessarily require recognizing *degrees* of humanness to account for the behaviors of premodern peoples. Indeed, Tattersall says that, despite his limited definition, he finds "great difficulty in denying Neanderthals human status" (1994:115).

All this may seem rather a matter of philosophical point of view—and, on some levels, it is. But scientifically, if we link being human to being included in certain taxonomic categories, then just how we classify groups of hominids will make a difference. If, for instance, we limit humanness to members of *Homo sapiens*, then it matters a great deal whether we accept a six-species or a one-species model for the evolution of our genus. This is the real issue of the Tattersall and Wolpoff pieces cited, and it leads directly to the consideration of the next chapter.

using luminescence dating (see Chapter 9), which is still somewhat experimental. There is other evidence that the Jinmium site may be only about 10,000 years old (Gibbons 1997c).

As the Upper Paleolithic continued, big game hunting became a way of life, especially for people living in glacial climates with limited plant resources. People no longer relied on caves or rock shelters for places of habitation, but began manufacturing shelters. From Mal'ta, for example, an 18,000-year-old site in south-central Russia, come the remains of a hut built on a wood frame supported by woolly mammoth bones and reindeer antlers and covered with animal hides.

Around 15,000 years ago, and possibly earlier, humans moved into North America, coming across a land bridge between Siberia and Alaska, which was exposed when the sea level dropped during glacial periods. They soon moved throughout the continent and into South America. Modern *Homo sapiens* had populated every landmass on the planet except Antarctica.

▽　　　▽　　　▽

SUMMARY

The record of the latest 2 million years of hominid evolution is complex. The fossils from the first 99 percent of this period are scarce, often fragmentary, scattered geographically, physically variable, and, in some cases, questionably dated. Not surprisingly, the interpretations of these fossils vary as greatly as do the fossils themselves. Our survey uses, as a starting point, the currently most elaborate model for classifying and naming these fossils—the recognition of six species within genus *Homo* after the early *H. habilis/rudolfensis* stage. I do not necessarily endorse this model but am beginning with it for the purpose of clearly organizing our discussion of a fairly complex topic.

The earliest species, *Homo ergaster,* is found only in Kenya, but a probable branch off this group, *Homo erectus,* spreads through the rest of Africa and into Asia and possibly southern Europe. These two species are characterized by virtually modern postcranial skeletons, brain sizes close to and even overlapping the modern human range, and the invention of more sophisticated stone tools and other cultural innovations, including the use of fire. In Java, *H. erectus* may have persisted until as recently as 27,000 years ago.

A geographically and chronologically scattered species, *Homo heidelbergensis,* appears next. The earliest examples of the species, from Spain, are placed by some authorities into a new species, *Homo antecessor.* Located from England to South Africa to China, *H. heidelbergensis* displayed brain sizes within the modern human range and at the modern human average, though their crania retained primitive features, giving them the label "archaic." They are known, starting about 200,000 years ago, for the invention of the Levallois stone toolmaking technique—a sophisticated way of "mass producing" flake tools. They may have done some hunting as well.

The most famous of the "archaic" humans are the Neandertals, a separate species, *Homo neanderthalensis,* according to many. Living in Europe and Southwest Asia from 200,000 to 36,000 years ago, this group exhibits traits that distinguish it from both *H. heidelbergensis* and later *Homo sapiens.* These traits include large, prognathous faces, ruggedly built skulls, and robust, muscular bodies—possibly adaptations to the cold glacial conditions many of their populations encountered. Neandertals are known for their retouched flake tools, which may have been used to carve bone and work wood; perhaps for the first use of hafting stone points on wooden shafts; and for abstract cultural achievements such as burial of the dead and care of the elderly and infirm.

Fossils transitional between archaic and modern *Homo* appear in Africa perhaps as early as 300,000 years ago, and the first fully modern *Homo sapiens* are found in Africa and Southwest Asia beginning around 120,000 years ago. From there, modern-appearing humans spread throughout the Old World and eventually onto the islands of the Pacific and into the Americas. Archaic peoples—or archaic traits—disappear. During this time, big game hunting developed, tool technology advanced, sophisticated shelters were built, and humans created art.

The questions now become: Just how many species of genus *Homo* are we actually dealing with? And, how are all these groups related evolutionarily? These are the questions addressed in the next chapter.

KEY TERMS

parsimony	tundra	postorbital
brow ridges	Acheulian	constriction
sagittal keel	hand axe	Levallois
torus	bifacial	Mousterian
Pleistocene	endocasts	haft
glaciers		

SUGGESTED READINGS

The *National Geographic* series "The Dawn of Humans," mentioned in the last chapter, also covers the topics of this chapter. The series appears in the issues of September 1995; January and March 1996; and February, May, July, and September 1997.

For other summaries of human evolution see three books by Ian Tattersall: *The Human Odyssey, The Fossil Trail,* and, most recently, *The Last Neanderthal.* He also has a brief summary article in the April 1997 issue of *Scientific American,* "Out of Africa Again . . . and Again?" Be aware that Tattersall is a splitter, advocating, at present, five species of *Homo* from *ergaster* on. A more technical general work is *Reconstructing Human Origins: A Modern Synthesis* by Glenn C. Conroy.

The intriguing story of the missing fossils of "Peking Man" are the topic of C. Janus's *The Search for Peking Man.* Some of the new evidence about *Homo erectus* is nicely summarized in an article by James Shreeve, "*Erectus* Rising," from the September 1994 issue of *Discover.*

The new finds from Atapuerca, Spain, are the topic of "The Face of an Ancestral Child," by Robert Kunzig in the December 1997 *Discover.*

For an up-to-date coverage of the archaeological record of early humans, see Kenneth Feder's *The Past in Perspective: An Introduction to Human Prehistory.*

CHAPTER

12

THE DEBATE OVER MODERN HUMAN ORIGINS

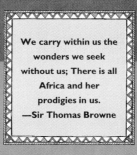

We carry within us the
wonders we seek
without us; There is all
Africa and her
prodigies in us.
—Sir Thomas Browne

My any of the current great debates in science involve, not surprisingly, the distant past. Scientists argue about the origin and early history of the universe, about the formation of our solar system and its planets, about the origin of life on earth, and about the causes and effects of mass extinctions seen in the fossil record. There are, of course, also debates about the early evolution of the hominids—the number of early hominid genera, for example, or the exact relationships among the groups of early hominids.

But no point in the history of our evolution is as contentious as the latest chapter—the origin of modern *Homo sapiens*. An astounding number of articles and books advocate one point of view or another, summarize and evaluate the various hypotheses, or analyze and interpret the debate itself. And this debate is far from peaceful. Arguments get heated at times, and some written pieces include accusations of poor scholarship or hidden agendas. Comments can get downright nasty.

Moreover, some investigators see, in the choice of hypotheses, implications that are not necessarily directly relevant to the issues being discussed (see the section below on "Race and Modern Human Origins"). These connections are picked up by the popular media and passed on to the public, who get the wrong impression of what the debate is really about. None of this helps us sort out, examine, and evaluate an issue that is already complicated enough. There are large amounts of data about the possible origin of modern *Homo sapiens*, much of it interpreted quite differently by different specialists. Even impartial and dispassionate accounts can still be detailed and confusing.

At the risk of adding yet another version, with yet another set of diagrams and names, I will try in this chapter to reduce the major competing hypotheses (or models) down to their essential elements in a way that relates them directly to the material we have covered so far, at a level of detail appropriate to this book. I hope that this approach will make sense in terms of the themes and data we have been dealing with, and that it will provide you with a basic framework to which you can add further information.

As confusing as the issue might be, it is a good example of science in action—as both a scholarly and a very human endeavor. Even summarizing the debate—with its different interpretations, different theoretical points of view, related agendas, and sometimes rancorous rhetoric—is to catch scientific progress "in the act."

This is a fascinating topic, and an understandably important debate, because, as I pointed out in the previous chapter, at stake is our very identity—our specific place in nature, our relationships to the other hominids, and our nature as products of the processes of evolution. We will address the following questions:

What are the major competing hypotheses regarding the origin of modern *Homo sapiens?*

What evidence has been offered—from the fossil record, from genetics, and from evolutionary theory—for and against each model?

Is there an alternative model, intermediate between the two major ones?

How is the issue of racial differences related to this debate?

THE MODELS

It would appear, based on current available evidence (see Table 11.4), that fully modern-*looking* people first appeared about 120,000 years ago, with transitional forms showing the beginnings of modern traits back as far as 300,000 years ago. It also appears that these traits first evolved in Africa. But at issue is the question, Do these traits accurately define and distinguish a new species of hominid, *Homo sapiens*, or is the collection of traits we think of as modern just the latest set of variable features in the evolution of a much older species? You should recognize these points of view as another way of stating the debate introduced in the previous chapter—between the single-species model of the evolution of genus *Homo* and the five- or six-species model.

In terms of the broad implications of this debate, we can give these models descriptive names. The single-species version is known as the **Multiregional Evolution** model (**MRE**). Models that recognize *Homo sapiens* as the most recent of several species of *Homo* are called by a number of names, most commonly the **Out-of-Africa** model. However, the MRE also recognizes our species as arising in and expanding out of Africa (it says that this evolution took place, just a lot earlier), so I prefer to call the second model the **Recent African Origin** model (**RAO**). Figure 12.1 has generalized diagrams that depict these models.

The Recent African Origin Model (RAO)

Major proponents of the Recent African Origin model are Christopher Stringer of the Natural History Museum in London (Stringer and McKie 1996) and Ian Tattersall of the American Museum of Natural History in New York (Tattersall 1997). Although various supporters of this model

Multiregional Evolution: The hypothesis that *Homo sapiens* is about 2 million years old and that modern traits evolved in geographically diverse locations and then spread through the species.

Out-of-Africa: Another name for the Recent African Origin model.

Recent African Origin: The hypothesis that *Homo sapiens* evolved as a separate species recently in Africa and then spread to replace more archaic populations.

FIGURE 12.1
Generalized models for the origin of *Homo sapiens.*

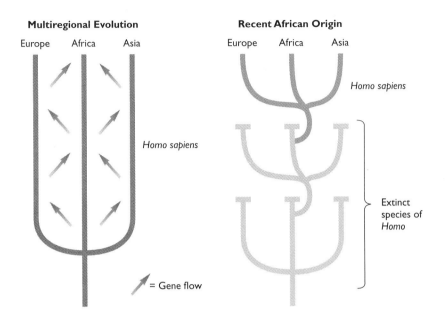

recognize different numbers of species within genus *Homo,* they all share the view that *Homo sapiens* is a separate species that branched from a preexisting *Homo* species in Africa around 150,000 to 200,000 years ago. This new species then spread over the Old World, replacing archaic populations when they came in contact, presumably because *H. sapiens* was a better-adapted species. (This model is sometimes called the Replacement model.)

Deductive predictions from this hypothesis include the following:

1. Transitional forms would be found only in Africa, the area of origin, with modern traits appearing first in Africa and later in other areas as the modern population spread.
2. Outside the area of origin, modern and archaic populations should overlap in time, since they are separate species and the process of replacement would not be instantaneous.
3. Humans should have relatively little genetic diversity since the species is young.
4. Modern populations should differ in the amount of genetic variation they possess, with the most diverse population in Africa, where the species first evolved, because this would represent the oldest group with the most time to accumulate genetic variation.

Figure 12.2 shows how this model interprets the relationships among the six species of *Homo* described in the previous chapter.

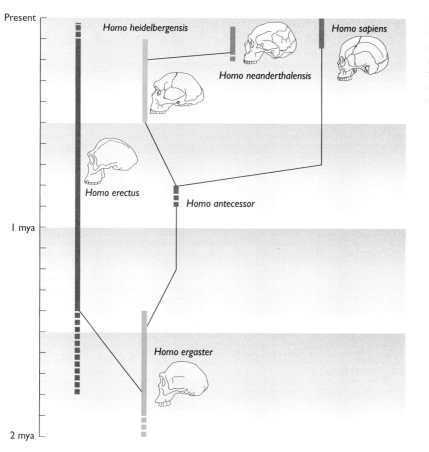

FIGURE 12.2
One possible set of relation-ships for the six proposed species of *Homo,* according to the Recent African Origin model. The data are the same as in Figure 11.1.

The Multiregional Evolution Model (MRE)

The name most often associated with the Multiregional Evolution model is Milford Wolpoff of the University of Michigan (Wolpoff and Caspari 1997). This model—a bit more complicated than the RAO—also claims that *Homo sapiens* arose in Africa, but it says that this event occurred 2 million years ago. Members of this new species (traditionally called *Homo erectus*) spread throughout the Old World, evolving genetic and pheno-typic regional differences in response to the wide variety of environmental circumstances they encountered, and in response to the complex popu-lation movements, isolations, mergings, and fissionings that must have taken place. The degree of species mobility resulted in sufficient gene flow to maintain a single species, as no population was isolated long enough or to a great enough degree for speciation to occur. As successful advanta-geous adaptive features arose, they were dispersed across the species. Phys-ical features we associate with modern humans appeared everywhere but may have been manifested in different ways in different populations and in different environments. Thus, we are today, and have always been, a variable species—but a single species.

Deductive predictions from this hypothesis include the following:

1. Transitional forms between archaic and modern humans should appear all over the Old World with different combinations of traits and at different times in various geographic locations.

2. Some traits characteristic of a particular region today may be traced back in time to older populations in that region.

3. Modern humans should show greater genetic diversity than that predicted by the RAO model, because we are an older species with more time to accumulate genetic variations.

4. The degree of genetic variation within each human group should be about the same, since the groups have all been evolving together as a single, interbreeding species.

Figure 12.3 shows how this model views the interrelationship among the regional fossil populations discussed in the previous chapter.

THE EVIDENCE

Clearly, the evidence for the last 2 million years of our evolution is limited. Fossils exist, but they are often fragmentary, and they are scattered across space and time. The same can be said for archaeological evidence of our ancestors' cultural activities. Genetic data are available, but only from fully modern populations alive today, or at least recently. And evolutionary theory is still being debated, both in general terms and especially when applied to the history of a specific group.

Thus, in reviewing the extensive literature on modern human origins, we find that different authorities have very different interpretations of the same data. Indeed, the same general data have been convincingly used to support either model, but proponents differ in which specific pieces of data they emphasize. It can become, as anthropologist David Pilbeam once said in another context (1984, 1986), like "peering" too closely at a pointillist painting or trying to look at a newspaper photo with a magnifying glass. The details become a bunch of "meaningless dots."

Below, then, is a general summary of the available evidence and interpretations by both "camps." There are, of course, more than two specific hypotheses, but understanding the extremes is the best starting point. Anyway, until recently, intermediate models have received little attention and their supporters seem to have been drawn toward one or the other of the major points of view (Smith and Harrold 1997).

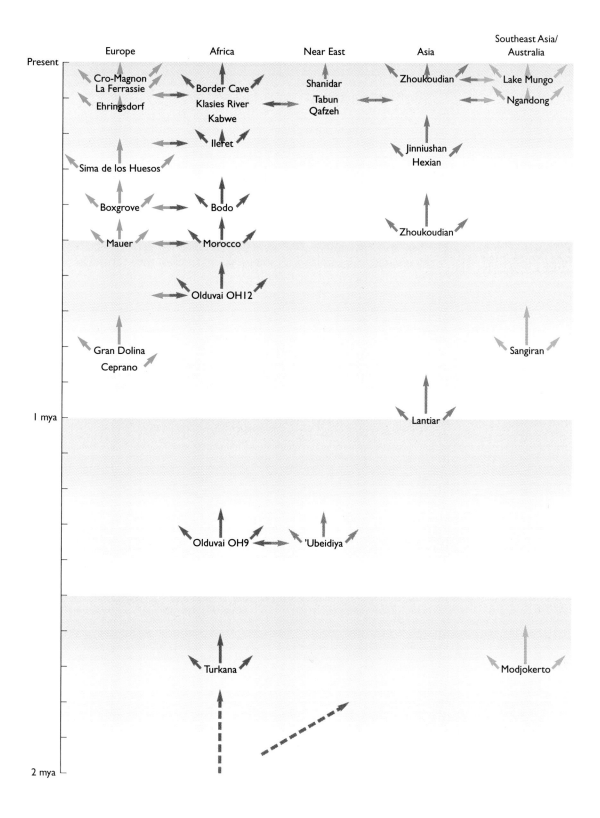

The Fossil Record

In using the multiple-species model as an organizing format for our discussion of genus *Homo* in the previous chapter, we have already presented the fossil evidence as interpreted by the RAO proponents. Look again at the tables and maps in Chapter 11.

Seen this way, the fossils support predictions 1 and 2 of this model. As suggested by prediction 1, forms transitional between archaic species (*H. heidelbergensis* and *H. neanderthalensis*) and *Homo sapiens* are found only in Africa. Modern forms appear first in Africa and then show up at increasingly recent dates as one moves away from that continent. And as prediction 2 states, archaics and moderns overlap in some areas. Note that the modern fossils from Skhul and Qafzeh in Israel actually predate the Neandertals in the same country, after which the two groups shared the area for a time (see Tables 11.3 and 11.4). In Java, if recent dating is correct, modern humans lived alongside the last remnants of *Homo erectus* until only 27,000 years ago. In other areas, replacement seems to have been quick and clear-cut. By the time modern *Homo sapiens* got to Europe, maybe 36,000 years ago, the Neandertals were nearly gone. According to Recent African Origin supporters, the European fossils from this time are unambiguously *either* of the two species, with no transitions.

In stark contrast, Wolpoff and Caspari assert that the variation seen within the fossil record of *Homo* does not warrant division into separate species. They claim, for example, that in broad perspective "just about every way *H. erectus* differs from its australopithecine ancestors also characterizes *H. sapiens*: virtually no features are unique to *H. erectus*" (1997:256). In other words, *H. sapiens* and *H. erectus* are the same species. They also contend that modern traits did not all arise in one location, but in many, and that they spread throughout the species, to be expressed differently in different geographic locations.

Moreover, Wolpoff and Caspari feel that "it has proved impossible to provide an acceptable [physical] definition of modernity" in the first place (1997:313). Some features proposed to define modern humans *do not* include all recent or living peoples. For example, it has been suggested that Neandertals' large, continuous brow ridges are a major diagnostic feature helping to distinguish them from modern humans. But some living indigenous people of Australia—fully modern biological humans in every sense of the word—also have large, continuous brow ridges (Figure 12.4). There is sufficient variation among modern humans, says Wolpoff, that modernity must be defined regionally, as no general definition includes all clearly modern humans and excludes all other proposed species. Thus, he believes that prediction 1 of the MRE model—transitions worldwide but in differing combinations and at different times—is upheld.

FIGURE 12.4
Two Tiwi from Melville Island, northern Australia. Note their large, continuous brow ridges—a trait associated with archaic humans, yet present here in fully modern *Homo sapiens*. The man on the right is in mourning, which requires that he paint his body and not feed himself, so he is receiving water from a friend.

Wolpoff and supporters also see continuity of individual traits in certain areas (prediction 2), especially Asia and Australia, where some modern regional features are said to resemble those from the Sangiran fossils identified as *Homo erectus*. He also says some features show continuity between Neandertal and modern populations in Europe. Especially important are nonadaptive traits, which would not be affected by environmental changes over time but *would* be affected by large-scale population replacement. An example is an opening for a nerve on the inside of the mandible (the mandibular foramen). A form of this opening (of no apparent adaptive significance) found only in European Neandertals is also found in high frequency in early moderns from Europe—and in *no* Asian or African populations—suggesting a direct evolutionary relationship.

David Frayer, another multiregionalist, addresses the issue of specimens labeled as transitional by the RAO proponents. Frayer reminds us that the unit of evolution is the population. Because *any* population displays variation, he argues, it is "impossible to identify transitional specimens. . . . [Only populations], not individuals, can be transitional" (Frayer et al. 1994). The so-called transitional specimens, then, cannot be representative of the range of variation and may not represent the average appearance of the populations from which they came.

I think that in regard to this debate the fossil record is ambiguous. It can clearly be interpreted to support either point of view, and there is wide disagreement between those points of view. Note that even splitters cannot agree on the exact number of premodern species of *Homo*. The fossils that do exist are usually incomplete, not necessarily representative of the populations from which they came, and often of questionable age. Moreover, many of the morphological features being used for these analyses are of unknown heritability; that is, we don't know how much they tell us about actual genetic distinctions (Minugh-Purvis 1995).

Finally, it is hard to translate physical features into species classification. As we saw in Chapters 4 and 5, some separate species look nearly identical, while other species can include an amazing amount of phenotypic variation (see again Figure 2.6). The RAO people see the variation in the fossil record as being outside the range of modern human diversity. The MRE people feel that the fossil variation is well within the potential range of our species, just different in specifics at different points in time from modern variation.

Along with fossil evidence, archaeological data have also been cited in support of the two models. Recent African Origin supporters note the appearance of sophisticated toolmaking techniques earlier in Africa than elsewhere (see Figure 11.31 for an example). They also see evidence of the fairly rapid replacement in Europe of tools associated with Neandertals by those associated with modern *Homo sapiens*.

On the other hand, Multiregional Evolution advocates claim that these early African tool forms are not all that different from the tools of Neandertals and that artifacts associated with modern fossils from Skhul and Qafzeh are virtually identical to those associated with nearby Neandertal finds. In other words, they say that tool type is not necessarily diagnostic of species, and that the variation, scattered nature, and questionable dating of some archaeological data present the same problems as does the paleontological record. (For more detail, but still a basic discussion, see Feder and Park 1997.)

Genetics

For several years now, genetic analyses have been seen as providing the strongest evidence for the Recent African Origin model. Using sophisticated biochemical technology, we can make detailed comparisons among species and among populations within species to examine their genetic differences. Specific genetic differences among populations are the results of the accumulation of genetic changes over time—most importantly from mutations. The more genetically variable a population is, the older it probably is. The more genes that differ between two groups, the longer those two groups have been evolutionarily separate.

Data from living populations show that the human species is quite genetically homogeneous. There is less variation in our populous and widespread species than in any species of great apes (Stringer and Andrews 1988). Our species, therefore, does not appear to be very old. Moreover, when regional populations of *Homo sapiens* are compared, the data show that the most diverse groups are those from sub-Saharan Africa. This is taken as evidence that these represent the oldest populations of modern humans, apparent support for predictions 3 and 4 of the RAO model.

One of the first studies—and certainly the most famous and initially influential—that specifically applied genetic analyses to the question of modern human origins was performed by Rebecca Cann, Mark Stoneking, and the late Allan Wilson (Cann et al. 1987). It was flawed and has been seriously questioned (not unusual for first tries) but can provide a fairly simple example of how all such studies work.

Cann and colleagues overcame some objections to the use of nuclear DNA by using **mitochondrial DNA (mtDNA)**. The mitochondria (see Figure 3.1) are the energy factories of the cells. They convert energy stored in nutrients into a form that the cells can use to power their functions. Mitochondria have their own DNA, distinct from the DNA in the cell's nucleus, even to the point of having differences in which amino acid a particular codon codes for. In fact, the mitochondria are thought to have once been separate organisms that, early in the history of life, formed a **symbiotic** bond with larger cells. Most human cells contain hundreds or thousands of mitochondria.

The importance of mtDNA comes from the fact that the actions of the mitochondria are mostly run by the DNA in the nucleus of the cell. The mtDNA, while still having some function, can thus accumulate mutations that may not be selectively important. The reproductive success of the organism is not as dependent upon the exact genetic makeup of its mitochondria as it is on the genes in its nuclei. Furthermore, mtDNA mutates five to ten times faster than nuclear DNA, and the mutation rate appears to be fairly constant. So, mtDNA changes rapidly and the changes—the mutations—are less likely to disappear through selection than are mutations of nuclear DNA. Moreover, the entire mtDNA genome is known (that is, all the base pairs have been identified), and there are large noncoding sequences. Studies focus on these sequences because changes in them must be the results of mutations only, since natural selection has no effect on them. And mtDNA offers one more benefit as an object of study: it is only inherited through females. Sperm cells have mitochondria, but the mitochondria are not normally involved in fertilization. This simplifies the tracing of mtDNA inheritance. You inherited your mtDNA from your mother. It is not a combination, as is your nuclear DNA, of the genes of both parents.

Thus, if populations were compared for their mtDNA, we would seem to get a more accurate assessment of their genetic differences, and thus their evolutionary differences, than if we used nuclear DNA. Mitochondrial DNA studies appeared to support the idea that the human species is genetically homogeneous and, therefore, relatively young. No human groups differ by even as much as 1 percent of their mtDNA. Chimpanzees may be ten times as variable in their mtDNA as we are.

mitochondrial DNA (mtDNA): The genetic material found in the cells' mitochondria rather than in the cell nucleus.

symbiotic: An adaptive relationship between two different species, often, but not necessarily, of mutual benefit.

FIGURE 12.5

Computer-generated tree showing the lines of descent of the 147 women sampled in the study described. The diagram is drawn as a "horseshoe" simply to fit on the page; mentally straighten it out and you have a more familiar-looking family tree. The higher the percentage figure at the point of divergence, the more different were the women's mtDNA and so the longer ago the divergence took place. Note the cluster of African women at lower right. They are distinct from other African women and all others (0.6 percent on the scale). They also show greater diversity in their mtDNA, as seen by the fact that their lines of descent converge closer to the center of the diagram, that is, in the more distant past.

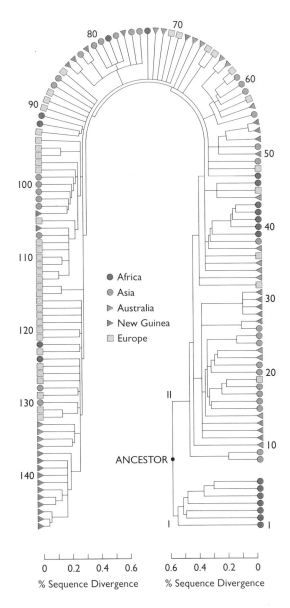

Cann and colleagues analyzed the mtDNA from 147 women from around the world and constructed, through a computer program, a tree of relationships among the groups represented by these women (Figure 12.5). The tree shows that the group from sub-Saharan Africa was relatively distinct from the others and was the most internally diverse. This coincides with RAO predictions 3 and 4.

Moreover, these researchers were able to suggest a date for the appearance of modern human mtDNA. Archaeological and biological evidence indicate that New Guinea was settled by a small number of original migrants about 40,000 years ago. Comparing the mtDNA of the New Guinea sample with that from Africa showed the African sample to be five times more diverse. Thus, mtDNA mutations have been accumulating in Africa $5 \times 40,000$ years, or 200,000 years. This date is in line with the fossil evidence for the first appearance of modern human traits. The research group concluded that we can all trace our mtDNA back to an African woman who lived about 200,000 years ago. This idea, as a result, came to be called the "Eve" hypothesis (see "Contemporary Reflections").

Recently, parts of this interpretation have been questioned. Even if mtDNA is mostly adaptively neutral and has a fairly constant mutation rate—and there is evidence *against* both of these ideas—it turns out that there are far more computer-generated family trees than the one depicted in Figure 12.5, depending upon just how the analysis is done. It has been suggested, in fact, that there may be millions of different trees that can reasonably be constructed. These trees differ in the relationships among the groups represented, and they do not all agree on which group is ancestral to the others.

However, as more studies of DNA have been carried out, using increasingly sophisticated techniques, the genetic evidence for a recent African origin seems to have been strengthened. Larger, more representative samples of human populations have been studied (some using thousands of people from dozens of populations) for variation not only in mtDNA but also in nuclear DNA and genes on the Y chromosome—the chromosome that, in an analogue to mtDNA, is passed down only through males. Using the same assumptions as the initial study by Cann and her colleagues, most of these seem to point to the beginning of *Homo sapiens* as a species in Africa about 150,000 to 200,000 years ago (see Stoneking 1993 for a summary).

Indeed, some recent studies of noncoding genes on the Y chromosome (Gibbons 1997d) found two important gene variants, marked by the presence of the base adenine (A) (see Chapter 3), that are shared by other primates and are found today only among Africans—mostly among Khoisan peoples, the groups once known as Bushmen and Hottentots. Thus, this variant is seen as the oldest version of the gene, and those populations as being the closest, genetically, to the first modern humans (Figure 12.6). According to the investigators' calculations, one of these markers mutated to a T (thymine) and one to a G (guanine) in some descendants of the first modern population around 100,000 to 200,000 years ago. Today, most Africans, and all men outside Africa, carry the newer variations. This is strong evidence in support of the RAO model.

FIGURE 12.6
Recent studies have indicated that the oldest versions of certain genes on the male-inherited Y chromosome are found among Khoisan men, like this !Kung San hunter from the Kalahari Desert in southern Africa (the "!" indicates a click sound). These data are taken to mean that Khoisan may be the closest living populations, genetically, to the earliest modern humans.

Finally, in 1997, some mtDNA was extracted from the humerus of the original Neandertal specimen found in 1856 (see Figure 11.20). The investigators (Krings et al. 1997) found three times more differences between the fossil DNA and modern human DNA than between pairs of modern humans. These differences placed the Neandertal mtDNA variation outside the range of modern human variation. Further, the Neandertal DNA showed no special similarity to that of modern Europeans; the sample was equally distinct from all modern human populations. These data were interpreted to mean that modern human mtDNA and Neandertal mtDNA began to diverge 690,000 to 550,000 years ago. "This suggests," say the investigators, "that Neandertals went extinct without contributing mtDNA to modern humans" (19). More support for the RAO model.

But can the genetic data also be seen as supporting the Multiregional Evolution model? The remarkable degree of overall genetic homogeneity in our species could, as the RAO model claims, be the result of our species' relative youth. MRE proponents, however, have suggested that the same homogeneity could have resulted with a much older origin if the species maintained sufficient gene flow to cause genetic variation to diffuse through the species. In fact, as gene flow increased through the years—with greater means of mobility and more motivation for mobility—genetic diversity might have decreased further.

The greater degree of genetic diversity in African populations can, according to MRE proponents, also be explained by the fact that Africa has, for most of human prehistory, had the largest population size, since that is where we first evolved. A large population, living on a large and environmentally diverse continent, would be expected to display a great deal of genetic variation (Relethford and Harpending 1995; but see Harpending and Relethford 1997, where they appear to change their minds). Thus, although predictions 3 and 4 of the MRE model seem not to be supported, there are other possible explanations.

In addition, according to biologist Alan Templeton (1997), a complex statistical analysis of the mtDNA data indicates no split between African and non-African populations. This split is required by the RAO model. Templeton claims that his analysis documents the continual gene flow that is at the heart of the MRE model.

Wolpoff and Caspari (1997:302) also note that the "history of mitochondrial DNA (or any other gene in the nuclear DNA) does *not* reflect population history." Rather, it reflects the history of a specific genetic system, in the same way that the history of "a single Scottish name might be different from the history of the Scottish people" (304). The evolutionary history of a population involves the histories of many genes. If there was a recent origin of a separate modern human species, then all genetic systems would have similar histories, which seems not to be the case. Wolpoff suggests that there were genetic bottlenecks in the past—different periods where, in regional populations, genetic diversity was greatly limited because of some event that decreased the population size or limited lines of descent. This would then differentially affect present diversity in genetic systems, limiting the diversity of some more than others. Thus, the great homogeneity of modern mtDNA (as well as the genes of the Y chromosome) might reflect a severe bottleneck in the past that had the effect of making the last common ancestor of mtDNA lines a

FIGURE 12.7

The different inheritance patterns of mitochondrial DNA and nuclear DNA. The four couples at the top each have one child. These children pair off and each pair has a child. These children then mate and produce the individual at the bottom. The colored dot in the center of each figure represents the mtDNA. The other colors represent nuclear DNA. Notice that the person at the bottom has inherited her mtDNA through only one line. The other mtDNA lines have become extinct because the other matings eventually produced a male who cannot pass on his mtDNA. The nuclear DNA of the individual at bottom, however, is a combination of the genes of *all* her ancestors. Her nuclear DNA, therefore, is much older than is her mtDNA. Similarly, all modern humans could have inherited their mtDNA from a recent common ancestor while tracing their nuclear DNA common ancestor back much further in time. (Drawn using the concept in a diagram from Hammer and Zegura 1996:122, after Jobling and Tyler-Smith 1995.)

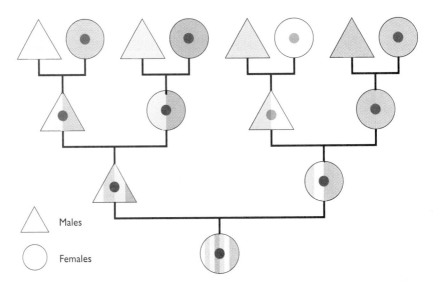

Males

Females

recent one, while our actual common ancestor could be much older (see the "Contemporary Reflections" feature).

Templeton (1997:353) also suggests that, because mtDNA is inherited only through females, it may show a more recent time of origin for all existing mtDNA than does nuclear DNA. Calculations based on certain features of the two forms of DNA suggest, says Templeton, that if all our current mtDNA can be traced to 200,000 years ago, it is likely that all our nuclear genes—which we inherit from both parents—have their point of origin at more than 1 or 2 million years ago—coincident with the MRE model (Figure 12.7).

The variety in histories of genes is being demonstrated by ongoing studies of new genetic systems, especially within nuclear DNA. Rosalind Harding of Oxford University, for example (Wong 1998), found a lineage of the betaglobin gene (the gene for the beta chain of hemoglobin, a mutation of which causes sickle cell anemia) that has been dated to 200,000 years ago. It is found in high frequency in Asia but is rare in Africa, suggesting that archaic populations in Asia contributed to the modern gene pool.

Also called into question are the dates derived by genetic analyses and offered by RAO supporters as evidence of their model. Wolpoff notes the wide range of dates for the age of the last common mtDNA and Y chromosome ancestors. Although many studies point to dates in the 150,000- to 200,000-year range, others have given dates for mtDNA as old as 500,000 years. A recent study of Y chromosome variation (Dorit et al. 1995) suggested a date of 270,000 years, while reinterpretations of the same data offered a date of half that or less (Donnelly et al. 1996, for example).

Finally, it has been noted that the mtDNA sample from a Neandertal came from a single individual and was a short genetic segment (397 base pairs). Considering, says geneticist Simon Easteal, that chimpanzees have much more mtDNA diversity within their species than do humans, the "amount of diversity [shown by the study] between Neanderthals and living humans is not exceptional" (Wong 1998). Clearly, more such fossil DNA data will have to be obtained and studied.

The genetic evidence, then, is still seen by most authorities as supporting the RAO model but can also reasonably be interpreted as evidence for MRE. Like the fossil and archaeological data, the genetic data are still far from conclusive.

Evolutionary Theory

From the above discussion, it is clear that much of the haggling over these two major hypotheses focuses on details of the data. What about some of the broader considerations of evolutionary theory? What happens when we step back and look at a bigger picture? A major issue in this perspective focuses on the plausibility of the gene flow required by the Multiregional Evolution model. Could it have taken place, and, if so, how?

Christopher Stringer (Stringer and McKie 1996:142 ff) thinks that such gene flow is unlikely at best, for four reasons. First, he says, until recent times, hominid populations were too thinly spread across the three continents of the Old World to be so connected by gene flow. The gaps between groups were too large for genes to move around as much as MRE requires.

Second, there were—again, until recently—too many geographical barriers. There are mountain, desert, and water barriers, and, over the last million years or so, the world has been in the grip of the Pleistocene Ice Ages, which caused extreme climatic disruptions and fluctuations. The flow of genes would have been severely limited by these geographical obstacles.

Third, even supposing that different human groups were potentially interfertile, would they have *wanted* to share their genes? Science writer James Shreeve (1995) offers the possibility that Neandertals and moderns in Southwest Asia never interbred because they looked so different they didn't even recognize members of the other group as potential mates. Quoting geneticist L. L. Cavalli-Sforza (Cavalli-Sforza et al. 1994), Stringer suggests that cultural and social barriers to fertility may have been very powerful, and interbreeding might have been considered "breaking a taboo."

Fourth, Stringer questions whether there is any biological precedent for the idea of a widespread species evolving "globally towards the same happy goal" (143). He quotes Stephen Jay Gould (1994a) as saying that we have no multiregional theory for rats or pigeons, two species that match us for success and geographical range. Why then "devise an entirely idiosyncretic . . . hypothesis" for humans? Most species initially arise in a single place and then spread.

There are—as you must suspect by now—responses to these questions from the MRE point of view. On the issue of population density, one estimate that Stringer quotes (Stringer and McKie 1996:144) uses mtDNA variation to calculate the number of females our species possessed in its early evolution. The figure derived is 7000 females, too few to have allowed much gene flow. But the use of mtDNA assumes the conclusion from other studies of that genetic system—that our species arose very recently from a localized group. The reasoning seems circular.

In addition, the apparently thin spread of early human populations across the Old World may be in part attributable to the nature of the fossil record. Remember that most individual hominids who ever lived did not leave fossilized remains, nor have we found but a fraction of all the fossil hominid remains that *were* left. The actual distribution of early populations may be quite different from the distribution of the fossils recovered.

Moreover, there are two processes involved in gene flow. One is the kind of genetic exchange Stringer cites, where "populations essentially sat still while genes passed through them" (144), exchanged between neighboring groups. But genes also flow as a result of migration. Hominids for the last 2 million years have been a migratory genus. In a short period of time, members of *H. erectus/ergaster* got all the way from Africa to Java. There is no reason why humans, having once arrived in these far-flung areas, would necessarily all stay put. They moved because they were following needed resources or looking for better conditions—and the Pleistocene climatic changes may have required a great deal of moving. As Templeton puts it (1997:357), "all that is needed is to have humans distributed throughout the Old World and able to disperse a little bit in any direction every generation."

Geographic barriers to human habitation and movement certainly existed, and still do. They did not, however, prevent the spread of human populations. Even if there were six different species of *Homo*, the fossil record shows that most managed to move around a bit (see the tables and maps in Chapter 11). And the climatic disruptions of the Pleistocene fluctuated. Barriers changed in severity and location. Sea levels rose and isolated some land areas but then dropped again. Dry periods followed wet periods. Glaciers covered huge masses of land but then retreated. Spread over a 2-million-year period, such temporary and changeable barriers might not have presented severe limitations to gene flow.

What can we say about behavioral barriers to interbreeding? Without a time machine, we obviously cannot conduct the only conclusive test. We do know, however, that different physical appearances have not been absolute barriers to interbreeding in modern humans. For example, despite claims by slave owners in this country that Africans were, at best, less civilized and, at worst, virtually a different species, genetic exchange (usually forced by the slave owners) still took place. Even cultural barriers that enforce **endogamy** (marriage within one's group) are temporary over long periods of time as rules and group definitions change, and such rules are not always adhered to anyway.

We even have evidence for interbreeding between nonhuman populations that we classify as different species. Different species of Darwin's finches on the Galápagos hybridize when climatic disruptions bring them into contact. Some species (or subspecies) within the baboon genus *Papio*—groups that are usually easily identified and distinguished, both by us and, presumably, by them—hybridize in zones where their ranges meet. So *our* assessment of physical differences among ancient human groups, and *our* assumptions about their behavioral taboos can't really tell us much about how they were really behaving.

Finally, there is the matter of there being no biological precedent for multiregional evolution. Gould says the human species is not, in terms of its evolution, unique. In general, it's not. As we have stressed in this book, humans play by all the same evolutionary rules as any other species. But we *are* unique in the sense of being at one end of a continuum of certain traits. Our big brains have allowed our genus to experience increasing control over our environments and our adaptations to those environments. We have placed an increasingly thick buffer between us and natural selection. As members of genus *Homo* spread into the far corners of the globe, they got increasingly good at surviving in an amazing variety of conditions through the extra-genetic mechanism of culture. We increasingly invented the means to move around, and we increasingly found motivations for doing so. We are not—to use Gould's examples—rats or pigeons. Gene flow, adaptive genetic changes, and behavioral influences on adaptation might be different in us to such a degree that we might be "idiosyncratic" in the specific way we have evolved.

Furthermore, Gould notes that "widespread species are stable for most of their history, and do not change in any substantial directional sense at all" (quoted in Stringer 1996:144). In other words, the amount of change in humans suggested by the MRE model is not in keeping with general evolutionary theory. But a period of history is relative. Perhaps 2 million years only seems a long period of time for genus *Homo* because those of us who study that genus belong to it. We have examined every minute variation in living humans and our fossil ancestors through a microscope—literally and figuratively. Perhaps, in doing so, we have misread

▼▼▼▼▼▼▼▼▼▼▼▼▼

endogamy: The restriction of marriage to members of the same culturally defined group.

the relative scale of our evolution. Maybe 2 million years is not a lot of time for a large, long-lived species with a long generation time. The changes seen by the MRE model might be a small slice of our species' oscillating selection (discussed in Chapter 5 with regard to Darwin's finches). A single species, as it responds to the processes of evolution through time, may change—although, over the long haul, the changes occur around some central adaptive theme that defines that species. Our central adaptive theme is our big brains and the resultant behaviors, especially culture, that they make possible. As Gould himself says (1997/98:64): "Stasis [species stability] is a dynamic phenomenon."

Thus, because we are still debating some generalities of evolutionary theory, the application of evolutionary processes to a particular species' history can be interpreted in a variety of reasonable ways.

IS THERE AN ALTERNATIVE MODEL?

The debate has been largely between the two diverse models discussed above. It should be clear that, although the proponents of each model adamantly stick to their point of view, most of the relevant data and the theoretical contexts can be read both ways. Not surprisingly, then, alternative models that are intermediate between these extremes have been proposed.

There seems to be a trend, even among RAO supporters, away from complete population replacement of archaics by moderns, and toward the assumption of *some* interbreeding (Bräuer and Stringer 1997, for example). Thus, *Homo sapiens* and archaics were not technically separate species. Models that are based on this idea see modern *traits* as having a single geographic origin, perhaps even quite recently. Then, because these traits were selectively advantageous, they replaced the typical archaic characteristics. These might be called **Genetic Replacement** models (Figure 12.8, and see Hammer and Zegura 1996 for brief descriptions of other specific alternatives).

Templeton (1997) summarizes the general idea. He says that "the genetic complex responsible for the features associated with anatomically modern humans arose first in a single geographic location in the range of ancient humans, which includes Africa[,] . . . then spread throughout the rest of humanity through gene flow amplified by selection, thereby resulting in the *morphological* replacement of the older human type by the modern type" (351). He supports the idea that selectively advantageous traits can spread across regionally differentiated populations by noting that "sickle-cell alleles of African origin have spread in certain European pop-

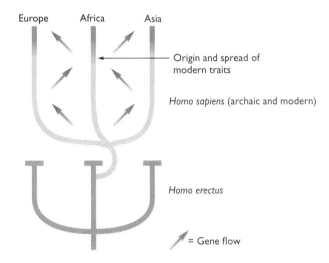

FIGURE 12.8
Genetic Replacement model
for the origin of *Homo
sapiens.*

ulations that are otherwise genetically and morphologically differentiated from Africans" (352).

Some recent studies lend further support to this sort of model. One of the Y chromosome studies noted before (Gibbons 1997d), besides concluding that an ancient genetic variant on that chromosome originated in Africa, found another variant that is common in Asians but also present in some Africans. Geneticist Michael Hammer suggests that some anatomically modern humans who migrated out of Africa interbred with Asians (presumably archaics) and then, because people were not just moving in one direction, migrated back to Africa, adding some ancient non-African genes to the modern genome.

A Genetic Replacement model, then, proposes that modern humanity—in terms of modern traits and the genes that code for them—has a recent origin probably in Africa. These modern traits conferred some adaptive advantage and spread throughout the entire species via migration and the exchange of genes between neighboring populations. Eventually the whole species, while still maintaining regional differences, shared modern characteristics.

Whenever major scientific hypotheses regarding some phenomenon are as diverse as the RAO and MRE models, something more "middle-of-the-road" often appeals simply as a reasonable compromise. Sometimes it turns out to be correct. It was long debated whether light was a wave or a particle. It turns out that, in a very complex manner, it's both.

A Genetic Replacement model has the benefit of describing a way in which two major points, one from each existing hypothesis, can work

Genetic Replacement:
The hypothesis that, although *Homo sapiens* may be an old species, modern human traits evolved recently in one area and spread from there, replacing archaic features.

together. It can accommodate a lumping of species within genus *Homo*, addressing a criticism that questions how so many (up to six) species could have arisen within one genus in a relatively short time. Especially since members of genus *Homo* are characterized by increasing intellectual and cultural control over their environments, it might seem implausible that the factors that lead to speciation—isolation and natural selection in different adaptive directions—could have taken place so many times. Such a model does not necessarily need to lump all *Homo* groups into a single species, but neither does it require *H. sapiens* to be a recent separate species. Modern humans may be seen as the same species as the Neandertals and even as *H. heidelbergensis/antecessor*. This is, in fact, the traditional division of *Homo* (excepting *H. habilis*) into two species, *H. erectus* and *H. sapiens*.

At the same time, a Genetic Replacement model still acknowledges the strong genetic evidence for a recent, localized (probably African) origin of modern humans—that is, those members of the species that possess modern traits. So the species itself may be very old, but the general traits that characterize contemporary humans—and thus the genetic complex responsible for those traits—may be of fairly recent origin.

I find attractive a model that can accommodate mutually exclusive parts of two more diverse models. Moreover, in a universe with the tendency to constantly prove itself more complex than we imagined, I think that the genetic and phenotypic history and the population dynamics of humans will be found to be complicated as well—neither five nor six clear-cut separate species, nor just one species with extensive gene flow that worked to maintain species identity for 2 million years. My leaning is toward some intermediate model of the Genetic Replacement type. The fascinating thing about science, however, is that the discovery of a new fossil, or a well-argued new interpretation, could change my mind overnight.

RACE AND MODERN HUMAN ORIGINS

"The Out-of-Africa model makes mincemeat of racial difference" reads a quote on the back of Christopher Stringer and Robin McKie's *African Exodus: The Origins of Modern Humanity* (1996). The title of Milford Wolpoff and Rachel Caspari's recent book (1997) is *Race and Human Evolution*, with the subtitle "A Fatal Attraction." What is the connection between race and the models we have been examining?

We will cover the topic of human biodiversity and the issue of race in detail in Chapter 14. For the moment, let me give away the punch line of that chapter and state that, in the view of modern biological anthropology, the human species *is not* and *cannot* be divided into *any* number of clearly defined subgroups that warrant the title race. To be sure, we display phenotypic variation—in everything from skin color to relative frequencies of blood types—and this variation sometimes has geographic correlations. We can often accurately identify people's regional backgrounds from their visible physical features. But those correlations are merely the results of different frequencies of alleles that have accumulated in different areas in response to some combination of environmental circumstances and population dynamics (in other words, in response to the operations of natural selection, gene flow, and genetic drift).

Genetically, the whole species is remarkably homogeneous, and the genetic variation is relatively evenly spread. For example, there is a good chance that I, of Irish-Scots-German descent, am more genetically similar overall to an indigenous sub-Saharan African than I am to, say, a southern European. It's just that a particular group of genes I share with that southern European makes the two of us more obviously physically similar. It is these outward physical similarities and differences that cultures use to divide humans into races. Race is a cultural construct.

The biological unity of our species, then, is now a well-documented fact, and it leads to certain socially relevant ideas and ideals—namely, that although individual humans vary in many ways, there exist no profound inherent differences *among human groups* that would warrant differential treatment in social and cultural environments. Skin color, for example, is no predictor of intellectual capabilities.

Indeed, a majority of anthropologists have leaned toward the Recent African Origin model not only because many believe the data support it but also because it neatly explains our species' current homogeneity. If our species is very young—only a few hundred thousand years at most—and if it arose from one localized population, then it could not possibly display deep and profound variations among its populations. There simply hasn't been enough time. If the RAO model is correct, human races could not exist. This makes the RAO model attractive indeed.

Moreover, it has been stated by some RAO supporters that one fatal problem with the multiregional model is that it *does* "suggest, at face value, that modern humanity's constituent races are divided by fundamental and deep-rooted differences" (Stringer and McKie 1996:60). If, such arguments go, local populations show continuity of features into the distant past, that implies that modern racial groups are themselves very ancient and profoundly different. Such a suggestion goes against current social ideals, not to mention the scientific facts regarding our relative homogeneity.

There were, to be sure, earlier models of a multiregional perspective that did make such suggestions. In his 1962 book, *The Origin of Races*, anthropologist Carleton Coon proposed that five subspecies or races of

Contemporary Reflections

Who Was "Eve"?

When that first groundbreaking research with mitochondrial DNA was completed in 1987, it was excitedly announced that the data showed all modern humans to be descended from an African woman who lived around 200,000 years ago. Naturally, it was tempting to dub her "Eve," a metaphorical reference to the creation story in Genesis, and the whole idea of a recent African origin became known as the "Eve hypothesis."

The name certainly captured the public's attention (a painting of Eve, along with an Adam, appeared on the cover of *Newsweek*), and many anthropologists found it rather gratifying that our field was receiving so much press. Indeed, one anthropologist has proposed that the naming was perhaps "a publicity stunt" (Groves 1997:326). And the trend has continued. More recent research on the male-inherited Y chromosome has pointed to the origin of those genes in an African man of about the same era as "Eve." Even as technical a publication as *Science* called him "Adam" (Gibbons 1997d).

These catchy names, however, led to two general misunderstandings, one fairly trivial, but the other more important. Indeed, even in some professional literature, it took a while for the second to be corrected.

First, mitochondrial Eve is not the Eve of the Bible. None of our scientific understanding of evolution is refuted by the mtDNA (or Y chromosome) studies. Some of the early media accounts, however, were sketchy, sensationalized, and confused and gave the clear impression that the actual mother of us all had been found.

The second misunderstanding occurred because some took the Eve data to mean that our *entire species* began with a single, 200,000-year-old African female. Obviously, there had to be a male involved, and, of course, no species begins with one couple. Whenever our species first evolved, it started with an interbreeding population, which came to be genetically different and isolated from its ancestral population.

What the Eve hypothesis says (and, of course, the conclusions are still debated) is that all modern *mtDNA* may have been inherited from a single, recent African female. Although our species began with a population of "Eves," the mitochondrial lines of all but one may have died out (see Figure 12.7).

An analogous phenomenon occurs with family names (Lewin 199:52–53). Begin with ten couples, each with a different surname. Assume that the surnames are passed down through the males and that each couple has two children. After twenty generations, the chances are very good that only one surname will remain. Why? In each generation one-quarter of the couples on average will have two boys, both of whom will pass on the name. But one-half will have a boy and a girl, so one of the children will not pass on the name, and one-quarter will have two girls, so that name will die out. The history of names is different from the history of biological lines. I could trace my last name back to its first occurrence, but that would be far more recent than my earliest biological ancestor.

The same is true for mtDNA inheritance, only through females. Add to this the real-life situations of different numbers of children born to different women, the fact that some women have no children, and the possibility of population bottlenecks, and it's quite possible that all modern humans are descended from a single, recent *mtDNA* line. That does *not* mean, however, that mitochondrial Eve is our *nuclear* DNA ancestor. The first members of *Homo sapiens* could be much older—even 2 million years old—with some individual modern gene systems such as mtDNA and the Y chromosome having different specific histories.

Homo erectus independently evolved into five major races of *Homo sapiens*, crossing "a critical threshold from a more brutal to a more *sapient* state" (1962:658). To make matters worse, he claimed that the different races crossed the "sapiens threshold" at different times, and that this accounted for some of the differences we see today in levels of cultural complexity. "If all races had a recent common origin," he asked, "why were the Tasmanians and many of the Australian aborigines still living during the nineteenth century in a manner comparable to that of Europeans of over 100,000 years ago?" (1962:4). It is clear who Coon thought crossed the threshold first and last. Such ideas may well have sensitized anthropologists against any model of our evolution that included great time depth and regional continuity of traits.

The modern multiregional model, however, is quite different from Coon's and other early ideas. The MRE does not claim that *populations* show continuity but that some regional *traits* do, especially traits that are found in fairly isolated areas such as Australia and other places on the margins of the human geographical range. So-called racial groups are not now, nor were they ever, completely isolated. Rather, the species has displayed continual gene flow, enough to maintain species identity and spread physical features and their genes all over the world. Say Wolpoff and Caspari (1997:208), "a past race has descendants in all living races, just as a living race has ancestors in all past ones."

But this is all really a non-issue. Even if the extreme single-species MRE model proves correct, today's human species is *still* genetically and physically homogeneous. We know this because of well-established, scientific studies of genetics and morphology. How we got to be this way doesn't change how we are, and either major model under debate could account for our current nature. As anthropologist Matt Cartmill puts it (1997:62): "We are what we are, not what our ancestors were. . . . The truth of racial egalitarianism hinges on the facts about living people. Their genealogies are irrelevant."

SUMMARY

The "hottest" current debate in bioanthropology is over the origin of modern *Homo sapiens*. Most authorities seem at present to support either of two major models. One, the Recent African Origin model (RAO), proposes that modern humans evolved as a separate species 200,000 to 150,000 years ago in Africa, having a set of characteristics that made them distinctly different from their ancestor species. They then spread throughout the Old World, replacing populations of archaic humans because of their better-adapted traits.

The second model, the Multiregional Evolution model (MRE), claims that our species is about 2 million years old and incorporates all other previously recognized species of genus *Homo* back through *H. erectus*. After first evolving in Africa, the species spread around the Old World, developing regional differences but always maintaining species identity through gene flow. As new and successful adaptations arose in different areas, they were shared across the species. Thus, "modern" humans are those of us—all 6 billion living today—who share a collection of traits that is the latest set of physical features in a very ancient species.

Intermediate models exist and are becoming increasingly supported. Most could be termed Genetic Replacement models. These models see our *species* as older than 200,000 years but see modern *traits* as having first evolved around that time, probably in Africa. Then, because of some adaptive advantage, these traits spread throughout the species and replaced earlier, archaic features.

The data from paleontology, archaeology, and genetics are ambiguous on this issue. Either model may be supported by the same basic facts. Moreover, neither model is eliminated by applying tenets of evolutionary theory. The attraction of the intermediate models lies in the fact that they incorporate aspects of both extreme hypotheses. Deductive testing and data collection continue, and it would seem that this debate will be ongoing for some time to come.

One related aspect of this debate—the connection to ideas about the nature and existence of human racial groups—has gotten considerable attention. The RAO has received some of its enthusiastic support because it nicely explains our species' current biological homogeneity. Some have interpreted the MRE as necessarily implying deep and profound differences among human groups. This issue may now be put to rest. Modern genetics has clearly shown that we display very little genetic diversity, with that diversity being shared across the species in a way that precludes division into racial groups. That fact is separate from the consideration of how we came to be that way. Any and all of the models proposed for our species' origin can account for our present nature.

KEY TERMS

Multiregional Evolution (MRE)

Out-of-Africa

Recent African Origin (RAO)

mitochondrial DNA (mtDNA)

symbiotic

endogamy

Genetic Replacement

SUGGESTED READINGS

There is extensive literature about this debate. I would especially recommend the two latest books by the major proponents of each point of view: *Race and Human Evolution* by Milford Wolpoff and Rachel Caspari in support of the MRE model, and *African Exodus* by Christopher Stringer and Robin McKie in support of the RAO model. The Wolpoff and Caspari book includes a good historical review of the issue.

For a collection of twenty-nine new articles on all aspects of the debate, see *Conceptual Issues in Modern Human Origins Research* edited by G. A. Clark and C. M. Willermet.

A fairly technical but accessible article by Michael Hammer and Stephen Zegura, "The Role of the Y Chromosome in Human Evolutionary Studies," not only discusses data about that chromosome but also gives a nice description of additional alternative hypotheses. Many of the other aspects of the debate are also addressed. A good review of the genetic evidence in general, as of 1993, is in Mark Stoneking's "DNA and Recent Human Origins."

On the topic of the race connection, see Matt Cartmill's "The Third Man" in the September 1997 issue of *Discover*, and have a look at Carleton Coon's *The Origin of Races* to see why that book caused such a furor.

We have followed the evolutionary history of the hominids up to *Homo sapiens* in its anatomically modern biological state. But the story of hominid evolution doesn't end just because we finally arrive at modern humans. Evolution continues to take place *within* each species. A species undergoes change through time, even as it remains a single species. Remember the peppered moths from Chapter 4.

Since the basic nature of our species was established, all the processes of evolution have continued to operate, acting on the human "theme" and changing us over time and across geographic space. As we divided ourselves into groups based on ethnic identity, nationality, language, and religion, we provided those evolutionary processes with new and varying breeding populations, or demes. Since evolution takes place in populations, the nature of those cultural groups also affected the further evolution of our species as a whole. So did the behaviors—the cultural systems—of the people in the populations. In other words, our biology and our culture are interrelated and affect one another.

As biological anthropologists, then, we are interested not only in how we evolved, but also in what we evolved into, how we have continued to evolve in the recent past, and how we are evolving even today. In this chapter, we will look at some of the ways bioanthropologists study living peoples in terms of genetic change, evolution within populations, the nature of our populations, the adaptive differences among populations, the influence of disease, and, finally, our individual life histories. We will address these questions:

How do we recognize genetic changes in populations and identify and study their causes?

What basic data do we gather in order to describe human populations? What sorts of trends can we see in populations within our species?

In what ways have humans adapted to the varying environments in which we live?

How have diseases influenced human populations?

What are the results of our species' evolution on the life histories—the "personal evolution"—of the human individual?

GENES IN POPULATIONS

In Chapter 4, I introduced the concept of allele frequency. The technical definition of evolution is *change in allele frequency through time*. A process of evolution is any process that alters the frequencies with which alleles of genes appear in a population. We can use allele frequency more specifically by applying actual allele frequency numbers in our study of human evolution.

The example of evolution we focused on in Chapter 4 was sickle cell anemia. Let's continue with that example. Suppose we can test a population for the sickle-cell genotypes at two points in time. Our first test gives the following numbers (based on an example in Relethford 1997):

AA (normal hemoglobin)	50 people
AS (sickle cell trait)	100 people
SS (sickle cell anemia)	50 people
Total	200 people

(A and S are *alleles of a single gene*, the *Hb* gene for hemoglobin.)

Now, when we return to test the population at some point in the future, we find the following numbers:

AA	35 people
AS	100 people
SS	10 people
Total	145 people

Obviously, some change has taken place in the frequency of the genotypes and in the total population size. Have the allele frequencies changed as well? In other words, has evolution taken place? To calculate the allele frequencies, you add up the total number of each allele and divide by the number of alleles in the population, which would be twice the number of people since each person has two alleles at each locus. Thus, for the first test, the number of A alleles is:

$(50 \times 2) + 100 = 200$,
    since each AA person has two A alleles and each AS heterozygote has one.

The frequency of A alleles in the population is thus:

200/400 (since each of the 200 people has two alleles) = .50 (50%).

Using the same reasoning, the frequency of the S allele is also .50 (50%).

Now, calculate the allele frequencies in the second test, after the obvious change in genotype frequency and number of people has taken place. Using the same procedure:

frequency of A = $([35 \times 2] + 100) / (145 \times 2) = .59$ (59%)
frequency of S = $([10 \times 2] + 100) / (145 \times 2) = .41$ (41%)

(The results are rounded for simplicity.) Thus, the frequency of the A allele has increased and that of the S allele has decreased. Evolution, by technical definition, is taking place.

The reason for this change is obvious because we understand sickle cell anemia. Those individuals with the SS genotype have a fatal disease, so only 20 percent (10 out of 50) of them survived between the two tests. Those with the AA genotype don't have sickle cell but may succumb to malaria. Here there was a 70 percent survival rate (35 out of 50) for the AA genotype. All of the heterozygotes survived since they had nonfatal symptoms of sickle cell and also possessed an immunity to malaria.

If, however, we did not already understand the situation, the calculation of these figures would show that *something* was happening and would indicate in which direction the change was taking place. It would be clear in this case that one allele is increasing in frequency because both homozygote genotypes are decreasing in number, but to different degrees. As a result of *this*, the heterozygote genotype is becoming more common. We would then have to try to figure out why.

Suppose, however, we could only examine the population once, as is often the case. How could we possibly see evidence for change over time? There is a formula, known as the **Hardy-Weinberg equilibrium,** that provides us with a tool. The formula is an example of a *null hypothesis*, a condition where nothing occurs. If you can state the conditions of *no change*, you can then compare them to a real situation and see whether or not change is taking place and, if it is, state the nature and direction of that change. The Hardy-Weinberg formula assumes that the genotype frequencies in a population will remain the same under certain conditions: that there is random mating (that is, everyone stands an equal chance of mating with anyone else of the opposite sex), and that there is no gene flow, no drift, no mutation, and no natural selection for any allele over another. In other words, none of the processes of evolution is taking place.

For example, using our two alleles for hemoglobin, A and S, we designate the frequency of A as p, and the frequency of S as q. (These letters, although they may make it a bit confusing at first, are used because of a mathematical convention.) So, for our population in the second test above:

$p = .59$ and $q = .41$

Now, we calculate the probability (the chance) of creating each of the possible genotypes *based solely on the percentages of the two alleles*. The probability is the product (the result of mutiplication) of the frequencies of the alleles that make up each genotype. How often a genotype is produced depends on how often the alleles of that genotype appear in the first place. Thus, the following applies:

GENOTYPE	PRODUCT OF FREQUENCIES
AA	$p \times p = p^2$
AS	$p \times q = pq$ ⎫
SA	$q \times p = qp$ ⎬ $= 2\,pq$
SS	$q \times q = q^2$

The heterozygote is counted twice because there are two ways of producing it, depending upon which allele comes from which parent. Because all genotypes are now accounted for,

$p^2 + 2pq + q^2 = 1$ (or 100%).
This is the Hardy-Weinberg formula for a two-allele gene.

We can now return to our population and see what its genotype frequencies would be if they were based only on the frequencies of the alleles, that is, if there were no evolutionary processes taking place and the percentages of the genotypes were strictly a matter of chance. For the AA genotype, for example, we calculate p^2 as $.59 \times .59$, which equals .3481. Now multiply this by the population size, 145, to show how many people would be *expected* to have this genotype if no evolution were taking place: $145 \times .3481 = 50$. Looking back, however, we observed that only 35 people actually possessed this genotype. We can do the rest of the calculations, producing the results shown in the table below.

GENOTYPE	EXPECTED FREQUENCY	EXPECTED NUMBER	OBSERVED NUMBER
AA	$p^2 = .59^2 = .3481$	$.3481 \times 145 = 50$	35
AS	$2pq = .59 \times .41 \times 2$ $= .4838$	$.4838 \times 145 = 70$	100
SS	$q^2 = .41^2 = .1681$	$.1681 \times 145 = 24$	10

(The numbers in the expected and observed columns should add up to the same figure but don't exactly because of rounding.)

The observed numbers of people possessing each genotype are not the same as those expected if chance alone were determining them. In evolutionary terms, then, our sample population is not in Hardy-Weinberg equilibrium. Something else is going on, namely, some evolutionary processes are in action.

In real life, we would still have to run certain statistical tests on our results because even if the expected and observed numbers do not match, that could still be the result of chance. For the record, I ran one such test, called Chi-Square, and found that the above results are not a matter of chance. They are, in mathematical terms, statistically significant.

Hardy-Weinberg equilibrium: The formula that shows genotype frequencies in a population under hypothetical conditions of no evolutionary change.

At any rate, we can note the direction of the differences. Again, comparing expected with observed frequencies, we see that there are large drops in the numbers of people with the AA and SS genotypes, and a large increase in those with the AS genotype. This hints that the heterozygote was being selected for and that the two homozygotes were being selected against. We know, of course, that this is the case with sickle cell anemia in malarial areas.

The other processes of evolution may also be quantified and studied in a similar fashion, by observing changes in allele frequencies through time or by calculating deviations from Hardy-Weinberg equilibrium, and then by noting the direction of change and determining probable causes of that change. Some references to more extensive coverage of mathematical population genetics are given at the end of the chapter.

EVOLUTION IN POPULATIONS

Using the techniques of population genetics introduced above, the processes of evolution taking place in living populations may be studied. But what about traits for which the genetic mechanism is unknown—in other words, what about the majority of phenotypic features? Is there any way these can still contribute to our understanding of evolution in living groups?

When I conducted my study of evolutionary processes among the Hutterites, I used **dermatoglyphics,** the study of the parallel ridges on the skin of the fingers, palms, toes, and soles. I focused on those of the fingers—in other words, fingerprints. I was not collecting data about the small features that make each individual's fingerprints absolutely unique from everyone else's. Rather, I was looking for the frequencies of various types of fingerprint patterns and for data about the size of the patterns, called ridge count. This is measured by counting the number of ridges between a reference point, the triradius, and the center of the pattern (Figure 13.1).

This research is an example of another way of examining evolution in living populations. If we know the genetic mechanism for a trait, as in the sickle cell example, we can see if the gene or genes for that trait change through time, that is, if they evolve. However, we don't know the genetic mechanism that gives rise to fingerprints, or, for that matter, the genetic mechanism for most phenotypic traits. But by comparing measures of phenotypic traits between populations and between groups within a population, we may estimate the degrees of genetic difference among these groups and thus gauge the extent to which the various processes of evolution are taking place.

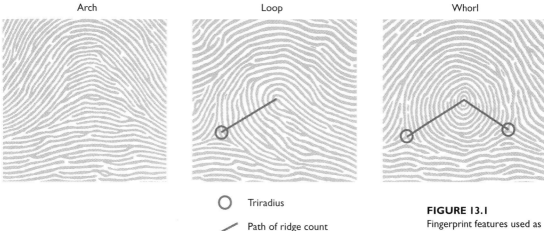

Arch   Loop   Whorl

○   Triradius

╱   Path of ridge count

FIGURE 13.1
Fingerprint features used as anthropological data. Arches have no triradius and, therefore, no ridge count. Whorls have two ridge counts; the largest is used as data.

We know that one's fingerprints are under some genetic control since certain features, especially ridge count, are similar among members of a family line. Moreover, certain unusual dermatoglyphic traits or characteristic frequencies of some traits have been correlated with abnormalities of known or suspected genetic origin. We also know, however, that other fingerprint traits are affected by prenatal environmental factors or simply by chance. Not knowing what genes are involved, I obviously couldn't calculate allele frequencies and run Hardy-Weinberg tests, so how did I use these features?

In 1973, I collected fingerprint data from everyone in each of two Hutterite colonies that were the result of the splitting of an original colony in 1958 (Figure 13.2). As you recall from Chapter 1, I was interested in examining the effects of gene flow and genetic drift. I examined 133 sets of fingerprints for pattern type, pattern size, and a few other variables (about 1330 individual prints—although many of the men in this farming society had fewer than ten fingers). I then statistically compared the fingerprint data of various subgroups to get a numerical *approximation* of the genetic distances among them. I used different methods of analysis to see if some dermatoglyphic data were better than others for estimating genetic distance.

First, I was specifically interested in seeing how much genetic change was brought about by splitting (fissioning) the population. This would measure the form of genetic drift known as the founder effect (see Chapter 4). Second, I wondered how much change took place between generations, and how much of that change was the result of the fact that about half of the mothers of the second generation had moved into the two colonies

dermatoglyphics: The study of the parallel ridges and furrows on the fingertips, palms, toes, and soles of the feet.

FIGURE 13.2
Hutterite colonies in the
study described. E and R are
code letters I used to identify each colony to maintain
my subjects' anonymity. The
original colony, in Alberta,
Canada, split in 1958. Half of
the families stayed in the Alberta colony (R1), and half
founded a new colony in Saskatchewan (E1). By 1973,
when I conducted my study
of the two colonies (R2 and
E2), a second generation had
been born.

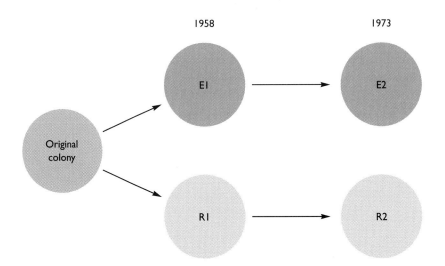

after marriage (gene flow). Natural selection was ruled out as a cause of change since there is no evidence that it makes any difference in repro-ductive success what ridge patterns you have and how big they are. Nor do people choose mates based on their fingerprints.

I felt I could apply what I found to a broader perspective on human evolution. The Hutterites nicely mirror the nature of many human pop-ulations during much of our history—small groups of interrelated families that split and merged in various ways as they moved about in search of resources.

I proposed and tested two hypotheses (Figure 13.3). First, I guessed that there would be a founder effect after the original population split in 1958 to create two new populations. That is, I hypothesized that the new populations would be genetically different from one another as a result of being founded by nonrepresentative samples of the original. I did not think the effect would be particularly extensive, however, since splitting a sam-ple into two nearly equal halves lessens the chance of a major difference between them. In addition, all the families involved were descended from seven brothers, so there would not be a whole lot of genetic variation to begin with.

As a second hypothesis, I expected a significant effect from gene flow, making the next generations after the split (E2 and R2 in the figures) different from their parental generations (E1 and R1). I expected the sec-ond generations of the two colonies to be even more different from one another than were the two founded colonies. As noted in Chapter 4, nearly three-quarters of the mothers of the second generation "flowed" into the colonies of their husbands at marriage, and families with one of these women accounted for about half the children of the second gener-

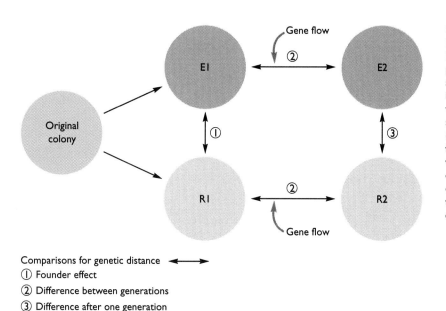

Comparisons for genetic distance ←——→
① Founder effect
② Difference between generations
③ Difference after one generation

FIGURE 13.3
Diagram of tests run: (1) Founded colonies were compared. These were reconstructed by using only those individuals still alive in 1973 who were involved in the split. (Most were still living.) (2) The members of the founded colonies in 1958 were compared to all the offspring born since that date. (3) All members of the 1973 colonies were compared.

ation. A lot of new genes were brought into each colony and all of the women carrying those genes became parents. The parents should be distinctly genetically different from the nonparents—a form of selection, although one not based on adaptation.

What did I find? For the first hypothesis, the data showed evidence of a founder effect, but there was more difference between the two founded populations than I expected. You obviously can't base a whole conclusion on one limited study, but my results did suggest that fission and the founder effect could be important processes not only within the Hutterites but in the small, interrelated human populations that they represent.

My second hypothesis was not supported by the evidence. The two second-generation populations were *more* similar to one another than were the founder populations. This was surprising at first, but then the reason became clear.

The colonies from which the flow group women came belonged to the same subgroup of Hutterites. The Hutterites are divided into three subgroups. Since World War I, these groups have been endogamous—members only marry within their group. Thus, the women were more closely related than if they had come from the Hutterite population in general.

Moreover, since the two colonies I studied were geographically close, the colonies from which the women came were also geographically close. Hutterites often find their mates in colonies they regularly visit. This increased the chances that the flow group women were themselves closely related to each other. The genes flowing into the two colonies were similar, so the differences between the colonies was lessened over time, even over a single generation. Differences among populations, then, can increase and decrease, back and forth, depending upon how the memberships of those populations are organized and exactly who marries whom. Culture, in other words, influences biology.

Finally, I observed which statistical tests most closely matched the predicted results (once I had figured out that gene flow *decreased* the genetic distance). I was able to suggest that ridge count (the size of the patterns) was the best dermatoglyphic feature to use in such a study.

This dermatoglyphic research on the Hutterites is just one of many examples of a population genetic study. It does, however, show the ways in which we can go about making genetic comparisons among various populations, and how we can then analyze the evolutionary processes behind the differences we find.

This example also points out the importance of collecting and organizing data about the populations we study. How do we do this and what can we learn from such data about the nature of the human species as a whole and of the groups into which we have divided ourselves?

DESCRIBING POPULATIONS

The statistical study of the size and makeup of human populations, and of changes in those measures, is called **demography.** Normally studied in detail by those who study human or cultural geography, demographic data are nonetheless of importance to biological anthropologists. Populations are, after all, the units of evolutionary change, and so the nature of the groups we study cannot be separated from the evolutionary processes that affect those groups. The Hutterite example clearly shows this.

The most obvious thing we need to know about a population is its size—how many people there are. Since we're interested in change over time, we also want to know to what extent and in what direction the size of a population has changed during a given period.

For example, we know that the population of Europe dropped from about 70 million in 1347 to 45 million by 1352—a 35 percent decrease over a mere five years. It then took 118 years (until 1470) for Europe to once again achieve a population of 70 million.

On the other hand, the number of Hutterites in North America has increased from about 300 in 1875 to about 30,000 at present. This is a hundredfold increase in 120 years.

We need to determine what causes such changes and, for that matter, any population changes anywhere. Clearly, there are three variables in-

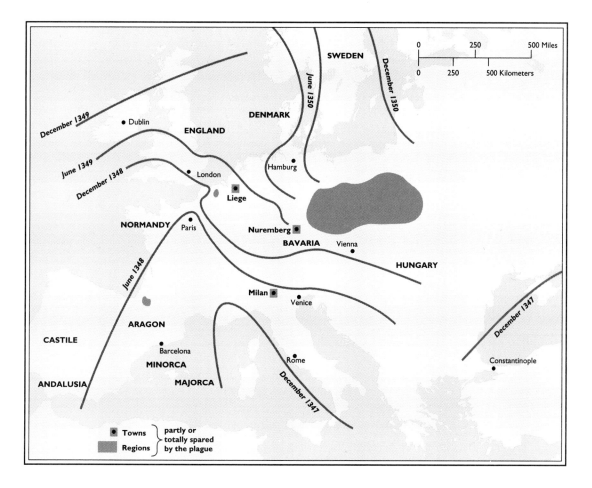

FIGURE 13.4
The progression of the Black Death across Europe in the fourteenth century, an event that, in five years, killed over one-third of Europe's people.

volved: births, deaths, and migration into or out of the population. When the birth rate exceeds the death rate, the population size increases. It decreases when the death rate is greater. Only in rare cases is migration a major factor, though it certainly may play a significant role.

In the case of fourteenth-century Europe, we know that the drop in population was the result of plague, mostly bubonic plague, a fatal bacterial disease carried by fleas that are, in turn, transported by rats. A major outbreak began in Italy in 1347 and spread rapidly across Europe over the next five years, killing 25 million people. The period came to be known as the Black Death (Figure 13.4). No birth rate could have made up for this. The fact that it took longer to replace the 25 million than to kill them off results from two facts. First, there were further, though smaller, outbreaks of plague over the next century that kept the death rates high.

demography: The study of the size and makeup of populations.

Second, a phenomenal growth rate of around 100 persons per thousand would have been required each year to put the population back in only five years. By comparison, the U.S. growth rate for 1970 was only about 9 persons per thousand. (Growth rate is birth rate minus death rate.)

Bubonic plague is older than the fourteenth century and is still around today. It spread so quickly in Europe during those years because of the dense populations of many of Europe's cities and because of the extensive trade networks that linked those cities. Rats that carried the fleas moved easily from place to place, and the bacteria easily moved from person to person. Culture affected a biological event, and the connection went the other way as well. Many aspects of European culture were affected by the Black Death—everything from economy to art.

The increase in the Hutterite population in North America can be attributed to the high birth rate among this group. They have, on average, 10.4 children per family, one of the highest recorded for any population. This results in a birth rate of about 46 births per thousand. The death rate is about 4 per thousand, yielding a growth rate of 42 per thousand. This high rate is the result of Hutterite religious beliefs—their firm adherence to the biblical injunction to "be fruitful and multiply"—and, most likely, because of the healthy lifestyle they lead, which includes hard work in nonurban areas and excludes drugs and all but occasional alcohol.

Biological anthropologists are also interested in the composition of populations. How many people are there of each sex, in each age group, and in various other ethnic, occupational, economic, and religious groups? We can display these data with a pyramid diagram. Figure 13.5 shows the age-sex structure of the Hutterite colonies I studied. The data here are typical for all Hutterites.

As you might expect for a group with such a high reproductive rate, the graph is wider on the bottom, showing that there are more children than adults. The fact that there are many more children between ages five and nine than between zero and four may indicate that the growth rate is slowing, at least in these colonies.

That females outnumber males (79 to 54) may indicate any number of factors that would have to be examined more closely. Perhaps male death rates are higher—they are in the general population. It could also be that, despite what I was told and what I calculated, I *did not* get to see everyone in the colonies. Maybe some of the men did not want to participate, and I never knew they existed.

Now, compare the graph for the Hutterites with one representing developing nations—nations like Mexico, where industrialization is fairly recent (Figure 13.6). This age-sex graph also shows larger numbers of children, but, unlike on the Hutterite graph, the numbers of adults rapidly decrease with age. This reflects higher death rates, especially as one gets older.

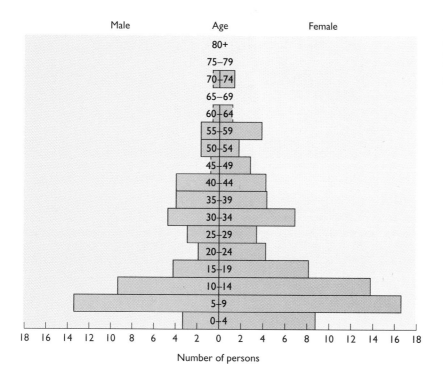

FIGURE 13.5
Age-sex graph of Hutterite colonies used in my study. This is typical of such graphs for the Hutterites in general.

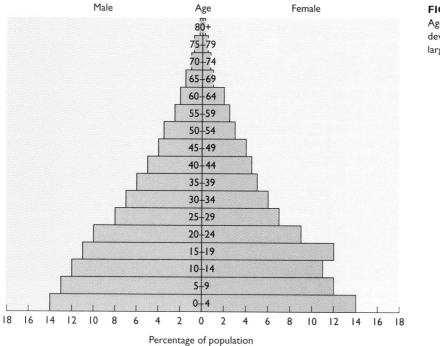

FIGURE 13.6
Age-sex graph for a typical developing nation, showing large numbers of children.

FIGURE 13.7

Age-sex graph for typical developed nations, which have fewer children and longer life expectancy.

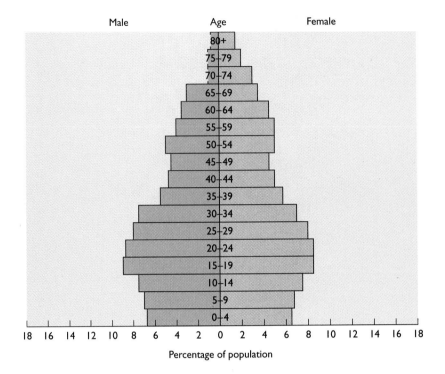

For adults, the Hutterites more closely resemble a graph for developed nations, like the United States, that have been industrialized for some time (Figure 13.7). Here the numbers of adults do not decrease as quickly with age, indicating that people in developed countries live longer in general. Regarding children, however, the developed nations differ from the Hutterites in having lower birth rates.

What are the cultural connections here? As we noted, the Hutterites are responding to their religious beliefs by having many children. Their communal, self-sufficient lifestyle can accomodate large families, and their practice of splitting colonies prevents local overpopulation.

Developing nations have high mortality rates. This provides one incentive to produce as many children as possible—simply to try to offset the deaths. In addition, birth control technology is not always available and there may be cultural rules against it. But, although the bottom of the pyramid diagram is wide for such populations, it narrows quickly. Because of poor medical care and poor nutrition and sanitation, people have a decreasing chance of living into the next age group. Recent data have shown, however, that family size is decreasing in many developing countries. This may eventually narrow the bottom of the graph for such countries (see Figure 13.6) and might lead to better living conditions that

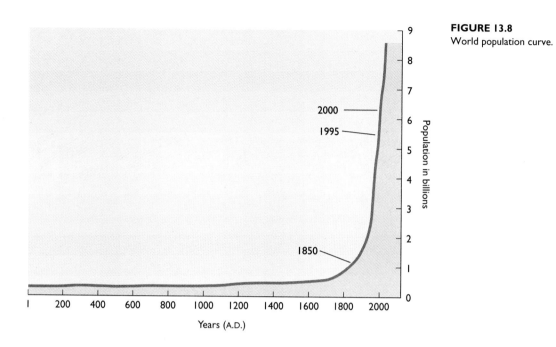

FIGURE 13.8
World population curve.

would, in turn, widen the top of the graph, as people increase their chances of longevity (see the "Contemporary Reflections" box at the end of this chapter).

In developed countries, there is increasing motivation to limit population, and there is access to the means of birth control. Moreover, the quality of medical care and diet in general allow people to live longer. Thus, the nearly vertical shape of the diagram.

Finally, what can we say from demographic statistics about the human species in general? One thing is certain—our total population is going to increase. Since the beginning of farming and animal domestication some 12,000 years ago, the rate of increase of the human population has accelerated, jumping sharply with the Industrial Revolution of the eighteenth century (Figure 13.8). As of January 10, 1998, the U.S. Census Bureau estimated the world population at 5,888,669,471. At current growth rates, the world population is expected to reach over 6 billion by the year 2000 and 8.5 billion by the middle of the next century.

In addition to a growing population, the structure of the population of the next century will change. As birth rates and death rates continue to drop in developed nations, and, perhaps, as other nations become increasingly developed, the age-sex pyramids will become top-heavy. There will be more older people than younger people. This will radically change the social and economic nature of such cultures.

Both of these changes carry implications that are beyond the scope of this book. Clearly, though, they will require responses and actions that will put a very different face on the world of the next generation, and that will profoundly affect *Homo sapiens* of the twenty-first century (see "Contemporary Reflections").

HUMAN ADAPTATIONS

Living human populations inhabit every continent except Antarctica (and there are small, temporary groups of people who live there, mostly doing scientific research). We have to deal with just about every imaginable set of environmental circumstances the earth presents, and we have been doing this for just about as long as modern *Homo sapiens* has existed. Indeed, even back in *Homo erectus* times, humans successfully moved into a wide range of environments.

One would expect, therefore, that different populations of our species would be differently adapted to those various environments. Obviously, most of our adaptations are cultural. We build shelters, manufacture clothing, make tools, and invent various technological devices that are specifically geared to the environmental conditions with which we have to contend (Figure 13.9).

Human populations also differ in their physical appearance and in features of their physiology. Our species displays **polymorphisms**—variations in phenotypic traits that are the results of genetic variation (that is, multiple alleles). Are some of these polymorphisms adaptive responses to different environments?

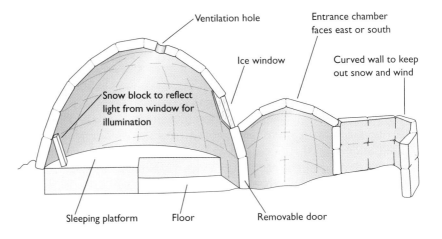

FIGURE 13.9
Cultural adaptation. The famous igloo of the Inuit has many ingenious features that make it remarkably adapted to life in a harsh climate.

Species Adaptations

As members of the same species, all humans certainly share many adaptations to variable conditions. One important environmental variable is temperature. All humans sweat as a means of dissipating heat from the body. As noted in Chapter 10, our relative hairlessness may be an adaptation to promote the quick evaporation of sweat. On the other hand, when it becomes too cold, we shiver, our metabolic rate increases, and our blood vessels alternately widen and narrow to increase or decrease the flow of blood, and therefore warmth, to various body parts.

Similarly, we are all exposed to ultraviolet radiation from the sun. An excess of UV can damage skin cells, alter the cells' DNA to cause skin cancer, and adversely affect the body's immune system. To protect tissues from UV damage, specialized skin cells called **melanocytes** produce the pigment **melanin** and deliver it to the upper layer of skin, where it absorbs UV radiation. Melanocytes respond to increased UV levels by increasing their melanin production and darkening the skin. This, of course, is tanning. Even dark-skinned individuals can exhibit a tanning response.

The low oxygen conditions at high altitudes can have damaging, even deadly effects on the human body, and all humans have some ability to respond biologically. After a time at higher-than-normal altitudes, a person's respiratory and heart rates will increase, as will red blood cell count. Hemoglobin concentration may go up as well. All this helps the body better acquire and use what oxygen is available.

Humans, however, live in such a variety of conditions—including those related to temperature, ultraviolet radiation, and high altitudes—that these species-wide responses may not be sufficient to adapt all populations to their environments.

Variation in Adaptations

Humans have settled in places from the hottest deserts and rain forests to the coldest reaches above the Arctic Circle. No matter how much we may sweat, shiver, increase our metabolic rate, and change the shape of our blood vessels, it may not be enough to deal with some environmental extremes. For example, there is no difference in the number of sweat glands among human populations, regardless of regional temperature. There are, however, other adaptations to temperature that do vary with location.

Populations that inhabit hot climates tend to be very linear in build, and those in cold areas tend to be stockier (Figure 13.10). This is because the linear individual has a greater surface area and so loses heat more rapidly, whereas the stockier person has a smaller surface area and so retains heat better. There is also a tendency for people in cold climates

polymorphisms: Variations in phenotypic traits that are the results of genetic variation.

melanocytes: Specialized skin cells that produce the pigment melanin.

melanin: The pigment largely responsible for human skin color.

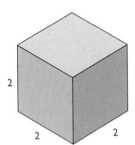

Volume = 2 × 2 × 2 = 8 in.³
Surface area = (2 × 2)(6 sides)
= 24 in.²
(Numbers in inches)

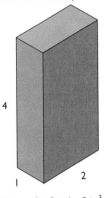

Volume = 1 × 2 × 4 = 8 in.³
Surface area = (1 × 2) (2) +
(1 × 4) (2) +
(2 × 4) (2)
= 28 in.²

FIGURE 13.10
The body build of the Inuit (left) is adapted to heat retention, while that of the Masai cattle herder from Kenya is built to promote heat loss. (Above) The relationship between surface area and shape for two solids of equal volume. This explains the adaptations of the two men pictured.

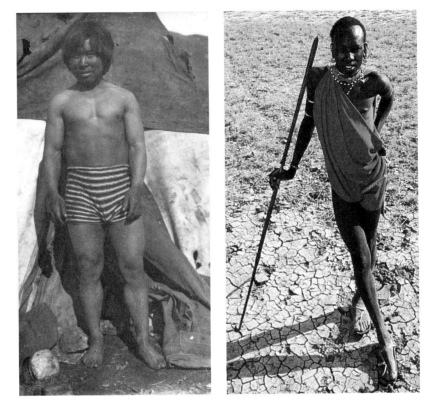

simply to be bigger in general than those in hot climates since, obviously, the larger person would have more body mass away from the surface and so retain heat more efficiently.

Ultraviolet radiation varies with latitude. Sunlight strikes the earth more directly at the equator, and at more of an angle the farther one gets from the equator. Hitting at an angle, the solar radiation also travels through more atmosphere, and thus more UV is absorbed by ozone in northern latitudes. Not only do humans have the ability to tan in response to increased UV levels, but, as is obvious to us all, populations are genetically programmed for differences in skin color, and these differences also vary by latitude. In general, peoples closer to the equator have darker skin. Skin color gradually gets lighter in populations away from the equator (Figure 13.11). It is generally agreed that the relationship between dark skin and high levels of UV radiation is an example of an adaptive response. Because of the damaging effects of UV, peoples in or near the equator have undergone selection for permanently higher levels of melanin production. Darker-skinned people do not have more melanocytes than lighter-skinned ones, just more melanin. An implication of this, of course,

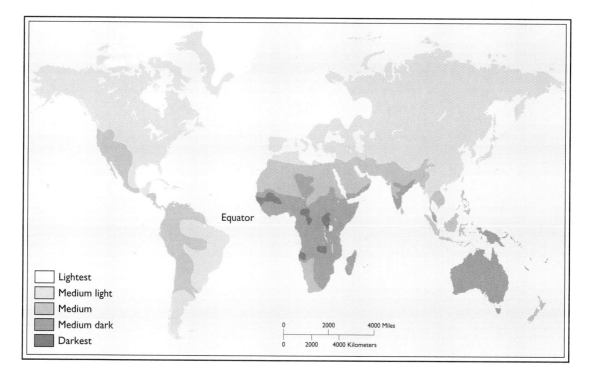

Lightest
Medium light
Medium
Medium dark
Darkest

FIGURE 13.11
Skin color distribution.
Darker skin is concentrated
in equatorial regions.

is that dark skin was the original human skin color, since—at least according to the latest evidence—our species first evolved in equatorial Africa.

The question then becomes, Why did populations who moved away from the equator evolve lower melanin production and therefore lighter skin? It is easiest to say that since dark skin was no longer needed, it became light. Evolution, however, doesn't really work this way. More likely, there was an adaptive reason why lighter skin was actively selected *for*.

A common answer has to do with vitamin D production. Vitamin D can be synthesized by the body, in the lower layers of skin, when a precursor of the vitamin is activated by UV radiation. This vitamin is important in regulating the absorption of calcium and its inclusion in the manufacture of bone. Deficiency in vitamin D can lead to a condition of skeletal deformity known as rickets in children. (There is an adult version of the abnormality as well.) Bones with rickets are also more prone to breakage, and the disease can cause a deformity of the pelvis that can make childbirth difficult.

It has been thought that, as populations moved away from the equator, those with darker skin could not manufacture sufficient vitamin D for normal bone growth and maintenance. Those with lighter skin, therefore, were at an adaptive and, thus, a reproductive advantage. Over time, lighter skin became the normal, inherited condition in these groups. Skin color was thus seen as a balancing act—dark enough to protect from the damaging effects of UV and light enough to allow the beneficial effects.

The vitamin D explanation has recently been questioned, however. Rickets is associated with recent urban populations (in narrow city streets, children get little direct sunlight) and is seldom found in rural areas. There is little evidence for it in the fossil record. Moreover, although dark skin does slow down the production of vitamin D, it can still allow for sufficient synthesis to maintain healthy levels. Vitamin D synthesis may not have been a selective factor for our ancestors.

Now, of course, we can also obtain vitamin D through vitamin supplements and by drinking vitamin D–fortified milk. It is also found in fish liver oils and egg yolks. A correlation between dark-skinned urban populations and rickets—once proposed as evidence for the adaptive connection—may be based more on socioeconomic matters resulting in poor diet than on skin color differences.

Another possibility for an active selective factor for light skin concerns injury to the skin from cold. Data from the military suggest that darker skin is more prone to damage from frostbite than is lighter skin (Post et al. 1975). Selection for light skin may not be related to ultraviolet radiation but to temperature, while selection for darker skin remains related to UV.

As these examples of body build and skin color demonstrate, our species, despite its ability to adapt through culture to a wide array of environments, has still undergone natural selection for and against certain features in response to those environments. The discussion of sickle cell anemia from Chapter 4 is another example. Although we might like to think we have buffered ourselves against this process of evolution, it has occurred in modern *Homo sapiens* and it continues to affect populations of our species.

Are All Polymorphisms Adaptively Important?

We can see, in the distribution of body build and skin color, some obvious correlations with environmental factors that lead us rather directly to our conclusions about the adaptive significance of these polymorphic traits. Other human polymorphisms, on the other hand, seem distributed among our populations in such a way that there is no obvious relationship to environmental circumstances.

The distribution of blood types in the ABO system (see Chapter 3) is a perfect example of a polymorphism unrelated to the environment (Figure 13.12). There seems to be no rhyme or reason to how the various

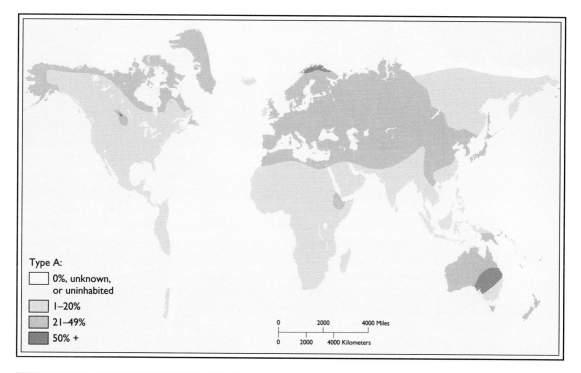

Type A:

- ⬜ 0%, unknown, or uninhabited
- ▨ 1–20%
- ▨ 21–49%
- ▨ 50% +

0   2000   4000 Miles

0   2000   4000 Kilometers

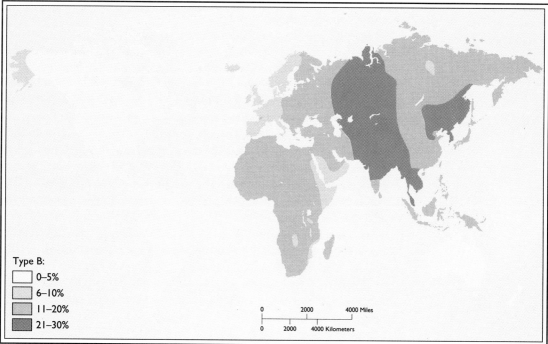

Type B:

- ⬜ 0–5%
- ▨ 6–10%
- ▨ 11–20%
- ▨ 21–30%

0   2000   4000 Miles

0   2000   4000 Kilometers

FIGURE 13.12

Approximate frequency distributions of type A and type B blood, demonstrating the lack of a pattern in the distribution of this polymorphism.

frequencies of the phenotypes are dispersed around the world. Type A, for example, is totally absent among some native South American groups, but is found in frequencies of over 50 percent in parts of Europe and native Australia and among a few native North American groups, where, however, it is generally found among less than a quarter of the population. Type O, the most common in the species, still ranges from 40 percent in parts of Asia to 100 percent among some native South Americans.

Are the variations of this genetic trait adaptively neutral; that is, do they make no difference in terms of differential reproductive success? We believe this to be the case for some other blood group systems. (There are about thirty different blood group systems besides the ABO system, that is, different chemical phenotypes in the blood that are the results of different genes with multiple alleles.)

The actual phenotypic trait involved in the ABO system is the presence or absence of certain proteins, called antigens, on the surface of the red blood cells. In addition, your blood plasma contains, from shortly after birth, other proteins that react against the alternate version of your antigen. For example, if you have antigen A, then antigen B is the alternate version. These other proteins are called **antibodies.** Table 13.1 shows how these are expressed in the ABO system.

The reactions between antigens and antibodies is the reason that blood used for transfusions must match the blood type of the recipient. As a type A person, if I received a transfusion of type B blood, my anti-B antibodies would recognize the B antigen of the transfused blood as foreign to my system. My antibodies would bind with the antigens on the transfused red blood cells and destroy the cells by causing them to burst (hemolyze). If extensive enough, this reaction could lead to shock or kidney failure. In emergencies, however, a person of any blood type may receive type O, since O has no antigens and therefore would stimulate no reaction.

Since antibodies of various sorts are important components of our bodies' immunological system, disease is one obvious factor to examine for an adaptive significance of the ABO polymorphism. Some microorganisms possess antigens that are similar to the A and B antigens, so perhaps certain blood types are predisposed to fight off certain infectious diseases. At the same time, if an infecting microorganism possesses antigens that are similar to your own, then your system may not be stimulated to produce the proper antibodies against the organism, making you more susceptible to that disease.

Some correlations between blood type and susceptibility to diseases have been suggested. Type A has been associated with bronchial pneumonia, smallpox, and typhoid, and type O has shown correlations with bubonic plague. Among the data that support some connections among these factors is the low frequency of type O in India, where there is a long history of frequent plague epidemics.

TABLE 13.1
ABO Blood Group Phenotypes and Antibodies

Genotypes	Phenotypes	Antigens	Antibodies
AA AO	A	A	anti-B
BB BO	B	B	anti-A
AB	AB	A, B	none
OO	O	none	anti-A, and anti-B

It should also be noted that there is some evidence that mosquitos are more attracted to type O persons. If so, then diseases carried by mosquitos, such as malaria, would also be influenced, although indirectly, by blood type.

There are correlations as well between blood types and noninfectious gastrointestinal diseases. Type O persons appear to have a greater chance of duodenal and stomach ulcers and type A persons of stomach cancer. Most people have blood group antigens in their body fluids, including their gastric juices, as well as in their blood, and so there may well be some reactions between these antigens and chemicals in the food one eats. The reactions may have a positive or negative effect on the digestive process itself, or they may lead to some irritation of the digestive tract. Thus, certain blood types may have been selected for, and others against, depending upon what foods were typically consumed in certain areas by certain populations.

Along the same lines, there may also be reactions between blood antigens in the digestive tract and some intestinal bacteria. Individuals of certain blood types may be more or less affected by bacterial ailments like infant diarrhea. Such ailments are major factors in infant mortality in many parts of the world. Thus, they are important selective factors, and any polymorphism that influenced the severity of these problems could be selected for or against.

What do blood type correlations tell us? Certainly these data indicate that a selective role for the ABO system is possible, especially with diseases that affect people during or before their reproductive period. We must demonstrate, however, that selection is, in fact, taking place. The fact that we have gained control over some of the diseases in question limits our ability to study them in the present, and so we have to rely, as with the plague connection, on historical records.

Moreover, we must establish a cause-and-effect relationship between antigen and disease, and we must also show if, and under what conditions,

antibodies: Proteins in the immune system that react to foreign antigens.

this would make enough of a difference to affect reproductive success. The ABO system is also found in chimps and gorillas, so the origin of the polymorphism itself may be hidden in our evolutionary past. Some of the more important connections are with diseases of dense urban populations. Thus selection for certain blood types, and their distribution, may be a fairly recent phenomenon.

As this single example shows, the topic is a complex one. We asked at the beginning of this section: Are all polymorphisms adaptively important? The answer is: We don't know for sure. Human polymorphisms need to be examined for their selective contributions to populations within the species. We may find, however, that some of our variable traits make no difference at all, or at least make no difference now.

DISEASE AND HUMAN POPULATIONS

We tend to think of diseases as abnormalities—and, for individuals suffering from them, they are. But diseases are as much a part of life as any other "normal" aspect of our biological world. Since many diseases are caused by other living organisms—viruses, bacteria, and protozoa—and are carried around by other species, they are really perfectly "natural." Disease-causing species have adapted to the biology of their hosts, and the hosts at least attempt to adapt to the disease-causing species. Diseases are thus excellent examples of evolutionary processes.

We also tend to think that our species, especially in modern times, has removed itself from many, if not most, such relationships. After all, those of us in developed countries virtually ignore diseases that, a generation ago, were serious threats. Polio (still a problem in my childhood) is gone; tuberculosis is rare in the United States, as are mumps and measles. In 1980, smallpox was declared eradicated worldwide. In the United States, only two of the twelve most common causes of death (pneumonia/influenza and AIDS) are infectious diseases (Figure 13.13).

But there are still diseases that disable and kill us, and new diseases or new strains of old diseases are even now emerging as the species that cause them continue to undergo the processes of evolution. And it should be clear that, in the past, disease has had direct effects on our evolution. We have already discussed the examples of sickle cell anemia, malaria, and plague, and there may well be evolutionary relationships between our blood types and certain diseases. These examples all show diseases as important factors of natural selection.

It has even been suggested (Linda van Blerkom, personal communication) that infectious diseases might have contributed to the hypothesized population bottlenecks and replacements that may have taken place

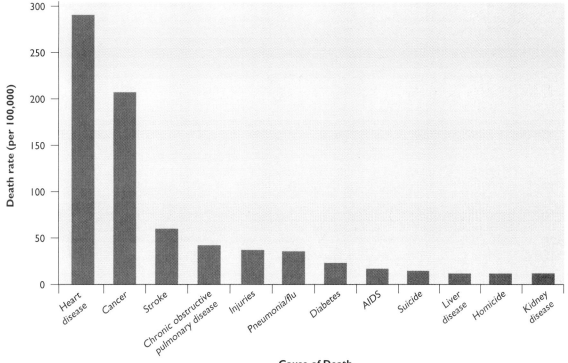

Cause of Death

FIGURE 13.13
The twelve leading causes of death in the United States in 1994. Note that only two, pneumonia/influenza and AIDS, are infectious diseases. (From Relethford 1997.)

at the origin and spread of modern *Homo sapiens* (see Chapter 12). Migrations out of Africa—where populations had time to develop immunity to certain diseases—could have carried pathogens to new human hosts who lacked evolved immunity to them. An analogous phenomenon occurred, for example, when the Spaniards conquered the Aztecs of Mexico in 1521. European diseases—smallpox, measles, and influenza—with which the Aztecs had no experience, and thus no immunity, probably did more to lead to their downfall than did the actions of Spanish soldiers. In addition, of course, migrating human hosts could have entered new areas and encountered new pathogens to which they had evolved no immunity.

Looked at from the evolutionary perspective we have used throughout this book, we may see general trends in the relationship between diseases and the human species. Anthropologist George Armelagos (Armelagos et al. 1996; Armelagos 1998) has outlined these trends and refers to them as three "**epidemiological** transitions."

For most of hominid evolutionary history, we lived in small, widely dispersed, nomadic foraging groups. Our ancestors certainly experienced diseases of various sorts and would have come into contact with new diseases as they migrated to new environments. But infectious diseases would

epidemiological: Pertaining to the study of disease outbreaks and epidemics.

not have had serious effects on large numbers of people since they would have had little chance of being passed on to many other humans.

When, starting about 10,000 years ago, some people began to settle down and produce their food through farming and animal domestication, the "first epidemiological transition" occurred. Now infectious diseases increased in impact, as larger and denser concentrations of people provided the disease vectors with greater opportunity to be passed from host to host. Animal domestication may have brought people into contact with new diseases previously limited to other species. Working the soil would have exposed farmers to insects and other pathogens. We have already seen how irrigation in some areas provided breeding places for mosquitos, increasing the incidence of malaria. Sanitation problems caused by larger, more sedentary populations would have helped transmit parasitic diseases in human waste, as would use of animal dung for fertilizer. In addition, agriculture also led to a narrowing of food sources over the varied diets of foragers. This could have resulted in nutritional deficiencies, and the storage of food surpluses attracted new disease carriers like insects and rats. Trade between settled communities, as we saw in the case of the Black Death in Europe, helped spread diseases over large geographic areas. Epidemics, in the sense of diseases that affect a large number of people at the same time, were essentially nonexistent until the agricultural revolution.

Beginning in the last years of the nineteenth century and continuing into the twentieth, we experienced the "second epidemiological transition." With modern medical science providing immunizations and antibiotics and with better public health measures and improved nutrition, many infectious diseases were brought under control or even, as with smallpox, eliminated. There was a shift, in terms of what ailed and killed us, to chronic, degenerative diseases such as cancers, heart and circulatory diseases, and pulmonary disease. The increase in many of these came not only from the fact that fewer people were dying from infectious diseases and were living longer, but also from the results of modern lifestyles in developed countries and among the upper classes of developing countries—a more sedentary life leading to less physical activity; more stress; environmental pollution; diets contributing to obesity, clogged arteries, and diabetes; and smoking and alcohol consumption. But at least, we thought, many of these problems were things we could potentially control; all those infectious epidemics were things of the past (or, at least, of developing countries).

But on the heels of the second transition has come the "third epidemiological transition," and we are in it now. New diseases are emerging, and old ones are returning. Both of these phenomena can be understood through evolutionary theory.

The return of old diseases is the result of the fact that microorganisms are evolving species. For example, new and serious antibiotic-resistant

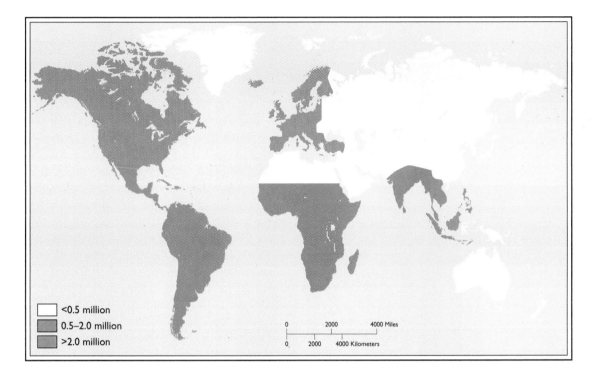

FIGURE 13.14
The distribution of the 18.5 million known adult infections of HIV-1, the more virulent of the two forms of the virus, from 1980 to 1995. HIV is still on the rise in Africa, Asia, and South America and is declining somewhat in North America and Europe. Evidence suggests strongly that the current epidemic first infected humans in the rain forests of west central Africa. (Data from Goudsmit 1997.)

strains of tuberculosis have recently appeared. This evolution may have been encouraged by what some authorities consider our overuse of antibiotics, giving microorganisms a greater chance to evolve resistance by exposing them to a constant barrage of selective challenges. Remember, some bacteria reproduce *hourly*, and so the processes of mutation and natural selection are speeded up in these species.

The emerging diseases are also the results of human activity in the modern world, which brings more people into contact with more diseases, some of which were unheard of even a few decades ago. As people and their products become more mobile, and as our populations spread into previously little-inhabited areas, cutting down forests and otherwise altering ecological conditions, we contact other species that may carry diseases to which they are immune but that prove deadly to us. HIV, the virus that causes AIDS, may have originated among African monkeys, who had evolved the ability to carry the virus without being adversely affected (Goudsmit 1997). Although the virus eventually kills its human hosts— seemingly a maladaptive behavior for the virus—it survives and proliferates because it has the adaptive ability to move easily from host to host via sexual contact (Figure 13.14). We have long known of one example of a deadly virus, rabies, that is successful because it can jump from species to species (Mills 1997). Hantavirus from rodents, ebola virus from an as yet unknown source, and *campylobacter*, a bacterium from chickens, are some other examples of pathogens that have recently jumped from other species to ours, with serious consequences.

Finally, and perhaps most frighteningly, are the prion proteins. Not living organisms, they begin as normal proteins (of as yet unknown function) in the nervous tissue of humans, other animals, and birds that (for as yet unknown reasons) sometimes fold up in an abnormal configuration. In this abnormal form the prions trigger the same folding up of the normally configured proteins and then build up in brain tissue, which they eventually destroy. The condition is called spongiform encephalopathy. "Mad cow" disease in cattle; Creutzfeld-Jakob disease in humans; and kuru, a disease described among the Fore people of highland New Guinea, are some examples, as are other manifestations in sheep, goats, and minks. Although the trigger for the abnormal shape of the protein may come, not surprisingly, from a genetic mutation (since, as you recall, genes code for the synthesis of proteins), the frightening thing about prions is that they can easily be transmitted across species. Moreover, they are very hard to destroy. Mad cow disease may have been spread because cattle in England were fed meal that contained the remains of other domestic animals. Even though these remains were rendered (cooked and processed into meal), the prions survived and passed to other cows through ingestion (Rhodes 1997). There are now 23 cases of Creutzfeld-Jakob disease in England that are thought to be traceable to human consumption of infected beef (Prusiner 1997). It should be noted that these diseases are still undergoing intensive investigation and that the nature of the prions is still being debated.

So the evolution of our species has been, and is still being, affected by diseases caused by, originating in, and carried by other species that are themselves evolving. An important source of understanding of these diseases, then, is evolutionary theory, which explains important factors about their source and transmission. In fact, this approach has been given the name "Darwinian medicine" (Oliwenstein 1995), and I imagine it will become increasingly important in the future.

THE BIOANTHROPOLOGY OF INDIVIDUALS

Individuals don't evolve, at least not in the sense that we are using the term here. And yet, bioanthropologists are interested in growth rates, developmental rates, and the timing of important events in the lives of individual members of our species. Why is this important to bioanthropology?

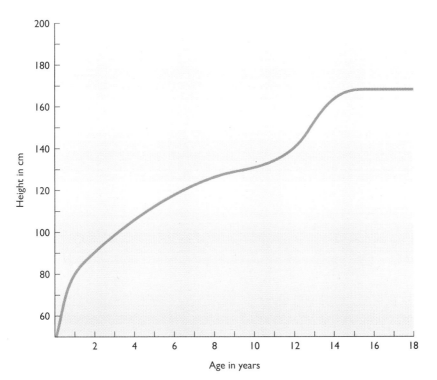

FIGURE 13.15
Distance curve for height
and age.

First of all, we are interested in these topics simply because they are part of our species' makeup. Studying just the adults of a species does not tell us everything about that species. We need to know such things as how developed an individual is at birth, how fast it reaches certain levels of growth, when it becomes sexually and physically mature, how long its reproductive span lasts, and how long it lives. We also look at rates at which certain components of the body grow and compare them to one another, and we compare all these data for different populations within a species and for different groups within populations—like males and females.

For example, we may plot a curve that shows the height of the members of a human population at certain ages (Figure 13.15). This type of curve is called a **distance curve.** We see from such a curve that change in height as people mature is not at a steady rate but alters at different stages. The sudden increase in height in early adolescence is obviously related to puberty and is called, in fact, the "adolescent growth spurt."

We all remember that the adolescent growth spurt did not occur at the same time in members of the two sexes. This and other differences in growth rate can be seen by comparing distance curves for males and females (Figure 13.16). These differences will be discussed in the next chapter.

distance curve: A graph that compares some variable at different points in time.

FIGURE 13.16

Distance curves for height and age in males compared to females.

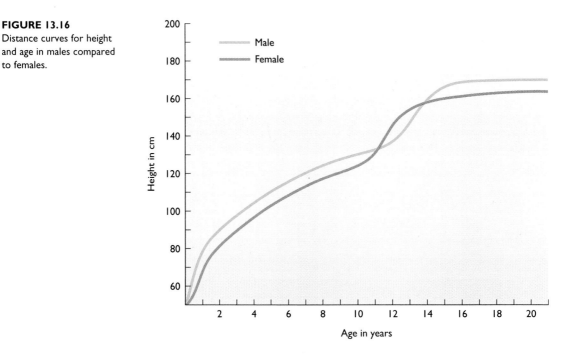

These changes can be seen in another way by plotting the rate of change for different ages. This is called a **velocity curve,** and it measures how *fast* changes are taking place, in this case, how many centimeters per year the plotted individual is growing (Figure 13.17). Note the increase (acceleration) of growth rate at early adolescence.

Not every part of the body, of course, grows at the same rate. Figure 13.18 compares height with brain size, using percent of final adult size as a scale. Note that, unlike increase in height, the fastest brain growth is in the first few years of life.

These and many other analyses show us the patterns of growth of our species in general and of different populations and groups within the species. Observing these patterns leads to other reasons for being interested in this topic.

First, we want to know what factors influence the differences we see between populations of our species and the changes within populations at different points in time. Two obvious influences on populations are nutrition and medical care. In societies where people are properly nourished, for example, girls grow faster, reach sexual maturity earlier, and achieve a larger adult body size. Over the last century, better nutrition and medical care have even made adult height greater and the age of sexual maturity

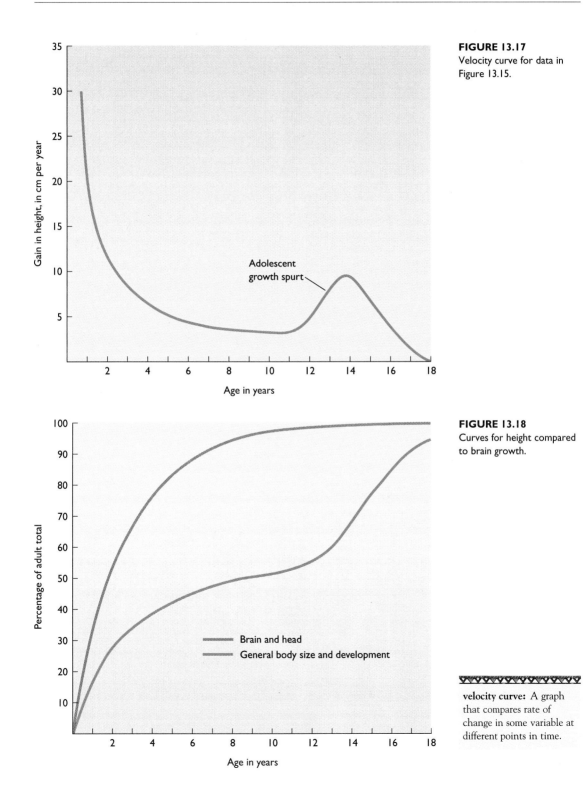

FIGURE 13.17
Velocity curve for data in
Figure 13.15.

FIGURE 13.18
Curves for height compared
to brain growth.

velocity curve: A graph
that compares rate of
change in some variable at
different points in time.

Contemporary Reflections

Where Is the Population Crisis?

A major influence on Darwin's thinking was the English economist Thomas Malthus (1766–1834). In *An Essay on the Principle of Population*, he wrote (1789:1), "Population, when unchecked, increases in a geometrical ratio. Subsistence increases only in an arithmetical ratio. . . . I can see no way by which man can escape from the weight of this law which prevades all animate nature." Malthus predicted famine and war if humans continued the population increase that even he in his day perceived. He should only have known.

Since Malthus's time, the human population has increased nearly sixfold (see Figure 13.8) and, given the war, famine, and environmental degradation we see around us, we have every reason to believe that Malthus was right and that, with our current 1.5 percent per year population increase, we will eventually run out of something—food, water, land, clean air, patience with one another—and our species and its world will be in for some very bad times indeed. The human species has even been likened to a cancer—growing uncontrolled, spreading, and eventually destroying its environment (Hern 1993, who even compares photos of malignant brain cancers to diagrams of the spread of London from 1800 to 1955 and to aerial photos of American cities!).

It is tempting to those of us in the developed West to place the blame for rampant growth on the developing countries of Latin America, Africa, and Asia, where some total fertility rates (the average number of births per woman) have been as high as 8. We tend to see no evidence of a population problem here in the United States and comfortably see the Malthusian predictions as affecting *other* countries. If only *they* would change, the problem could be solved.

In fact, many *are* changing. In some undeveloped and developing nations, frequent birth was traditionally practiced in order to make up for high infant mortality and high mortality rates in general. But

earlier in the United States. There are still differences in age of **menarche** between poor women and those of more affluent means within this country. At the same time, however, age at **menopause** is no different in populations of different nutritional and medical levels, nor has better food and health expanded the overall human lifespan, which remains about a hundred years at most (Hill 1993). Culture can affect some aspects of our stages of life, but not others.

The second reason we are interested in life course data is that it may help explain how we evolved. A new approach called **life history** collects such data and compares it within and between groups of organisms to try to draw some general rules about the life histories of living things and therefore explain the differences between them.

To give but one example (Hill 1993), we see major differences in the life histories of modern humans and our closest kin, the chimpanzees. Chimps reach sexual maturity about four years earlier than humans, but humans have an *adult* lifespan (from maturity to death) that is three times as long as a chimpanzee's (forty-two years compared to fourteen). Further, many developing countries are experiencing a fairly rapid decline in birth rates (Robey et al. 1993), and this is the result not of becoming more like the West but of having better education about and access to contraceptive technology. People in many of those countries realized the problems inherent in overpopulation but lacked the means to address it. In Thailand, to give just one example, fertility dropped by 50 percent from 1975 to 1987 (Robey et al. : 61).

It is rather arrogant to think that *we* are not part of the problem. We do live, as the cliché says, in a global village. All parts of the world are now interrelated in every way imaginable. Global ecological effects are well known. Politics and economics are no different. (As I'm writing this, a monetary crisis in the Pacific Rim is affecting stock prices on Wall Street.) *Every* new human, no matter where they live, will help use up world food, water, and energy resources and will contribute to the buildup of waste products. *Every* new human adds to the population density of the world and encourages the further spread of people, with its resultant alteration of environments (and also, as we have seen, possible contact with new pathogens).

Moreover, to think that there is no population problem in this country is simply incorrect. Although we might in theory be able to feed, clothe, and house all the people of the United States, the fact is we don't. Resources here are unevenly distributed, as they are in the rest of the world. Many of the children born in this most affluent of societies are unwanted. One survey concluded that of the 5.4 million pregnancies among American women in 1987, 57 percent were unintended (Cohen 1996).

Aspects of the population problem are still, to be sure, being debated. There are arguments as to how many people the planet could ideally support, as well as arguments as to how best to (or if it is even possible to) bring about those ideal conditions. But, that there *is* a population problem is undeniable. And to think that it is not *everyone's* concern is complacent at best.

in human females, half of that time is spent in a postreproductive stage, whereas chimps reproduce pretty much all their adult lives. Yet, despite the longer time we have to reproduce, humans still reproduce more often than chimps. Because reproduction takes a great deal of energy, this suggests that either human females are more efficient at acquiring and using energy than are chimp females, or that human females acquire energy from an additional source—such as human males. This coincides with the idea that one important change in hominid evolution was the addition to the basic primate family unit of a bonded male, one who would aid in protection and provisioning (see Chapters 7 and 8).

Life history studies are trying to explain these differences and to establish when the human life history pattern first evolved. It appears, by looking at the dental development pattern of the Taung Baby, that *Australopithecus africanus* did not share our life history and may have been more similar to chimpanzees (Smith 1993). These studies are still in their infancy but should provide further insight in the future into this important and relatively unstudied aspect of our evolutionary history.

menarche: A woman's first menstrual period.

menopause: The end of a woman's reproductive cycle.

life history: The study that examines the timing of life cycle events such as fertility, growth, and death.

▽   ▽   ▽

SUMMARY

While a major focus of bioanthropology is on the evolutionary history of the hominids, the nature of the product of that evolution—modern *Homo sapiens*—is also important. We study living populations of our species from several different yet interrelated approaches.

If we know the genetic mechanism for a particular phenotypic trait, we can calculate the frequencies of the alleles of the gene involved and then see what changes in allele frequency take place in populations over time. Since evolution is technically defined as change in allele frequency, this allows us to see if evolution is in operation for that phenotype and to try to determine what processes of evolution are involved. The use of the Hardy-Weinberg equilibrium lets us make this analysis even if we cannot examine a population at several different time periods.

Even if we don't know the genetic mechanism of a trait, we may still use that trait to study processes of evolution, provided it is under some genetic control. By statistically comparing populations, or groups within a population, for such a trait, we may estimate their genetic distances. In this way, we can hypothesize what sorts of evolutionary changes are taking place.

The use of demographic variables for size and composition of populations lets us describe the groups we study and observe changes in those variables that may denote certain biological or cultural trends. Indeed, when we analyze such data, we see that the biology of demographic changes is intimately linked to cultural variables of the studied populations.

Since humans live in such a wide range of environmental circumstances, it stands to reason that human groups would have different adaptations to those environments. Most adaptations of our species are cultural, but we still exhibit a number of polymorphic traits. There is evidence that our variation in these traits is the result of natural selection at some point in our evolution to climatic and other environmental variables.

Among the environmental factors to which humans respond evolutionarily are diseases. Many diseases are caused by or carried by other species, so evolutionary theory may be applied to our understanding of their epidemiology. Viewed from this perspective, we may see some general trends in the relationship between our species and other disease-causing species, in the past and in the present.

Finally, we understand that we need to study not only adult members of our species but also the growth and development of immature members, who are in the process of becoming adults. When certain changes take place and how fast they do so are part of our species' characteristics. Understanding how these changes and rates of change differ from those of other species is beginning to shed more light on the nature and course of our evolution.

KEY TERMS

Hardy-Weinberg
   equilibrium
dermatoglyphics
demography
polymorphisms

melanocytes
melanin
antibodies
epidemiological
distance curve

velocity curve
menarche
menopause
life history

SUGGESTED READINGS

This chapter merely skimmed the surface of the study of population genetics. For a more detailed treatment, with specific reference to humans, see *Human Variation and Human Microevolution* by Jane Underwood. For some classic examples of human population studies, try *The Structure of Human Populations* edited by G. A. Harrison and A. J. Boyce.

If you would like to know more about dermatoglyphics, the standard work is *Finger Prints, Palms, and Soles* by Harold Cummins and Charles Midlo.

There are many texts available that cover human demography. Richard Tullar's *The Human Species* gives a nice introduction, as does John Relethford's book of the same name.

For more detail on human polymorphisms and their adaptive significance, see Stephen Molnar's *Human Variation: Races, Types, and Ethnic Groups*, and for a well-known work that covers all of these topics and more, try *Human Biology* by Harrison, Weiner, Tanner, and Barnicot.

On the topic of the emerging diseases, see Frank Ryan's *Virus X: Tracking the New Killer Plagues* for a general treatment; *Viral Sex: The Nature of AIDS* by Jaap Goudsmit on that disease; and Richard Rhodes's *Deadly Feasts* on prion protein diseases. The perspective of Darwinian medicine is described by Lori Oliwenstein in "Dr. Darwin" in the October 1995 issue of *Discover*.

For a good introduction to life history studies, see "Life History Theory and Evolutionary Anthropology" by Kim Hill in *Evolutionary Anthropology*.

CHAPTER

14

HUMAN
BIOLOGICAL
DIVERSITY

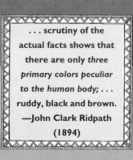

... scrutiny of the
actual facts shows that
there are only *three
primary colors peculiar
to the human body;* ...
ruddy, black and brown.
—John Clark Ridpath
(1894)

In the previous chapter we discussed some human polymorphic traits. The distribution of some, like skin color, points fairly clearly to an explanation involving natural selection to varying environmental conditions. Others, like blood type, are distributed in such a way as to make them seem adaptively neutral, or, at least, with an adaptive significance that is complex and not immediately obvious.

If our interest in phenotypic variation among modern humans was limited to describing and explaining the distribution of polymorphisms, we would still have a challenging task. But our biological variation has further meaning to us. Some of our variable traits—whether they have adaptive significance or not—are distributed with some geographic regularity, enough so that one can very often tell from what part of the world a person comes.

People look European, or Asian, or African, or Native American. We can often be more specific: People from Japan don't on average look like people from China. Swedes don't look like Italians. Masai from East Africa don't look like the Khoisan from the Kalahari. Inuit don't look like Maya.

Look at Figure 14.1. The photographer in the center and his highland New Guinea subjects—though all are demonstrably members of the same species, *Homo sapiens*—are about as different looking as humans could be. Even if you had not been told where these people were from, you could still probably venture a good guess as to their geographic origin. We seem to have evidence, in other words, that our species is divided into some number of fairly distinct subgroups. The term usually applied to such groups is *race*. It seems, on the surface, a logical assumption. Indeed, for much of the history of anthropology, a focus has been on discovering just how many human races there are and on identifying them.

However—as noted in Chapter 12—races, on a biological level, don't exist within the human species. Races *are* real, but they are *cultural* categories. Cultures respond to and interpret objective reality—in this case human biological and cultural diversity—and create subjective categories that have meaning within given cultural systems. A good example of this process, and a somewhat more clear-cut one, is the way in which different cultures interpret the biological categories of sex into the cultural categories of gender.

These ideas require more detailed examination, and such an examination is, perhaps, one of the more important contributions of biological anthropology. Let's look at the following questions:

How are the two human sexes interpreted differently by different cultures? How can we use this as a model for examining "racial" variation?

Is race a valid biological concept?

Are there human biological races?

FIGURE 14.1
A European American photographer who is 6 feet 2 inches tall with a group of Yali people from the highlands of Irian Jaya (the western half of New Guinea). There is little doubt as to who is who, nor that members of our species can display a striking degree of phenotypic variation. The major question then becomes: Does this degree of variation mean that there are distinguishable human races?

What, then, *are* human races?

How can bioanthropology contribute to understanding some of the problems that the idea of race has presented?

SEX AND GENDER

Most human beings are unambiguously either biologically male or female. As noted in Chapter 9 with regard to skeletal features, we exhibit sexual dimorphism—varying phenotypic traits that distinguish the two sexes. In living humans there are more clearly dimorphic traits—hair distribution, for example. And other differences exist as well.

Human males, on average, are larger and more heavily muscled than females. They have relatively larger hearts and lungs, a faster recovery time from muscle fatigue, higher blood pressure, and greater oxygen-carrying capacity. Males are more susceptible than females to disease and death at all stages of life. During the first year of life, one-third more males die, mostly from infectious disease. Males are also more likely to have speech disorders, vision and hearing problems, ulcers, and skin disorders.

Females have a greater proportion of body fat than do males. They mature faster at almost all stages of life, most notably exhibiting earlier puberty and the adolescent growth spurt. They are less likely than males to be thrown off their normal growth curve (see Figure 13.16) by disease or other factors and, if they are, will recover more quickly than males. Although females appear to have a greater tendency than males to become obese, males suffer more from the effects of too much weight—strokes, for example. Females seem to be more sensitive to touch and pain and perhaps to higher sound frequencies, and they are said to be better at locating the sources of sounds. (For more detail, see Barfield 1976.)

These dimorphic features are not completely understood, and there is a good deal of overlap in the range of variation of these traits—for example, there are *some* females who are more heavily muscled than *some* males. But the above tendencies do suggest an adaptive explanation. Many of the characteristics of the human male are aimed at sustained, stressful physical action at the expense, however, of overall health. Females' overall better health, earlier sexual maturity, and greater sensitivity to stimulation of the senses might be geared toward their reproductive and child-rearing roles. Perhaps some basic themes of primate dimorphism (we find these size and strength differences in apes as well) were retained and some others selected for in our early ancestors as their small, cooperative bands (described in Chapter 10) confronted the challenges of life in the changing environments of Africa.

At any rate, although there is some individual and regional variation in the degree and nature of our sexually dimorphic traits, in general we rarely have any difficulty telling the **sex** of another human being. Male and female are two biological categories that are objectively real and are common to all human groups.

As these two real categories are incorporated into various cultural systems, however, differences arise. The identity, place, and role of males and females under different cultural systems vary depending upon the nature of those systems—their economies, politics, family organizations, and abstract beliefs. Thus, *males* and *females* of the human species become the *men* and *women* of a particular society practicing a particular culture. We refer to the cultural interpretation of biological sex categories as **gender** (Figure 14.2).

From cultural anthropology we acquire data about the incredible range of variation in gender identity and gender roles among the world's cultures. The variable factors include the roles of genders in economic activities,

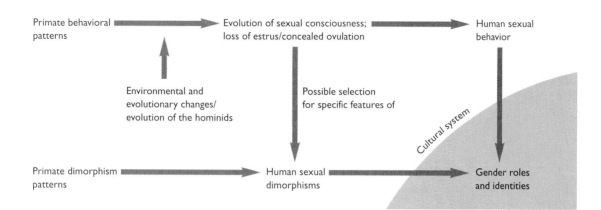

FIGURE 14.2
The evolved sexual identities and roles common to all members of the human species are translated by individual cultural systems into gender identities and roles.

differences in political and other decision-making power and influence, and expected norms of behavior.

For example, in the United States only a century ago, men were seen as the gender that properly had political, economic, and social power and that, therefore, should be educated. Women were far less likely to receive a college education, seldom held any sort of management position (if they did any work outside the home at all), and until 1920 were not even allowed to vote. Women were sometimes thought of as "the weaker sex." Obviously, things are different now, at least to a degree. As our culture has changed over the last hundred years, our gender roles and identities have changed to fit our evolving cultural system.

We refer to culturally defined categories as **folk taxonomies,** or cultural classifications. A society of people orders its world in ways that reflect objective reality as its people see and understand that reality, and that also meet its particular cultural needs and fit the totality of its cultural system.

To take an example from a different area, our society has a scientific viewpoint about the causes of disease. We understand that diseases are the results of natural processes, and one way we classify them is by the nature of their cause. Diseases are genetic, bacterial, viral, parasitic, environmental (drugs, radiation, pollutants), nutritional, congenital (where the development of the embryo is disrupted), emotional, and so on.

The Fore (Fo-RAY), a farming people of Papua New Guinea (Lindenbaum 1979), also classify disease by cause, but the causes are very different. The Fore believe that all disease is the result of the malicious intent of either sorcerers or spirits. Life-threatening diseases are thought to be caused by sorcery—malevolent action of one person against another. This reflects the political and economic tensions, rivalries, and jealousies that have become prevalent parts of Fore lives. Less severe diseases are caused by nature spirits inhabiting important places or by the ghosts of the recently deceased. These diseases are punishments for violating im-

sex: The biological categories and characteristics of males and females.

gender: The cultural categories and characteristics of men and women.

folk taxonomies: Cultural categories for important items and ideas.

FIGURE 14.3
Hijras, emasculated men who dress and behave like women, make up a third gender category in India. These *hijras* are blessing a child, one important ritual function they perform.

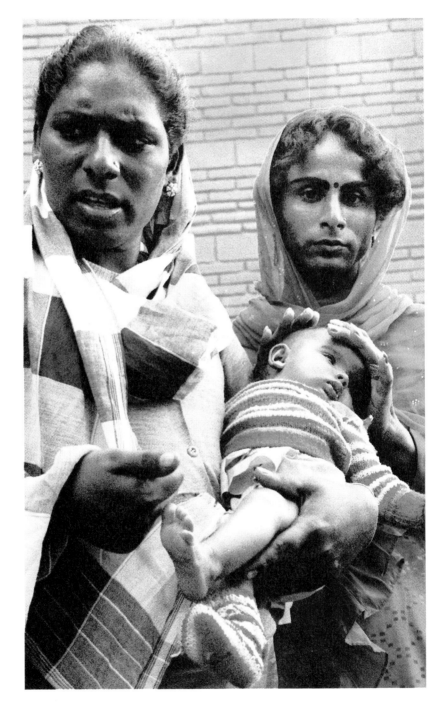

portant norms with regard to nature or the dead. Minor illnesses are attributed to a person's having violated some social rule among the living. The Fore folk taxonomy for disease, though it differs a great deal from our own, makes perfect sense within the context of the Fore cultural system.

Similarly, folk taxonomies for gender differ to a great degree among the cultures of the world even though we are all dealing basically with two sexes and two gender categories. We need to note, however, that biological sex is not always unambiguous. There are people born with underdeveloped sexual characteristics or with characteristics (including genitalia) of both sexes. In addition, there are those who are ambivalent toward their own sexual identity. As a result, some cultures recognize more than two genders.

A striking example is the *hijras* of India (Nanda 1990). The word means "not men," and, indeed, *hijras* are men who have been voluntarily surgically emasculated. They make up a third gender, and they have very specific identities and roles within the culture of Hindu India. Although often mocked and ridiculed because of their exaggerated feminine expressions and gestures, they are also in demand as performers at important rituals such as marriages and births (Figure 14.3).

A less extreme example comes from a number of Native American cultures where some men dressed as women and assumed the occupations and behaviors of women. Such men have been referred to by the term *berdache* (a French term with derogatory implications but still in common use). In some cases, they engaged in sexual relations with other men, and certain rituals could be performed only by them. In the cultures in which they were found, *berdaches* were not considered abnormal but were thought of as another gender.

It appears, then, that some societies acknowledge that certain of their members are, or think of themselves as, ambiguous with regard to the two standard sex categories. These societies have evolved third or even fourth gender classifications to accommodate them, and these classifications have developed defined places, identities, and roles within those societies' cultures. Sex is biological. Gender is a folk taxonomy. So, as we will see, is race in humans.

RACE AS A BIOLOGICAL CONCEPT

The processes of evolution ensure that each species of living thing possesses genetic variation and displays some degree of phenotypic variation. Some species are more variable than others, depending upon the nature of the species' geographic distribution and the variety of specific environments to which its members are adapted.

FIGURE 14.4

The caribou, *Rangifer tarandus*. This woodland caribou of Alaska and Canada is sometimes classified as subspecies *Rangifer tarandus caribou*. Well adapted to a wide range of environments, the caribou has such traits as hollow outer guard hairs that give it extra bouyancy for swimming and extra insulation for warmth. This feature makes caribou hides a favorite material among the Inuit for making parkas.

As noted in Chapter 5, some species are said to be specialized. They inhabit a relatively small geographic area or are adapted to a highly specific set of ecological circumstances—a narrow niche. Such species, of course, tend to be relatively homogeneous genetically and phenotypically. Natural selection has selected for essentially the same characteristics in all members of specialized species. A classic example is the koala, which lives only in Australia and eats primarily the leaves of the eucalyptus tree. We would not expect koalas to show a whole lot of variation, and they don't.

A species that inhabits a wide geographic range and is adapted to many specific niches is said to be generalized. Selection will promote different versions of the species' basic traits in response to the environments found in different parts of its range. Such species are more variable.

To remain a single species, of course, all males and females of the group must be potentially capable of interbreeding. There must be sufficient gene flow to prevent one or more groups from becoming completely isolated. Gene flow, however, is not always even. Members of a species may be clustered into breeding populations, or demes (see Chapter 4).

More genes are exchanged within demes than between different demes, often because some geographic barrier prevents extensive gene flow or because the environments to which the species are adapted come in clusters themselves with gaps between them that limit steady genetic exchange (see Figure 4.6).

Demes may be thought of as an important stage in many cases of speciation. If a deme becomes so isolated that virtually no genes are exchanged, if its environment is different enough to cause selection for a distinct set of traits, and if enough time elapses, the deme may eventually become a separate species, unable to interbreed with what were formerly other demes of the same species.

If, however, isolation is not complete or the conditions above have not been going on for a long enough time, the demes may represent phenotypically distinguishable regional populations within the same species. Such a species is said to be **polytypic** ("many types"), and such demes may be referred to as **subspecies** or **races.**

For example, reindeer of Europe and Asia and caribou of North America are classified as a single species, *Rangifer tarandus* (Figure 14.4). Now isolated from one another in separate hemispheres, the reindeer and caribou were no doubt once able to interbreed when Alaska and Siberia were joined during the Pleistocene, connecting the Old and New Worlds. Reindeer and caribou, then, have been separated for only a few thousand years, generally not enough time for speciation to have occurred. Enough time has elapsed, however, for the two populations to become physically distinguishable. They may be considered subspecies or races of a single species.

The North American population of this species has been further classified into at least four subspecies, the result of their distribution in different environments of Alaska, Canada, and Greenland. These subspecies, some woodland and some tundra dwellers, are distinguishable by such features as size, antler shape, and coat color (Figure 14.5). There are, then, five named subspecies or races of *Rangifer tarandus*, at least one in the Old World and four in the New World.

The utility of the race/subspecies concept, however, has been questioned. The identification and naming of subspecific groups is rather arbitrary. Zoologists Paul Ehrlich and Richard Holm (in Montagu 1964) noted two problems with the idea. First, we need to decide *what* phenotypic traits we should choose in defining racial groups within a species. Are all traits equally useful, or are some more useful than others? If so, which ones?

Second, we need to decide *how much* difference in phenotypic characters should be recognized as amounting to subspecific difference. A certain number of traits? A particular degree of difference in the measurements of certain traits?

polytypic: A species with physically distinguishable regional populations.

subspecies: A physically distinguishable population within a species.

races: In biology, the same as subspecies. In culture, cultural categories to classify and account for human physical diversity.

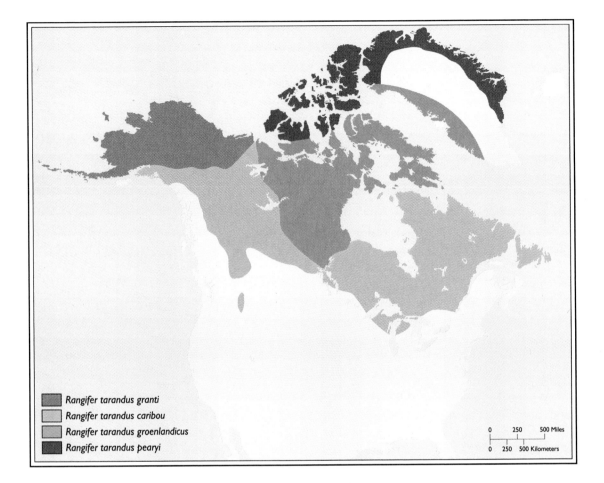

Rangifer tarandus granti
Rangifer tarandus caribou
Rangifer tarandus groenlandicus
Rangifer tarandus pearyi

0   250   500 Miles
0   250   500 Kilometers

FIGURE 14.5

North American populations of caribou are considered by some to represent subspecies or races.

One might well be justified in calling the caribou and reindeer subspecies, but their complete isolation in separate hemispheres for the last 10,000 years might mean they are on the way to becoming separate species. This state is better acknowledged with the use of the term **semispecies**—populations at an intermediate state between being a single interbreeding group and being different species. They still *can* interbreed (it has been done artificially), but they *don't*.

The four North American races pose a different problem. Because all the groups of caribou do exchange genes as members of a single species, it really becomes a matter of judgment as to whether their different environments, geographic ranges, and phenotypic features constitute distinct enough differences to warrant subspecific or racial designations.

Recent books in evolutionary biology seem either to treat race as one of the steps toward the evolution of new species (for example, Mettler et al. 1988) or to not mention either "subspecies" or "race" at all (for example, Ridley 1996). Indeed, the latter makes the point that all species show some variation among their populations and that, more often than not, the distribution of this variation is in the form of a **cline**—a contin-

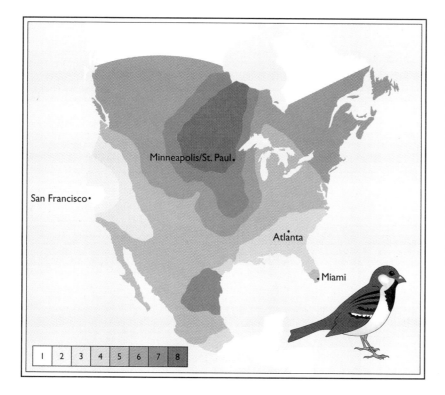

FIGURE 14.6
Distribution of size variation in male house sparrows, determined by sixteen skeletal measurements. The larger the number, the larger the sparrow. The classes, however, are arbitrary. If a line is drawn from Atlanta to St. Paul or from St. Paul to San Francisco, the size variation in the sparrows is distributed as a cline, a continuum of change from one area to another. (Notice also that the birds tend to be larger in the north, another example of this adaptation to cold; see Chapter 13.)

uum of change from one area to another, as opposed to sudden and absolutely distinct changes (Figure 14.6). Many biologists, then, do not recognize the subspecies or race concept as a valid description for what actually occurs in a natural species. The only named division within a species is the semispecies, as in the case of the Old and New World caribou/reindeer populations. With these views in mind, we can now address the question of human biological races.

ARE THERE HUMAN RACES?

Based upon the discussion above, the easiest answer would be to say that, because there are many who find no validity in the biological concept of race to begin with, there simply *cannot* be any human races. But the human species does display a number of visible polymorphic traits, many of which show some regularity in terms of their geographic distribution (see again Figure 14.1). Could we, then, be like the caribou of North America—distributed in distinct enough breeding populations that the concept *could* be applied, arbitrary though it may be? After all, we have applied it, even in anthropology.

semispecies: Populations of a species that are completely isolated from one another but have not yet become truly different species.

cline: A geographic continuum in the variation of a particular trait.

We may formalize the conditions required for subspecific classification by those who apply the concept. These conditions are (1) some degree of population isolation with limited gene flow, (2) environments different enough to promote adaptive selection in different directions, (3) genetic variation among the populations, and (4) enough time. How well does our species meet these criteria?

Even if our species has existed for only a few hundred thousand years, this is, theoretically, enough time even for *speciation* to have occurred if all the other conditions have been met. However, while we have been spreading and moving about, no human population has been isolated long enough, or to a complete enough degree, to allow even moderately separate and independent genetic events to take place. During all this time, humans have in fact become increasingly mobile, and it seems fair to say that we exchange genes at most every opportunity.

To be sure, cultural rules of endogamy exist, and they do tend to genetically isolate certain populations at certain times. The rules, however, change, and the political, ethnic, and religious populations defined by the rules change through time. The rules, in addition, are not always fully upheld. Endogamy is a temporary condition.

Gene flow, then, is the norm for our species, and, as widespread as we are, we still manage to exchange enough genes—through intermediary populations—even between the most far-flung of our peoples. As Stephen Jay Gould puts it, "I do not belong to a separate species from my brethren in Brazil just because I have never been there" (1992:43).

What about different environments? As noted in the previous chapter, some of our polymorphisms may be attributed to natural selection in response to differing environmental circumstances. But culture is our major adaptive mechanism. Even where natural selection has had an effect on certain traits of our species—such as skin color or maybe blood type—these adaptive differences are minor compared to our major adaptation of culture, with its values, social systems, and technologies.

The cultural adaptation was well developed and part of our hominid line long before modern humans arose. Think of the place of culture in the success of *Homo erectus*. Big brains—the basis for the cultural potential—are shared by all modern humans and are so basic to our modern identity that they are unlikely to show much major variation. Furthermore, the products of the cultural ability—social systems, beliefs, technologies—act as a buffer against much of the effect of biological natural selection. Had I been a Neandertal only 40,000 years ago, I might well have been selected out long ago, even if my group took care of me. But, today, my eyeglasses, blood pressure medication, and an emergency appendectomy—among other things—have kept me going well beyond average Neandertal life expectancy. Culture, in a sense, *is* our environment. Thus, it may well be said that we all share that environment and that there is, in this respect, little environmental variation in our species.

Finally, as recent genetic studies have shown, we are not a very genetically diverse species to begin with. About 75 percent of all human genes are monomorphic (having only one allele); that is, all humans are identical for three-quarters of the human **genome** (Lewontin 1982:120). This is a higher percentage than in chimpanzees. The genetic variation that does exist—the remaining 25 percent of our genes with multiple alleles—is actually fairly evenly distributed. Richard Lewontin (1982:123) calculates that if some great cataclysm left only Africans alive, that remnant of the human species would still retain 93 percent of the total genetic variation of the former population of the species, although certain traits, like skin color, would have different *average* expressions.

The human species, then, fails in theory to meet the criteria for division into subspecies. And we may strengthen the argument by looking at the variable traits themselves. Examined closely, we see that no real boundaries exist between trait expressions. Although I divided skin color into five categories for the sake of the map in Figure 13.11, those divisions were arbitrary. Skin color does not change abruptly as the map may imply. It changes gradually in populations closer to or farther from the equator. In other words, skin color is distributed as a cline. It does not come in neat packages with clear geographic limits. Neither, for example, does blood type, as a look at Figure 13.12 clearly shows.

Moreover, when we compare the distributions of human polymorphisms, we see that the distributions are "discordant." The distribution of one trait rarely matches the distribution of any other. Thus, a subspecific or racial division based on the distribution of one trait will invariably differ from that based on another (Figure 14.7, and compare again Figures 13.11 and 13.12). At the biological level, then, *human variation exists, but human races don't.*

Does this mean, however, that our species is one gigantic "stew" of people with no discernable groups and thus no way to trace and understand the history of our populations? Whereas phenotypic traits only serve to confuse the matter, our increasing knowledge of genetics does allow us to compare living populations to one another, to understand what genetic variation does exist, and to begin to build a family tree determining where populations originated, how they are related, and how they spread.

Such an analysis is essentially an extension of that done with mitochondrial DNA as described in Chapter 12. Figure 12.5 showed a tree of relationships among populations from which the mtDNA samples were drawn. Those data were limited, however. A more extensive study was done by L. L. Cavalli-Sforza and colleagues (Cavalli-Sforza 1991; Cavalli-Sforza and Cavalli-Sforza 1995; Cavalli-Sforza et al. 1994) that used more

genome: The total genetic endowment of a species.

FIGURE 14.7

Diagram of discordant variation. Each layer represents the geographic variation in one polymorphism. Each "core," or cylinder, represents a sample of individuals from a particular area. Notice that each core is different and that any other four cores are very likely to be different as well. The expression of one trait does not predict a particular expression of another. There are no natural racial divisions based on specific combinations of traits.

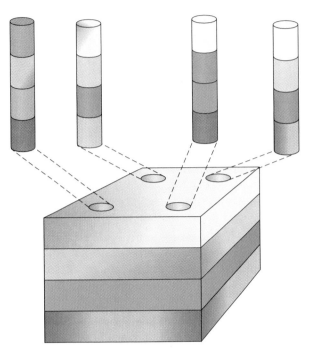

than 100 different inherited traits of 3000 individuals taken from 1800 populations. The study compared proteins, the direct products of the genes. A second study used actual DNA code sequences. There was marked agreement among the analyses.

These studies were able to plot the distributions of small genetic differences within and between populations and to estimate how long ago various populations shared common ancestors. From these data, family trees of population relationships were drawn and routes for major migrations of modern humans described (Figure 14.8). It should be noted that Cavalli-Sforza is a proponent of the Recent African Origin model (see Chapter 12), and so the migration map assumes an interpretation of the genetic data that supports that point of view. Those data, as you recall, can also be interpreted to support a multiregional model. The important point, however, is that with sophisticated techniques that allow us to compare the smallest genetic differences among human groups, we are able to begin to paint a picture of the detailed biological history of our species' populations.

The distribution of genes coincided to a great degree with the distribution of languages. Languages and genetic populations can be correlated because, as human populations split and separate, "each fragment evolves linguistic and genetic patterns that bear marks of shared branching points. . . . [Furthermore], linguistic differences [and the cultural differ-

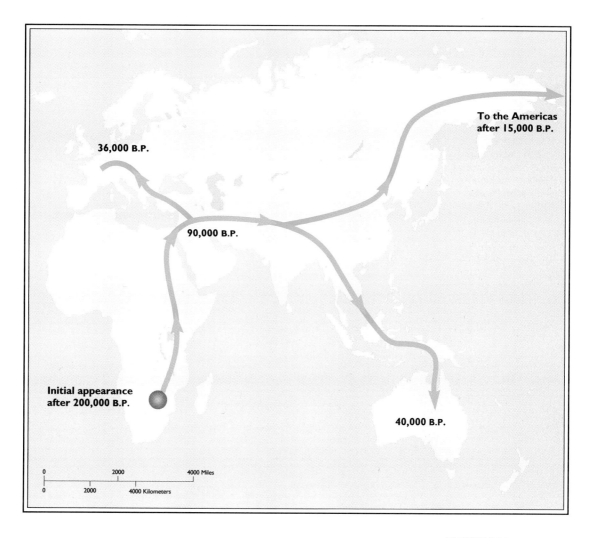

Initial appearance
after 200,000 B.P.

90,000 B.P.

36,000 B.P.

To the Americas
after 15,000 B.P.

40,000 B.P.

0   2000   4000 Miles

0   2000   4000 Kilometers

ences they reflect] may generate or reinforce genetic barriers between populations. Hence, some correlation is inevitable" (Cavalli-Sforza 1991:109). Figure 14.9 is a simplified diagram of this correlation.

We can conclude that our species does not sort itself into clear-cut and profoundly different racial or subspecific groups. We are too mobile, too genetically homogeneous, and too culturally adapted. But the richness of our genetic, ethnic, and cultural variety is not lost within some worldwide melting pot. There *are* human populations, identified by correlated biological and, mostly, cultural factors. And this brings us to the next question.

FIGURE 14.8
Movement over time of modern *Homo sapiens* (according to the Recent African Origin model) or of the histories of some modern genes (in the view of the Multiregional Evolution model). The map was drawn using DNA comparisons of modern populations.

WHAT, THEN, *ARE* HUMAN RACES?

Like gender categories, human races are folk taxonomies. Several years ago I gave one of my classes a weekend assignment to ask ten people,

Genetic Groups · Living Populations · Linguistic Groups

Genetic Groups	Living Populations	Linguistic Groups
African	San	Khoisan
	Masai	Nilo-Saharan
	Mbuti	Niger-Congo
	Ethiopian	Afro-Asiatic
Caucasoid	Southwestern Asian	
	Mediterranean	Indo-European
	Northern European	
	Indian	
American	North American	Amerind
	Central American	
	South American	
Arctic	Eskimo	Eskimo-Aleut
	Siberian	Altaic
Northeast Asian	Japanese	
	Korean	
	Tibetan	Sino-Tibetan
Mainland Island Southeast Asian	Southern Chinese	
	Indonesian	Austronesian
	Philippine	
Pacific Islands	Polynesian	
	Melanesian	Indo-Pacific
	New Guinean	Australian
	Australian	

FIGURE 14.9
Chart of the correlation between genetic and linguistic groups in modern humans. The living populations listed are a representative sample. Note that where populations live close to one another under similar environmental conditions, as with Ethiopians and Southwest Asians, they may speak languages of the same group even though they are genetically different.

preferably from different backgrounds and of different ages and both sexes, two questions: How many races are there? What are they?

Nearly all the responses were versions of a familiar set of categories: "white," "black," and "yellow," or "Caucasian," "Negro," and "Oriental," or some other terms that varied with the individual. The similarity of most responses is an indication that some basic taxonomy is shared among members of our culture.

However, there was some interesting variation in the responses as well. One respondent said there were three races, "black," "white," and "Polish." Jews were considered a race by some, as were Hispanics. A few people, who I guessed had done some reading on the subject, added Native Americans and native Australians to the usual three. This showed that, despite the similarities, there was no universally agreed-upon classification, as there would be for some scientific fact like the number of planets in the solar system. Specific responses were as variable as the individual back-grounds of the respondents.

Cultures classify other people relative to themselves. Isolated societies with some knowledge that others exist will have a very simple racial clas-sification: us and them. As knowledge accumulates among more mobile or cosmopolitan groups and as the relations among people become more varied, the classifications become more complex. Knowledge about other groups includes such things as their cultural practices, their relations with your group, and their physical appearance. Thus, a racial taxonomy also carries implications about a society's attitude toward others. In short, race—which differs from society to society—is a folk taxonomy, used by a particular society, at a particular time, for particular, culturally based reasons.

The categories of race that we in the United States recognize are no exception. The categories' origins can be traced to European knowledge and attitudes first acquired during the Age of Exploration. European ex-plorers, using mostly water transporation, were limited in the range and distribution of human variation they could observe. They sampled points along the continuum of human variation. Because points along a contin-uum can differ greatly from one another, depending upon how far apart they are, it appeared that human variation fell into a number of relatively discrete categories (Figure 14.10 and see again Figure 14.1).

In addition, the peoples contacted were not seen as simply different human beings; instead, they were compared to and ranked against Euro-pean peoples, usually unfavorably. They were, after all, of different ap-pearance, with different cultures, often with less complex technologies, and—this was important to the Europeans—with non-Christian religions. Furthermore, the motivation for the explorers' voyages was less to acquire knowledge than to find new territories, sources of labor, spices, and gold. A dominant attitude was built in to the European's relationships with these new peoples. Witness the way in which Europeans would claim new lands "in the name of the crown," entirely ignoring the fact that there were already people to whom the lands belonged. Obviously, it was thought, the indigenous people were too primitive to really have laws of ownership.

The racial folk taxonomy that resulted from these cultural events was formalized, and thus made more real, by Linnaeus. In the final edition of his taxonomy in 1758, he included *Homo sapiens* and divided the species into varieties or races. Not surprisingly, he recognizes four races of humans (five if you count a category called "wild man," apparently a catch-all to account for populations, mostly mythical, that did not fit the other four). His main races are American, European, Asiatic, and African, and his descriptions of these races are a blend of biological generalizations and, as Stephen Molnar says (1992:10), "personality profiles" based on European

FIGURE 14.10
Columbus's first contact with natives of the New World. To the Europeans, the Indians were so strikingly different in physical and cultural features that it was natural to consider them as a distinct category of human. Notice the men planting the cross to claim the land as theirs. (From a seventeenth-century Spanish version of a 1594 engraving by de Bry. The Granger Collection.)

perspectives. Here is Linnaeus's description of Africans, for example (Kennedy 1976:25).

> Black, phlegmatic [sluggish], relaxed. Hair black, frizzled; skin silky; nose flat; lips tumid [swollen]; crafty, indolent, negligent. Anoints himself with grease. Governed by caprice [impulse].

Europeans, of course, were "brawny," "gentle," "inventive," "covered with cloth vestments," and "governed by laws."

Because the history of the United States has been so influenced by European cultures, it stands to reason that the European folk taxonomy with regard to race—the categories and the attitudes they implied—was carried over and affected our country's culture. Our racial categories are real. They may not reflect universal biological reality on the species level, but they do have meaning within our cultural system, for better or for worse.

RACE, BIOANTHROPOLOGY, AND SOCIAL ISSUES

The issue of race in the human species is not just a matter of whether or not to apply the biological concept of subspecies. Would that it were. Rather, the idea of race can be, and is, used to make prejudgments about people and to determine a person's place in society, often without regard to that person's individual characteristics. This is **racism.** The moral dimension of this problem, though it should be important to everyone, is not something we can or should deal with in a brief book about science. We may, however, show how bioanthropology, through the use of science, can examine some claimed connections between racial categories and biological traits. In so doing, we can help make ourselves more informed about just what race is and what it is not.

Let's briefly look at one topic. If your goal is to limit the social position and power of a particular group, one of the strongest arguments you can propose is that the population in question possesses some unalterable biological difference that inherently limits their abilities and therefore justifies their lower social status. The practice of slavery in the United States was often justified by the claim that the black slaves were biologically less intelligent than the whites and therefore could never hope to attain the dominant race's social, political, and intellectual level. Claims like this have been quite common, even during the last century (Gould 1996b).

Such broad statements about race and intelligence, or even race and evolutionary level, are so clearly motivated by social and economic situations as to be at least questionable, if not obviously false. Perhaps more dangerous, however, are the more subtle correlations whose propositions are based on scientific investigation. Ideas that sound scientific are often treated more seriously, especially because, even today, many people feel that science is something so complex and obscure that only a handful can really understand it. Many people take the position that if something sounds scientific and they don't get it, it must be valid.

Such is the case for the claimed connection between the American black and white races and IQ (intelligence quotient). The most famous (or infamous) example is educational psychologist Arthur Jensen's 1969 article in the *Harvard Educational Review* titled "How much can we boost IQ and scholastic achievement?" The article is 123 pages long and quite scientific in its wording, logic, and methodology, and it includes a lengthy mathematical formula or two. As a result, many people, both supporters and critics of Jensen's work, have never bothered to actually read it. A more recent and perhaps better-known work, *The Bell Curve* by Herrnstein and Murray (1994), repeats and greatly expands the same essential argument. See Gould (1996b) for a detailed critique.

racism: Judging an individual based solely on his or her racial affiliation.

A focus of Jensen's article was the documented fact that American black children score, on average, fifteen points lower on IQ tests than American white children. Jensen wondered why programs aimed at the obvious solution of culturally enriching children's lives had basically failed. Some studies showed that the fifteen-point IQ difference remained. Hence, the title of his article (emphasis mine for the right intonation): "How much *can* we boost IQ and scholastic achievement?"

Jensen embarks on a scientific investigation. His first conclusion is that IQ tests measure something called *g*, or general intelligence—a biological, inherited entity. This entity, *g*, has a **heritability** of .80 (80 percent). This means that 80 percent of the variation in intelligence within a population is explained by genetic differences. Only 20 percent is the result of members of that group having been brought up in different cultural environments. (It bears restating that heritability measures the amount of *variation within a group* that is due to genetic differences. It does not measure the amount of genetic control of a trait in an individual. It does not say that 80 percent of my intelligence is genetically determined.)

The obvious conclusion, then, is that the difference in intelligence between the two racial groups in question must be largely the result of some genetic difference, and, thus, all the cultural enrichment programs in the world can only have a limited effect. The answer to the question in Jensen's title is, "Not much." He states, "No one has yet produced any evidence based on a properly controlled study to show that representative samples of Negro and white children can be equalized in intellectual ability through statistical control of environment and education" (1969: 82–83).

Jensen went further, however. He compared scores from different parts of IQ tests and concluded that the different IQs of blacks and whites is the result of their having different kinds of intellectual abilities. Whites are better at problem solving and abstract reasoning, while the abilities of blacks are focused on memorization, rote learning, and trial-and-error experience. His ultimate conclusion was that education should be as individualized as possible, taking into account not only individual differences in ability and skill but these racially based differences as well.

As you can imagine, Jensen's article caused a great deal of controversy. He was labeled a racist, and, certainly, those with racist leanings embraced his work enthusiastically. I don't know what Jensen's social attitudes were, but we can look at his article from a scientific point of view, drawing especially on what we have learned from anthropology.

First, the idea that IQ tests measure some innate mental ability is fraught with problems. It has been said that IQ tests measure the ability to take IQ tests. This is not, as it sounds, just a sarcastic remark. IQ tests, in fact, measure particular knowledge and abilities that are largely learned through one's culture. They are valuable. They may, in fact, point out some learning disability that may turn out to be biologically based. Because they measure the kinds of skills required by education in our culture as well as by many occupations, they do have predictive value as to one's success within those aspects of our cultural system.

We do not even know, however, what intelligence is. How can we—through a test given in a cultural language, in a cultural setting, with cultural problems—apply a single number to such a complex and multi-faceted concept? When we do this, we commit the logical error called **reification.** With IQ scores we have reified intelligence—translated a complex idea into a single entity, in this case, a number, which we then use to classify people into groups such as different learning tracks in schools.

Let's put this another way. As anthropologist Jonathan Marks suggests, there is a difference between *ability* and *performance* (Marks 1995: 240 ff). One's score on an IQ test is a score of one's performance. Certainly some internal factor—one's innate intellectual abilities, whatever those are—plays a part in one's performance on an IQ test. But that performance is also affected by all sorts of external factors. In test taking, for example, your cultural background, quality of education, personality, home life, even your mood on the day of the test can all affect your performance on a test. We cannot, therefore, infer innate abilities from the score on a test, any more than we can, say, infer a person's athletic abilities from their performance in one game. We cannot do so, in part, because there *are* so many external influences; and we have no way of accounting for them, controlling them, or even knowing what they are. More importantly, though, to make such an inference from IQ is to reify intelligence—to take the measurement of performance on a test and assume that it is also a measurement of an innate ability. As Marks puts it, "We can't measure ability; we can only measure performance" (1995: 241).

But what about the claimed heritability of IQ? This is a complicated issue (see Gould 1996b for the best discussion), but there is one major problem we can point out here. Heritability studies—estimating the genetic and environmental components of the phenotypic variation in a population—are done regularly, but these studies are done on organisms like fruit flies, where the genetic mechanisms for phenotypic traits are well known (and can even be manipulated) and where the environmental variables can be controlled in detail. Numbers may be placed on these genetic and environmental variables that may then be plugged into the heritability formula. This is the formula that Jensen reproduces in his article.

To apply the heritability formula to humans, however, is virtually impossible. What numbers can we place on the external environmental variables that affect us? How, in other words, can we reify culture? What number is applied to having a culturally enriched childhood, to being a member of a minority group, or to having a poor early education?

heritability: The amount of variation of a particular trait within a population that is caused by genetic differences.

reification: Translating a complex set of phenomena into a single entity such as a number.

Heritability has been *estimated* for humans based on twin studies. Because identical twins have no genetic variation between them, any phenotypic difference, including intelligence, must be the result of environmental differences. IQ scores of identical twins are generally very similar, even in twins raised separately, and this seems to indicate that environment has little effect on intelligence. We must remember, however, that IQ does not measure intelligence, but rather performance on an exam. Therefore, IQ is measuring, to a great extent, the results of environmental influences in the first place and not the results of genetic endowment. Even in twins raised apart, it may well be that their environments are similar enough to result in similar IQ scores. On those rare occasions when identical twins are separated shortly after birth, it is likely that they are raised in homes of similar socioeconomic level and so receive educations of similar quality. It cannot be denied that identical twins are probably similar in whatever those innate abilities are that we call intelligence, but studies based on the IQ scores of such twins are reflecting a whole lot more than those innate abilities.

To further claim that two races have different kinds of intellectual abilities is to ignore the very nature of the modern human species. This claim says that there is a major degree of difference in the very abilities—to solve problems or to formulate abstractions and generalizations—that are a hallmark of our species' evolution. Certainly, we express individual variation in some of these abilities, and some of this variation may well be based on some sort of biological difference. I have no doubt that Beethoven and Einstein had some fundamental innate processes going on in their brains that I don't. But to think that natural selection would promote, in two different groups, profoundly different expressions of the major adaptive mechanism of a species makes little sense in light of what we know about the workings of adaptive evolution.

Finally, if you are looking to make biological comparisons between two groups, the groups need to be biologically defined. American whites and American blacks are decidedly not biological races. We have already established that race is not a biological concept for the human species (or, perhaps, for any other species) in the first place. What variation does exist is distributed in such a way as to make distinct, discrete groups of *Homo sapiens* nonexistent. We perceive differences in these two groups—average skin color, major geographic area of origin, frequency of diseases like hypertension, and even frequency of some genes such as that for sickle cell anemia—but the groups themselves are cultural. There's simply not much genetic difference, certainly not on the level of genes for different intellectual abilities. Indeed, it has been estimated that about 15 percent of all genes in African Americans have come from European Americans because of the extent of gene flow between the two populations over the last several hundred years (Lewontin 1982).

So, the difference in performance on IQ tests can be seen as heavily influenced by the socioeconomic limitations imposed on African Americans for the past several centuries, limitations that have resulted in separate and often poor-quality education, limited access to various forms of cultural enrichment, and even the psychological effects of being identified as members of a minority group. These are all intangible factors that are impossible to fully control or even identify. Scores on IQ tests certainly involve some aspect of a person's innate intellectual abilities, but, again, because of all these external factors, we cannot infer those abilities from the results of test performances. And we certainly cannot make a biological generalization about a culturally defined group of people based on those performance results.

Our folk taxonomies are powerful and influential. We respond to them often without realizing that they are *our* culture's way of ordering *our* world and are not necessarily scientific universals. The influence of the American folk taxonomy for race can easily be seen in Jensen's work. By understanding what race is, and what it's not, and by applying what we know about the workings of genetics and evolution, we may see the fallacies of this and similar pieces of research. This perspective is an important one for helping us deal with the other issues of race that confront us almost daily.

SUMMARY

Human societies need to find order in, and to make sense of, the environments in which they live. Objective reality is, thus, translated into categories that have meaning within particular cultural systems. We call these categories folk taxonomies.

So important are the relationships between the sexes and the relative places in society of males and females that different cultural systems have evolved very different folk taxonomies for sex. These are gender roles and identities and, in some societies, may even include more than two genders if those societies have the need to formally classify persons of ambiguous sex or sexuality.

That humans in general display variable traits is obvious, on some level, to all societies, and so all cultural systems also include folk taxonomies for race. On a biological level, however, races or subspecies do not exist for our species. Indeed, the concept is falling from use in biology in general. But even if we attempt to apply the race concept to humans, we find that the biological nature of our species does not lend itself to division into clear-cut, discrete units.

Contemporary Reflections

Are There Racial Differences in Athletic Ability?

Having established that race has no biological meaning (at least for the human species), we can translate the question to ask whether there are average differences in athletic ability among populations from different geographic regions. Of course there are. How many heavyweight boxers could hail from the highlands of New Guinea (see Figure 14.1) where people, on average, are much smaller than most Europeans or Africans? Could the average Inuit (see Figure 13.10) compete very successfully in a 400-meter sprint? There are phenotypic differences within the human species, and some of these would certainly have an effect on performance in particular athletic contests.

The question, however, is commonly posed in the context of American sports, where even a casual look at a National Basketball Association game would give one the clear impression that African Americans are better basketball players than European Americans. The biggest stars of the game are African Americans like Michael Jordan, Shaquille O'Neal, and Charles Barkley. The idea has become part of our folk culture—we say jokingly that "white men can't jump," but we probably really believe it. How reasonable is the inference, however?

For one thing, we cannot infer a generalization about a whole group of people from a small sample. Professional basketball players are those who, due in large measure to some innate abilities and physical features (like, for example, above-average stature), excel at the skills required for the game. In no way does it follow that all blacks have those skills, any more than it follows that all white European males have the ability to write the Ninth Symphony. It does not even follow that blacks are *more likely* to possess those skills than whites.

Why, then, the prevalence of blacks in the sport? As Jonathan Marks has pointed out (1995:240 ff), sports involve innate skills, but, like IQ tests, they are also performances and, as such, are influenced by complex external factors. The difference in socioeconomic status of those identified as white and black has made a difference in the opportunity that people have to play certain sports. In fact, just a few generations ago, most professional basketball players were white, because, except for boxing, blacks had little or no opportunity to participate in professional sports.

Even now that sports are open to all groups, the effects of those socioeconomic differences have an influence. To practice the skills of basketball, one needs only a hoop of some sort, an area to play, and a ball. These prerequisites can be found in every neighborhood. Swimming pools, golf gear and courses, tennis courts, even baseball equipment are more expensive and not as readily available. Moreover, with career choices traditionally more limited for black youths than for whites, an easily practiced sport becomes an increasingly popular focus. There may well be many white youths who have the innate abilities of a Jordan, O'Neal, or Barkley, and people from all groups enjoy the game at an avocational or scholastic level, but more athletically inclined black youths are interested in a *career* in basketball and so pursue it. Thus, more men who become professional basketball players are black, and this is a major reason for the skewed "racial" distribution within that sport.

Does this cultural explanation preclude the existence of some physical or physiological feature related to basketball prowess that shows an average difference between Americans of African descent and those of European descent? Certainly not. There are other features—most notably skin color—that show an average difference. To my knowledge, no one has found any such trait, but if they did, so what? We each possess features that both enable and limit us in terms of what we can do—intellectually, artistically, and athletically. Some of these features may relate to our geographic heritage. Better to understand the facts behind such features and their effects than to concoct myths about them and to prejudge an individual's abilities based simply on the group to which he or she belongs.

So powerful is the folk taxonomy for race that our categories take on a reality beyond that which is warranted, and we find that we use them as cues to tell us how to think about other groups of people and how to treat them. We can all too easily confuse culture and biology, and this effect can even be seen in scientific investigations, such as those that look for some biological racial difference in the cultural measure of intelligence called IQ.

KEY TERMS

sex	subspecies	genome
gender	races	racism
folk taxonomies	semispecies	heritability
polytypic	cline	reification

SUGGESTED READINGS

A good book on sex and gender from an anthropological perspective is *Female of the Species* by M. Kay Martin and Barbara Voorhies. Despite the title, it is really about both sexes and all the gender categories found in various cultural systems. The fascinating case of India's *hijras* is documented in *Neither Man Nor Woman: The Hijras of India* by Serena Nanda.

On race, I highly recommend Stephen Molnar's *Human Variation: Races, Types, and Ethnic Groups* for a text covering the entire issue as a part of anthropology. It includes sections on our polymorphic traits. Another treatment of the same subject, but from a biologist, is Richard Lewontin's *Human Diversity*. The newest book on the subject, and the one that includes an extended discussion of race and athletic ability, is Jonathan Marks's *Human Biodiversity: Genes, Race, and History*.

For a collection of articles on the nonexistence of human biological races, see *The Concept of Race* edited by Ashley Montagu, and for a nice treatment of the history of race studies, try Kenneth A. R. Kennedy's *Human Variation in Space and Time*.

The analysis of human genetic differences and what they tell us about the history of human groups is nicely covered by Luigi Luca Cavalli-Sforza and Francesco Cavalli-Sforza in *The Great Human Diasporas: The History of Diversity and Evolution*.

The best book on racism, emphasizing an examination of scientific attempts to find correlations between race (and sex) and intelligence is Stephen Jay Gould's *The Mismeasure of Man*.

CHAPTER

15

BIOLOGICAL ANTHROPOLOGY: APPLICATIONS AND LESSONS

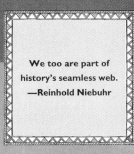

We too are part of
history's seamless web.
—Reinhold Niebuhr

A s I am writing this, the second trial in the Oklahoma City bombing case has just ended. One man has been convicted of blowing up, and one of conspiring to blow up, a federal office building in that city on April 19, 1995. The death toll in the bombing was 168. Many of the bodies were difficult to identify because they were literally blown apart by the blast, which left only fragments.

One of the people involved in the grim task of identifying the dead was forensic anthropologist Clyde Snow, himself an Oklahoman. Though certainly not to everyone's taste, such work is one of the ways that biological anthropology can make a tangible contribution to our lives. It is, of course, unfortunate that such skills are needed. But they are, and the work of identifying human remains and, sometimes, of identifying the cause of their deaths, is an important one, bringing some comfort to the survivors and justice to the slain.

Although the work of all biological anthropologists is useful in its contribution to knowledge, there are some practical ways in which our field can be applied and some lessons all people can learn from biological anthropologists' unique perspective on our species. In this last chapter, we will address the simple question:

What are some of the applications and lessons of biological anthropology?

FORENSIC ANTHROPOLOGY: READING THE BONES

Forensic means relating to courts of law or public discussion or the application of science to legal matters. The skills anthropologists use to retrieve information from ancient skeletons (see Chapter 9) have also proved useful in retrieving information from more modern ones—the victims of violent crimes and accidents. Forensic anthropology is increasingly called upon to examine skeletal remains and the conditions under which they were found to determine identity, time and cause of death, and any other information that may prove helpful to law enforcement agencies. In turn, some of the methods that have been developed by forensic anthropologists have been applied to older remains that are of strictly scientific, rather than legal, interest.

Perhaps the best-known case of the latter is the well-publicized "Ice Man." He was found by hikers in September 1991, at over 10,000 feet in the Alps, just on the Italian side of the border with Austria. He had been naturally mummified by the dehydrating action of the cold and the wind and was in a remarkable state of preservation. This became all the more remarkable when carbon-14 dating of the body itself, and of grass with

FIGURE 15.1
The Ice Man's body, pre-
served for over 5000 years
in the Italian Alps, was naturally mummified by cold and
wind. Pressure from the ice
disfigured his nose and lip
and pushed his left arm into
this odd position. We are
still learning about his life
and death from his preserved
body, which includes his
brain and internal organs.

which he had stuffed his boots, provided a date of 3300 B.C. The body was over 5000 years old.

The Ice Man was found with a fascinating array of artifacts, including much of his clothing and some tools. Details on these may be found in the references I'll give at the end of the chapter. Here, we'll concentrate on the body itself (Figure 15.1).

Investigators x-rayed the body and, using techniques we discussed in Chapter 9, determined that it was that of a male about 5 feet 2 inches tall. Initially, he was thought to have been in his late twenties or early thirties when he died, but more recent analysis has indicated he was around 50. Oddly, he had only eleven pairs of ribs, instead of the usual twelve, and eight ribs had been broken at one time or another but were healed, or were healing, at the time of his death. He had arthritis of the neck, lower back, and right hip, and the joints of his knees and ankles were worn. There is some evidence of hardening of the arteries, and his lungs were blackened, probably by smoke from open fires.

There are odd sets of parallel lines on the Ice Man's lower back, left thigh, and right ankle that resemble tattoos. One hypothesis is that these are related to the arthritic and joint pain he probably suffered in those areas. Some cultures are known to use hot brands as treatments for such ailments.

There is a good deal of wearing down of the Ice Man's teeth, some of which can be clearly seen on his upper incisors. This probably indicates that he used his teeth as tools, perhaps for leather working, and that he ate a tough diet including dried meat and the products of flour from grains that had been mixed with sand to aid in grinding. Both practices are known from the archaeological record.

His diet, however, may not have been particularly good. Patterns on a fingernail recovered later (the others had fallen off) are consistent with signs of periods of reduced nail growth from disease or malnutrition.

How did the Ice Man die? We may never know for sure, but we may make a good guess. There was no evidence that insects had laid any eggs on his body, and some sloe berries were found along with him. These facts point to his death in late summer or early fall, when insect reproductive activity has ceased and when the berries are available. It is a time when the weather in that area can turn suddenly and unexpectedly bad. Given his ill health and possible poor diet, he may simply have been caught in foul weather and froze to death.

Finally, in part to put to rest the inevitable questions about a possible fraud, mitochondrial DNA analysis was performed. It indicated that the Ice Man was a European and that he was related to living populations from the northern Alps. Techniques of reconstruction have even given us an idea of what he looked like (Figure 15.2).

All this information, and more, can be gleaned about a mummified corpse over fifty centuries old. When the Ice Man died, writing was just being invented in Mesopotamia, the great pyramids of Egypt had yet to be built, and the lives of Julius Caesar and Jesus were over 3000 years in the future.

As famous as the Ice Man is, we do not, of course, know his name. Forensic studies, however, have provided us with new information about some famous people whose names we are very familiar with. For example, the late forensic anthropologist William Maples (Maples and Browning 1994) helped identify the skeletal remains of the assassinated Russian tsar Nicholas II and his family. (The bones did not, by the way, include those of Anastasia, the tsar's daughter, said to have survived and escaped to the West.) Maples also examined the remains of U.S. president Zachary Taylor to prove that he was not murdered by arsenic poisoning. He also helped identify the true remains of Spanish conquistador Francisco Pizarro and proved that a mummy reported to be Pizarro's was actually someone else's.

Clyde Snow, another well-known forensic anthropologist, identified a skeleton found in Brazil as that of Nazi war criminal Josef Mengele. The standard information about the skeleton fit what was known about Mengele, but Snow clinched it by superimposing images of the skull over photographs of the man known as the "Angel of Death." They matched, and the identification was verified shortly after when Mengele's dental records were discovered. Snow has also been involved in a review of the assassination of John F. Kennedy and has, as mentioned earlier, searched in Bolivia for the remains of the famous outlaws Butch Cassidy and the Sundance Kid, so far without success.

More important, however, than these cases of the rich and famous are those involving the remains of common, everyday people who, for one reason or another, need to be identified and who, perhaps, require justice. Clyde Snow has, for example, examined and tried to identify the remains of some of the more than 10,000 people who "disappeared" during the military rule in Argentina from 1976 to 1983. His evidence has been used to help prosecute some of those responsible. He has done similar work in the Philippines and in Southwest Asia, and he has helped identify the victims of airline crashes, such as one that took place in Chicago in 1979 killing 273 people.

Investigating smaller tragedies, however, is not outside the activities of the forensic anthropologist. For a typical example, we can look at one of Clyde Snow's cases, a case that, ironically, began around Oklahoma City (Snow and Luke 1970). In the summer of 1967, two young girls, aged 5 and 6 years, disappeared in the Oklahoma City area within a few weeks of one another. In November of that year, two hunters found some bones, including a human cranium, in a rural area outside the city. The bones were scattered on the surface of the ground. Further investigation, however, revealed a crude grave that contained more bones and children's clothing. An extensive excavation was conducted. Among the several hundred bones eventually recovered—most of which belonged to various nonhumans—were those of a young child. Snow investigated further to see if the bones could reveal a specific identity and perhaps a cause of death. There was a good chance that these were the bones of one of the missing girls, and perhaps even both.

Snow determined that the bones had been buried fairly recently. They still had the greasy texture of fresh bone, and there were no signs of

weathering that would indicate they had been there over winter. Although the bones had been damaged by scavengers, there were no rodent gnaw marks on them. Rodents gnaw well-weathered bones as sources of minerals and protein. The bones were recent, but how recent?

They were completely skeletonized, but this could certainly have happened during the previous summer. It was shown that, in Oklahoma's climate, a child's body would be reduced to bone within two to six weeks. There were spider webs and other signs of insect activity in the skull, so it was determined that the bones had been completely exposed before cold weather set in and those creatures became inactive. Burial had occurred in early September at the latest.

Soon, the possibility that more than one human was represented was ruled out. The cause of death was a problem, though. Much of the skeleton was missing, and the bones that remained were found scattered about. Some bones were damaged, and some teeth missing. None of this, however, could be clearly attributed to trauma before death or purposeful dismemberment afterward. More likely, it was the result of decomposition and the work of carnivorous scavengers that dug up the grave, scattered the bones, and carried off those with fleshy parts.

Determining the sex of the skeleton was difficult. No pelvis was found, nor was there enough of the remainder of the skeleton to make a good

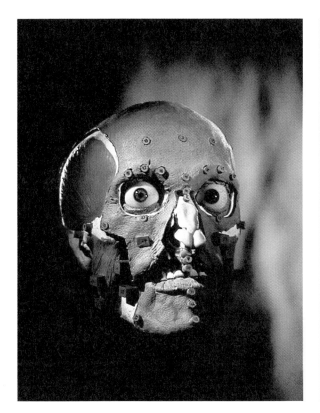

FIGURE 15.2

Artist John Gurche reconstructed the face of the Ice Man. He began with measurements, computer images, X rays, and CAT scans and produced a model of the Ice Man's skull. Next, he added clay to resemble the mummified face and then, like a plastic surgeon, rebuilt the face, reconstructing the nose and adding fatty tissue and muscles (represented by the red pegs) using anatomical data and his own interpretation from anthropological training.

assessment for a preadolescent. The clothing found was that of a little girl, however.

Both the missing girls were white, and the presence of a Carabelli's cusp on one of the remaining teeth pointed to that population. Carabelli's cusp is a small dental feature found in about 50 percent of U.S. whites, 34 percent of blacks, and only 5 percent to 20 percent of Native Americans. The incisors were not shovel-shaped, a form found in over 80 percent of Native Americans. It was important to rule out Native Americans since Oklahoma has a high Native American population. Some remaining hair verified the assessment, as its color and shape were those common to white populations.

Age was determined through cranial sutures, epiphyseal union, and dental eruption and development (see Chapter 9). In addition to the four separate bones of the cranial vault, each bone itself grows in separate pieces. The occipital, at birth, is in four pieces, which fuse together at 4 or 5 years of age. The occipital found was completely fused with no trace of sutures.

The epiphyses at the proximal (closest to the body) femur and radius, and the distal (farthest from the body) humerus were all open. These close at 17, 14, and 14 years respectively. Taken with the evidence from the occipital, an age range of 4 to about 15 was determined. This was narrowed to 5 to 12 years by looking at further sites of bone union in the vertebral column.

Both first permanent molars were fully erupted. The central incisors were missing, but the size and form of the sockets indicated that they too had erupted. Taking into account the range of variation at which eruption occurs among individuals, these data provided an age range of about 5½ to 8 years. In addition, teeth, of course, develop below the gum line before they erupt, and X rays of the child's teeth further narrowed the age range to about 6 to 8 years. The evidence, then, favored the skeleton being that of the older missing girl. Finally, stature was estimated using formulas that compare the length of various long bones to total height. The skeleton was estimated to have belonged to someone about 50 inches tall. The older missing girl was about that height, while the younger was 8 inches shorter.

Snow concluded that the remains probably belonged to one of the two missing girls. There had been no other unsolved cases of missing girls of that age from the area in several years. The bones most likely were those of the 6-year-old. Sadly, the remains of the other girl have not been found, and no suspect has been identified. But Snow's forensic work helped strengthen the identification, which would have been little more than a good guess without the precise information he was able to extract by reading the bones.

LESSONS FROM THE PAST

Besides applying the skills of the biological anthropologist to legal matters, we may also apply the perspective of our discipline to areas of modern life. Our evolutionary perspective tells us that we are not a species that suddenly appeared a few million years ago nor are we, as modern humans, what evolution was somehow directed toward all along.

Rather, humans evolved from previous primate species. We are variations on the primate theme. We retain many of the major primate characteristics, and our unique features are still based on them. Moreover, in no way can we say that the modern manifestation of our species is the culmination or the best-adapted form of our evolutionary line. We have manipulated our environment, our very biology, and our behavior through culture, so our present environment may not be the one to which our species was biologically adapted. We may well learn a few valuable lessons by taking a closer look at what we were like in the past, before culture played so great a part in our lives.

For instance, anthropologists Marcia Thompson and David Harsha (1984) have looked at the daily routines of people in modern industrial societies and compared them with those of people in nonindustrial cultures and nonhumans living in the tropics. They conclude that, in the common structure of our work days, we are violating a pattern that evolved in our tropical ancestors and cousins that programs us for a two-peaked rhythm of daily activity, one peak in the late morning and another in the late afternoon, with a lull in between. That period of tiredness we often feel after lunch may have nothing to do with eating.

Tropical animals and people in many human societies take an afternoon break that originally may have been a response to the heat of the midafternoon sun but may now in humans be a real biological decrease in activity level. After all, they note, other bodily functions—more than 100 physiological and performance variables—fluctuate in predictable cycles during the twenty-four hours of our day. Thus, the afternoon nap is a natural phenomenon. (I knew it!)

Thompson and Harsha suggest that the best way we could respond to this, given that most of us can't nap, at least during weekdays, would be to move lunch back a few hours to correspond to the afternoon lull. As it is, we often take lunch during one of our peak activity periods. By taking into account a possible biological pattern, we might make ourselves more productive in our modern cultural environment.

Another anthropologist, James McKenna (Small 1992), has looked at sleep behavior of other primates and of people in other cultures and has noted that it is common for young babies to sleep with their parents. In the West, we have long been advised that babies should sleep by themselves, probably as a response to our emphasis on independence and the idea that the parents' lives, perhaps especially in bed, are separate from those of their children.

McKenna suggests that, in fact, infant nonhuman primates and human babies seem better off psychologically and physically if they sleep with their parents. In humans, this may even extend to help in learning to breathe properly. For humans, speech is so important that we have two kinds of breathing—automatic and controlled—and we need to learn to switch between kinds. In addition, remember that the vocal tract of infants is different from that of adult humans and is like that of chimpanzees in being higher in the throat at first. As the vocal tract begins to drop early in life, the baby goes through a great physical change.

These two facts—the development of the two kinds of breathing and the physical change in the vocal tract—may explain Sudden Infant Death Syndrome (SIDS), where babies inexplicably die in their sleep. It is thought that, perhaps because of miscues in regulating breathing, these babies stop breathing and fail to wake up so they can start again. Sleeping with a parent may help prevent this because such situations cause the baby to wake up periodically in response to the parent's movement and so the infant learns better how to jump between kinds of breathing. McKenna notes that SIDS is twice as common in the United States as in Japan, where infants normally sleep with parents. A more recent study (Mosko et al. 1997) has also suggested that close proximity to the mother while sleeping, especially in face-to-face orientation, may also provide the infant with increased levels of CO_2 from the mother's respiration, which might help stimulate its breathing.

We may also learn lessons about disease. The evolutionary perspective that sheds light on the nature of sickle cell anemia may also be applied to other diseases, especially those associated with particular populations. Biologist Jared Diamond (1991) offers an intriguing evolutionary explanation for the high frequency of Tay-Sachs disease among Eastern European (Ashkenazic) Jews and their descendants. Tay-Sachs is a lethal disease caused by a recessive gene. In homozygotes, it results in the body's inability to produce an enzyme that breaks down a particular fatty substance. This substance accumulates in nerve cells and literally destroys the victim's nervous system. Most sufferers die by age 4. The disease is incurable and cannot be prevented.

Tay-Sachs has a frequency of about 1 in 400,000 worldwide but is found in 1 of every 3600 Ashkenazim. Other Jewish populations have Tay-Sachs no more often than the general population. The usual explanation for this incredibly high frequency is the founder effect. The founders of the Ashkenazic populations happened to have a high frequency of the gene, which then persisted through genetic drift, aided by the fact that it was usually hidden from natural selection as a recessive. Some of the other ten diseases that are overrepresented among Ashkenazim have been explained in this way (Glausiusz 1995), as has the high frequency of Tay-Sachs in a Pennsylvania Dutch population (see Chapter 4).

But Diamond contends that the founders of the Ashkenazim were large populations, and that their communities in Eastern Europe were widespread. The founder effect has significant results only in small populations. In the numerous and widespread communities, drift would have increased the frequency of the gene in some but decreased it in others. In addition, since these communities were first founded almost a thousand years ago, one would expect natural selection to have had sufficient time to decrease the frequency of this lethal gene to that found in the general population.

Moreover, it seems as if there are several different mutations along the same segment of DNA that can cause Tay-Sachs, and that two of them are overrepresented among the Ashkenazim. It is unlikely that the same random evolutionary events could have happened twice. In addition, two of the other diseases that are more common in Eastern European Jews than in the general population also result from the excess accumulation of fatty substances.

Diamond suggests that, as with sickle cell, the heterozygous condition for Tay-Sachs must confer some selective advantage. He notes that Ashkenazic Jews were confined to towns for much of the last 2000 years. They were forbidden to own land and so lived as businessmen in confined, urban areas. (This is the origin of the term *ghetto*.) A common ailment in such towns was TB (tuberculosis). In the early twentieth century, for example, TB caused up to 20 percent of all deaths in Eastern Europe. One study, however, indicates that relatively few Jews died from TB (1 in 306 people for whom data were available, a far cry from 20 percent). Thus, a reasonable hypothesis is that heterozygotes for Tay-Sachs, who do not exhibit symptoms of the disease, nevertheless have slightly elevated levels of the fatty substance, and this—for reasons that are still unknown—may provide some immunity to TB.

Though the cause-and-effect relationship has not been established, this hypothesis provides a basis for further investigation and is an example of how our knowledge of evolutionary processes can provide a possible answer to a question involving modern human populations.

Finally, S. Boyd Eaton and Melvin Konner propose that the major chronic illnesses that we in the industrialized West suffer from are caused by a "mismatch between our genetic constitution" and factors in our modern lifestyles, including diet, exercise, and exposure to such things as alcohol and tobacco. Our genes, they suggest, "must now function in a foreign and, in many ways, hostile Atomic Age [environment]" (Eaton and Konner 1985:1).

FIGURE 15.3

The !Kung San (the ! represents a click sound) from the Kalahari Desert in Namibia and Botswana are, of course, fully modern humans. Yet their way of life, until recently that of hunters of wild game and gatherers of wild plants, can give us a window into the lives of our ancestors before the invention of farming and animal domestication. Here, members of a !Kung San family are on the move, carrying with them their children, tools, weapons, and other possessions. The lives of the !Kung San have been forever changed by political and military events in southern Africa. (See also Figure 12.6.)

They note that some studies indicate that our ancestors who lived before the advent of farming, about 12,000 years ago, were taller and more heavily muscled than we are. Their teeth also showed a much smaller percentage of dental caries (tooth decay). By looking at the lives of recent hunter-gatherer groups, we may, suggest the authors, have a "window" into the world of our Stone Age ancestors (Figure 15.3). (They are careful, of course, to caution that recent hunter-gatherer groups are fully modern humans with technologies, such as the bow and arrow, that were not available until about 15,000 years ago.) One thing we note right away is that such people have a lower incidence of coronary heart disease, emphysema, hypertension, and cancer of the breast, prostate, colon, and lung.

When the diets of fifty hunter-gatherer groups were analyzed, it was seen that, on average, they ate more red meat than we do now. This sounds bad at first, until we understand that wild game has much less saturated fat than do domestic animals, and most of that is "structural" fat (rather than "storage" fat), which is largely polyunsaturated—not the harmful kind, in other words. Thus, our ancestors ate about three times the protein we do, but only about half the fat.

Most of the plant foods eaten, because they were wild and unprocessed, had a higher nutritional value, fewer calories, more complex

Contemporary Reflections

What Can One Do with a Degree in Bioanthropology?

It's safe to say that most people who work as professional biological anthropologists (or, for that matter, any sort of professional anthropologist) have at least a master's degree and, more likely, a Ph.D. The majority of these do what I do—teach in a college or university while researching and writing. Although acquiring a Ph.D. requires, on average, four additional years of university classwork and a variable number of years after that to complete a doctoral dissertation (I took six years), it is a career I can highly recommend. Essentially, you get paid to learn about and think about the subject you're most interested in, and then to impart that knowledge to your students. There's a good deal of (often inconsequential) committee work and other related activities required, but, all in all, it's a good deal, and a very rewarding life.

Unfortunately, at the moment, there are more Ph.D.s and near Ph.D.s in anthropology than there are university faculty jobs. The job market, however, has improved and worsened several times in the twenty-five years I've worked at my university, and the situation could improve again. You shouldn't let current conditions dissuade you if a Ph.D. and a university position are your goal.

Some bioanthropology Ph.D.s work in other departments of universities. It is not uncommon to find them in medical, dental, and nursing programs, or in biology, genetics, psychology, public health, or physical therapy departments. Others work outside academia. I glanced through the list of current members of the American Association of Physical Anthropologists and found people who worked for museums, medical research and forensics institutes, the armed forces, and government agencies such as the Bureau of Land Management. As I mentioned, the Connecticut State Archaeologist is a former student of mine who has his Ph.D. in bioanthropology.

Most of you reading this book, however—if you are working toward a degree in anthropology—will get a B.A. It has been said that one bachelor's degree is as good as another in terms of finding jobs that require a college education. On a practical level, that may well be true. What a four-year degree means is that you have shown mastery of a certain core curriculum at a certain level with a focus on a particular discipline, and that you have the skills, dedication, and persistence to achieve that degree. In terms of specific skills needed for a certain job, the college degree essentially tells an employer that you will have the ability to learn and use those skills.

But *what* degree you get may have deeper meaning, and—although I'm clearly biased—I think a degree in biological anthropology is a good choice. The breadth of knowledge inherent in the field is wide. There is the focus on scientific methodology, but with the need—because it *is* anthropology—to understand other areas of knowledge and other cultures. The central theme of evolution necessarily involves a deep understanding of biology in general and of the biology of other species in particular. Genetics, anatomy, physiology, behavior, ecology, chemistry and physics (for dating techniques), geology, paleontology, and medical topics are all integral parts of the field. The number of careers to which such topics, such a breadth of knowledge, and such a perspective could be applied is huge—limited only by your imagination.

The only barrier might be the fact that many people have little understanding of what bioanthropology is, and so might not at first think your degree would be appropriate to certain jobs you may wish to apply for. I tell my students that, in such cases, they must be prepared to make their case, to explain to potential employers what bioanthropology is and why that background would be ideal for their job.

For some sound practical advice, read *Careers in Anthropology* by John T. Omohundro (1998). In the meantime, the answer to the question about what you can do with a degree in bioanthropology is: Just about anything you want.

carbohydrates (rather than simple ones that turn to fat), more fiber, and less salt (a contributor to hypertension). They drank mostly water and seldom were exposed to alcohol and tobacco.

Additionally, rather than concentrating on one sort of exercise, our ancestors were more like "decathlon athletes," responding to the harsh physical demands of their lives with a varied "exercise program" that changed daily and seasonally.

The lessons from all this are obvious and are, indeed, suggestions we hear all the time. We know we're supposed to eat low-fat foods, cut down on salt, get plenty of fiber, and exercise regularly. Evolution, though, provides an explanation and rationale for following those suggestions.

SUMMARY

Biological anthropology studies the human species, past and present, from the perspective of evolutionary processes, change, and adaptation. To understand how these affected our ancestors, we have developed skills that allow us to squeeze an amazing amount of information out of the meager skeletal remains that those ancestors left us. These skills are now being increasingly recognized and used by law enforcement agencies in the identification and analysis of skeletal remains of missing persons and accident and murder victims. Forensic anthropology is a fast-growing specialty within our field.

Our evolutionary perspective can also be useful in more abstract ways. By understanding the nature of our adaptations as a species, we may evaluate some of our behaviors and practices in light of the recent cultural environment we have made for ourselves. We find that some of our cultural adaptations may be out of step with our biological ones. Using the evolutionary viewpoint to look at daily biological rhythms, sleep patterns, the nature of our breathing, diseases that affect us, our diet, and our exercise habits—among other aspects of our lives—may enable us to change how we do things so as to be more in line with how our species is actually adapted and, in so doing, improve our lives.

In the end, however, it must be noted that, to be useful and important, information need not have a practical, concrete application. There is nothing wrong with the idea of knowledge for its own sake, and, certainly, learning about our species—where we came from, what processes brought about our evolution, who we are and where we fit in the natural world—should be important to us as individuals and as members of our own society and the society of all the world's peoples.

SUGGESTED READINGS

The Ice Man story is summarized by Konrad Spindler in *The Man in the Ice*. Paul Bahn's review of that book, which adds some additional information, is in the May/June 1995 issue of *Archaeology* magazine. The June 1993 issue of *National Geographic* includes an article, "The Ice Man," by David Roberts that covers the Ice Man as well as some of the related archaeology of his time and place. For a more technical article, see "The Stone Age Iceman from the Alps" by Torstein Sjøvold in *Evolutionary Anthropology*.

Two recent situations involving, like the Ice Man, mummified bodies, have been reported from western China and from Peru. See "The Silk Road's Lost World" by Thomas B. Allen in the March 1996 *National Geographic* and "Peru's Ice Maidens" by Johan Reinhard in the June 1996 issue of that magazine.

More on the reconstruction of ancient faces can be found in John Prag and Richard Neave's *Making Faces*.

On forensic anthropology, see *Dead Men Do Tell Tales* by William R. Maples and Michael Browning and *Bones: A Forensic Detective's Casebook* by Douglas Ubelaker and Henry Scammell.

The Clyde Snow case covered in this chapter is recounted in detail in "The Oklahoma City Child Disappearances" by Snow and James Luke, in Podolefsky and Brown, *Applying Anthropology*. A profile of Snow is in the December 1988 issue of *Discover* in a piece by Patrick Huyghe called "No Bone Unturned."

Glossary of Human and Nonhuman Primates

Adapidae (ah-da'-pih-day) Group of early primates from the then-connected landmass of North America and Europe, dating to more than 50 mya and thought to be ancestral to prosimians such as lemurs and lorises.

Aegyptopithecus (ee-gyp'-toe-pith'-ah-cuss) Extinct monkey genus with several apelike traits. Discovered in Egypt and dating to more than 25 mya, it may represent a form of primate ancestral to Old World monkeys and apes.

Ankarapithecus (ahn-ka-ra-pith'-ah-cuss) Fossil ape genus from Turkey dated at 9.8 mya, which shows similarities to *Sivapithecus*.

Anthropoidea (an-throw-poi'-dee-ah) According to the traditional taxonomic system, one of the two suborders of the order Primates (the other is **Prosimii**). Means "humanlike" and includes monkeys, apes, and humans.

Ardipithecus ramidus (ar-di-pith'-ah-cuss rah'-midus) Recently identified hominid genus from Ethiopia and dated at about 4.4 mya. It is based on skeletal fragments and teeth. Not yet fully documented or accepted, it is thought by its discoverers to represent the earliest species in the hominid line. Thus, the species name, which means "root" in the local language.

Australopithecus afarensis (os-trail-oh-pith'-ah-cuss ah-far-en'-sis) Fossil species from East Africa, the oldest well-established species in the hominid line. Dated from 4 to 3 mya, *afarensis* had a small, chimp-sized brain but walked fully upright.

Australopithecus africanus (os-trail-oh-pith'-ah-cuss ah-frih-cane'-us) A fossil hominid species

from South Africa dated from about 3 to 2.3 mya. It is similar to *A. afarensis* and may well be a direct evolutionary descendant of the earlier species. It retains the chimp-sized brain and is fully bipedal.

Catarrhini (cat-ah-rhine'-eye) One of two infraorders of suborder **Anthropoidea** (the other is infraorder **Platyrrhini,** the New World monkeys). Catarrhini is the infraorder of the Old World monkeys, apes, and hominids. Along with the geographical distinction, catarrhines can be distinguished from platyrrhines by their narrow nose shape, fewer premolar teeth, and lack of a prehensile tail.

Cercopithecoidea (sir-co-pith-ah-coy'-dee-ah) The superfamily of all monkeys of Europe, Africa, and Asia.

Eosimiidae (ee-oh-sim-ee'-ih-day) A group of early primates from Asia, dated at around 45 mya, that may represent direct ancestors of monkeys, apes, and hominids.

Gigantopithecus (ji-gan-toe-pith'-ah-cuss) Genus of fossil apes, from 12 to perhaps 1 mya in China, India, and Vietnam. They may have reached a height of 12 feet when standing erect and may have weighed 1200 pounds, making them the largest primate known.

Gorilla gorilla (go-rill'-a go-rill'-a) The gorilla (well, duh), one of the three great ape species from Africa and the largest living primate.

Haplorhini (hap-low-rhine'-eye) According to the cladistic taxonomic system, one of two suborders of the order **Primates** (the other is **Strepsirhini**).

Haplorhini are primates lacking a moist nose and other primitive features. Includes the tarsier and all primates traditionally included in suborder **Anthropoidea.**

Hominidae (ho-mih′-nih-day) The family of modern and extinct human species, defined as the primates that are habitually bipedal. Members of this group are called hominids.

Hominoidea (ho-min-oy′-dee-ah) The superfamily that includes the large, tailless primates: apes and hominids, living and extinct.

Homo antecessor (ho′-mow an-tee-sess′-or) A newly proposed species from Spain and dated at 780,000 years or more. The fossils show a mix of primitive and modern human features and are interpreted by their discoverers as possibly ancestral to *Homo heidelbergensis* and *H. neanderthalensis.* This species is not widely recognized at present.

Homo erectus (ho′-mow ee-wreck′-tuss) Fossil hominid species dating from at least 1.8 mya to 100,000, or perhaps fewer, years ago. First appearing in Africa, *H. erectus* was the first hominid species to expand beyond that continent. Fossils are found throughout Africa and Asia, and there is possible evidence from Europe. Members of this species had a brain size average about two-thirds that of modern humans, made advances in stone tool technology, and late in their existence were able to control fire.

Homo ergaster (ho′-mow er-gas′-ter) The earliest *H. erectus* fossils from Kenya, said by some researchers to be sufficiently different that they represent a separate species that was ancestral to both *H. erectus* and, later, *Homo sapiens.*

Homo habilis (ho′-mow ha′-bill-us) Fossil hominid species dating from about 2.2 to 1.5 mya, and found in East Africa. Fully bipedal, and with an average brain size of 680 ml, *H. habilis* was the first confirmed hominid stone toolmaker. Because this was the first hominid with a brain larger than that of a chimpanzee, and because of the association with stone tools, this is thought to be the earliest member of our genus, *Homo.*

Homo heidelbergensis (how′-mow high-del-berg-en′-sis) Proposed species from Africa, Asia, and Europe dated from between 475,000 and 200,000 years ago. They had a modern human brain size but retained primitive features such as brow ridges, prognathism, and postorbital constriction.

Homo neanderthalensis (ho′-mow knee-an-dir-tall-en′-sis) Proposed species from Europe and Southwest Asia dated from between 225,000 and 36,000 years ago. They have more pronounced versions of some of the cranial features of *Homo heidelbergensis,* such as brow ridges and prognathism. The postcranial skeletons were robust and heavy, with short arms and legs, possibly adaptations to cold climates.

Homo rudolfensis (ho′-mow rue-dolf-en′-sis) Thought by some authorities to be a separate species made up of the East Turkana, Kenya, specimens traditionally placed in *Homo habilis.*

Homo sapiens (ho′-mow say′-pee-ens) Taxonomic name for modern humans. There is debate as to whether or not this name covers certain other species, including *Homo erectus, ergaster, antecessor, heidelbergensis,* and *neanderthalensis.*

Hylobatidae (high-low-bat′-ah-day) Family that includes the gibbons and siamangs, the arboreal, so-called lesser apes of Southeast Asia. They are highly efficient brachiators.

Kenyapithecus (ken-ya-pith′-ah-cuss) Fossil genus from East Africa dated at 14 million years ago. A possible candidate for the first hominoid.

Morotopithecus (more-row-tow-pith′-ah-cuss) Fossil genus from Uganda dated at 20 million years ago. A possible candidate for the first hominoid, it may have been capable of occasional upright walking.

Omomyidae (oh-mow-me′-ah-day) A group of early primates that lived in the then-connected landmass of North America and Europe. Dating to more than 50 mya, they are thought to be ancestral to tarsiers and may have been ancestral to **Anthropoidea** as well.

Ouranopithecus (oo-ran′-oh-pith′-ah-cuss) An ape from Greece dated at 9 or 10 mya. Based on some hominidlike features, it is thought by some to be a member of the ape line that led to the hominids.

Pan paniscus (pan pan-iss′-cus) The bonobo, sometimes called the pygmy chimpanzee, one of the three great apes species from Africa.

Pan troglodytes (pan trog-low-dye'-tees)   The chimpanzee, one of the three great ape species from Africa.

Papio (pah'-pee-oh)   A genus within superfamily **Cercopithecoidea** (the Old World monkeys) comprised of the several species of baboons, large monkeys living in social groups on the African savannas.

Paranthropus aethiopicus (par-an'-throw-pus ee-thee-o'-pih-cus)   Species from East Africa dating from 2.8 to 2.2 mya. They are the first members of the so-called robust early hominids, having large, rugged features associated with chewing, although their other features, including brain size, are very similar to those of members of genus *Australopithecus*. Many authorities still include them in that genus. It is thought they were adapted to tough, gritty, hard vegetable foods. The most famous, and first, specimen of this species was the "Black Skull."

Paranthropus boisei (par-an'-throw-pus boys'-ee-eye)   The East African robust hominid from 2.2 to 1 mya. It had large features associated with chewing, although less pronounced than in *P. aethiopicus*. The first specimen was "Zinjanthropus." Sometimes included in genus *Australopithecus*.

Paranthropus robustus (par-an'-throw-pus row-bus'-tus)   The Southern African robust hominid, dated from 2.2 to 1.5 mya. It is marked by robust chewing features, although they are less robust than in either *P. aethiopicus* or *P. boisei*. The postcranial skeleton and the brain size remain similar to those of *Australopithecus*. It is sometimes included in that genus.

Platyrrhini (plat-ee-rhine'-eye)   One of two infraorders of the suborder **Anthropoidea** (the other is infraorder **Catarrhini,** the Old World monkeys, apes, and hominids). Platyrrhines comprise the New World monkeys. Members of this group can be told apart from the catarrhines by their broad nose shape, greater number of premolar teeth, and the fact that several species have prehensile tails.

Pongidae (pon'-jih-day)   Family of the so-called great apes, the orangutans of Southeast Asia and the gorillas, chimpanzees, and bonobos of Africa.

Pongo pygmaeus (pon-go pig-may'-us)   The orangutan, the only great ape from Southeast Asia.

Primates (pry-mate'-ees)   Order within class Mammalia. Large-brained, arboreal mammals with stereoscopic color vision and grasping hands (and sometimes feet). Includes prosimians, monkeys, apes, and hominids.

Prosimii (pro-sim'-ee-eye)   According to the traditional taxonomic system, one of two suborders of the order **Primates** (the other suborder is **Anthropoidea**). Prosimians are the more primitive of the two suborders in that they retain features of some of the oldest primate fossils. Many lack color vision, are nocturnal, and have limited opposability of the thumb.

Sivapithecus (she'-vah-pith'-ah-cuss)   Genus of fossil ape from India and Pakistan dated from 15 to 12 mya. Thought to be ancestral to the orangutan.

Strepsirhini (strep-sir-rhine'-eye)   According to the cladistic taxonomic system, one of two suborders of the order **Primates** (the other is **Haplorhini**). Primates with a moist nose and other primitive features. Includes all primates traditionally in suborder **Prosimii** except the tarsier.

Glossary of Terms

absolute dating technique Dating method that gives a specific age, year, or range of years for an object or site. See **relative dating technique.**

Acheulian A toolmaking tradition associated with *Homo erectus/ergaster* in Africa and Europe. Includes hand axes, cleavers, and flake tools.

adapted When an organism has physical traits and behaviors that allow it to survive in a particular environment.

adaptive radiation The evolution and spreading out of related species into new **niches.**

allele frequency The percentage of times a particular **allele** appears in a population. The same as **gene frequency,** but the preferred term.

alleles Variants of a genetic **locus.** Most loci possess more than one possible allele, the different alleles conveying different instructions for the development of a certain **phenotype** (for example, different blood types).

altruistic Behavior that benefits others without regard to one's own needs or safety.

amino acids The chief components of **proteins.** Each "word" in the genetic code stands for a specific amino acid.

analogies Traits shared by two or more species that are similar in function but unrelated evolutionarily, for example, the wings of a bird and of an insect. See **homology.**

anthropology The **holistic** study of the human species. Anthropology includes the study of human biology, human physical **evolution,** human cultural evolution, and human adaptation.

antibodies **Proteins** in the immune system that react to foreign **antigens.**

antigens The **proteins** used by the body's immune system that distinguish between "self" and "non-self." The antigens of the ABO blood group system are examples.

applied anthropology **Anthropology** used to address current practical problems and concerns.

arboreal Organisms that are **adapted** to life in the trees.

archaeology Subfield of **anthropology** that studies the human cultural past and the reconstruction of past cultural systems.

argon/argon dating A **radiometric** dating technique that uses the decay of radioactive argon into stable argon gas. Can be used to date volcanic rock with greater accuracy and smaller samples than **potassium/argon** dating.

asexually Reproducing without sex, by fissioning or budding.

belief systems Ideas that are taken on faith and cannot be scientifically tested. Examples are religions, philosophies, and ethical and moral beliefs. See **scientific method.**

bifacial A stone tool that has been worked on both sides.

bioanthropology Another name for **biological anthropology.**

biological anthropology Subfield of **anthropology** that studies humans as a biological species.

bipedal Walking on two legs.

bottleneck A severe reduction in the size of a population such that only certain genes survive and come to characterize the descendant population.

brachiation Locomotion using arm-over-arm swinging.

breeding populations Populations within a **species** that are genetically isolated to some degree from other populations.

brow ridges Heavy, bony ridges over the eyes.

carbon dating A **radiometric** dating technique using the decay rate of a radioactive form of carbon found in organic remains.

carnivore An organism adapted to a diet of mostly meat. See **omnivore.**

catastrophists Those who believe the history of the earth is explained by a series of global catastrophes, either natural or divine in origin. See **uniformitarianism.**

chromosomal mutations Mutations of a whole **chromosome** or a large portion of a chromosome. See **point mutations.**

chromosomes Strands of **DNA** in the nucleus of a cell.

cladistics A classification system based on order of evolutionary branching, rather than on present similarities and differences. See **taxonomy.**

cline A geographic continuum in the variation of a particular trait.

codominant When both **alleles** of a pair are expressed in the **phenotype.**

codons The sections of **DNA** that code for specific **amino acids.**

comparative anatomy Comparing the anatomical features of various **species.** Used to reconstruct a fossil species from fragmentary remains.

competitive exclusion When one **species** outcompetes others for the resources of a particular area.

core tools Tools made by taking flakes off a stone nucleus. See **flake tools.**

crossing over When sections of **chromosomes** switch between chromosome pairs during **meiosis.** See **recombination.**

cultural anthropology Subfield of **anthropology** that focuses on human cultural behavior and cultural systems and the variation in cultural expression among human groups.

culture Ideas and behaviors that are learned and transmitted. Also, the system made up of the sum total of these ideas and behaviors that is unique to a particular society of people. Nongenetic means of adaptation.

Darwinian gradualism The view, held by Darwin, that **evolution** is slow and steady with cumulative change. See **punctuated equilibrium.**

deduction Suggesting specific data that will be found if a **hypothesis** is true, a step in the **scientific method** involving the testing of hypotheses. See **induction.**

demes Populations within a **species** that are genetically isolated to some degree from other populations. Same as **breeding population,** but sometimes implies physical distinctions.

demography The study of the size and makeup of populations.

deoxyribonucleic acid (DNA) The molecule that carries the genetic code.

dependency The period after birth during which offspring require the care of adults to survive.

dermatoglyphics The study of the parallel ridges and furrows on the fingertips, palms, toes, and soles of the feet, commonly referred to as fingerprints, palm prints, and so on.

distance curve A graph that compares some variable at different points in time, for example, height and age. See **velocity curve.**

diurnal Active during the day. See **nocturnal.**

DNA See deoxyribonucleic acid.

dominance hierarchy A social pattern among animal **species** where there are recognized individual differences in power, influence, and access to resources and mating. Found in many **primate** species.

dominant In a **heterozygous** pair of **alleles,** the one that is expressed in the **phenotype.** See **recessive.**

electron spin resonance dating (ESR) An **absolute dating technique** that measures the number of electrons excited to higher energy levels by natural radiation and trapped there. Can be used to date tooth enamel, shells, corals, mineral cave deposits, and volcanic rock, but does not work well on bone.

endocasts Natural or human-made casts of the inside of a skull. The cast reflects the surface of the brain and allows us to study the brains even of extinct species.

endogamy   Restricting marriage to members of the same culturally defined group.

environmental   Any nongenetic influence on the phenotype. Also refers to the conditions under which an organism exists, such as climate, altitude, other species, food sources, and so on.

enzymes   **Proteins** that control chemical processes.

epidemiological   Pertaining to the study of disease outbreaks and epidemics.

estrus   The period of fertility. The signals indicating this condition.

ethology   The study of the natural behavior of animals under natural conditions.

evolution   Systematic change through time, usually with reference to biological **species,** but may also refer to changes within cultural systems.

fission   A process of **evolution** that involves the splitting up of a population to form new populations.

fitness   The relative adaptiveness of an individual organism, measured ultimately by reproductive success.

flake tools   Tools made from the flakes removed from a stone core. See **core tools.**

folk taxonomies   Cultural categories for important items and ideas. **Gender** and **race** are examples of folk taxonomies.

foramen magnum   The hole in the base of the skull through which the spinal cord emerges and around the outside of which the top vertebra articulates.

forensic anthropologist   One who applies anthropology to legal matters. Usually used with reference to the identification of skeletal remains and the assessment of time and cause of death.

fossils   Remains of life forms of the past.

founder effect   A process of **evolution.** Genetic differences between populations produced by the fact that genetically different individuals established (founded) those populations.

gametes   The cells of reproduction, commonly sperm and egg, which contain only half the **chromosomes** of a normal cell.

gamete sampling   A process of **evolution.** The genetic change caused when genes are passed to new generations in frequencies unrepresentative of those of the parental generation. An example of **sampling error.**

gender   The cultural categories and characteristics of men and women. The translation of **sex** into a **folk taxonomy.**

gene flow   A process of **evolution** that involves the exchange of genes among populations through interbreeding.

gene frequency   The percentage of times a particular **allele** appears in a population. See **allele frequency.**

gene pool   All the **alleles** in a population.

generalized   **Species** that are adapted to a wide range of environmental **niches.** Such species tend to be genetically and physically variable. See **specialized.**

genes   Those portions of the **DNA** molecule that code for specific traits. Roughly a synonym for **locus.**

Genetic Replacement   The hypothesis that, although *Homo sapiens* may be an old species, modern human traits evolved recently in one area and spread from there, replacing archaic features. See **Multiregional Evolution** and **Recent African Origin.**

genome   The total genetic endowment of a **species.**

genotypes   The **alleles** possessed by an organism. See **phenotypes.**

glaciers   Massive sheets of ice that expand and move. Found on the polar ice caps and in mountains.

grooming   Cleaning the fur of another animal, which promotes social cohesion. Common among **primate** groups.

haft   To attach a handle or shaft, such as to a spear point.

half-life   The time needed for one-half of a given amount of a radioactive substance to decay.

hand axe   A **bifacial,** all-purpose stone tool, shaped somewhat like an axe head. First invented by *Homo erectus* and usually associated with that **species.**

Hardy-Weinberg equilibrium   The formula that shows **genotype** frequencies in a population under hypothetical conditions of no evolutionary change.

heritability   The amount of variation of a particular trait within a population that is caused by genetic, as opposed to **environmental,** differences.

heterozygous   Having two different **alleles** in a gene pair. See **homozygous.**

holistic   Assuming an interrelationship among the parts of a subject. **Anthropology** is a holistic discipline.

hominids   Modern human beings and our ancestors, defined as the **primates** who stand erect. Technically, the members of family Hominidae.

homologies   Traits shared by two or more species through inheritance from a common ancestor. An example would be the arms of a human and the wings of a bat. We assume that many similar behaviors among humans and chimpanzees are also homologies. See **analogies.**

homozygous   Having two of the same allele in a gene pair. See **heterozygous.**

human ecology   Specialty of **anthropology** that studies the relationships between humans and their environments.

hunter-gatherers   Societies that rely upon naturally occurring sources of food. They have no domestic plants or animals except, perhaps, dogs.

hypotheses   Educated guesses to explain natural phenomena. In the **scientific method,** hypotheses must be testable. See **theory.**

inclusive fitness   The idea that fitness is measured by the success of one's genes, whether possessed by the individual or by that individual's relatives.

independent assortment   When genetic **loci** on different **chromosomes** segregate to **gametes** independently of one another.

induction   Developing a general explanation from specific observations. The step in the **scientific method** that generates **hypotheses.** See **deduction.**

inheritance of acquired characteristics   The incorrect idea, associated with Lamarck, that adaptive traits acquired during an organism's lifetime can be passed on to its offspring.

inorganic   A molecule not containing carbon. See **organic.**

intelligence   The relative ability of the brain to acquire, store, retrieve, and process information.

Levallois   Tool technology involving striking uniform flakes from a prepared core. See **core tools** and **flake tools.**

life history   The study that examines the timing of life cycle events such as fertility, growth, and death.

linkage   When genetic **loci** occur on the same chromosome and are inherited together.

locus (plural **loci**)   The location on a **chromosome** of the genetic code for a specific trait. This term has become preferable to **gene.**

luminescence dating   An **absolute dating technique** that measures trapped electrons by releasing their energy in the form of light. Can be used to date fired clay, pottery, brick, and burned stones. It may have some application to soil dating.

macromutations   **Mutations** with extensive and important physical results. The mutations for sickle cell anemia and Down syndrome are examples.

meiosis   The process of cell division in which **gametes** are produced, each gamete having one-half the normal complement of **chromosomes** and, therefore, only one **allele** of each original pair. See **mitosis.**

melanin   The pigment largely responsible for human skin color.

melanocytes   Specialized skin cells that produce the pigment **melanin.**

menarche   A woman's first menstrual period.

Mendelian genetics   The basic laws of inheritance, discovered by Gregor Mendel in the nineteenth century.

menopause   The end of a woman's reproductive cycle.

messenger ribonucleic acid (mRNA)   The molecule that carries the genetic code out of the nucleus for translation into **proteins.** See **transfer RNA.**

mitochondrial DNA (mtDNA)   The genetic material found in the cells' mitochondria, rather than in the cell nucleus. The mtDNA does not play a role in inheritance and thus may give a more accurate measure of the genetic differences among populations.

mitosis   The process of cell division that results in two exact copies of the original cell. See **meiosis.**

monogenic   A trait coded for by a single **locus.** The ABO blood group system is a monogenic trait.

Mousterian   The culture associated with the European Neandertals.

Multiregional Evolution   The hypothesis that *Homo sapiens* is about 2 million years old and that modern human traits evolved in geographically diverse locations and then spread through the species. See **Genetic Replacement** and **Recent African Origin.**

mutation Any mistake in an organism's genetic code.

natural selection Evolutionary change based on the differential reproductive success of individuals within a **species.**

niche The environment of an organism and its adaptive response to that environment.

nocturnal Active at night. See **diurnal.**

notochord A stiff cartilaginous rod that supports the body and protects the dorsal nerve. The evolutionary precursor of the vertebral column.

nucleotide The basic building blocks of **DNA** and **RNA,** made up of a sugar, a phosphate, and one of four bases.

omnivore An organism with a mixed diet of animal and vegetable foods. See **carnivore.**

opposability The ability to touch (oppose) the thumb to the tips of the other fingers.

organic Molecules that are part of living organisms. They are based on the chemistry of carbon and contain mostly hydrogen, oxygen, carbon, and nitrogen. Even carbon-based molecules that are not found in living things are sometimes referred to as organic. See **inorganic.**

osteology The study of skeletal anatomy and function.

Out-of-Africa Another name for the **Recent African Origin** model.

paleoanthropology Specialty that studies the human **fossil** record.

Pangea The supercontinent that included parts of all present-day landmasses. It formed around 280 mya and began breaking up around 200 mya.

parsimony Use of the simplest explanation in formulating a scientific **hypothesis.**

particulate The idea that biological traits are controlled by individual factors rather than by a single all-encompassing hereditary agent.

petrified A **fossil** that has turned to stone. As the **organic** material decays it is slowly replaced by minerals, leaving a cast in stone of the organism or some of its parts.

phenotype The chemical or physical results of the genetic code. See **genotypes.**

photosynthesis The process by which plants manufacture their own nutrients from carbon dioxide and water, using chlorophyll as a catalyst and sunlight as an energy source.

physical anthropology The traditional name for **biological anthropology.**

plate tectonics The movement of the plates of the earth's crust caused by their interaction with the molten rock of the earth's interior. The cause of continental drift.

Pleistocene The geological time period, from 1.6 million to 10,000 years ago, characterized by a series of glacial advances and retreats. See **glaciers.**

point mutations **Mutations** of single **codons.** The mutation that causes sickle cell anemia is an example. See **chromosomal mutations.**

polygenic A trait coded for by more than one **locus.** Skin color is a polygenic trait.

polymorphisms Variations in phenotypic traits that are the results of genetic variation. Human skin color is a polymorphic trait; human clothing styles are not polymorphic because they are not genetic.

polytypic A species with physically distinguishable regional populations.

postorbital constriction A narrowing of the skull behind the eyes, as viewed from above.

potassium/argon (K/Ar) dating A **radiometric** dating technique using the rate at which radioactive potassium, found in volcanic rock, decays into stable argon gas. See **argon/argon dating.**

prehensile Having the ability to grasp.

primates Large-brained, tree-dwelling mammals with three-dimensional color vision and grasping hands. Humans are primates.

primatology Specialty of **anthropology** that studies nonhuman **primates.**

prognathism The jutting forward of the lower face and jaw area.

progressive In **evolution,** the now discounted idea that all change is toward increasing complexity.

prosimian A member of the group of **primates** with the most primitive features, that is, that most closely resemble the earliest primates.

proteins Molecules that make cells and carry out cellular functions. Proteins are made of **amino acids.**

protein synthesis The process by which the genetic code puts together **proteins** in the cell.

provenience The precise location of **fossils** or archaeological artifacts.

pseudoscience Scientifically testable ideas that are taken on faith, even if tested and shown to be false. **Scientific creationism** is a pseudoscience.

punctuated equilibrium The view that **species** tend to remain stable and that evolutionary changes occur fairly suddenly. See **Darwinian gradualism.**

quadrupedal Walking on all fours.

races In biology, the same as **subspecies.** In culture, cultural categories to classify and account for human diversity. See **folk taxonomy.**

racism Judging an individual based solely on his or her racial affiliation.

radiometric Referring to the decay rate of a radioactive substance. See **argon/argon dating; carbon dating;** and **potassium/argon dating.**

Recent African Origin The hypothesis that *Homo sapiens* evolved as a separate species recently in Africa and then spread to replace more archaic populations. See **Multiregional Evolution** and **Genetic Replacement.**

recessive The **allele** of a **heterozygous** pair that is not expressed. For a recessive allele to be expressed it must be **homozygous.** See **dominant.**

recombination Genetic change that results from **crossing over.**

reification Translating a complex set of phenomena into a single entity such as a number. IQ test scores are an example.

relative dating technique Dating method that indicates the age of one item in comparison to another. **Stratigraphy** provides relative dates by indicating that one layer is older or younger than another. See **absolute dating technique.**

reproductive isolating mechanism Any difference that prevents the production of fertile offspring between members of two populations. Necessary for the production of separate **species.**

reproductive strategies Behaviors that evolve to maximize an individual's reproductive success.

RNA See **messenger RNA** and **transfer RNA.**

sagittal keel A sloping of the sides of the skull toward the top, as viewed from the front.

sampling error When a sample chosen for study does not accurately represent the population from which the sample was taken.

savanna The open grasslands of the tropics. The savannas of Africa are, according to latest evidence, where **hominids** first evolved.

science The method of inquiry that requires the generation, testing, and acceptance or rejection of **hypotheses.**

scientific creationism The belief in a literal biblical interpretation regarding the creation of the universe, with the connected belief that this view is supported by scientific evidence. An example of a **pseudoscience.**

scientific method The process of conducting scientific inquiry. See **science.**

segregation In genetics, the breaking up of **allele** pairs in the production of **gametes.**

semispecies Populations of a **species** that are completely isolated from one another but have not yet become truly different species.

sex The biological categories and characteristics of males and females. See **gender.**

sexual dimorphism Physical differences between the sexes of a species not related to reproductive features. See **sex.**

sexually Reproducing by combining genetic material from two individuals. See **asexually.**

sites Places that contain evidence of human presence.

sociobiology The scientific study that examines evolutionary explanations for social behaviors within species.

specialized Species adapted to a narrow range of environmental **niches.** See **generalized.**

speciation The evolution of new **species.**

species A group of organisms that can produce fertile offspring among themselves but not with members of other groups. A closed genetic population, usually physically distinguishable from other populations.

stereoscopic vision Three-dimensional vision; depth perception.

strata (singular **stratum**) Layers; here, the layers of rock and soil under the surface of the earth.

stratigraphy The study of the earth's **strata.**

subspecies Physically distinguishable populations within a **species.** See **races.**

symbiotic An adaptive relationship between two

different species, often, but not necessarily, of mutual benefit.

symbolic   A communication system that uses arbitrary but agreed-upon sounds and signs for meaning.

systematists   Another name for **taxonomists.**

taphonomy   The study of how organisms become part of the paleontological record—how **fossils** form and what processes affect them through time.

taxon   Any category within a taxonomic classification. See **taxonomy.**

taxonomists   Those who classify and name living organisms.

taxonomy   A classification based on similarities and differences. In biology, the science of categorizing organisms and of naming them so as to reflect their relationships. See **cladistics.**

theory   A **hypothesis** that has been well supported by evidence and testing. In **science,** *theory* is a positive term.

torus   A bony ridge at the back of the skull, where the neck muscles attach.

transfer ribonucleic acid (tRNA)   RNA that lines up amino acids along mRNA to make proteins. See **messenger RNA.**

trephination   Cutting a hole in the skull, presumably to treat some illness, a practice within some societies with prescientific knowledge.

tundra   A treeless area with low-growing vegetation and permanently frozen ground. Located in the Arctic today, tundra conditions were found during the **Pleistocene** in the vicinity of **glaciers** far to the south.

uniformitarianism   The idea that present-day geological and biological processes can also explain the past history of the earth and its life. See **catastrophism.**

velocity curve   A graph that compares rate of change in some variable at different points in time, for example, rate of growth at different ages. See **distance curve.**

vertebrates   Organisms with backbones.

zygote   The fertilized egg before cell division begins.

Bibliography

Aiello, L., and C. Dean. 1990. *An Introduction to Human Evolutionary Anatomy.* London: Academic Press.

Allen, T. B. 1996. The Silk Road's lost world. *National Geographic* 189 (3): 44–51.

Appleman, P. 1979. *Darwin: A Norton Critical Edition.* 2nd ed. New York: Norton.

Armelagos, G. 1998. The viral superhighway. *The Sciences* 38 (1): 24–29.

Armelagos, G., K. C. Barnes, and J. Lin. 1996. Disease in human evolution: The re-emergence of infectious disease in the third epidemiological transition. *AnthroNotes* 18 (3): 1–7.

Bahn, P. G. 1995. Last days of the iceman. *Archaeology* (May/June): 66–70.

Barfield, A. 1976. Biological influences on sex differences in behavior. In *Sex Differences,* ed. M. S. Teitelbaum. Garden City, N.Y.: Anchor Press/Doubleday.

Bass, W. 1971. *Human Osteology: A Laboratory and Field Manual of the Human Skeleton.* Columbia: Missouri Archaeological Society.

Bermúdez de Castro, J. M., J. L. Arsuaga, E. Carbonell, A. Rosas, I. Martinez, and M. Mosquera. 1997. A hominid from the Lower Pleistocene of Atapuerca, Spain: Possible ancestor to Neandertals and modern humans. *Science* (May 30): 1392–95.

Binford, L. 1985. Ancestral life ways: The faunal record. *Anthroquest* 32 (1): 15–20.

Binford, L. R. 1987. *Bones: Ancient Men and Modern Myths.* Orlando, Fl.: Academic Press.

Binford, L., and K. Chuan. 1985. Taphonomy at a distance: Zhoukoudian, "The cave home of Beijing Man." *Current Anthropology* 26: 413–43.

Binford, L., and N. M. Stone. 1986. Zhoukoudian: A closer look. *Current Anthropology* 27: 435–76.

Boesch, C., and H. Boesch-Achermann. 1991. Dim forest, bright chimps. *Natural History* (September): 50–57.

Bordes, F. 1972. *A Tale of Two Caves.* New York: Harper and Row.

Bower, B. 1997a. Ancient roads to Europe. *Science News* (January 4): 12–13.

Bower, B. 1997b. Ancient ape shuffles to prominence. *Science News* (October 18): 244.

Bowlby, J. 1990. *Charles Darwin: A New Life.* New York: Norton.

Boyd, R., and J. B. Silk. 1997. *How Humans Evolved.* New York: Norton.

Bramblett, C. A. 1994. *Patterns of Primate Behavior,* 2nd ed. Prospect Heights, Ill.: Waveland Press.

Bräuer, G., and C. Stringer. 1997. Models, polarization, and perspectives on modern human origins. In *Conceptual Issues in Modern Human Origins Research,* eds. G. A. Clark and C. M. Willermet. New York: Aldine de Gruyter.

Bräuer, G., Y. Yokoyama, C. Falguères, and E. Mbua. 1997. Modern human origins backdated. *Nature* (March 27): 337.

Cann, R. L., M. Stoneking, and A. C. Wilson. 1987. Mitochondrial DNA and human evolution. *Nature* 325: 31–36.

Cartmill, M. 1992. New views on primate origins. *Evolutionary Anthropology* 1 (3): 105–11.

Cartmill, M. 1997. The third man. *Discover* (September): 56–62.

Cavalieri, P., and P. Singer. 1993. *The Great Ape Project: Equality Beyond Humanity.* New York: St. Martin's.

Cavalli-Sforza, L. L. 1991. Genes, peoples, and languages. *Scientific American* 265: 104–10.

Cavalli-Sforza, L. L., and F. Cavalli-Sforza. 1995. *The Great Human Diasporas: The History of Diversity and Evolution.* Reading, Mass.: Addison-Wesley.

Cavalli-Sforza, L. L., P. Menozzi, and A. Piazza. 1994.

The History and Geography of Human Genes. Princeton, N.J.: Princeton University Press.

Ciochon, R., J. Olsen, and J. James. 1990. *Other Origins: The Search for the Giant Ape in Human Prehistory.* New York: Bantam Books.

Clark, G. A., and C. M. Willermet, eds. 1997. *Conceptual Issues in Modern Human Origins Research.* New York: Aldine de Gruyter.

Cohen, J. E. 1996. Ten myths of population. *Discover* (April): 42–47.

Conroy, G. C. 1997. *Reconstructing Human Origins: A Modern Synthesis.* New York: Norton.

Coon, C. 1962. *The Origin of Races.* New York: Knopf.

Coppens, Y. 1994. East side story: The origin of humankind. *Scientific American* 270: 88–95.

Cowen, R. 1995. *History of Life,* 2nd ed. Boston: Blackwell Scientific Publications.

Cummins, H., and C. Midlo. 1961. *Finger Prints, Palms, and Soles: An Introduction to Dermatoglyphics.* New York: Dover.

Darwin, C. R. 1898. *On the Origin of Species by Means of Natural Selection,* 6th ed., 1872. New York: Appleton.

De Bonis, L., and G. D. Koufos. 1994. Our ancestor's ancestor: Ouranopithecus is a Greek link in human ancestry. *Evolutionary Anthropology* 3 (3): 75–83.

de Waal, F. B. M. 1995. Bonobo sex and society. *Scientific American* (March): 82–88.

de Waal, F. B. M., and F. Lanting (photographer). 1997. *Bonobo: The Forgotten Ape.* Berkeley: University of California Press.

Diamond, J. 1991. Curse and blessing of the ghetto. *Discover* (March): 60–65.

Dobzhansky, T. 1970. *Genetics of the Evolutionary Process.* New York: Columbia University Press.

Donnelly, P., S. Tavaré, D. J. Balding, and R. C. Griffiths. 1996. Technical comments: Estimating the age of the common ancestor of men from the ZFY intron. *Science* 272: 1357–58.

Dorit, R. L., H. Akashi, and W. Gilbert. 1995. Absence of polymorphism at the ZFY locus on the human Y chromosome. *Science* 268: 1183–85.

Eaton, S. B., and M. Konner. 1985. Diet: Paleolithic genes and twentieth century health. *Anthroquest,* The L. S. B. Leakey Foundation, 1985.

Edey, M., and D. Johanson. 1989. *Blueprints: Solving the Mystery of Evolution.* Boston: Little, Brown.

Eldredge, N. 1991. *The Miner's Canary: Unraveling the Mysteries of Extinction.* New York: Prentice-Hall.

Eldredge, N. 1995. *Dominion.* New York: Henry Holt.

Fagan, B. 1994. *In the Beginning: An Introduction to Archaeology,* 8th ed. New York: HarperCollins.

Feder, K. L. 1996. *The Past in Perspective: An Introduction to Human Prehistory.* Mountain View, Calif.: Mayfield.

Feder, K. L. 1997. Indians and archaeologists: The conflicting views of myth and science. *Skeptic* 5 (3): 74–80.

Feder, K. L. 1999. *Frauds, Myths, and Mysteries: Science and Pseudoscience in Archaeology,* 3rd ed. Mountain View, Calif.: Mayfield.

Feder, K. L., and M. A. Park. 1997. *Human Antiquity: An Introduction to Physical Anthropology and Archaeology,* 3rd ed. Mountain View, Calif.: Mayfield Publishing.

Fedigan, L. M., and L. Fedigan. 1988. *Gender and the Study of Primates: Curricular Module for the Project on Gender and Curriculum.* Washington, D.C.: American Anthropological Association.

Ferris, Timothy. 1988. *Coming of Age in the Milky Way.* New York: William Morrow.

Fleagle, J. G. 1988. *Primate Adaptation and Evolution.* San Diego: Academic Press.

Fossey, D. 1983. *Gorillas in the Mist.* Boston: Houghton Mifflin.

Francione, G. L. 1996. *Rain Without Thunder: The Ideology of the Animal Rights Movement.* Philadelphia: Temple University Press.

Frayer, D. W., M. H. Wolpoff, A. G. Thorne, F. H. Smith, and G. G. Pope. 1994. Getting it straight. *American Anthropologist* 96: 424–38.

Fuentes, A., and P. Dolhinow. In press. *The Nonhuman Primates.* Mountain View, Calif.: Mayfield.

Galdikas, B. 1995. *Reflections of Eden: My Years with the Orangutans of Borneo.* Boston: Little, Brown.

Gebo, D. L., L. MacLatchy, R. Kityo, A. Deino, J. Kingston, and D. Pilbeam. 1997. A hominoid genus from the early Miocene of Uganda. *Science* (April 18): 401–4.

Gibbons, A. 1997a. Tracing the identity of the first toolmakers. *Science* (April 4): 32.

Gibbons, A. 1997b. A new face for human ancestors. *Science* (May 30): 1331–33.

Gibbons, A. 1997c. Doubts over spectacular dates. *Science* (October 10): 220–22.

Gibbons, A. 1997d. Y chromosome shows that Adam was an African. *Science* (October 31): 804–5.

Gish, Duane T. 1979. *Evolution: The Fossils Say No!* San Diego: Creation-Life Publishers.

Glausiusz, J. 1995. Unfortunate drift. *Discover* (June): 34–35.

Goodall, J. 1971. *In the Shadow of Man*. Boston: Houghton Mifflin.

Goodall, J. 1986. *The Chimpanzees of Gombe: Patterns of Behavior*. Cambridge, Mass.: Belknap Press.

Goodall, J. 1990. *Through a Window: My Thirty Years with the Chimpanzees of Gombe*. Boston: Houghton Mifflin.

Gore, R. 1993. Explosion of life: The Cambrian period. *National Geographic* (October): 120–36.

Gore, R. 1997a. Expanding worlds. *National Geographic* 191 (5): 84–109.

Gore, R. 1997b. The first Europeans. *National Geographic* 192 (1): 96–113.

Goudsmit, J. 1997. *Viral Sex: The Nature of AIDS*. New York: Oxford University Press.

Gould, S. J. 1977. *Ever Since Darwin*. New York: Norton.

Gould, S. J. 1980. *The Panda's Thumb*. New York: Norton.

Gould, S. J. 1983. *Hen's Teeth and Horse's Toes*. New York: Norton.

Gould, S. J. 1985. *The Flamingo's Smile*. New York: Norton.

Gould, S. J. 1989. *Wonderful Life: The Burgess Shale and the Nature of History*. New York: Norton.

Gould, S. J. 1991. *Bully for Brontosaurus*. New York: Norton.

Gould, S. J. 1992. What is a species? *Discover* (December): 40–45.

Gould, S. J. 1993a. *Eight Little Piggies*. New York: Norton.

Gould, S. J., ed. 1993b. *The Book of Life*. New York: Norton.

Gould, S. J. 1994a. In the mind of the beholder. *Natural History* 103 (2): 14–23.

Gould, S. J. 1994b. The evolution of life on the earth. *Scientific American* 271 (4): 84–91.

Gould, S. J. 1995a. *Dinosaur in a Haystack: Reflections in Natural History*. New York: Harmony.

Gould, S. J. 1995b. Of tongue worms, velvet worms, and water bears. *Natural History* 104 (1): 6–15.

Gould, S. J. 1996a. *Full House: The Spread of Excellence from Plato to Darwin*. New York: Harmony Books.

Gould, S. J. 1996b. *The Mismeasure of Man*, 2nd ed. New York: Norton.

Gould, S. J. 1997/1998. The paradox of the visibly irrelevant. *Natural History* 106 (11): 12–18, 60–66.

Greene, J. C. 1959. *The Death of Adam*. New York: Mentor Books.

Hammer, M. F., and S. L. Zegura. 1996. The role of the Y chromosome in human evolutionary studies. *Evolutionary Anthropology* 5 (4): 116–34.

Harpending, H., and J. Relethford. 1997. Population perspectives on human origins research. In *Conceptual Issues in Modern Human Origins Research*, eds. G. A. Clark and C. M. Willermet. New York: Aldine de Gruyter.

Harris, C. L. 1981. *Evolution: Genesis and Revelations*. Albany: State University of New York Press.

Harrison, G. A., and A. J. Boyce, eds. 1972. *The Structure of Human Populations*. Oxford: Clarendon.

Harrison, G. A., J. S. Weiner, J. M. Tanner, and N. A. Barnicot. 1977. *Human Biology: An Introduction to Human Evolution, Variation, Growth, and Ecology*, 2nd ed. Oxford: Oxford University Press.

Hern, W. M. 1993. Is human culture carcinogenic for uncontrolled population growth and ecological destruction? *BioScience* 43 (11): 768–73.

Herrnstein, R. J., and C. Murray. 1994. *The Bell Curve: The Reshaping of American Life by Difference in Intelligence*. New York: Free Press.

Hill, K. 1993. Life history theory and evolutionary anthropology. *Evolutionary Anthropology* 2 (3): 78–88.

Holliday, T. W. 1997. Postcranial evidence of cold adaptation in European Neandertals. *American Journal of Physical Anthropology* 104: 245–58.

Holloway, R. 1980. Indonesian "Solo" (Ngandong) endocranial reconstructions: Preliminary observations and comparisons with Neandertal and *Homo erectus* groups. *American Journal of Physical Anthropology* 53: 285–95.

Holloway, R. 1981. The Indonesian *Homo erectus* brain endocasts revisited. *American Journal of Physical Anthropology* 55: 503–21.

Hostetler, J. A. 1974. *Hutterite Society*. Baltimore: Johns Hopkins University Press.

Huyghe, P. 1988. No bone unturned. *Discover* (December): 34–37.

Ingmanson, E. 1996. Tool-using behavior in wild *Pan paniscus*: Social and ecological considerations. In *Reaching into Thought: The Minds of the Great Apes*, eds. A. Russon, K. Bard, and S. Taylor. Cambridge: Cambridge University Press.

Ingmanson, E., and H. Ihobe. 1992. Predation and meat eating by *Pan paniscus* at Wamba, Zaire. Paper presented at the 61st Annual Meeting of the American Association of Physical Anthropologists, Las Vegas.

Ingmanson, E., and T. Kano. 1993. Waging peace. *International Wildlife* (November/December): 30–37.

Janus, C. 1975. *The Search for Peking Man*. New York: Macmillan.

Jensen, A. R. 1969. How much can we boost IQ and scholastic achievement? *Harvard Educational Review* 39 (1, Winter): 1–123.

Jobling, M. A., and C. Tyler-Smith. 1995. Fathers and sons: The Y chromosome and human evolution. *Trends in Genetics* 11: 449–56.

Johanson, D. C., and M. A. Edey. 1981. *Lucy: The Beginnings of Humankind*. New York: Simon and Schuster.

Johanson, D., and J. Shreeve. 1989. *Lucy's Child: The Discovery of a Human Ancestor*. New York: William Morrow.

Johnson, T. C., C. A. Scholz, M. R. Talbot, K. Kelts, R. D. Ricketts, G. Ngobi, K. Beuning, I. Ssemmanda, and J. W. McGill. 1996. Late Pleistocene desiccation of Lake Victoria and rapid evolution of cichlid fishes. *Science* (August 23): 1091–93.

Jolly, A. 1985. *The Evolution of Primate Behavior*. New York: Macmillan.

Jolly, A. 1988. Madagascar's lemurs: On the edge of survival. *National Geographic* 174 (2): 132–61.

Kano, T. 1990. The bonobos' peaceable kingdom. *Natural History* (November): 62–71.

Kay, R. F., C. Ross, and B. A. Williams. 1997. Anthropoid origins. *Science* (February 7): 797–804.

Keith, A. 1927. *Concerning Man's Origin*. London: Watts.

Kennedy, K. A. R. 1976. *Human Variation in Space and Time*. Dubuque, Iowa: W. C. Brown.

Kerr, R. A. 1996. New mammal data challenge evolutionary pulse theory. *Science* (July 26): 431–32.

Kingston, J. D., B. D. Marino, and A. Hill. 1994. Isotopic evidence for neocene hominid paleoenvironments in the Kenya rift valley. *Science* 264: 955–59.

Krings, M., A. Stone, R. W. Schmitz, H. Krainitzki, M. Stoneking, and S. Pääbo. 1997. Neandertal DNA sequences and the origin of modern humans. *Cell* 90 (1): 19–30.

Kunzig, R. 1997. The face of an ancestral child. *Discover* 18 (12): 88–101.

Leakey, M. G., C. S. Feibel, I. McDougall, and A. Walker. 1995. New four-million-year-old hominid species from Kanapoi and Allia Bay, Kenya. *Nature* 376: 565–71.

Leakey, R., and R. Lewin. 1992. *Origins Reconsidered: In Search of What Makes Us Human*. New York: Doubleday.

Leakey, R., and R. Lewin. 1995. *The Sixth Extinction: Patterns of Life and the Future of Humankind*. New York: Doubleday.

Lemonick, M. D. 1994. One Less Missing Link. *Time* (October 3): 68–69.

Lewontin, R. 1982. *Human Diversity*. New York: Scientific American Books.

Lindenbaum, S. 1979. *Kuru Sorcery: Disease and Danger in the New Guinea Highlands*. Mountain View, Calif.: Mayfield.

Lyell, C. 1873. *The Geological Evidences of the Antiquity of Man*. London: Murray.

Malthus, T. R. 1789. An Essay on the Principles of Population as It Affects the Future Improvement of Society with Remarks on the Speculations of Mr. Godwin, M. Condorcet and Other Writers. London: Macmillan (facsimile of the first edition, 1926).

Maples, W. R., and M. Browning. 1994. *Dead Men Do Tell Tales*. New York: Doubleday.

Marks, J. 1994. Book reviews. *Human Biology* 66: 1113–17.

Marks, J. 1995. *Human Biodiversity: Genes, Race, and History*. New York: Aldine de Gruyter.

Marks, J., and R. B. Lyles. 1994. Rethinking genes. *Evolutionary Anthropology* 3 (4): 139–46.

Martin, M. K., and B. Voorhies. 1975. *Female of the Species*. New York: Columbia University Press.

Martin, R. D. 1993. Primate origins: Plugging the gaps. *Nature* (May 20): 223–24.

McCrossin, M. L. 1997. New postcranial remains of

Kenyapithecus and their implications for understanding the origins of hominoid terrestriality. Paper delivered at the 66th Annual Meeting of the American Association of Physical Anthropologists, St. Louis.

Menon, S. 1997. Neanderthal noses. *Discover* (March): 30.

Mettler, L. E., T. G. Gregg, and H. E. Schaffer. 1988. *Population Genetics and Evolution*. Englewood Cliffs, N.J.: Prentice-Hall.

Mills, C. 1997. The deadliest virus. *The Sciences* (January/February): 34–38.

Minugh-Purvis, N. 1995. The modern human origins controversy: 1984–1994. *Evolutionary Anthropology* 4 (4): 140–47.

Molnar, S. 1992. *Human Variation: Races, Types, and Ethnic Groups*, 3rd ed. Englewood Cliffs, N.J.: Prentice-Hall.

Montagu, A., ed. 1964. *The Concept of Race*. New York: Collier Books.

Morris, H. M. 1974. *The Troubled Waters of Evolution*. San Diego: Creation-Life Publishers.

Mosko, S., C. Richard, J. McKenna, S. Drummond, and D. Mukai. 1997. Maternal proximity and infant CO_2 environment during bedsharing and possible implications for SIDS research. *American Journal of Physical Anthropology* 103 (3): 315–28.

Mowat, F. 1987. *Woman in the Mists*. New York: Warner Books.

Nanda, S. 1990. *Neither Man nor Woman: The Hijras of India*. Belmont, Calif.: Wadsworth.

Napier, J. R., and P. H. Napier. 1985. *The Natural History of the Primates*. Cambridge, Mass.: M.I.T. Press.

Nichols, M., J. Goodall, G. B. Schaller, and M. G. Smith. 1993. *The Great Apes: Between Two Worlds*. Washington, D.C.: National Geographic Society.

Oliwenstein, L. 1995. Dr. Darwin. *Discover* (October): 111–17.

Omohundro, J. T. 1998. *Careers in Anthropology*. Mountain View, Calif.: Mayfield.

Orgel, L. E. 1994. The origin of life on the earth. *Scientific American* 271 (4): 76–83.

Park, M. A. 1979. Dermatoglyphics as a Tool for Population Studies: An Example. Unpublished doctoral dissertation, Dept. of Anthropology: Indiana University, Bloomington.

Park, M. A. 1982–83. Palmistry: Science or hand-jive? *The Skeptical Inquirer* VII (2): 21–32.

Park, M. A. 1997. *Biological Anthropology: An Introductory Reader*. Mountain View, Calif.: Mayfield.

Passingham, R. 1982. *The Human Primate*. New York: W. H. Freeman.

Pfeiffer, J. 1969. *The Emergence of Man*. New York: Harper and Row.

Pilbeam, D. 1984. The descent of the hominoids and hominids. *Scientific American* 250 (3): 84–96.

Pilbeam, D. 1986. Human origins. *David Skomp Distinguished Lecture in Anthropology*. Bloomington: Indiana University.

Podolefsky, A., and P. J. Brown, eds. 1994. *Applying Anthropology: An Introductory Reader*. Mountain View, Calif.: Mayfield.

Post, P. W., F. Daniels, Jr., and R. T. Binford. 1975. Cold injury and the evolution of "white" skin. *Human Biology* 47: 65–80.

Potts, R. 1984. Home bases and early hominids. *American Scientist* 72: 338–47.

Potts, R. 1996. Evolution and climate variability. *Science* (August 16): 922–23.

Power, M. 1991. *The Egalitarians—Human and Chimpanzee: An Anthropological View of Social Organization*. Cambridge: Cambridge University Press.

Prag, J., and R. Neave. 1997. *Making Faces: Using Forensic and Archaeological Evidence*. College Station: Texas A&M University Press.

Prusiner, S. B. 1997. Prion diseases and the BSE crisis. *Science* (October 10): 245–51.

Reinhard, J. 1996. Peru's ice maidens. *National Geographic* 189 (6): 62–81.

Relethford, J. H. 1997. *The Human Species: An Introduction to Biological Anthropology*, 3rd ed. Mountain View, Calif.: Mayfield.

Relethford, J. H., and H. C. Harpending. 1995. Ancient differences in population size can mimic a recent African origin of modern humans. *Current Anthropology* 36 (4): 667–74.

Rhodes, R. 1997. *Deadly Feasts: Tracking the Secrets of a Terrifying New Plague*. New York: Simon and Schuster.

Ridley, M. 1996. *Evolution*, 2nd ed. Boston: Blackwell Scientific Publications.

Rischer, C. E., and T. A. Easton. 1992. *Focus on Human Biology*. New York: HarperCollins.

Roberts, D. 1993. The Ice Man. *National Geographic* 183 (6): 36–67.

Robey, B., S. O. Rutstein, and L. Morris. 1993. The fertility decline in developing countries. *Scientific American* (December): 60–67.

Rowe, N. 1996. *The Pictorial Guide to the Living Primates*. East Hampton, N.Y.: Pogonius Press.

Ryan, F. 1997. *Virus X: Tracking the New Killer Plagues Out of the Present and Into the Future*. Boston: Little, Brown.

Sagan, C. 1977. *The Dragons of Eden: Speculations on the Evolution of Human Intelligence*. New York: Random House.

Sagan, C. 1996. *The Demon-Haunted World: Science as a Candle in the Dark*. New York: Random House.

Schadewald, R. 1981–82. Scientific creationism, geocentricity and the flat earth. *The Skeptical Inquirer* VI (2): 41–48.

Schultz, E., and R. Lavenda. 1998. *Anthropology: A Perspective on the Human Condition*, 2nd ed. Mountain View, Calif.: Mayfield.

Schwartz, J. H. 1995. *Skeleton Keys: An Introduction to Human Skeletal Morphology*. New York: Oxford University Press.

Semaw, S., P. Renne, J. W. K. Harris, C. S. Feibel, R. L. Bernor, N. Fesseha, and K. Mowbray. 1997. 2.5-million-year-old stone tools from Gona, Ethiopia. *Nature* (January 23): 333–36.

Sharer, R. J., and W. Ashmore. 1993. *Archaeology: Discovering Our Past*, 2nd ed. Mountain View, Calif.: Mayfield.

Shea, J. 1989. A functional study of the lithic industries associated with hominid fossils in Kebara and Qafzeh Caves, Israel. In *The Human Revolution: Behavioural and Biological Perspectives in the Origins of Modern Humans*, eds. P. Mellars and C. Stringer (pp. 611–25). Princeton, N.J.: Princeton University Press.

Shipman, P. 1981. *Life History of a Fossil: An Introduction to Taphonomy and Paleoecology*. Cambridge, Mass.: Harvard University Press.

Shipman, P. 1984. Scavenger hunt. *Natural History* 93 (4): 20–27.

Shipman, P. 1986. Scavenging or hunting in early hominids: Theoretical frameworks and tests. *American Anthropologist* 88: 27–43.

Shipman, P., and J. Rose. 1983. Evidence of butchery and hominid activities at Torralba and Ambrona: An evaluation using microscopic techniques. *Journal of Archaeological Science* 10: 465–74.

Shreeve, J. 1994. *Erectus* rising. *Discover* (September): 80–89.

Shreeve, J. 1995. The Neanderthal peace. *Discover* (September): 70–81.

Shreeve, J. 1996. Sunset of the savanna. *Discover* 17 (7): 116–25.

Simons, M. 1996. New species of early human reported found in Africa. *The New York Times* (May 23): A8.

Sjøvold, T. 1992. The stone age iceman from the Alps: The find and current status of investigation. *Evolutionary Anthropology* 1 (4): 117–24.

Small, M. F. 1992. A reasonable sleep. *Discover* (April): 83–88.

Smith, B. H. 1993. Life history and the evolution of human maturation. *Evolutionary Anthropology* 1 (4): 134–42.

Smith, J. M. 1984. Science and myth. *Natural History* 93 (11): 10–24.

Smith, S. L., and F. B. Harrold. 1997. A paradigm's worth of difference? Understanding the impasse over modern human origins. *Yearbook of Physical Anthropology* 40: 113–38.

Smuts, B. 1985. *Sex and Friendship in Baboons*. Hawthorne, N.Y.: Aldine de Gruyter.

Smuts, B. 1995. Apes of wrath. *Discover* (August): 35–37.

Snow, C. C., and J. L. Luke. 1970. The Oklahoma City child disappearances: Forensic anthropology in the identification of skeletal remains. In *Applying Anthropology*, eds. A. Podolefsky and P. J. Brown. Mountain View, Calif.: Mayfield.

Spindler, K. 1995. *The Man in the Ice*. New York: Harmony Books.

Stanford, C. B. 1995. To catch a colobus. *Natural History* 104 (1): 48–55.

Steudel, K. 1996. Limb morphology, bipedal gait, and the energetics of hominid locomotion. *American Journal of Physical Anthropology* 99 (2): 345–56.

Stoneking, M. 1993. DNA and recent human evolution. *Evolutionary Anthropology* 2 (2): 60–73.

Stringer, C. B., and P. Andrews. 1988. Genetic and fossil evidence for the origin of modern humans. *Science* 239: 1263–68.

Stringer, C. B., and R. McKie. 1996. *African Exodus: The Origins of Modern Humanity*. New York: Henry Holt.

Strum, S. 1987. *Almost Human*. New York: Random House.

Susman, R. L. 1994. Fossil evidence for early hominid tool use. *Science* (September 9): 1570–73.

Suwa, G., B. Asfaw, Y. Beyene, T. D. White, S. Katoh, S. Nagaoka, H. Nakaya, K. Uzawa, P. Renne, and G. WoldeGabriel. 1997. The first skull of *Australopithecus boisei*. *Nature* (October 2): 489–92.

Tattersall, I. 1992. The many faces of *Homo habilis*. *Evolutionary Anthropology* 1 (1): 33–37.

Tattersall, I. 1993. *The Human Odyssey: Four Million Years of Human Evolution*. New York: Prentice-Hall.

Tattersall, I. 1994. What do we mean by human— and why does it matter? *Evolutionary Anthropology* 3 (4): 114–16.

Tattersall, I. 1995a. *The Fossil Trail: How We Know What We Know About Human Evolution*. New York: Oxford University Press.

Tattersall, I. 1995b. *The Last Neanderthal: The Rise, Success, and Mysterious Extinction of Our Closest Human Relatives*. New York: Macmillan.

Tattersall, I. 1997. Out of Africa again . . . and again? *Scientific American* (April): 60–67.

Templeton, A. R. 1997. Testing the out of Africa replacement hypothesis with mitochondrial DNA data. In *Conceptual Issues in Modern Human Origins Research*, eds. G. A. Clark and C. M. Willermet. New York: Aldine de Gruyter.

Thompson, M. J., and D. W. Harsha. 1984. Our rhythms still follow the African sun. *Psychology Today* (January): 50–54.

Time-Life Books, eds. 1973. *The First Men*. New York: Time-Life Books.

Todd, T. W. 1920. Age changes in the pubic bone. *American Journal of Physical Anthropology* 3: 285–384.

Tullar, R. M. 1977. *The Human Species: Its Nature, Evolution, and Ecology*. New York: McGraw-Hill.

Ubelaker, D., and H. Scammell. 1992. *Bones: A Forensic Detective's Casebook*. New York: HarperCollins.

Underwood, J. H. 1979. *Human Variation and Human Microevolution*. Englewood Cliffs, N.J.: Prentice-Hall.

Vrba, E. S. 1993. The pulse that produced us. *Natural History* 102 (5): 47–51.

Weaver, Robert F. 1984. Changing life's genetic blueprint. *National Geographic* (December): 818–47.

Weiner, J. 1994. *The Beak of the Finch: A Story of Evolution in Our Time*. New York: Knopf.

White, F. J. 1996. *Pan paniscus* 1973 to 1996: Twenty-three years of field research. *Evolutionary Anthropology* 5 (1): 11–17.

White, T. D., and P. A. Folkens. 1991. *Human Osteology*. San Diego: Academic Press.

White, T. D., G. Suwa, B. Asfaw. 1994. Australopithecus ramidus, a new species of early hominid from Aramis, Ethiopia. *Nature* (September 22): 306–12.

Wilford, J. N. 1994. Fog thickens on climate and origin of humans. *New York Times* (May 17): C1, C8.

Wilmut, I., A. E. Schnieke, J. McWhir, A. J. Kind, and K. H. S. Campbell. 1997. Viable offspring derived from fetal and adult mammalian cells. *Nature* (February 27): 810–13.

Wilson, Edward O. 1992. *The Diversity of Life* (College Edition with Study Materials). New York: Norton.

Wolpoff, M. 1994. What do we mean by human— and why does it matter? *Evolutionary Anthropology* 3 (4): 116–17.

Wolpoff, M., and R. Caspari. 1997. *Race and Human Evolution*. New York: Simon and Schuster.

Wong, K. 1998. Ancestral quandry. *Scientific American* 278 (1): 30–32.

Yoon, C. K. 1996a. Lake Victoria's lightning-fast origin of species. *New York Times* (August 27): C1, C4.

Yoon, C. K. 1996b. Parallel plots in classic evolution. *New York Times* (November 12): C1, C7.

Photo Credits

Chapter 1 CO1, © William F. Keegan; Fig. 1.1, From John Hostetler. *Hutterite Society.* page 156, © 1974, 1997. Reprinted by permission of the Johns Hopkins University Press; Fig. 1.2, Courtesy of the author; Fig. 1.3, Courtesy of the author; Fig. 1.4, © William F. Keegan; Fig. 1.5, Photograph by Michael Kodas/The Hartford Courant, 7/25/93

Chapter 2 CO2, Courtesy K.L. Feder; Fig. 2.1, © Julia Margaret Cameron/National Portrait Gallery, London; Fig. 2.2, from J. Best Publishing Co.; Fig. 2.3, Courtesy K.L. Feder; Fig. 2.4, Courtesy NASA; Fig. 2.6, © Robert F. Sisson/National Geographic Society Image Collection

Chapter 3 CO3, © David Robert Austen; Fig. 3.4, © David Robert Austen; Fig. 3.6, © CNRI/SPL/ Science Source/Photo Researchers, Inc.

Chapter 4 CO4, © Michael Tweedie/Photo Researchers, Inc.; Fig. 4.1 (left), Courtesy K.L. Feder; Fig. 4.1 (right), Courtesy J.M. Beatty; Fig. 4.2, © March of Dimes; Fig. 4.3, © Michael Tweedie/Photo Researchers, Inc.; Fig. 4.9, © AP/Wide World Photos

Chapter 5 CO5, © Stephen Dalton/Animals Animals; Fig. 5.2 (top left), © Stephen Dalton/Animals Animals; Fig. 5.2 (top right), © Zigmund Leszczynski/Animals Animals; Fig. 5.2 (bottom), © Robert Lubeck/Animals Animals; Fig. 5.4, Neg. #K12654. Courtesy Department of Library Services, American Museum of Natural History; Fig. 5.6, Courtesy Janet M. Beatty

Chapter 6 CO6, *The Age of Reptiles,* a mural by Rudolph F. Zallinger. © 1966, 1975, 1985, 1989, Peabody Museum of Natural History, Yale University, New Haven, Connecticut.; Fig. 6.2, © Fred Bavendam/Peter Arnold, Inc.; Fig. 6.5, © Marvin Mattelson/National Geographic Society Image Collection; Fig. 6.7, *The Age of Reptiles,* a mural by Rudolph F. Zallinger. © 1966, 1975, 1985, 1989, Peabody Museum of Natural History, Yale University, New Haven, Connecticut.; Fig. 6.8, Courtesy of the author

Chapter 7 CO7, © Frans Lanting/Minden Pictures; Fig. 7.1, From Barnes et al., *The Invertebrates: A New Synthesis,* © 1988. Reprinted by permission of Blackwell Science, Inc.; Fig. 7.4, © Frans Lanting/Minden Pictures; Fig. 7.6, Courtesy Marine World Africa USA/Darryl Bush; Fig. 7.8 (top left), © Noel Rowe; Fig. 7.8 (top right), © Noel Rowe; Fig. 7.8 (bottom left), © Noel Rowe; Fig. 7.8 (bottom right), Courtesy of the author; Fig. 7.9, Courtesy of the author; Fig. 7.10 (top), © Noel Rowe; Fig. 7.10 (bottom), © Stewart Halperin/Animals Animals; Fig. 7.13, © Noel Rowe; Fig. 7.14, © Noel Rowe; Fig. 7.15, © Andrew L. Young; Fig. 7.16, © Noel Rowe; Fig. 7.17, © Noel Rowe; Fig. 7.18 (top left), © Ron Garrison/ Zoological Society of San Diego; Fig. 7.18 (top right), Courtesy of the author; Fig. 7.18 (bottom left), © Steve Turner/Animals Animals; Fig. 7.18 (bottom right), © Ron Garrison/Zoological Society of San Diego; Fig. 7.19, © Jane Goodall/ National Geographic Society Image Collection; Fig. 7.20, Courtesy of the author

Chapter 8 CO8, © Frans Lanting/Minden Pictures; Fig. 8.2, © T.W. Ransom/Biological Photo Service; Fig. 8.3, © Irven DeVore/ Anthro-Photo; Fig. 8.4, © Zig Leszczynski/Animals Animals; Fig. 8.5, © Kennan Ward/DRK Photo; Fig. 8.6, © Frans Lanting/Minden Pictures; Fig. 8.7, © Noel Rowe

Chapter 9 CO9, © Enrico Ferorelli/National Geographic Image Collection; Fig. 9.1, Gorilla illustration by Enid Kotschnig. Cat illustration by Rudolf Freund.; Fig. 9.4, Illustrations by Enid Kotschnig; Fig. 9.5, Reprinted from *Identification of Pathological Conditions in Human Skeletal Remains,* Orter and Putschar (Washington, DC: Smithsonian Institution Press), pages 195,198, by permission of the publisher. © 1985; Fig. 9.6, © E.E. Kingsley 1984/Science Source/Photo Researchers, Inc.; Fig. 9.7, © Enrico Ferorelli/National Geographic Image Collection; Fig. 9.8, From Price and Feinman, *Images of the Past.* Mayfield Publishing Company, Mountain View, CA; Fig. 9.10, Courtesy of the Greenland National Museum and Archives; Fig. 9.11, Courtesy Marsha Park Herman; Fig. 9.12, Reprinted with permission from J.J. Yunis et al., "The Striking Resemblance of High-Resolution G-Banded Chromosomes of Man and Chimpanzees," *Science,* 208 (1980), 1145-1149. Copyright 1980, American Association for the Advancement of Science.

Chapter 10 CO10, © 1985 David L. Brill; Fig. 10.2, Illustration by Rudolf Freund.; Fig. 10.3, From R.D. Martin, *Primate Origins and Evolution: A Phylogentric Reconstruction,* p. 61. Used by permission of Chapman & Hall; Fig. 10.4, © David L. Brill, 1985; Fig. 10.6, Stephen D. Nash/ © 1997. Reprinted with permission of Discover Magazine; Fig. 10.7, Courtesy Dr. Ian

Index